Foreign Bodies

Foreign Bodies: Eating Disorders, Childhood Sexual Abuse, and Trauma-Informed Treatment addresses the association between eating disorders and childhood sexual abuse, proposing a new way of treating those suffering from eating disorders who were sexually abused as children. Based on testimonies of survivors of abuse who subsequently developed eating disorders, it offers a new form of diagnosis and treatment, arguing that the eating disorder field often ignores the traumatic sources of eating disorders, leading to some treatment programmes not being commensurate, and at times conflicting, with the principles of childhood sexual abuse treatment.

The case studies used to highlight the link between childhood sexual abuse and eating disorders are presented from the perspective of the women involved, in their own words. Their voices are supplemented by Gur's own stance as a clinician specializing in the treatment of sexual abuse and CPTSD. The book is divided into three parts: the first deals with eating disorders, childhood sexual abuse, and the association between them; the second examines the treatment of eating disorders and childhood sexual abuse; and the third offers a new form of diagnosis and treatment for eating disorders.

This book will be of great interest to researchers and postgraduate students in the eating disorder field of psychotherapy, psychology, or psychiatry, plus those studying the treatment of trauma. It will also be of interest to clinical dieticians, psychologists, social workers, doctors, nurses, eating disorder specialists, and policymakers in the mental health field, as well as eating disorders sufferers and those who care for them.

Anat Gur, MSW, PhD, is a social worker and psychotherapist specializing in the treatment of women and survivors of sexual abuse and Complex PTSD. She is the professional director of the Women's Therapy Centre: Women's Wisdom in Israel and head of the two-year programme for treating sexual abuse at Bar-Ilan University.

Foreign Bodies

Eating Disorders, Childhood Sexual Abuse and Trauma-Informed Treatment

Anat Gur
Translated by Liat Keren

Routledge
Taylor & Francis Group
LONDON AND NEW YORK

First published 2019
by Routledge

2 Park Square, Milton Park, Abingdon, Oxfordshire OX14 4RN
52 Vanderbilt Avenue, New York, NY 10017

Routledge is an imprint of the Taylor & Francis Group, an informa business

First issued in paperback 2020

British Library Cataloguing-in-Publication Data
A catalogue record for this book is available from the British Library

Library of Congress Cataloging-in-Publication Data
A catalog record for this book has been requested

ISBN: 978-1-138-60092-8 (hbk)
ISBN: 978-0-367-48925-0 (pbk)

Typeset in Bembo
by Apex CoVantage, LLC

Contents

Acknowledgements xi
Preface xii
Introduction xviii

PART I
Eating disorders, childhood sexual abuse, and the link between them 1

Introduction 1

1 **Eating disorders** 3
The definition of eating disorders 4
The history of eating disorders 7
The aetiology of eating disorders 8
Eating disorders and gender 8
A chronicle of an eating disorder: listening to women's voices 10
Anorexia 10
Natasha: 'The repertoire of what I eat is more like that of autistic children' 10
Grace: 'Every time I stepped on the scales and saw that I'd lost weight, it was the greatest feeling in the world' 11
Lily: 'If I'm thin I'll be less disgusting' 12
Shirley: 'People on the outside don't understand, but it's amazing' 13
Bulimia 14
Liliana: 'I didn't throw up calories. I threw up myself, from inside myself' 14
Debby: 'It's a cunning, accursed disease, it's like cancer' 15
Bingeing 15
Naomi: 'This fat is what protects me' 15
Orna: 'Eating and filling something that's broken inside' 16

2 **Childhood sexual abuse: from witchcraft and hysteria to CPTSD** 19
The clinical picture of childhood sexual abuse 20
An historical review of childhood sexual abuse 22
A chronicle of childhood sexual abuse 25
Natasha: father-daughter incest 26
Liliana: older brother-younger sister incest 27
Liora: grandfather-granddaughter incest 29
Maggie: father-daughter incest 29

3 **The relation between childhood sexual abuse and eating disorders: a meta-view of the professional literature** 32
The rates of correlation between childhood sexual abuse and eating disorders – Research and clinical assessments 33
Theoretical and clinical explanations of the link – A review of the professional literature 34

4 **Women speak of the association between childhood sexual abuse and eating disorders** 39
Women talk about the association 42
Is there a link between childhood sexual abuse and eating disorders? 43
'Of course there's a connection' 43
Denial of the link 44
Eating disorders as a 'disguised language of secrets too terrible for words' 46
Eating disorders as an expression of self-blame, self-destruction, and self-harm 52
Eating disorders as a form of slow suicide and a way of being rid of the exploited body 52
Eating disorders as self-destruction and self-punishment: 'To strike the sin I didn't commit' 54
Eating disorders as an illusion of regaining control 56
Eating disorders as a way of 'self-medicating' the damage caused by the abuse 59
Food, eating, and sexual abuse 60
Not eating as a way of recalling elements of the abuse 62

5 **Eating disorders in the service of dissociation** 65
Dissociation and dissociative disorders 66
Childhood sexual abuse and dissociation 69

Eating disorders and dissociation 72
Women speak of eating disorders as a way of dissociating 72
Eating disorders and dissociative amnesia 73
Eating disorders and depersonalization 81
Eating disorders and identity confusion 83
Eating disorders and dissociative identity disorder 83
Eating disorders as addiction and distraction: 'It's instead of feeling' 85

6 The betrayed/betraying body: eating disorders as ways of coping with the feminine body, sex, and sexuality in the wake of childhood sexual abuse 91
The female body in patriarchal society 92
The betrayed/betraying body: childhood sexual exploitation, the female/feminine body, and eating disorders 93
The body as a source of vulnerability, shame, guilt, and revulsion: 'Not dealing with the body is the eating disorder' 95
Punishing the body: eating disorders as hurting the body on which the abuse was perpetrated 99
Eating disorders as purging the body and soul: 'To clean your insides out' 101
Eating disorders as an expression of defending and protecting the body and soul after being abused 106
Obesity and fat as a defence against men and sexuality 106
Thinness as a defence against men and sexuality 108
Fear of menstruation and the attempt to prevent it by self-starvation 112

PART II
Treatment of eating disorders and childhood sexual abuse 115

Introduction 115

7 Treating eating disorders 117
Eating disorder treatment methods: a review of the literature 119
Studies evaluating eating disorder treatment from the client's perspective 119
The feminist critique of eating disorder treatment 121
The treatment of childhood sexual abuse within the field of eating disorders 121
Women talk about treatment in eating disorder frameworks 121

Focus on the body and diet: 'They only deal with food and . . . the body and not with the person inside' 122
Coercive and punitive methods: 'Force is not the way, not with girls like us' 125
Sexual abuse in the framework of eating disorders 130
The ignoring of sexual abuse 130
Childhood sexual abuse treatment in eating disorder frameworks 132
Hospitalization for eating disorders 135
Stories of hospitalization on eating disorder wards 136
Hospitalization on eating disorder wards as a haven 141
Psychiatric hospitalization 144
Family therapy and mother/daughter-relations treatment 147
'Not in our school': transfer to other frameworks due to lack of specialization 150
'The operation was a success but the patient died': How getting rid of symptoms can interfere with vital survival strategies 153
Optimal treatment: 'If there are monsters, then he's the fairy godmother' 156
Summary: childhood sexual abuse, eating disorders, and appropriate eating disorder treatment 159
Focus on the eating disorder symptoms 159
Getting rid of the symptoms without providing safe alternative coping strategies: 'My anorexia is my chemotherapy' 160
Focus on the body and neglect of the psyche 160
Reenactment of the misuse of power, authority, and specialist status 160
Invasiveness and lack of respect for privacy 161
Focus on pathology rather than the survivor's personal strengths 161
'Nodding therapists' 162
'Not in our school': transfer of clients from one framework to another 162
Conclusion 163

8 Specialist sexual abuse treatment 166
Childhood sexual abuse treatment 166
The stories of women treated in sexual abuse centres 168

PART III
A new diagnosis and treatment proposal 175

Introduction 175

9 Women, 'madness', and a new diagnosis 177
Eating disorders, hysteria, and 'madness' in women 178
A new diagnostic definition 181
Complex Post-Traumatic Stress Disorder 182
A controversial diagnostic concept 183

10 Treating CPTSD 189
The CPTSD treatment model 189
Three stages of recovery 190
Neurobiological and developmental implications for treatment 191
The sociocultural context of extreme trauma and clinical practices 192
Recognition of the primacy and uniqueness of each client 194
Personal empowerment 194
Recognition of clients' strengths and resilience 195
Creation of a therapeutic alliance characterized by trust, collaboration, mutuality, and non-authoritarianism 195
Safe boundaries 197
Encouraging a support system outside the therapy 198
The hazards of listening: the challenge of treating childhood sexual abuse survivors 199
Transference and countertransference 200
Vicarious trauma 201
The ABC Model – awareness, balance, and connection 203

11 Eating disorders, CPTSD, and appropriate treatment 207
Turning eating disorder services into trauma-informed services 208
An appropriate and integrative eating disorder treatment approach 211
The incorporation of eating disorder treatment within sexual assault centres 212
The incorporation of eating disorder treatment within centres for at-risk women 212

Epilogue 215
Appendix: Dawn's story 218
Bibliography 238
Index 249

Acknowledgements

I am deeply grateful to all the women who agreed to be interviewed for this study; their accounts form its heart and soul. Responding to a call I issued, they surprised and moved me by their willingness to make their voices heard, exhibiting a sense of female solidarity, responsibility, and commitment to helping others and a hope that their experiences can affect the way in which eating disorders are treated in the future. As always, while both the telling of their stories and their reading are painful and disturbing, they also hold out a promise of change and advance in both theory and practice.

My thanks go to Dawn in particular. A remarkable young social worker, she contacted me after her interview and sent me a written version of her story that now constitutes the Appendix. The step demanded great courage and was taken out of a profound desire to better the lives of young girls and women still suffering in agony and equip the therapists who seek to bring them out on the other side with the tools with which to do so.

Numerous other people contributed significantly to the present volume. Liat Keren very generously and capably translated the original document into English. Prof. Rivla Tuval-Mashiach, Dr. Einat Zubery, Dr. Zivya Seligman, Prof. Eli Somer, Prof. Ariela Fridman, Dr. Effi Ziv, Ziva Skurnik, Lilach Ben Moshe, Dr. Orit Kamir, Giora Rosen, Debbie Eylon, Nurit Zubery, Amnon Abraham, Ronit Assia, and Michal Heiman all supported me in various ways while I was writing my doctorate and revising it into book form. Dr. Timothy Brewerton and Dr. Phyllis Chesler provided me with constructive criticism on the original English draft. To all, I express my sincere gratitude.

Preface

Throughout history, 'mad' women have been described, diagnosed, and 'treated' by men belonging to the hegemonic patriarchal establishment. The dramatic emotional and physical damage caused to rape victims has been exemplified through history in various and diverse, historically culture-dependent ways as demonic possession of the soul and body. In the Middle Ages, Christian clergy burnt at the stake women thought to be possessed by demons. Members of the hegemonic male establishment of the period – beginning with mediaeval Christian clergy and through to the contemporary medical/psychiatric establishment – consistently 'diagnosed' women via stigmatizing ailments. Towards the end of the nineteenth century, doctors shut up 'hysterical' women in closed institutions, stripping them naked, tying them up, and 'treating' them with various instruments and hard streams of water. Contemporary psychiatrists diagnose women as suffering from a variety of stigmatizing ailments. Blind to the traumatic sources of their difficulties, they continue patriarchal practices by subjecting them to rigid treatment methods, such as coercion, locking away, binding, and force feeding.

The voices of the women themselves are never heard in these depictions of women and 'madness'. Only with the rise of feminism in the 1960s and '70s did women from the therapeutic professions begin to reexamine the field of 'women and madness' from the perspective of women themselves. Phyllis Chesler's *Women and Madness*, published in 1972, was a seminal force in prompting a revisiting of what women in need of treatment at the hands of (male) mental health figures – psychiatrists, psychologists, and psychotherapists – have been experiencing since the days of Freud. This groundbreaking work was based on the very difficult personal accounts of women who had been hospitalized or sought therapy.

The present volume – published forty years after the first edition of *Women and Madness* – is also based on the testimony of women themselves, presenting their viewpoint in their own words: how they perceive their eating disorders, the reasons for them, and the treatment they received. This is supplemented by my own personal perspective as a clinician specializing in treating sexual abuse victims.

The women's evidence was collected for a study I conducted in the framework of my doctoral dissertation, which analysed 'The Link between Childhood Sexual Abuse and Eating Disorders from the Perspective of Women Victims of Childhood Sexual Abuse and Eating Disorders' (Gur, 2011). This study set out to examine the nature of the link between eating disorders and childhood sexual abuse and investigate whether the standard treatment of women within the framework of eating disorders met the needs of women and girls who had been the victims of childhood sexual abuse. I found myself venturing into far broader regions – ancient historical ones that dealt with women and 'madness' and the link between these and between them and the systematic rape of women and girls in a patriarchal culture as a means of dominating, controlling, and subjugating women and preserving and concretizing male superiority.

The findings of this study clearly demonstrate how eating disorders form part of a long chain across the generations of the rape of children and women that leads to severe feminine physical and mental health problems. Contemporary eating disorders are merely another link in the chain of the distress of female rape victims expressed via the disturbed rhetoric of their bodies and souls.

The field of eating disorder treatment has developed over the past thirty years in parallel with the development of treatment of childhood sexual abuse. From my personal perspective as a childhood sexual abuse specialist, I had long suspected that eating disorders are a direct consequence of childhood sexual abuse. At first glance, eating disorders present a rebellion against femininity; the lack of will to mature and become a woman; the desire to conceal the female body under a mantle of fat or extreme thinness; the wish to die, disappear, and hide; and the urge to throw up the secret and disgust and make it public. All these symptoms are prominent features of childhood sexual abuse.

As a therapist who has dealt with childhood sexual abuse for over thirty years, I am intimately acquainted with the experience of girls who grow up being sexually exploited by close relatives and ignored and/or silenced by other adults tasked with taking care of, protecting, and safeguarding them. My estimation is thus that eating disorders are an innate and self-evident expression of mortal afflictions.

While the rich professional literature published over the past thirty years on the subject of childhood sexual abuse recognizes eating disorders as an integral part of the complex spectrum of symptoms caused by childhood sexual abuse, the eating disorder field lags well behind in acknowledging that childhood sexual abuse frequently constitutes a central aetiological cause in the development of eating disorders. Experts in this focus prefer to focus on explanations linking eating disorders with a vast range of other factors, ignoring the history of sexual trauma.

Only in recent years, in the wake of an increase of studies and clinical experience that point to the possible link between eating disorders and childhood sexual abuse, has the eating disorder field begun to address this issue. My first acquaintance with the eating disorder field was when I was invited, as a childhood sexual abuse specialist, to provide professional supervision in the treatment of sexual abuse within the framework of eating disorders. This overture demonstrates that the academic and clinical eating disorder world today is welcoming childhood sexual abuse specialists within its doors, thereby making a significant effort towards the integration of the two fields. From my perspective as a childhood sexual abuse specialist, however, recognition of the growing number of childhood sexual abuse survivors amongst eating disorder patients requires deeper and more substantial changes in both diagnosis and treatment.

Opining that eating disorder treatment centres are still not ready for the significant development that must occur in order to provide an optimal framework for sexual abuse survivors, I chose to go out into the field and talk with women who suffer – or suffered – from eating disorders and childhood sexual abuse and listen to their voices. I wanted to know how they perceive the link between sexual abuse and eating disorders and how they experienced treatments in the past when they suffered from eating disorders.

I believed that my lengthy clinical experience in treating women in general and childhood sexual abuse survivors in particular would help me listen to what they found so hard to express, interviewing them about the so-hard-to-talk-about subject of childhood sexual abuse and eating disorders in the best and most empowering way I could. I was convinced that the possibility of speaking and influencing would be an empowering and reparative experience for women whose voices had been silenced, who feel helpless and flawed not only due to having been abused in childhood but also because of their experiences of the therapeutic system.

The book is also based on over thirty years' clinical experience in treating women criminals who are drug addicts exploited in prostitution. Having gained experience working with women in prison, I established and worked for many years as the director of a half-way house for released women prisoners. The steering committee set up to examine the grounds for rehabilitating released women prisoners decided – on the basis of the professional literature that discusses the chances of rehabilitating of women prisoners across the globe – that the prognosis for women who had been in prison was extremely low. In my first years at the half-way house, it did indeed appear that the chances were minimal, most of the women leaving and returning to the world of crime, drugs, and prostitution.

The conventional treatments for women prisoners at the time were based on a diagnosis of personality disorder – primarily 'antisocial personality disorder' and 'borderline personality disorder'. The approaches customary then – and to a large extent still today – for people suffering from criminality and addictions were rigid, authoritative, and punitive, designed as a way of rehabilitating people regarded as 'disturbed', violent, and manipulative. As long as the treatment methods and rehabilitation at the half-way house were based on these principles, they failed to help the women.

Close acquaintance with the women and their traumatic stories led me to believe that beyond the stigmatizing diagnoses the abuse and neglect they had experienced in childhood and throughout their lives were directly linked to the severe disorders from which they currently suffered. I began to understand that what led women and girls into crime, drugs, and prostitution was their traumatic history, their symptoms and lifestyle – awful as they might be – forming their only way of surviving and coping with the traumas they had endured. Many women amongst the inmates had also suffered from severe eating disorders – primarily bulimia – which would erupt when they stopped taking the drugs that served as self-medication for their eating disorder symptoms.

During this period, the feminist professional literature began to evince a greater understanding of the link between girls in distress and women criminals and juvenile delinquents addicted to drugs and exploited as prostitutes and their history of childhood sexual trauma. In parallel, the professional literature regarding appropriate methods for the treatment of trauma began to develop, frequently subversively challenging conventional methods. The transition from stigmatizing diagnoses to the diagnosis of post-trauma childhood sexual abuse and the shift from rigid, authoritative, punitive treatment methods to empowering, mutual, and egalitarian methods led to a seminal breakthrough in the rehabilitation of women criminals.

This book is also largely based on an impressive change in the treatment of women criminals – one made possible only by a change in diagnosis and the matching of treatment principles to the treatment of childhood sexual abuse survivors.

This volume hopes to contribute to the shift away from the stigmatizing diagnoses given to women criminals towards recognizing the traumatic sources of their problems. It challenges the customary diagnoses of eating disorders found in multitudes of psychiatric definitions, claiming that we must ask: is it right to classify eating disorders as an independent mental disorder when we know that they form part of the spectrum of symptoms resulting from complex traumas?

As I finished writing the first draft of this book, in May 2013, DSM-5 – the 'Bible of mental disorders' – was about to appear and the subversive attitude received unexpected support from central bodies in the psychiatric establishment itself. A few weeks before the tome's publication, psychiatric specialists were arguing that it lacks any 'scientific validity'. According to the director of the National Mental Health Institute in the United States, not reflecting the complexity of many disorders, its categorization of mental illnesses should not guide research: 'As long as the research community takes the D.S.M. to be a bible, we'll never make progress. People think that everything has to match D.S.M. criteria, but you know what? Biology never read that book' (Belluck & Carey, 2013). I thus do not endorse the biological approach to common mental disorders, my clinical experience teaching me that their source lies rather in complex childhood trauma.

This book is critical of the conventional methods with which women eating disorder sufferers who were sexually abused in childhood have traditionally been treated. From my viewpoint as a specialist childhood sexual abuse clinician, the diagnoses in the eating disorder field appear to be blind to the traumatic sources of eating disorders. Some of the accepted methods of treatment in the eating disorder field are not only inconsistent with but at times even downright contrary to the fundamental principles of childhood sexual abuse treatment.

While my decision to study the subject from the perspective of the women themselves was born out of my critical stance regarding the customary methods of eating disorder treatment, the women's critical voices are clearly and poignantly conveyed in the direct quotes from the interviews I conducted with them. These paint a picture of their experience in their own words.

My distinctive viewpoint as a clinician from outside the eating disorder field gives me a vantage point not always afforded to those working within it. At the same time, it may also mean that I only see part of the picture, important elements eluding my eyes. My goal in this book is thus to present a complementary viewpoint to that offered by eating disorder specialists in their important work with especially challenging and difficult clients – a perspective that reflects the latter's own perceptions and voices, so frequently unheard within therapeutic frameworks and quantitative studies. While I hope that readers will understand the limitations of this observation post, I also believe that the information it contains can supplement rather than replace traditional approaches.

A certain measure of truth exists in the claim that, prompted by the sense that existing methods of treatment must be revised, my perspective is *a priori* biased. The stories of the women nonetheless stand in their own right, some of them being very difficult and disturbing. I found myself committed to making the voices of the girls and women who told me their stories heard – lucid, clear, and critical voices, voices that surprised me in their ability to identify and express their essential point and unfortunately too often confirmed my fears that women do not always receive optimal treatment.

The stories of the women who participated in the study of their childhood experiences are shocking and disturbing. The decision to include a number that detail the sexual abuse they experienced in their childhood stemmed from my desire to concretize the terrible abuse: only when we begin to understand the depth of the horror can we begin to empathically understand the severe 'madness' on display. Only if we agree to listen and attend to the stories of intolerable trauma can we apprehend how, like the hysteria, demon possession, and witchcraft that preceded them, the severe disorders they produce serve as essential survival and coping strategies – 'unspeakable' cries directed towards those who refuse to allow women to be heard.

I believe that the social epidemic of childhood sexual abuse affects all of us – men, women, and children – in a society that abandons many of its daughters and allows them to experience severe trauma. Whether we ourselves have been the victims of childhood sexual abuse or not, we all pay the heavy price of living in a culture in which rape, prostitution, pornography, and other forms of violence towards women and children are still common, daily rituals. The little I can do is to make use of my professional knowledge, writing, and communicative skills, and conversations with women victims as a channel through which the authentic voices of the women who agreed to share their experiences and hurts with me can be heard and thus contribute, however modestly, to improving the treatment of women and girls against whom such abuse has been perpetrated.

References

Belluck, P., & Carey, B. (2013). Psychiatry's guide is out of touch with science, experts say. *New York Times*, May 6, 2013. Retrieved October 22, 2017, from www.nytimes.com/2013/05/07/health/psychiatrys-new-guide-falls-short-experts-say.html?pagewanted=all&_r=0

Chesler, P. (1972). *Women and madness*. New York, NY: Avon.

Gur, A. (2011). *The relationship between childhood sexual abuse and eating disorders from the perspective of women who experienced childhood sexual abuse and suffer from eating disorders* (PhD diss.). Bar-Ilan University (Hebrew, Ramat Gan Israel).

Introduction

This book is based on a narratival study documenting the many, diverse, and complex ways in which childhood sexual abuse is linked to eating disorders and the treatment those suffering from them received. The stories of the women interviewed paint a clear picture of the nature of the links between childhood sexual abuse and eating disorders and between childhood sexual abuse, eating disorders, and dissociative disorders. One of the central findings of the study on which this volume is based was that many women who suffer from eating disorders do not remember the sexual abuse they experienced when their eating disorders are acute – or, in professional terminology, suffer (or suffered) from significant dissociative disorders, including full or partial amnesia of the abuse. The results indicate that the eating disorders themselves serve – in diverse forms – as ways of forgetting and dissociating from the abuse, frequently constituting dissociative expressions of sexual traumas that have not been mentalized or worked through and from which their victims are cut off (see Chapter 5).

The study's findings provide a picture of a substantial lag in eating disorder treatment centres in matching diagnoses and treatment methods to childhood sexual abuse treatment. In addition to eating disorders, the majority of women also suffer from a number of other characteristic symptoms, such as personality disorders, dissociative disorders, suicidal thoughts/attempts, etc. – all of which form part of the spectrum of Complex PTSD symptoms that are the result of childhood sexual abuse. Diagnosed as suffering from 'comorbidity', the treatment they receive is inappropriate and fragmentary, failing to provide a comprehensive and optimal response to the original trauma or amelioration of the spectrum of severe symptoms that are its direct and intrinsic consequences. The sexual abuse in a client's history remains voiceless, shrouded in a veil of secrets, shame, denial, and dissociation. Blind to the traumatic sources of the disorders, the diagnoses and treatment methods prevalent in the eating disorder field reflect the silencing commonly practiced by society – as amongst the victims themselves – of sexual abuse.

While women who suffer from eating disorders have been the subject of numerous medical studies, only recently have they begun being given the opportunity to give voice to their experience from their own perspective. This study joins pioneering research whose goal is to let women eating disorder sufferers speak and document their experiences from their own viewpoint. The study reported the women's narratives relating to sexual abuse, eating disorders, the link between the two, and the appropriate methods of treatment. This discourse is vitally important for balancing the scientific-medical discourse regarding the link between childhood sexual abuse and eating disorders – a discourse paralyzed, disguised, and accompanied by fierce controversies in the eating disorder field (Wooley, 1994).

The women interviewed were women who had been sexually abused in childhood and suffered/were suffering from eating disorders who responded to a call I issued, volunteering to be interviewed. They represent strong survivors who wished to recount their experiences in order to convey a message to their co-sufferers – and their therapists – and thus influence treatment methods. The majority were no longer in treatment, some of them today possessing a retrospective view of the treatment they received in the past. Some of them also had experience with childhood sexual abuse treatment and thus could compare the treatments offered. Most of them had been in therapy, this circumstance allowing them to relate the course of their lives, their sexual abuse, and eating disorders with awareness, insight, and an analytic mind. It is possible that women who suffer from eating disorders today and have not yet received psychotherapy would not relate to or interpret the link between eating disorders and childhood sexual abuse in the same way.

One of the important findings indicates that some of the women dissociated from the childhood sexual abuse they had experienced when they were suffering from eating disorders. At that point in time they completely denied any possible link between childhood sexual abuse and their eating disorders. Similar research conducted with clients suffering from acute eating disorders might have not evinced similar results.

The women's stories demonstrate that when the two phenomena of childhood sexual abuse and eating disorders are not regarded as one continuum, those suffering from eating disorders who were sexually abused in childhood are condemned to fragmentary treatment that only relates to some of their severe and complex symptoms. Today, treatment centres are divided into eating disorder treatment centres that do not give sufficient place to specialized childhood sexual abuse treatment and childhood sexual abuse treatment centres that do not make room for specialized eating disorder treatment.

The high rates of correlation between childhood sexual abuse and eating disorders demand a revision of both the diagnoses and current conventional methods of treatment in the eating disorder field. The study findings demonstrate the need to revisit the diagnoses and treatment methods currently employed in the eating disorder field and their alignment with innovative professional knowledge pertaining to the diagnosis and treatment of the complex traumas of childhood sexual abuse. They also challenge the field of childhood sexual abuse treatment to find proper ways of treating the high numbers of clients suffering from eating disorders.

The clinical knowledge over the last three decades being developed by eating disorder and childhood sexual abuse experts (e.g., Wooley & Kearney-Cook, 1986; Wooley, 1994; Kearney-Cook & Striegel-Moore, 1994) evinces similar findings with respect to understanding the link between childhood sexual abuse and eating disorders and the attitude towards appropriate treatment methods. Studies examining the perspective of eating disorder clients (e.g., de la Rie, Noordenbos, Donker, & van Furth, 2006; Rosenvinge & Klusmeier, 2000) also yield similar findings with respect to the critique of the conventional methods of treatment in the eating disorder field.

One of the central claims arising from this study is that the spectrum of severe and complex symptoms that are the well-known result of childhood sexual abuse challenges the psychiatric diagnostic institution and prevalent methods of treatment. Despite the fact that people with complex trauma histories make up the bulk of clients seen in mental health centres, they remain nameless and homeless. The treatment of chronically traumatized individuals fundamentally continues to play itself out on a village level of oral traditions and anecdotes. The profound clinical wisdom that results from intimate exposure to chronically traumatized people continues to be largely anecdotal and transmitted in supervision sessions, small conferences, and informal discussions among colleagues (van der Kolk, 2009).

We are thus faced with the question of the extent to which numerous mental illnesses – such as hysteria – and other phenomena defined as witchcraft or demon possession throughout history are in fact (primarily judgmental and stigmatizing) names given to the inherent consequences of childhood sexual abuse. Challenging the psychiatric diagnostic institution, this book reveals how often abused women become victims once again within the mental health system, suffering from false diagnoses and inappropriate – and frequently damaging – treatment methods.

Understanding the direct link between childhood sexual abuse and eating disorders is of seminal importance for finding methods to prevent the emergence of the latter and offer appropriate methods of treatment. This study calls for a reexamination of the therapeutic views that lie at the basis of the eating disorder field of knowledge and revision of numerous therapeutic procedures – from the multi-participant intake that broadcasts to clients, from the moment they enter therapy, that even here their privacy is not respected through to the intrusive and violent procedures of being locked up in cooling down rooms, tied up, and force fed.

A large segment of women who suffer from eating disorders also exhibit a complex spectrum of other symptoms. Women frequently turn to specialized treatment centres at their own initiative. Some of the women interviewed in this study went to centres dedicated to treating eating disorders, while others sought help from centres specializing in childhood sexual abuse or therapy with general therapists. In most of the treatments, the therapists found it difficult to provide an adequate response to the full range of their complex symptoms, some of the women being referred from one framework to another. The implications for intervention thus highlight the importance of establishing a series of integrative treatment centres.

The study's findings also challenge the nature of the diagnoses and existing therapeutic distinctions with respect to syndromes produced by childhood sexual abuse – such as women addicted to drugs, women offenders, etc. The various symptoms from which these women suffer forming part of the complex spectrum of childhood sexual abuse manifestations, centres that develop expertise in one area can only give fragmentary and partial treatment. Frequently, the focus is directed towards alleviating symptoms, leading – in the best case – to their removal. In the absence of any consideration of their source, however, they will simply be replaced with others. In the worst case, no progress will be achieved and the client will be dismissed due to non-cooperation or transferred from one specialized framework to another. Hereby, they reexperience the sense of being unacceptable, abandoned, and betrayed by the therapist. These feelings reenact the original trauma.

The research highlights the need for additional studies to expand our knowledge of children, girls, and women who suffer from eating disorders from the perspective of their childhood traumas. Great importance exists in finding research methods that will give place and space to the authentic voices of clients. Quantitative studies conducted via questionnaires struggle to document childhood sexual abuse and eating disorders because of the secrecy involved. This fact explains the vast gaps that exist between studies, clinicians, and reports on the link between childhood sexual abuse and eating disorders today. Qualitative research must be conducted that will allow women and girls to express their own voice and bring their own perspective into therapeutic fields and research.

Clients with a history of childhood sexual abuse challenge therapists because their experience is one of betrayal and abandonment by close caretakers. It is thus difficult for us who represent institutional frameworks and authority to build relations of trust and healing with them. The epidemic of childhood sexual abuse is spawned by the authoritative, aggressive patriarchal society in which we grow up and by which we are influenced. This serving as fertile ground for the growth of abuse and exploitation of the subordinate and helpless, we must find structures that challenge social conventions and the treatment procedures offered in them and develop innovative, subversive, and creative treatment methods that can provide true healing for abused women.

The book is divided into three parts. The first deals with eating disorders, childhood sexual abuse, and the link between them. The second examines eating disorders and childhood sexual abuse treatment. The third proposes a new diagnosis and treatment that is essentially trauma-informed. The appendix brings Dawn's story, which is a perfect example of what this book has set out to address.

References

Kearney-Cooke, A., & Striegel-Moore, R. H. (1994). Treatment of childhood sexual abuse in anorexia nervosa and bulimia nervosa: A feminist psychodynamic approach. In M. F. Schwartz & L. Cohn (Eds.), *Sexual abuse and eating disorders* (pp. 155–175). Bristol, PA: Brunner/Mazel.

Rie, S. de la, Noordenbos, G., Donker, M., & van Furth, E. (2006). Evaluating the treatment of eating disorders from the patient's perspective. *International Journal of Eating Disorders, 39*(8), 667–676.

Rosenvinge, J. H., & Klusmeier, A. K. (2000). Treatment for eating disorders from a patient-satisfaction perspective: A Norwegian replication of a British study. *European Eating Disorders Review, 8*, 293–300.

van der Kolk, B. (2009). Afterword. In C. A. Courtois & J. D. Ford (Eds.), *Treating complex stress disorders* (pp. 455–466). New York, NY: Guilford Press.

Wooley, S. C. (1994). Sexual abuse and eating disorders: The concealed debate. In P. Fallon, M. A. Katzman, & S. C. Wooley (Eds.), *Feminist perspectives on eating disorders* (pp. 171–211). New York, NY: Guilford Press.

Wooley, S. C., & Kearney-Cooke, A. (1986). Intensive treatment of bulimia and body-image disturbance. In K. D. Brownell & J. P. Foreyt (Eds.), *Handbook of eating disorders: Physiology, psychology, and treatment of obesity, anorexia and bulimia* (pp. 476–502). New York, NY: Basic Books.

Part I

Eating disorders, childhood sexual abuse, and the link between them

Introduction

The close link between childhood sexual abuse and eating disorders has only begun to come to the attention of those working in the field of eating disorders in recent years, following the publication of professional studies and clinical accounts reporting the high rate of childhood sexual abuse amongst women suffering from eating disorders. The increased awareness of childhood sexual abuse may be attributed to the growing public discourse with regard to the sexual abuse women suffer, a discourse that, legitimizing the breaking of the cycles of shame and silence amongst women suffering from eating disorders, allows them to speak about the sexual abuse they experienced as children.

Controversy nevertheless still rages within the eating disorders field over various issues – such as the rate of childhood sexual abuse amongst the eating disorder population, the existence of a causal relation between traumatic history and eating disorders, whether childhood sexual abuse is a central risk factor in the aetiology of eating disorders, and whether they are widespread amongst women in general.

The studies that have examined the rates of childhood sexual abuse amongst women suffering from eating disorders differ widely. Today, more and more, in particular clinical reports are documenting high levels – around 70 to 80 percent – of a history of childhood sexual abuse amongst women with eating disorders (Oppenheimer, Howells, Palmer, & Chaloner, 1985; Kearney-Cooke & Striegel-Moore, 1996).

The rates of childhood sexual abuse are very difficult to assess due to the secrecy, shame, silence, and dissociation characteristic of this type of molestation. Children are frequently sexually abused by close and loved family members at an age when they are too young to understand what is happening and are thus unable to conceptualize it or remember it with any certainty. Women with eating disorders find it particularly difficult to identify the phenomenon because, as we shall see below, these often serve as a means of dissociation from the sexual abuse and its horrors. The rates of childhood sexual abuse amongst women suffering from eating disorders may thus be far higher than reported, many women not speaking of their traumatic history due to full or partial amnesia of the events and the great difficulty in speaking about having been sexually abused.

In Part I, I review the various forms of eating disorders as defined in DSM-5 and the history of the development of the tendency to define them as a disorder. We shall examine the reasons behind the emergence of eating disorders as defined in the professional literature and the link between them and gender. I then look at childhood sexual abuse and its features and consequences, citing its close association with eating disorders and the theories adduced to explain this link. This is followed by accounts of eating disorders and childhood sexual abuse from women who have suffered from both and descriptions and narratives given by those interviewed for the study upon which this book is based regarding the link between childhood sexual abuse and eating disorders. The findings indicating that this connection is also closely linked with dissociative disorders, I shall also review the latter as defined in the DSM. Here, too, we shall hear the stories of women who suffer from such phenomena. The final chapter in this part addresses the associations between sexual abuse, eating disorders, and the female body.

References

Kearney-Cooke, A., & Striegel-Moore, R. H. (1996). Treatment of childhood sexual abuse in anorexia nervosa and bulimia nervosa: A feminist psychodynamic approach. In M. F. Schwartz & L. Cohn (Eds.), *Sexual abuse and eating disorders* (pp. 155–175). Bristol, PA: Brunner/Mazel.

Oppenheimer, R., Howells, K., Palmer, L., & Chaloner, D. (1985). Adverse sexual experiences in childhood and clinical eating disorders: A preliminary description. *Journal of Psychiatric Research, 19*, 157–161.

2) Rumination disorder: Repeated regurgitation (re-chewing, re-swallowing, or spitting out of food) on a frequent basis – at least twice a week and often every day – over a period of at least one month that is not due to a medical condition nor occurs exclusively in the course of other eating disorders.
3) Avoidant/restrictive food intake disorder: An eating/feeding disturbance manifested in a persistent failure to meet appropriate nutritional and/or energy needs that leads to significant loss of weight (or failure to achieve expected weight gain/faltering growth in children), significant nutritional deficiency, dependence on external feeding or oral nutritional supplements, and impaired psychosocial functioning.
4) Anorexia nervosa: The three principal features of anorexia nervosa are: a) persistent restriction of energy intake; b) an intense fear of gaining weight/ becoming fat or persistent behaviour that interferes with weight gain; and c) disturbance in the way body weight or shape is experienced, undue influence of body shape and weight on self-evaluation, or persistent lack of recognition of the seriousness of the current low body weight (the latter being defined as falling below the minimal normal level suitable to body form, age, sex, developmental trajectory, and physical health). Although anorexia nervosa is linked to significant loss of weight, it can also manifest itself in children and adolescents in the form of normal development problems – such as growth or height. Its incidence is 0.4 percent, the correlation between women and men being estimated at 10:1.
5) Bulimia nervosa: Recurrent episodes of binge eating during a discrete period of time (e.g., within any two-hour period) of a larger amount of food than that eaten by most people during a similar period of time and under similar circumstances accompanied by a sense of lack of control (e.g., a feeling that one cannot stop eating or control what/how much one is eating). Recurrent inappropriate compensatory behaviours are also engaged in in order to prevent weight gain – self-induced vomiting, misuse of laxatives, diuretics or other medications, fasting, or excessive exercise. The binge eating and inappropriate compensatory behaviours occur on average at least once a week for a period of three months. Self-evaluation is unduly influenced by body shape and weight. The incidence of bulimia nervosa is between 1 and 1.5 percent. Although it is not clear how many males it affects, the correlation between women and men is estimated at 10:1.
6) Binge-eating disorder: Recurrent episodes of binge eating over a discrete period of time (e.g., within any two-hour period) of a larger amount of food than that most people would eat during a similar period of time and under similar circumstances and a sense of lack of control over eating during the episode. This disorder is associated with eating much more rapidly than normal, eating until feeling uncomfortably full, consuming large amounts of food when not feeling physically hungry, eating alone because of feeling embarrassed by how much one is eating, and feeling disgusted

with oneself, depressed, or guilty afterward. The incidence of this disorder is 1.6 percent amongst women and 0.8 amongst men.

7) Other specified feeding or eating disorder: These are situations in which the symptoms of feeding or eating disorders cause clinically significant distress and impairment in areas of social or professional functioning but do not fully meet the criteria for any other feeding or eating disorder. A diagnosis may then be allocated that specifies a specific reason why the presentation does not meet the specifics of another disorder (e.g., low-level bulimia nervosa).
8) Unspecified feeding or eating disorder: Behaviours that cause clinically significant distress/impairment of functioning but do not fully meet the criteria of any of the feeding or eating disorder criteria. This category is appropriate for cases in which clinicians choose not to specify why the criteria are not met, including presentations in which insufficient information is available to make a more specific diagnosis (e.g., in emergency room settings).

The changes made in DSM-5 were introduced in order to reduce the number of unspecified eating disorder diagnoses. Thus, for example, 'refusal' to maintain proper weight has been deleted from the anorexia nervosa criteria due to the difficulty in measuring it. The criterion of no menstrual cycle has also been dropped because in some cases the remaining criteria are met but the menstrual cycle continues. It is also irrelevant to men, pre-pubescent girls, and postmenopausal women. With respect to bulimia nervosa, the frequency of binge-eating sprees and purging rituals has been reduced to twice a week. As this edition was nearing publication, however, clinicians and scholars in the field estimated that the revisions have not resolved the problems attendant upon the definition of eating disorders (Fairburn & Cooper, 2010).

The interviews conducted for this study clearly indicate that eating disorders do not constitute a distinct and precisely defined category classifiable according to the criteria found in the psychiatric diagnostic manuals. Several of the women interviewed had suffered from various forms before they finally found an appropriate way to convey the horror of the sexual abuse they had experienced as children. They related how they had suffered from an undefined problem, seeking ways to express their distress that included diverse eating disorders – avoiding eating, vomiting, and bingeing. Olivia, for example, who had been sexually abused by her father but until recently had had no memory of the abuse, related that as she entered puberty she began to starve herself. Losing a lot of weight and receiving many compliments from those around her and her mother, she became anorexic. Because she loved food, however, she found it difficult not to eat and began bingeing instead. As she put on weight, she became a binge eater, a condition that lasted several years. When she was conscripted into the army to do her regular two years' service, her friends introduced her to the 'patent' of throwing up as a way of dealing with her obesity. She began vomiting regularly, thus becoming a bulimic. Together with these eating disorder symptoms, she suffered from numerous others, such as revictimization, self-injury, prostitution, etc. Her story demonstrates that, as part of an undiagnosed problem, she began unconsciously 'choosing' ways to express her distress – some of which took the form of eating disorder symptoms. The culture of slimness serves as a convenient and acceptable social means of expressing post-traumatic distress. All young girls and women wanting to be slim, this state becomes an easy and acceptable social default for articulating unspeakable distress.

The history of eating disorders

Although phenomena such as self-starvation, vomiting, and overeating are documented in the literature over the centuries, their classification as mental disorders is a relatively new development. Anorexia nervosa, bulimia nervosa, and atypical eating disorders were first included in DSM-III in 1980 (APA, 1980), the latter – considered rare during this period (Thomas, Vartanian, & Brownell, 2009) – referring to eating disorders of a clinical magnitude that do not meet the criteria of anorexia nervosa or bulimia nervosa.

A historical review of the definition of eating disorders as a 'disease' indicates that anorexia was identified and gained its name in Victorian England during the 1870s, as medicine began emerging as a profession. Etymologically, anorexia signifies 'without appetite'. The 'birth' of this disease was linked to the new authority medicine gained during this period and the changes in the structure of society, both of which were of great import for women. Joan Jacobs Brumberg (1988) argues that pubescent girls in modern society face sociocultural pressures that cause them to feel that looking good is more important than cultivating inner qualities. Anorexia thus first arose as part and parcel of the development of Western industrial-capitalist society and bourgeois living, which introduced factors such as intimacy, marital life, parenthood, gender labour division, power, and sexuality.

The diagnostic criteria of anorexia nervosa were first outlined in 1972, and they were included in DSM-III in 1980 (G. F. M. Russell, 1986). The term bulimia nervosa – from the Greek *bous* = ox and *limos* = hunger (i.e., ox-hunger) – only entered the English language in 1977 (Gordon, 2000), being recognized as a mental disorder in 1979 (G. F. M. Russell, 1995). The term 'eating disorder not otherwise specified' (EDNOS) was coined in 1994 for DSM-IV (APA, 1994) to designate clients suffering from clinically significant eating disorders that did not meet any of the diagnostic criteria of anorexia nervosa or bulimia nervosa (Walsh & Garner, 1994). As noted above, the various definitions of eating disorders in the official psychiatric manuals – the DSM and ICD (International Classification of Diseases) – are continually being revised.

A historical survey of eating disorders evinces the provisionality and relativity of their definition, together with the influence of the perspective from which the psychiatric diagnoses are made – commonly and erroneously regarded as 'scientific' and absolute. Diagnosis is of great import for clinical treatment and research directions (G. F. M. Russell, 1995). The question arises of the extent to which contemporary official diagnoses of eating disorders in fact serve the male hegemonic medical establishment as a way of classifying and branding women seeking to express the distress caused by the sexual abuse they have suffered. I shall discuss this issue in the chapter on eating disorders, hysteria, and 'madness' amongst women.

The aetiology of eating disorders

The aetiology of eating disorders remains obscure, scholars today still being unable to point to the prime cause of their development. They are commonly accepted, however, to be the result of a combination of a large number of biological, personality, psychological, family, and sociocultural factors (Fairburn & Harrison, 2003). Numerous studies have addressed the issue of the risk factors specifically associated with the development of eating disorders (Striegel-Moore & Bulik, 2007). In a survey of the findings relating to this question in the professional literature, Jacobi, Hayward, de Zwaan, Kraemer, and Agras (2004) found that over thirty are adduced, including demographic factors (e.g., gender and ethnic origin), psychological factors (e.g., preoccupation with weight, negative body image, and feeding and low self-image in childhood), and biological factors (e.g., childhood obesity). The most commonly accepted paradigm is the bio-psycho-social model (Polivy & Herman, 2002), which takes into account a broad range of factors – from cultural, biological, and familiar to social, cognitive, learnt, personality, etc.

The plethora of causes suggested and fierce dispute over the aetiology of eating disorders may reflect the persistent tendency amongst eating-order specialists to ignore a central factor – namely, childhood sexual abuse. The present study indicates that the trauma caused by childhood sexual abuse lies at the heart of eating disorder aetiology, the other key factors referred to in the literature – such as relational difficulties with the mother and family problems – are being a byproduct of this initial trauma. In most cases of childhood sexual abuse, other aetiological factors also exist. For example, many girls who suffer from childhood sexual abuse develop great rage towards their mothers for having failed to protect them and prevent the abuse.

Eating disorders and gender

As noted above, eating disorders are an overwhelmingly female complaint, estimates indicating that 85–95 percent of all those who suffer from anorexia nervosa, bulimia nervosa, and unspecified eating disorders and 65 percent of all bulimics are women (NIMH, 2008). Although gender plays a more important role in eating disorders than in any other field, its precise contribution towards their development remains obscure (Fallon, Katzman, & Wooley, 1994). Numerous scholars associate the acute suffering experienced by eating disorder sufferers with the difficulties women face in society. Carrying the deepest fears of all women in our culture and their own as-yet-unidentified problems, they express them in a body language that still remain to be learnt (Fallon et al., 1994). Linked with the over-preoccupation in our society with the female body image, they are thus anchored in female social inequality (Orbach, 2006).

Others argue that the pursuit of slimness serves as a form of male impersonation in an age in which women who strive to influence society equally with their male counterparts must deny their 'otherness' in order to gain their goal (Fallon et al., 1994). Additional explanations adduce the religious traditions of asceticism and monasticism, flight from sexuality, and a return to childhood (Fallon et al., 1994). Anorexia is also thought to reflect female confusion over the extent of the space women are able to attain in the world (Orbach, 2006). Some scholars have sought to examine the role hormones may play, particularly in pubescent and adolescent girls. Studies have also found that girls who start menstruating early are at high risk of developing eating disorders (NIMH, 2008).

Feminist psychoanalysts posit that women use their bodies to express the inner conflicts they experience as a result of the social context into they are born, develop, and become adults. Some scholars thus assert that eating disorders form a complex personal response to a series of interpersonal, intrapsychic, political, and cultural phenomena that determine women's relationships with themselves and others (Orbach, 1986). Avoidance of food may form a function of a girl/woman's need to control her body as representing her emotional needs (Orbach, 1986). Some feminist clinicians thus contend that, unable to tolerate feelings and experiencing their emotional life as an attack upon themselves, anorexics seek ways to negate who they are – needy, hungry, angry, yearning – in order to turn themselves into someone they find more acceptable (Orbach, 1986).

Many scholars adduce the ever more oppressive norms regulating female appearance. In less than two decades, the ideal woman size has decreased by a third, an expectation most women cannot meet. As the efforts to conform to this standard become ever more strenuous and demand more and more resources, weight norms have become an accepted form of female oppression (Fallon et al., 1994). Orbach (2009) asserts that 'body anxiety' and 'body hatred' constitute a widespread problem from which millions of women in the world suffer in silence. While taken as self-evident, it nevertheless remains undefined. Not liking their bodies, women make them the object of conflict. The body has also become commercialized in modern society, all of its parts being subject to intense scrutiny. Today, myriads of treatments exist designed to intervene in normal developmental process, women spending vast amounts of money in an attempt to alter their appearance.

This sense of dissatisfaction with one's appearance and endeavour to change it is being bequeathed to younger and younger girls, who are being told that positive feelings towards their bodies can only be achieved via the use of beauty products, styling, diets, cosmetic surgery, fashion, and body sculpting. All these industries – whose sole purpose is to sell more and more products – make millions from girls and women unhappy with their appearance, the unrealistic visual images on billboards and computer and television screens that surround us encouraging uniformity by means of digital images of ideal women that have no relation to reality. Girls see adverts portraying the female sex as attractive, arousing, enticing, slim, and sleek, and they seek to conform to them.

A chronicle of an eating disorder: listening to women's voices

Beyond the psychiatric diagnostic criteria and experts who define eating disorders, it is vitally important to listen to the voices of those who suffer from them themselves and their own descriptions of their experiences. Like the stories of sexual abuse, these are difficult to hear – embarrassing, humiliating, and shameful. Women thus find it difficult to give a full account of them. The decision to quote examples here was taken in order to illustrate these problems and demonstrate the direct link between eating disorders and childhood sexual abuse. The women interviewed for the study were all sexually abused as children, their descriptions of their eating disorders giving voice to the various ways in which they attempted to deal with this trauma – the feelings of shame and disgust, the need to get rid of everything inside that has no words, the desire to 'scream out' the abuse, the effort to regain control over their bodies, etc.

Anorexia

Natasha: 'The repertoire of what I eat is more like that of autistic children'

It . . . it began when . . . I think I was at university, that at some stage, somewhere in the middle of the first year, I think . . . in general . . . every situation began to deteriorate, like . . . it was hard to understand that it was deteriorating because I was simply on a high all the time. But I almost stopped sleeping and eating. I could eat, but I didn't want to, and I lost some 8 kilos just like that, in about half a year, or less. I ate really little for a long time. And then somehow, gradually, I started eating more. Then there began a period of bingeing. I would get up in the night and empty the fridge. That went on for about three years and I put on a lot of weight. Then there was another long period when I virtually stopped eating. This time it got more serious. If the first time, during the first period, I could still eat a bit, because I didn't want to deteriorate altogether, I didn't want, I didn't want to find myself hospitalized or something. Then in the second period it was already . . . there were weeks when I couldn't eat at all, for a week or two. I could eat perhaps a crisp a day. I couldn't, I couldn't swallow unless it dissolved in my mouth. And then all the time I had . . . even when I did eat, I was nauseous all the time. A feeling of nausea . . . gradually, over the years, during these years things became a bit more balanced. But always when I had some . . . some periods of tension, I would go back to this and I wouldn't eat. I . . . say all the time, I almost wouldn't eat anything cooked.

Still today, the repertoire of what I eat is more like autistic children. Like, it comes in waves. There are times when I eat A, B, C, D and there are times when I eat E . . . One thing, like . . . But it's always specific things. And . . . often I eat really little. In general, say a long period, two or three years, I eat on average between eight hundred and a thousand calories a day, when I know I'm supposed to eat one thousand eight hundred.

Grace: 'Every time I stepped on the scales and saw that I'd lost weight, it was the greatest feeling in the world'

I wasn't that fat, in general, I was athletic and that, like, I had a great body (laughs). And then I stopped eating. And it began, it began with replacing food with all sorts of diet things – diet coca cola, diet ice cream, diet everything. Then I started eating more vegetables . . . to began to count calories, to understand calories, sport, more, ah . . . everything possible to lose weight.

At then at a certain point . . . I began using laxatives, and then . . . it began with one pill, to two, three, until it got to 120. Until, you know, the body quite broke down. I would shower sitting down, everything was already . . . and then I told my mother, if you don't go and get more pills I'll kill myself (laughs). It was like that . . . already in fact . . . no, not because of guilt towards her, but it was difficult to send Mum, it's like going to get drugs. And she went and got them for me, because of course that was better than my killing myself. Somehow, my Dad gave up at some point, like, I understood that he told my Mum: 'Look, I'm raising my hands'. Like, with the suicide thing and all . . . and then it became a situation in which everything I ate it was 120 laxatives and nothing was left, my whole body had began to be consumed.

At some stage, seeing is no longer rational. I just stood in front of the mirror and if I did something like this and, like, there was just a tiny bit flesh, then I was fat. Now when I went to the beach, I was already like that, you can see in pictures today and that. People used to look at me, and I always thought that they were looking because I was fat – not because I was so, so, so thin. And I always had this thing, all the time I could hold something that was fat on me, all the time there was flesh on me, then I was fat, I had to lose more weight.

I liked hurting myself, like it was . . . it was fun. Look, in my feelings I already understood that I was going and fainting, that I was going to work and I was dizzy, that, like, it was hard to stand up. There are some things that are understandable. But losing weight was the most powerful thing. Nothing around me was of any interest, I don't know if I felt that, like, I presume so, that I understood that I was putting myself in danger at some point. But it didn't – it didn't really interest me. It was excitement, every time I stepped on the scales and saw that I'd lost weight, it was the greatest feeling in the world. Because I was in control, as it were. In control but losing control. Then, thank God, I was in control – no one else. I got down to 30 kilos.

Lily: 'If I'm thin I'll be less disgusting'

The eating disorder really began when I became an adolescent. I was . . . I mean, it wasn't that I was a fat child, I was always thin and athletic and all sorts of things like that. Like, very not . . . like I didn't need to diet, that wasn't the point, I didn't begin by starting diets. I mean, it wasn't anorexia from starting diets. What it was, I think, was that I was simply awfully depressed. I mean, I remember myself primarily, primarily what I felt was awfully alone. And at some stage, like, I didn't stop eating, it wasn't something that happened all at once, but I began to become preoccupied with this issue . . . I wasn't into food. I mean, food interested me less. And not sweets, let's presume, that I wasn't a great fan of sweets. And then I remember . . . like I remember that it began happening, like in the sense of a disorder. That I began to become preoccupied with calories, for example . . . and I really remember the beginning. Like, something like this, that I said to myself: 'Why are you dealing with this? Like, what's the story now?' But it's something that got out of control.

I started menstruating, for example, at a relatively young age. Like, to me it seemed awfully early. I was 12½, which seemed to me very quick. I was like a short child, small, thin, not really developed. I'm talking on the physical level. Or even of sexuality, on the chest level, then . . . I wore a bra because everyone did, but what was there? (laughs) But ok.

There's something that's really difficult apparently, when losing control, to understand exactly where you lose it there. But I lost control over this. I mean, it was something that I was dealing with every day, all the time. At the same time as all my matriculation exams, all the time. Really all the time. On the level of a cucumber. Like the thing that most . . . I don't know what. Like how many calories is this? And how many calories is that? And how much am I putting into my body now and how much I'm putting in now?

And at the same time as dealing with this, yes, what I remember is really strong, is myself in the mirror. If I spoke before about the feeling of disgust, then it's really disgusting. Really. I mean, disgusting, revolting, fat, disgusting. I mean, I looked ugly to myself, simply ugly, like something disgusting. And that's what I saw, I mean, that's what was in my head. I didn't see someone else. I didn't see something else. I didn't see myself as I looked.

And that's it, it went on for a long time. Something like 2½ years. People spoke to me, at school as well. I had a history teacher, I don't know why – why he in particular came to talk to me. He asked me what was happening with me and why I was so thin. I got down to 32 kilos, I mean I was really . . . I didn't eat. No, I ate from time to time because I *was* hungry. But if I ate then I would have awful pangs of conscience. And I would count, like, what I had eaten, and do the calculations, like, of if I eat this then I can't eat for a week because, I don't know what.

True, I looked fat to myself. But what was most in my head was that I was simply disgusting, other people, and . . . even myself. And then if I was thin . . . it wasn't connected, it wasn't connected to reality, but then I . . . If I would be thin I would be less ugly.

Shirley: 'People on the outside don't understand, but it's amazing'

When I was in the army, I began an ordinary diet. It began like something very, very ordinary, because I wanted to be thinner. But I think that gradually I began to cut down on what I was eating. I didn't eat every day and only ate when I went home, and then when I went home I had a certain meal – say schnitzel, rice, and something else. Then I began to cut down on amounts. Instead of two spoonful of rice, I would have one. I decided that I also had to leave something on the plate. And I began to become addicted to everything connected with this issue. I also began to do lots and lots of sports – like an obsession. I began to do push-ups and I told myself that I had to do 60, and every time I persuaded myself that I'd miscounted. I could get up to 5000 by convincing myself that I'd counted wrongly.

I also used laxatives, of course, in huge amounts. I began with, say, two and then I said, Ok, I'll double the amount, like with the push-ups, and I got up to some 15 pills at a time.

Then at a certain stage I lost a lot of weight. I weighed 42 kilos and I was still going around with coats on and everyone caught on and the head of my section called my Mum and told her that if she was taking care of me she would send me to a mental health officer. It was very extreme, I lost some 17 kilos.

Then I started therapy and they sent me to a dietician. And with the dietician I began to relinquish control a bit. I put on weight very quickly, I was in shock over it, and I was very, very angry. I was angry with everyone because they'd hurt me – look what you've done to me. My waves were like this, of losing a lot, a lot of weight and putting it back on very quickly.

After I was released from the army, there were episodes of some months of losing lots of weight, months of putting it on, low weight, like a yo-yo. It was really strange because the people who worked with me, I would go from a size 26 to a size 42. With huge disparities. People on the outside don't understand, but it's amazing. Then they diagnosed me with clinical depression and I got anxious. It was like off and on.

Bulimia

Liliana: 'I didn't throw up calories. I threw up myself, from inside myself'

With respect to eating disorders, first of all, I was curvaceous, feminine, as a girl, I always had a big chest, and I remember the first time I dieted, Mum put me on a diet when I was 17 – 17 or 16. A proper diet, that Mum put me on, three meals a day, a piece of chocolate a day, and that's it. It began, as you know, when you want to be a bit thinner, more sculpted, and such like.

And then I got to know a good friend – who's still a good friend today – from whom I first heard the word vomit. And my eyes lit up. To the person who tells you that throwing up is all acid, stinking, regurgitated food, I so much know that, that it sits in the hole so much . . . it's like a hole that's just waiting for it. It's a hole, that sits . . . I'd never thrown up food, I, I, never thought about calories. I didn't throw up calories. I threw up myself, from inside myself. It's like a cycle. You feel bad, not just physically, after you throw up, because you say: 'Everything I've undergone – and none of things I wanted to come out have come out'. What I wanted to come out didn't come out. But at the same time it's a wonderful feeling, it's a feeling . . . Today I don't have the strength to get to that level any more. But until you get to the bile in the stomach and you've already got cramps, when you already don't need to do anything. Because I know techniques of soap and such like, and all sorts of tricks like that, you already don't do anything. There are these natural cramps. That you're already thin and your ribs are caught in . . . the rib is caught in this bone, and everything like this, everything is cramping, and I don't know, perhaps I prayed that my body would come out through my pharynx, through my oesophagus. Because there's s★★★ inside. There some sort of s★★★ inside. There's s★★★ inside that has to come out.

It makes me feel good and it makes me feel bad. It's simply . . . first of all, it's also bad physically. It's really hard, tiring, exhausting. It also doesn't give, it doesn't give real relief. But all the time you hope that it will. In other words, there's a form of relief. It's a physical relief, that's the first thing. First of all, there's physical relief, first of all because, you know, space has been made, it's always good. And . . . and it's almost . . . it's really like that, it's like something suddenly appears, you . . . it doesn't have words, I'm really sorry, it's *without words*. But it's like if I try to translate the feelings, again, because it's not the words I had then in my head. But it's like saying, 'Look, look, here I am, here's the feeling, now it's just physical, the relief will come in a moment'. And perhaps some relief and then you say 'pak', really not, apparently it's impossible. Then you try again, and again, and again. But it's not, it's not conscious. It's not entirely conscious. It's not that you say to yourself, I didn't say to myself: 'Here, I'm throwing up. . .' I don't know what, the smell. No. I understand, but when something is sitting inside you and you want to get it out.

Look, the vomiting is with me until today. I virtually don't throw up, but I can tell you that with my present partner – we've been together a year and a half – some months after we became an item, then . . . he, I won't say what, he did something that in my opinion you don't do. And I didn't want to talk to him about it. So I told him: 'Get out, we've got nothing in common, we're two different worlds'. And I went to the bathroom and used my largest finger and just felt as though I was throwing him up. That I was throwing up the bad thing he had done to me. I don't have many situations like that, I – I'm talking to myself, but it's a really, really easy and effective solution. I don't recommend it to you.

Debby: 'It's a cunning, accursed disease, it's like cancer'

In my opinion, my bulimia got worse before I went into the army. From there, it really became systematic. I take laxatives regularly, I throw up every day, and I'm sad that I'm like that. I'm sad. But it's part . . . I don't know how you treat . . . I don't know what to do, I scream.

I would eat, eat, eat, I remember it was cornflakes with chocolate milk. It really made me feel that I had to throw up. So I would eat a full bowl of cornflakes with chocolate milk and . . . get rid of it all.

The whole subject of bulimia . . . people don't . . . don't understand. Like once I told a friend during the period when I joined a group that I'm a bulimic, so she says to me, 'What fun! I wish I could vomit'. Like just like that. And I tell her, 'Yo, like, you don't understand how difficult it is?' Like it's . . . it's a disease, it's a cunning, accursed disease, it's like cancer. Really. It's impossible, I . . . sometimes I say, no, today I'm only going to eat healthy things that don't have any calories and today I'm not going to throw up. It's not. It's not. It's not. I throw up every day. Whenever I eat. Or I don't eat so that I won't have any need to throw up, because it's so awfully, awfully tiring, and I'm so, so exhausted after all the throwing up. So then I really try not to eat too much on one day.

But it's an accursed disease. Simply to see yourself every day in . . . in . . . your image reflected . . . not nice to say . . . like in . . . in . . . the toilet like . . . Yes, it's not nice.

Sometimes I'm afraid that nothing will come out . . . there's already no gag reflex. In other words, the gag reflect is already ah . . . ah . . . yes, it's sad . . . it's rather embarrassing to talk about it, but yes. It's a disease, what can you do? So yes, to do some motion of vomiting and everything comes out. And to drink lots. In other words, after eating to drink lots and lots and lots in order to bring everything to the top and vomit. Today, I'm 39½. And it's almost more than 20 years. . .

Bingeing

Naomi: 'This fat is what protects me'

When I became an adolescent, and men and women – in fact it's not men, it's boys and girls – I gradually started becoming fatter and like, it's not something that happens boom, in one go, but it begins with eating improperly, eating at night, and wasting almost all your money, your pocket money, on food. So I would do lots of babysittering during that time and spend all my money really on these treats that were linked with food. And then it continued, like, also when I was in the army.

Although it developed gradually, it was like suddenly going from a girl who worked out and played basketball and I was in the school long jump team and all sorts of things like that, suddenly I became plump. Since then I've virtually been living with the thing of 'on and off' – of diets, ordinary states, or feeling good about myself and not good about myself, and each time something else.

And that's it, but food was always my best friend, like even out of my love of cooking, like I make ice cream and chocolates, and I worked in restaurants, I mean this is essentially what I wanted to do, so food was always around me, I mean, it was never a problem. But there were always . . . it was connected to the fact that, to the whole thing of . . . other than the fact that people saw me eat, it was always around, and every time I got some feedback from the other sex, and it was only things that I see every day, in retrospect, because at the time I didn't see them, so I went and gave myself feedback with food. And that's it, that's the issue that has gone on for about eight years already. My top was plus another 30 kilos, I was around 140 kilos at my top weight. This fat is what protects me.

Orna: 'Eating and filling something that's broken inside'

I was very, very fat. From a young age, I was fat. In Grade 6, they took me to a doctor and a dietician to see what was happening with me. I was already 106 kilos, in Grade 6. I remember it. After that, I only got fatter and fatter, and in Grade 10, I think, they again took me to a doctor and he told me that I wouldn't live to 12 because in another two years I would surely be dead because I weighed 140, something like that.

With respect to eating disorders, obesity, so I was born a big girl. I was the biggest of all my siblings. And all my life I was fat. All my childhood and all my life. Once, the . . . when, linked to this issue, I was 9, so my Mum was very angry at me, again, that I was fat and that I couldn't stay on the diet and that I . . . not . . . like, that it's not alright, so I told her I wasn't fat, I was pregnant. And so she told me I couldn't be pregnant. She asked me why I could be pregnant. I told her . . . I warned her not to tell my Dad, but I explained to her why I was pregnant and then she . . . she simply ignored it completely. She only told me that I couldn't be pregnant and that was it, and that from her point of view it was over and only that I needed to lose weight – and that was the end of the story.

Towards my army service, I wasn't conscripted because I was too fat. But then I lost 75 kilos in one go. I simply didn't eat. I was hungry for half a year.

I simply didn't eat anything. Perhaps an olive a day, really nothing. And then I was conscripted and then it was alright and all.

But after I was released I put on weight again. And then once again I got to 160 kilos. 160½. All my life I've been fat. All my childhood and all my life. I used to eat lunch and then I would eat more. Like, this was my pleasure, food. This was my happiest moments, this was my escape. I escaped, I escaped simply there. And until today, by the way, this . . . this I absolutely know, that I eat out of emotion. In other words, when I don't feel good I eat, completely. I remember once that my Mum said, 'Dad is awfully worried when he looks at you and you're so fat'. There were all sorts of expressions . . . coming down hard on me, on my dimensions, on my figure, these were the expressions then at home. And really to hurt me, and 'don't eat that'. And then you learn to eat in secret. It's easy – really, really easy. But yes, all the time a feeling of guilt, that you need to lose weight and lose weight and I'm awfully fat, I'm not ok.

And then, to avoid the insults and humiliations, I would eat in secret. Up until today, I find it difficult to eat in front of people. I generally only eat when I'm alone. Eating . . . overeating, is generally when I'm alone. I don't eat that much in front of other people. In front of other people I eat in a very proper, orderly fashion. People have told me they don't understand why I'm fat.

My eating disorder is overeating. I remember that I thought that if I was very fat then I wouldn't . . . perhaps I would turn other people off, and I wouldn't be attractive. So yes, it was part of the issue. It didn't really work. But it was there . . . but still, even after the story with my brother was over, there were still some other abuses. Then it was probably that . . . that story wasn't really a success.

And there's also the matter of eating and filling something that's broken inside, then, like, to fill it with food. And there's also the matter of erasing tastes from the point of view . . . like there's a nasty taste in the mouth from something that happened, then I eat something else to stop it. But the taste doesn't stop and then you eat more and more until it does stop.

Note

1 A medical student, Noga sent me an email because she wanted to be interviewed for this study. Although I had already finished the interview stage, she so badly wanted to share her difficult experience and contribute to an improvement in the treatment of eating disorders that she recounted her story in an email. All the names of the interviewees have been changed to protect their identity.

References

APA (American Psychiatric Association). (1980). *Diagnostic and statistical manual of mental disorders* (3rd ed.). Washington, DC: American Psychological Association.

APA (American Psychiatric Association). (1994). *Diagnostic and statistical manual of mental disorders* (4th ed.). Washington, DC: American Psychological Association.

Brumberg, J. J. (1988). *Fasting girls: The emergence of anorexia nervosa as a disease*. Cambridge, MA: Harvard University Press.

Dana, M., & Lawrence, M. (1999). *Nashim okhlot et atzman: Al anorexiya, bulimiya ve-akhila kefiyatit* [*Women eating themselves: On anorexia, bulimia, and forced eating*]. Tel Aviv: Modan (Hebrew).

Fairburn, C. G., & Bohn, K. (2005). Eating disorder NOS (EDNOS): An example of the troublesome 'not otherwise specified' (NOS) category in DSM-IV. *Behavior Research and Therapy*, *43*(6), 691–701.

Fairburn, C. G., & Cooper, Z. (2010). Eating disorders, DSM-5 and clinical reality. *British Journal of Psychiatry*, *198*, 8–10.

Fairburn, C. G., & Harrison, P. J. (2003). Eating disorders. *The Lancet*, *361*, 407–416.

Fallon, P., Katzman, M. A., & Wooley, S. C. (1994). *Feminist perspectives of eating disorders*. New York, NY: Guilford Press.

Gordon, R. A. (2000). *Eating disorders: Anatomy of a social epidemic* (2nd ed.). Malden, MA: Wiley-Blackwell.

Jacobi, C., Hayward, C. de Zwaan, M., Kraemer, H. C., & Agras, W. S. (2004). Coming to terms with risk factors for eating disorders: Application of risk terminology and suggestions for a general taxonomy. *Psychological Bulletin*, *130*, 19–65.

Latzer, Y., Hochdorf, Z., Bachar, E., & Conetti, L. (2003). Treatment as a 'secure base': Family therapy as a secure-based attachment in eating disorders. *Sihot*, *3*, 1–9 (Hebrew).

NIMH (National Institute of Mental Health). (2008). *What are eating disorders?* Retrieved October 22, 2017, from www.nimh.nih/health/topics/eating disorders?/index.shtml

NIMH (National Institute of Mental Health). (2015). *Eating disorders*. Retrieved October 22, 2017, from www/nimh.nih.gov/health/topics/eating disorders/index.shtml

Orbach, S. (1986). *Hunger strike: The anorectic's struggle as a metaphor for our age*. Harmondsworth: Penguin.

Orbach, S. (2006). *Fat is a feminist issue: The anti-diet guide*. London: Arrow.

Orbach, S. (2009). *Bodies*. New York, NY: Picador.

Polivy, J., & Herman, C. P. (2002). Causes of eating disorders. *Annual Review of Psychology*, *53*, 187–213.

Russell, G. F. M. (1986). The changing nature of anorexia nervosa. In G. I. Szmukler, P. E. Slade, P. Harris, D. Benton, & G. F. M. Russell (Eds.), *Anorexia nervosa and bulimic disorders* (pp. 101–112). Oxford: Pergamon.

Russell, G. F. M. (1995). Anorexia nervosa through time. In G. Szmulkler, C. Dare, & J. Treasure (Eds.), *Handbook of eating disorders: Theory, treatment and research* (pp. 5–17). Chichester: Wiley-Blackwell.

Striegel-Moore, R. H., & Bulik, C. B. (2007). Risk factors for eating disorders. *American Psychologist*, *62*, 181–198.

Thomas, J., Vartanian, L. R., & Brownell, K. D. (2009). The relationship between eating disorders not otherwise specified (EDNOS) and officially recognized eating disorders: Meta-analysis and implication for DSM. *Psychological Bulletin*, *135*(3), 407–433.

Walsh, B. T., & Garner, D. M. (1994). Diagnostic issues. In D. M. Garner & P. E. Garfinkel (Eds.), *Handbook of treatment for eating disorders* (pp. 24–33). New York, NY: Guilford Press.

Chapter 2

Childhood sexual abuse

From witchcraft and hysteria to CPTSD

Childhood sexual abuse is a widespread phenomenon that has been met with denial and disavowal throughout history. Only over the past forty years, with the rise of feminism in the 1960s and '70s, has a broad body of knowledge begun to develop that has alerted professional and social forums to the proportions of the problem and the mental and physical damage it causes (Courtois, 1988; D. E. Russell, 1986). Even today, however, society still shrouds childhood sexual abuse in a cloud of silence and negation, mental health professionals themselves participating in the debate.

From the very beginnings of the psychoanalytic movement, sexual molestation in childhood was understood to play a significant role in the development of mental disorders in adulthood. Freud, who treated women diagnosed as suffering from 'hysteria', heard from them stories of what he termed 'a precocious experience of sexual relations . . . resulting from sexual abuse'. He identified these as 'the specific cause of hysteria . . . not merely an agent provocateur' (1896/1962, p. 195; cited in van der Kolk, Weisaeth, & van der H art, 1996, p. 54). For reasons that remain obscure, he later dismissed this 'seduction theory' in favour of the conflict between the drives, claiming that his clients had merely oedipally fantasized the sexual experiences they reported. Professionals in the field thus virtually completely ignored the phenomenon of childhood sexual abuse and the damage it inflicts on its victims.

When the feminist movement emerged in the 1960s and '70s, millions of women across the Western world began forming consciousness raising groups to raise awareness of their status and treatment. Amongst these were many who shared their life stories, recounting the violence and sexual violence they had experienced as children and adults. In contrast to the professionals, who cast doubt on the reality these women reported, regarding it as an oedipal or masochistic fantasy, the feminist groups accepted and supported these accounts. Help centres for childhood sexual abuse victims and safe havens for women suffering from intimate-partner violence across the Western world thus began to be formed. Established by the feminist movement rather than the health-clinical establishment, many women began turning to these instead of medical and mental health institutions. As the scale of sexual violence against women and children gradually revealed itself, a feminist analysis of its meaning emerged, together with the development of appropriate modes of diagnosis and treatment.

According to an extensive epidemiological survey of over 900 women conducted by D. E. Russell (1983) in the United States in the 1980s, one of every four women had been raped and every one of three had been sexually abused as children. Today, it is estimated that one in every three girls has been exposed to unwanted and inappropriate sexual advances before the age of 18 (D. E. Russell, 1983; Finkelhor, 1979, 1994), one in every seven having been the victim of incest (D. E. Russell, 1986) – defined as the sexual abuse of a child by an older family member. Across the world, it is estimated that one of every four girls and of every five boys have been sexually abused (United Nations, 2006). Over the past two decades, numerous clinical and epidemiological studies have thus evinced that childhood sexual abuse is a key public-health issue.

According to other estimates in the United States, between 3 and 25 percent of men and 11 and 62 percent of women were sexually abused as children (Salter, 1992). In the National Violence Against Women Survey (Tjaden & Thoennes, 2000), which contacted 16,000 men and women, 17.6 percent of the women reported that they had been raped or been the subject of an attempted rape. More than half of these were girls under 18. In the United States today, childhood sexual abuse is regarded as the number one public-health concern. Exposure to interrelational trauma during childhood can lead to chronic and severe problems in psychological, social, cognitive, and biological development, exacting very heavy social and economic costs.

Sexual crimes against women form a way of preserving male control and feminine subjugation (Brownmiller, 1975; MacKinnon, 1989). Feminist thought views rape, sexual abuse, and battering as the use of superior male power against women in order to create and preserve feminine inferiority and subordination within male society. Rather than a rare incidence committed by disturbed individuals, as traditionally held, sexual violence against women is a widespread, systematic phenomenon that occurs across all segments of society.

Violence against women is similarly conceptualized as a ritual deeply imprinted within the psychology and social construct of patriarchy and supported and sanctioned by tradition and the establishment. Rape is frequently enacted ritually, as in the case of gang rape. These acts of sexual violence are often greeted with denial and dismissal or explained away or forgiven, the victims being silenced, blamed, and shamed (Mendelsohn et al., 2011). Even mental health professional relate to the traumatic sources of the severe mental disorders they treat in this fashion, giving no place to historical trauma either in their diagnoses or treatment methods.

The clinical picture of childhood sexual abuse

Childhood sexual abuse is a stressor with many traumatic characteristics that put the victim at risk of a range of initial and long-term effects (Courtois, 1997).

Today, it is known to be a strong predictor of adult psychopathology (Molnar, Buka, & Kessler, 2001). Trauma that occurs in childhood and adolescence directly impinges upon physical and mental development, identity-formation, and personality, preventing normal development processes. It thus differs from trauma in adulthood, which 'only' affects already-existing personality structures. In the majority of cases, childhood abuse does not consist of a single event but is ongoing and repeated, being committed by a close and loved family member or someone in authority. Because children are unable to contain and integrate the split between the perpetrator and loved one, they shut off or dissociate the experience and its memory, becoming day children who have no recollection of what happened during the night and night children burdened with keeping an awful secret. This significantly interferes with their ability to communicate with others and themselves.

Childhood sexual abuse creates abnormal states of consciousness that form a fertile breeding ground for the development of a vast array of symptoms (Herman, 1997), violating the child's physical, psychological, and spiritual space and thus gravely impairing her psychological and interpersonal development (Cole & Putnam, 1992).[1] Today, we know that childhood sexual abuse is a direct contributor to severe adult psychopathology – including mental disorders, depression, self-injury, drug, and alcohol addiction, eating disorders, dissociative disorders, adolescence runaways, promiscuous behaviour, juvenile delinquency, prostitution, etc. (Courtois, 1997). Numerous studies – amongst both clinical clients and the general population – indicate the correlation between childhood sexual abuse and a broad array of psychiatric disorders (MacMillan et al., 2001).

Clinical descriptions of the grave effects of childhood sexual abuse evince a high degree of consistency (Courtois, 1997). Gelinas (1983), who provided one of the initial portraits of the phenomenon, found that adult survivors of childhood sexual abuse frequently present a picture of depression accompanied by impulsive and abnormal complications and features. To these are added strong emotions such as shame, an exaggerated sense of responsibility, and self-guilt and illogical guilt that aggravate the depression associated with it. As she notes, victims tend to exhibit a variety of anxiety disorders, including panic, agoraphobia, and a range of simple phobias – frequently directly towards or symbolically linked to the original trauma. A proclivity also exists towards self-destruction, including suicidal ideation, self-injury, and re-victimization as a result of obsessive repetition, reenactment, naivety, the ignoring of self needs, and risk-taking. Self-destruction also takes the form of addictions and obsessive behaviour designed to cope with distress – these stratagems then becoming serious problems in their own right.

The survivors of childhood sexual abuse also suffer from an existential crisis due to the trauma of betrayal (D. E. Russell, 1986). Many experience severe damage to their identity and sense of self-worth, finding it difficult to trust others, whom they expect to exploit them for their own gratification or abandon and fail to protect them. They also tend to experience a strong sense of loss of faith, personal meaning, and security in the world.

Childhood sexual abuse has a direct impact on personality structure, affecting the sense of self, the ability to regulate emotions, the sense of the completeness of the self, and the capacity to trust others and develop intimate relations (Chu, 1992; Cole & Putnam, 1992). Victims suffer from complex identity distortions, feel that their self has been contaminated, are ridden with guilt, and think of themselves as bad. They experience a fragmentation of the self that may develop into multiple personality disorders. They also suffer from a broad array of common physical symptoms, including actual physical injury, psychosomatic symptoms, digestive problems, urinary and gynaecological problems, headaches, neurological and auto-immune problems, muscle and spinal pain, impaired sexual function and performance, fertility and pregnancy complications, sexual distress (including STDs), and dissociation from various physical sensations (Courtois, 1988).

The trauma of childhood sexual abuse affects all the aspects of the internal organization of adult survival – cognitive, emotional, behavioural, and relational. The parent's/close relative's incomprehensible antithetical representations, together with those of responsible adults who stood by and failed to protect the child, induce a split in the self that develops around unfathomable object relations. This impossible situation being intolerable, it can only be dealt with through the defensive process of dissociation. The child exists within a never-ending nightmare of pain, loneliness, and death – without time, objects, or a self. The abuse is constantly remembered, the memories taking the form of graphic images, radical and inexplicable changes of mood, somatic symptomology, panic attacks, etc. (Davies & Frawley, 1994).

An historical review of childhood sexual abuse

Throughout history, gender power relations have muted and silenced women, preventing any talk or acknowledgment of childhood sexual abuse. As Judith Herman notes (1997, p. 7), more powerful the perpetrator, the greater is his prerogative to name and define reality and the more completely his arguments prevail. Despite their common occurrence and the mental and physical damage they cause, sexual crimes have thus remained on the margins of social and professional discourse. In the absence of words and the social legitimacy to give voice to the agonies they endure, victims are thus forced to give expression to their distress via severe and complex symptoms. The nature of the symptoms changes in accordance with the time and culture.

Over the generations – and in many cases still today – these symptoms have been diagnosed and treated within the framework of a male hegemonic patriarchy, from the mediaeval religious/ecclesiastical establishment through to the modern medical-psychiatric system. Herein, the symptoms that express the severity of childhood sexual abuse are diagnosed without any regard to their traumatic sources, the effect they have on the victims, or the pathologies they create. On many occasions, the mode of treatment dictated by the hegemonic male establishment appears to be a continuation of the social oppression of women.

Up until the late nineteenth century, phenomena such as demon possession, witchcraft, exorcism, and religious ecstasy were defined primarily by religious figures. From the Victorian period onwards, hysteria – a female complaint no longer recognized in the medical world – became a medical condition, commonly adduced to account for a wide range of symptoms, including fainting, nervousness, insomnia, fluid retention, heaviness in the stomach, muscular spasms, shortness of breath, lack of appetite, lack of libido, and a tendency towards 'making trouble' (Micale, 1993). Doctors believed it to be a specifically female ailment rooted in the uterus, this giving rise to its name. The concept served as a 'catch all' diagnosis, covering a vast array of undefined phenomena.

At the end of the nineteenth century, the French neurologist Charcot began investigating hysterical symptoms that resembled nerve damage – motor paralysis, loss of feeling, seizures, and amnesia. Demonstrating that these were in fact mental symptoms that could be treated through hypnosis (Herman, 1997; Micale, 1993), he and his disciples linked them with the cases of witchcraft, demon possession, and bizarre behaviour described in art and culture as hysteria. In 1880, one of his students claimed that many of the women shut up in the Salpêtrière would at other times have been burnt at the stake, their disease being regarded as a crime (Herman, 1997, p. 16). Freud (1986, p. 224) also acknowledged that the belief in demon possession held by mediaeval religious courts was identical to his own diagnosis of split consciousness, observing the resemblance between the confessions extracted through torture by mediaeval religious authorities and the stories told him by his clients.

The sufferers themselves felt that their severe symptoms brought witchcraft and exorcism to mind. Abused by her father, Sylvia Fraser compares her bizarre symptoms with the descriptions given by demon-possessed women in the Middle Ages, suggesting that in a superstitious society she might have been diagnosed as demon possessed: 'What in fact I had been possessed by was daddy's forked instrument – the devil in man' (1987, pp. 222–223). She also notes the numerous psychiatric symptoms from which she suffered – including hysterical convulsions and psychotic amnesia that began in childhood, anorexia, adolescent promiscuity, sexual dysfunction, poor intimate relations, depression, and adolescent suicidal ideation (ibid).

As diagnostic tools became more sophisticated, more and more of these symptoms began receiving different diagnoses – until virtually no symptoms specific to hysteria remained (Micale, 1993). During the first half of the twentieth century, the number of cases diagnosed as hysteria sharply declined, although some argued that it had not disappeared but was merely being classified under different categories (Micale, 1993).

As early as the late nineteenth century Freud recognized cases of trauma, primarily childhood sexual trauma, and severe mental disorders amongst women. In 'The Aetiology of Hysteria', published in 1896, he wrote:

> I therefore put forward the thesis that at the bottom of every case of hysteria there are one or more occurrences of premature sexual experience, occurrences which belong to the earliest years of childhood but which can be reproduced through the work of psycho-analysis in spite of the intervening decades. I believe that this is an important finding, the discovery of a *caput Nili* {source of the Nile} in neuropathology.
>
> (1995, p. 103)

Within a year, however, he had already renounced this theory, casting clients back into silence, denial, and shame for the next century (Herman, 1997). Following in his footsteps, mental health clinicians continued to preserve this stance. Thus, for example, one of the pillars of psychiatric literature, the *Comprehensive Textbook of Psychiatry* (Kaplan & Sadock, 1975), asserts that incest in all forms only affects one in every million people. Clinicians also commonly hold that children lie about sexual abuse, dismissing the allegations of childhood abuse as fantasies (Herman, 1981/2000).

Around half a century after Freud, incest was rediscovered – not by mental health clinicians, who would not allow themselves to recognize it, but by social scientists uninfluenced by psychoanalytic traditions (Herman, 1981/2000). Between 1940 and the 1980s, four assessment studies were conducted across a broad sample of women in the United States (Kinsley, Pomeroy, Martin, & Gehard, 1953; Gagnon, 1965; Landis, 1956; Finkelhor, 1979). All produced similar results: between 20 and 33 percent of all the women reported an incident of childhood sexual abuse with a known male adult, between 4 and 12 percent reporting sexual abuse by their father or stepfather (Herman, 1981/2000).

Despite the fact that 80 percent of the women claimed to have been scared and frightened, these high rates were not regarded as problematic. Children, it was argued, do not suffer any consequences in the wake of such experiences. If they do, it is only because virtuous parents or teachers make them feel 'hysterical' (Kinsley et al., 1953). Only in the wake of the Women's Liberation Movement of the 1970s did the fact of violence and sexual violence towards women and children and the severe post-traumatic mental injury they cause gain validity once more (Herman, 1997). In the 1970s and '80s, a study of incest and childhood sexual abuse reported the high incidence of the phenomena. This led to an unprecedented public awareness of incest and childhood sexual abuse (Courtois, 1997). Documenting the severe mental damage such abuse causes, this report prompted clinicians to begin developing prevention programmes and specific treatment methods.

The first treatment models for adult survivors of childhood sexual abuse began to emerge at the end of the 1980s and beginnings of the '90s (e.g., Briere,

1989; Kluft, 1990; Herman, 1992). Over the next two decades, the body of knowledge regarding the clinical picture of childhood sexual abuse and methods of treatment specific to this problem gradually increased. Today, it is still being developed (Herman, 2009). As the movement gained momentum, however, it triggered a predictable counter-reaction in the form of continued efforts to deny sexual violence against women and children. The rise in reports of childhood sexual abuse and research advances in the field of traumatic memory and the conceptualization of the phenomena associated with it – such as amnesia, repressed memories, and flashbacks – led to a wave of lawsuits against the perpetrators (Courtois, 1997). This led to the creation of the False Memory Syndrome Foundation, an organization whose members believed that therapists suggested false memories to their clients, no abuse in fact ever having occurred. 'False memory syndrome' proponents argued that people have a large range of memories of things that, while they never actually happened, appear real to them. Never gaining professional approval, this alleged syndromeis not recognized by DSM to this day (Somer, 2004).

Historical experience teaches that mental-trauma research did not develop due to clinicians working in the field but rather in consequence of political movements that opposed the stigmatizing diagnoses given to women trauma survivors by male mental health practitioners. Thus, for example, war trauma research only began to develop after Vietnam War veterans established a strong political anti-war movement in the 1970s, one of whose goals was to focus public attention on the mental health problems suffered by soldiers. Together with the expansion of the activities of the feminist movement during the 1960s and '70s, which highlighted the mental health implications of the epidemic of interpersonal violence and trauma for women, these led to the first definition of post-traumatic stress disorder (PTSD) in DSM-III (Herman, 1997).

Despite the impressive gains made in recent years in the treatment of childhood sexual abuse, we cannot rest on our laurels. The field of eating disorders forms a striking example of the fact that room still exists to fight for recognition of the traumatic history of women survivors and their right to receive treatment that meets their specific needs – enabling them to receive proper diagnosis and care alike.

A chronicle of childhood sexual abuse

Trauma in general and childhood sexual trauma in particular is by definition an incomprehensible event that cannot be put into words. Frequently, the people around the victim resist being witnesses to such unfathomable and unspeakable behaviour, the natural human instinct being to turn one's eyes away, not to see, hear, or know (Herman, 1997).

In order to understand how severe symptoms serve as an essential coping strategy for victims of childhood sexual abuse, we must first agree to become witnesses and listen to and hear the stories of sexual abuse. If the link between childhood sexual abuse and eating disorders – the latter frequently being accompanied by a complex range of other problems – is to be traced, we must expose ourselves to the horrific accounts of abuse and listen to the stories women tell through their symptoms. We must open ourselves up to a chronicle of sexual molestation of daughters by fathers, granddaughters by grandfathers, sisters by brothers, to the experience of being a child victim, and to the fragmented and dissociated ways in which they describe what they endured.

When reading the testimonies of childhood sexual abuse victims, it is important to pay attention to the incredible difficulty finding words poses. The traumatic experience leaves a lacuna that cannot be represented. This is the awful nature of trauma, which cannot be articulated in words. At a certain point, no explanation or description is valid any longer, every representation is 'unrepresentable' (Goldberg, 2006).

We must thus listen to the silences as much as to the things actually uttered. This is the vacuum the symptoms of eating disorders and various other symptoms seek to fill. Only when we understand the meaning of the sexual exploitation of a child can we treat the severe symptoms of eating disorders and other complex symptoms (such as dissociation, personality disorders, etc.) with the requisite empathy and apprehend the way in which they form vital coping and survival strategies.

Natasha: father-daughter incest

In principle, the primary sexual abuse was by my father who . . . in general, it wasn't just one time. Because he . . . in general there was a problem with boundaries in the house. Since I was a small child, he would also make lots of sexual remarks. He was a teacher, my father. My mother was always on the side. Even when my father beat me or shouted at me. She could have told him to stop, say no more. Like, she sat on the side and had no way to cope, to stand up against him. Don't know, she was very weak, and very swayed, very dependent on him. She was always depressed, too. And it was also he who supported her, she was very, very dependent on him in that respect. And I always remained on the side somehow.

When I was 10, my mother got sick and was hospitalized for a month. And then I was really left for a month with my father. He was drunk all the time and then he abused me sexually the most . . . in the most . . . way, the most, I don't know if worst or . . . like something I, that . . . that feels central to me. Like, the central abuse. Apart from all that . . . his whole behaviour.

But even before then, before 10, there was something I've just remembered. We were at the beach by the lake in a tent. It was dark, night, we went to sleep and I felt something with my hand, I didn't understand what it was, it was too slight to be a hand and I didn't . . . I didn't understand what it was. He says today that he wanted to explain how you make babies. He decided to demonstrate on himself and . . . and . . . that . . . and so he . . . and so he explained to me that look, for example then, he really liked it that I touched him and . . . I don't remember what else, but like, he demonstrated to me some . . . that it was very nice for him.

And then when I was 9 and my mother was hospitalized, one night he called me into his room, into their bedroom. Like, it was also the lounge, because there were only two rooms and they slept in the lounge. So he called me into the room and told me it was time he explained the relationship between men and women to me. I don't remember if I knew before then or not. I haven't a clue. In principle, in Russia, it wasn't customary to explain at a young age as it is now. In general, there was a taboo against talking about it. And he just began to explain to me and demonstrate on himself. He took off his pants and began to show me. And . . . so that I would understand better he told me that I should touch, that I should rub, and that he understands how it is. And that I should see how it feels, how it looks. And . . . he explained to me the differences between men and women and told me that I should . . . not . . . not feel ashamed that his was so big and mine was so small and that I would grow up and mine would get bigger as well. And . . . that's it, more or less. Like, he mostly only . . . only talked and told me to touch. And then, if I remember rightly, he told me that I should sleep in his bed that night, because he didn't want to be alone, so I thought. And then, I don't remember. And then it was . . . there were several occasions on which he came into my room and . . . and also . . . like . . . he asked me questions, he would tell me, he was very interested in how I was made down below and he told me that . . . he saw how it looked in babies and how it looked in women and was very interested in how it looked at my age. And he told me to show him and explain to him and . . . and then he would start touching and . . . pushed his face there. It was revolting and I know, made all sorts of horrible noises . . . that's what I remember. I don't . . . like it's two things I remember, I don't . . . those are all my memories from childhood. It's very fragmented like, from the flashes I remember, bits and pieces.

Later, when my mother was already home again and he tried again. I don't really remember, not completely, but I remember that he would come into my room at night. And I . . . I don't know how many times, but I remember once, he came in and started touching me and then I . . . and then it was really revolting, I told him that I . . . would shout, so that my mother would wake up. And then he told me, No, no and . . . stopped. And went, I think.

Liliana: older brother-younger sister incest

Let's start with the real matter. The truth is that I don't . . . I don't really remember everything. I remember that . . . I remember smells, I remember the idea. I had a dream once. I very rarely dream, but once I had a dream in which I really remembered like what happened. Let me first tell you the frame story, and then, if you want, I'll get down to the details. First of all, the person who forced himself on me, that's what I call it, was my brother, who all in all is two years older than me. And you know, I'm telling you this because I say, Ok, I'll talk. Because this, many years, this is what I heard and listened to, and I tried to check it out a bit, even when I was a bit older, so that . . . all the time to check if I'm normal. I mean or if it was really so awful, the feeling I feel, where's the justice and where's the injustice? Because what happened in my childhood is that I very quickly grasped, I mean, I understood, that the first feeling was total guilt. Like, as a child I tried very hard to reconstruct it, and I think it began when I was 10 and stopped at around age 12½, something like that, I think. Or 13 like that, tops.

Of course, first thing I thought it wasn't right, and secondly I immediately thought that *I wasn't right*. And then very quickly, and that was the luck, and it's something that's important for me to say, I very quickly understood that it wasn't my fault. And then . . . I can't say it was a dialogue because . . . there are things I'll tell you that maybe will make me want to throw up, but I – I'll say them.

I remember once I told him that it really wasn't right, what he was doing. So he told me: 'What nonsense are you talking? I'll take care of you'. And I felt disgusting, the most disgusting you can feel. I mean, all the things you can say about a person who . . . I'm talking about a specific feeling at that moment. Of a person like of someone who's screwed up, who's sick. And it's not . . . even in retrospect it didn't matter at all to me that he was a child.

First of all, he never penetrated me, not once. He, he rubs himself against me, that's all, that's all. Like when he was about 12, he was big, he was strong. Yes, yes, with all the respect due to him, with all the stink. He was also . . . it was with power, too, not to get to where he had to use force, *the power was clear*. Because he was big. The power was clear and yes, it also got to where he threatened me: 'I'll say you took my mobile phone'. And I was a good girl, I didn't have anything to be afraid of. I mean, I didn't do anything that this . . . not even small things. He would threaten me all the time. It wasn't a negotiation, you understand? It wasn't a negotiation, that was clear. I try . . . between these threats all around . . . perhaps I don't really remember? I – I can't tell you that it was with force, but I remember the . . . I remember him making me lie down. I don't remember, I don't know . . . I – I have to admit that I don't know if it was with force. If the force was only clear to me or it was actually physical force.

I really don't remember . . . I, during that period no, because I was still a child, I don't, I don't I don't remember . . . I don't have a clue. My mother says things like, that he was crazy about me when I little, he was always protecting me and defending me. I don't have a clue, I don't remember. I don't remember that we ever said anything, I don't remember anything. Nothing. I only remember afterwards, I don't remember. . . . All the time, when I was there, all the time I said, all the time I prayed it would end. Constantly, all the time. All the time, and the smell of the sweat, and the wet clothes . . . Yes, at that moment, there, only that it would stop. You can't understand how much I understood it wasn't right. How much I understood that he was crazy, that he was crazy. Really like that, like that . . . very quickly, the first time I'll kill . . . like at the beginning, I couldn't tell you if it was the first time, that you feel so much . . . You don't know the definition of this, but you feel – not a whore, a daughter of a whore, mother of a whore, f**ked in the ass. Sorry for saying that, but that's the *feeling of . . . that you're nothing*, that things like that don't happen. And it's instinctive. I'm so, you know, today I talk with people and I say: 'You'll never understand it'. It's like finding new words that no one, that you've never heard in your life. You don't understand them, you, your body performs them. How you're nothing.

Liora: grandfather-granddaughter incest

I discovered that when I was four my grandfather raped me. Once I remember that . . . he made me go down on him. I was . . . I remember myself as a small child, you know, everything's big. I remember his feet, and his trousers, and his nails . . . everything. Once I remember that . . . that it was on the couch and he penetrated me with his fingers, and I also, I remember the light bulb, and my mother also . . . one of the things I'm working on.

Let's start with the fact that I remember my grandfather, his wife, she saw it all and said nothing. I mean, she lay on the couch and . . . peeked and saw and did nothing. I mean, she lay on the sofa and . . . watched and saw and did nothing. And when after about an hour Mum came to take me, she didn't see anything about me either. Another time I remember it . . . it was in a very, very large bed and he . . . he was on top of me, something like that . . . that afterwards he gave me sweets so I would keep quiet.

Maggie: father-daughter incest

I used to wait awake. I went to sleep at eight, seven. And . . . I would wait already awake, like . . . half watching half not watching the door. The room was dark and there was always light in the corridor. I smelt him coming even before he came. There was the matter of . . . and then I shut my eyes. When his silhouette was at the door I would close my eyes and . . . this is the part I hate the most about the story with myself, that I still have a lot of difficulty with, that I continued to suck my thumb . . . that he was just there . . . very close, I mean . . . very close . . . I could feel the . . . he didn't touch but I could feel the . . . his presence there . . . his breath . . . I also knew what happens according to the . . . how he breathed . . . through the whole thing his breathing was the . . . the time indicator. I don't . . . I don't know like . . . I don't know if it's logical. It would start suddenly. Like within this endless time it would suddenly start. He never spoke to me. I didn't move. I didn't resist. I didn't shout. (Silence.) It was very violent, very painful. There was a lot of blood . . . I was already in the shower to clean off the blood . . . and the . . . sweat. It was mixed together . . . the ritual at the beginning was really that I was always choked. No, no . . . not in the sense of choking me to death. It sounds awful but . . . part of his rise came from the feeling that I was choking . . . it was part of what turned him on . . . it was the part

I know how to dissociate from the pain, when it's in a specific place. But when it's several places together, I don't know, but from choking, I don't know how to dissociate. Choking until . . . everything disappears, goes grey, I can't . . . then I find a way into the cracks in the walls, the electric sockets, I mean I know how to hide in places . . . when it hurts . . . most of all if hurts here or there but when it's several places all together . . . when I choke . . . the choking controls me . . . I said, 'That enough, I don't want any more'. I've even got physical scars . . . it left physical scars.

Note

1 Although boys are also abused, the present study relates primarily to girls and thus employs feminine language.

References

Briere, J. (1989). *Therapy for adults molested as children*. New York, NY: Springer.

Brownmiller, S. (1975). *Against our will: Men, women and rape*. New York, NY: Simon and Schuster.

Chu, J. A. (1992). The therapeutic roller coaster: Dilemmas in the treatment of childhood sexual abuse survivors. *Journal of Psychotherapy Practice and Research, 4*, 383–390.

Cole, P., & Putnam, E. (1992). Effect of incest on self and social functioning: A developmental psychopathology perspective. *Journal of Consulting and Clinical Psychology, 60*, 174–184.

Courtois, C. A. (1988). *Healing the incest wound: Adult survivors in therapy*. New York, NY: W.W. Norton.

Courtois, C. A. (1997). Healing the incest wound: A treatment update with attention to recovered-memory issues. *American Journal of Psychotherapy, 51*(4), 464–496.

Davies, J., & Frawley, M. (1994). *Treating the adult survivor of childhood sexual abuse: A psychoanalytic perspective*. New York, NY: Basic Books.

Finkelhor, D. (1979). *Sexually victimized children*. New York, NY: Free Press.

Finkelhor, D. (1994). Childhood sexual abuse: An evidence-based perspective. *Developmental Clinical Psychology and Psychiatry, 40*, 409–417.

Fraser, S. (1987). *My father's house: A memoir of incest and of healing*. New York, NY: Harper and Row.

Freud, S. (1896/1962). Heredity and the aetiology of the neuroses. In J. Strachey (Ed.), *The standard edition of the complete psychological works of Sigmund Freud* (vol. 3, pp. 141–156). London: Hogarth.

Freud, S. (1986). *The complete letters of Sigmund Freud to Wilhelm Fliess, 1887–1904*. Cambridge, MA: Belknap.

Freud, S. (1995). The aetiology of hysteria. In P. Gay (Ed.), *The Freud reader* (pp. 96–111). New York, NY: W.W. Norton.

Gagnon, J. (1965). Female child victims of sex offenders. *Social Problems, 13*, 176–192.

Gelinas, D. (1983). The persisting negative effects of incest. *American Journal of Psychiatry, 46*, 313–332.

Goldberg, A. (2006). Preface. In *Dominic LaCapra: Writing history, writing trauma* (pp. 7–27). Tel Aviv: Khidekel (Hebrew).

Herman, J. L. (1981/2000). *Father-daughter incest*. Cambridge, MA: Harvard University Press.

Herman, J. L. (1992). Complex PTSD: A syndrome in survivors of prolonged and repeated trauma. *Journal of Traumatic Stress, 5*, 377–391.

Herman, J. L. (1997). *Trauma and recovery*. New York, NY: Basic Books.

Herman, J. L. (2009). Foreword. In C. A. Courtois & J. D. Ford (Eds.), *Treating complex traumatic stress disorders* (pp. xiii–xvii). New York, NY: Guildford Press.

Kaplan, V. A., & Sadock, B. J. (1975). *Comprehensive textbook of psychiatry*. Baltimore: Lippincott Williams & Wilkins.

Kinsley, A. C., Pomeroy, W. B., Martin, C. E., & Gehard, P. H. (1953). *Sexual behavior in the human female*. Philadelphia: Saunders.

Kluft, R. P. (1990). *Incest-related syndromes of adult psychopathology*. Washington, DC: American Psychiatric Press.

Landis, J. T. (1956). Experiences of 500 children with adult sexual deviation. *Psychiatric Quarterly Supplement, 30*, 91–109.

MacKinnon, C. (1989). *Toward a feminist theory of the state*. Cambridge, MA: Harvard University Press.

MacMillan, H. L., Fleming, J. E., Streiner, D. L., Lin, E., Boyle, M. H., Jamieson, E., . . . Beardslee, W. R. (2001). Childhood abuse and lifetime psychopathology in a community sample. *American Journal of Psychiatry, 158*(11), 1878–1883.

Mendelsohn, M., Herman, J. L., Schatzow, E., Coco, M., Kallivayalil, D., & Levitan, J. (2011). *The trauma recovery group*. New York, NY: Guilford Press.

Micale, M. S. (1993). On the 'disappearance' of hysteria: A study in the clinical deconstruction of a diagnosis. *Isis, 84*, 496–526.

Molnar, B., Buka, S. L., & Kessler, R. C. (2001). Child sexual abuse and subsequent psychopathology: Results from the National Comorbidity Survey. *American Journal of Public Health, 90*(5), 753–760.

Russell, D. E. (1983). The incidence and precedence of interfamilial and extra-familial sexual abuse of female children. *Child Abuse & Neglect*, 7, 133–146.

Russell, D. E. (1986). *The secrete trauma: Incest in the lives of girls and women*. New York, NY: Basic Books.

Salter, A. C. (1992). *Epidemiology of child sexual abuse*. New York, NY: Lawrence Erlbaum.

Somer, (2004). To be or not to be: Childhood trauma and dissociative disorders. In Z. Seligman and Z. Solomon (Eds.), *Critical and clinical perspectives on incest* (pp. 164–192). Tel Aviv: Hakibbutz Hameuchad/Tel Aviv University (Hebrew).

Tjaden, P., & Thoennes, N. (2000). *Full report of the prevalence, incidences, and consequences of violence against women: Findings from the national violence against women survey (NCJ 183781)*. Washington, DC: US Department of Justice.

United Nations. (2006). *UN Secretary-General's study on violence against children*. Retrieved from www.unviolencestudy.org/

van der Kolk, B., Weisaeth, L., & van der Hart, O. (1996). History of trauma in psychiatry. In B. van der Kolk, A. C. McFarlane, & L. Weisaeth (Eds.), *Traumatic stress: The overwhelming experience on mind, body, and society* (pp. 47–76). New York, NY: Guilford Press.

Chapter 3

The relation between childhood sexual abuse and eating disorders

A meta-view of the professional literature

Much of the professional literature relating to eating disorders ignores their correlation with a history of childhood sexual abuse. While in recent years scholarly and clinical reports have begun to note the linkage between the two phenomena, the association is still not widely recognized. Those that do acknowledge it (Brewerton, 2007, 2011, 2015) relate to various types of (childhood) trauma – childhood maltreatment (emotional, sexual and/or physical in nature) (Molendijk, Hoek, Brewerton, & Elzinga, 2016) or childhood trauma (Guillaume et al., 2016) – rather than making a distinction between childhood sexual abuse as a specific factor in the development of eating disorders.

The most comprehensive meta-analysis of the association between childhood maltreatment exposure and EDs to date (Molendijk et al., 2016) found that childhood maltreatment is strongly associated with all types of eating disorders and the severity that characterizes them, often in codependent fashion. A recent systematic review and meta-analysis designed to estimate the association between distinct types of child abuse – sexual, physical, and emotional – and various eating disorders (Caslini et al., 2016) found a consistent and positive association between CSA and both BN and BED. The correlation with CSA and AN was not significant.

Various forms of child abuse being differentially associated with eating disorders, the role of other intervening and moderating factors deserves investigation as helping to explain the link between child abuse and eating disorders. Early screening of survivors of child abuse may lead to better preventive and treatment programmes for eating disorders. A review of the professional literature reveals the existence of a fierce debate amongst eating disorder experts on the relationship between childhood sexual abuse and eating disorders (Wooley, 1994; Vanderlinden & Vandereycken, 1996). Those who write about eating disorders maintain that the dispute over the role childhood abuse plays in the aetiology and treatment of eating disorders is still unclear, being difficult to document due to the fact that the debate is conducted in corridors and informal meetings rather than on the pages of professional journals, books, or lecture rooms (Wooley, 1994). According to Wooley (1994), the fact that most eating disorder clients are women who frequently prefer to speak about the sexual trauma they experienced with female rather than male therapists makes gender a significant factor. Disclosure of the rates of sexual abuse carrying divergent emotional meanings for men and women, this further compounds the debate between male and female therapists. In her opinion, this constitutes one of the reasons why eating disorder research lags behind other therapeutic fields in the integration of new findings regarding childhood sexual abuse into theory and treatment models.

The rates of correlation between childhood sexual abuse and eating disorders – Research and clinical assessments

In the last three decades, increasing numbers of clinical reports regarding significant traumatic experiences – in particular those of physical and sexual abuse – have begun appearing amongst anorexia nervosa (AN) and bulimia nervosa (BN) clients (Brewerton, 2004, 2007, 2011, 2015; Finn, Hartman, Leon, & Lawson, 1986; Goldfarb, 1987; Guillaume et al., 2016; Hall, Tice, Beresford, Wooley, & Hall, 1989; McFarlane, McFarlane, & Gilchrist, 1988; Molendijk et al., 2016; Oppenheimer, Howells, Palmer, & Chaloner, 1985; Root & Fallon, 1988; Schechter, Schwartz, & Greenfield, 1987; Sloan & Leichner, 1986; Torem, 1986; Vanderlinden & Vandereycken, 1996; Waller, 1991; Wonderlich et al., 1997; Wooley & Kearney-Cooke, 1986). A close scrutiny of the prevalence of sexual trauma amongst clients suffering from eating disorders indicates a worrying rate. Oppenheimer et al. (1985) reported that 70 percent of participants in a sample of seventy-eight women suffering from eating disorders had a history of childhood/adolescent childhood abuse. Herzog, Stoley, Carmody, Robbins, and van der Kolk (1993) found that 65 percent of twenty women suffering from eating disorders had experienced childhood sexual abuse.

In a sample of seventy-five women suffering from bulimia (Kearney-Cooke, 1988), 58 percent had a history of sexual trauma. Root and Fallon (1988) found that 65 percent of 172 women with eating disorders had experienced physical abuse, 23 percent had been raped, 28 percent had been sexually abused as children, and 23 percent were exhibiting inappropriate attitudes in present relationships. Hall et al. (1989) found that 40 percent of 158 women with eating disorders had been sexually abused. Carter, Beewell, Blackmore, and Woodside (2006) found that 48 percent of 113 female patients hospitalized diagnosed as suffering from AN had experienced childhood sexual abuse. Some studies claim that bulimics report more traumatic experience than anorexics (Vanderlinden & Vandereycken, 1996).

Other studies have found that childhood sexual abuse is linked to comorbidities that accompany eating disorders. In a sample of bulimic women in the community, Rorty and Yager (1996) found that childhood sexual abuse was associated with personality disorders. Two studies found that a history of sexual abuse was linked with self-injury in female eating disorder clients (Favaro &

Santonastaso, 2000; Nagata et al., 1999). Anderson, LaPorte, Brandt, and Crawford (1997) found that women sufferers from eating disorders with a history of childhood sexual abuse reported higher rates of depression and anxiety than those without any such history. Carter et al. (2006) found that women clients with a history of childhood sexual abuse reported severer psychiatric disorders – including a higher rate of depression and anxiety, low self-image, greater interpersonal difficulties, and obsessive/compulsive symptoms – than those without. Female clients with a history of childhood sexual abuse also reported more serious eating disorder psychopathology.

Other studies, however, have found a low rate of a history of childhood sexual abuse amongst women suffering from eating disorders. In a sample of 112 women bulimics whose weight was normal, only seven were found to have experienced childhood sexual abuse that had included physical contact, 3.6 percent of the participants reporting incest, but only 1.8 percent childhood incest (Lacey, 1990).

The inconsistent findings in the scholarly literature with respect to the potential link between childhood sexual abuse and eating disorders can be attributed to various factors. The professional literature is subject to various methodological limitations, including divergent definitions of sexual abuse. These affect the differences in rates of reported abuse (Miller, 1996). Participants do not always report sexual abuse due to shame and embarrassment (Smolak & Murnen, 2002). Some clients do not remember childhood sexual abuse (Goodman, Bottoms, Rudy, Davis, & Schwartz-Kenney, 2001). The heterogeneity in the findings likewise attests to the complexity of the association between eating disorders and childhood sexual abuse (Smolak & Murnen, 2002).

A significant disparity also obtains between the reports of the levels of childhood abuse that arise from clinical work with clients and the rates reported in studies. Clinicians – in particular female therapists – report high levels of a history of childhood sexual abuse in female sufferers of eating disorders – up to 80 percent (Kearney-Cooke & Striegel-Moore, 1996; Rorty & Yager, 1996; Vanderlinden & Vandereycken, 1996; Wooley, 1994). This reflects, at least in part, the difficulty in disclosing the awful secret of childhood sexual abuse in impersonal studies compared to treatment settings where the therapeutic alliance established with the therapist allows clients to feel sufficiently safe to recount their traumatic experience.

Theoretical and clinical explanations of the link – A review of the professional literature

Very little attention is paid in the professional literature on eating disorders to the question of the association between childhood sexual abuse and eating disorders. Herein, I shall survey some of the scholarly articles and papers based on clinical experience that suggest possible explanations for the link between the two phenomena.

Significantly, right at the beginning of psychoanalysis Freud adduced a connection between childhood sexual abuse and eating disorders while working with 'hysterical' women. In *Studies on Hysteria* (1895), he describes the case of Katharina, abused as a child by her father: 'There then followed a short period of working-out, of "incubation", after which the symptoms of conversion set in, the vomiting as a substitute for moral and physical disgust. This solved the riddle. . . . this could only be the memory of the attempt on her at night when she had "felt her uncle's body"' (p. 131).[1]

Clinical experience demonstrates that many women interpret their eating disorders as directly or indirectly linked with the trauma of childhood sexual abuse (Rorty & Yager, 1996; Goldfarb, 1987; Hall et al., 1989; Sloan & Leichner, 1986; Tice, Hall, Beresford, Quinones, & Hall, 1989). Clinicians describe the way in which eating disorders serve as a forceful metaphor for the traumatic experience or a means of symbolic relief (Root & Fallon, 1988; Tice et al., 1989; van der Kolk, 1989). AN is portrayed as a means of avoiding sexual contact or feelings, functioning as a method of making the perpetrator into someone repugnant who can thus be fended off (Hall et al., 1989; Sloan & Leichner, 1986; Tice et al., 1989). Bulimic women speak of their disorder as serving as an indirect way of expressing their rage at the perpetrator, directed inwards as a form of punishment or a strategy for coping with guilt, self-hatred, helplessness, and post-traumatic symptoms linked to the violation of personal space and boundaries. It also helps them feel non-sexually attractive (Hall et al., 1989; Tice et al., 1989; Root & Fallon, 1988), the fat functioning as a 'shield' against abuse and the self-hatred and anxiety associated with it (Hall et al., 1989; Tice et al., 1989). Eating disorders are described as connected to low body image (Andrews, 1997).

Some eating disorder clinicians (Kearney-Cooke & Striegel-Moore, 1996) address the link between childhood sexual abuse and eating disorders from a feminist perspective, associating the need for self-control – a central element of AN – with a history of sexual abuse. During the latter, victims feel that they have no control over the situation, thereby impairing their ability to feel that they can govern the negative or dangerous events in their lives. They thus become particularly sensitive to control issues. According to these therapists, eating disorder symptoms help to prevent the re-experiencing of post-trauma symptoms, this being especially true of binge-purge AN clients (Kearney-Cooke & Striegel-Moore, 1996; Carter et al., 2006).

In summary, a survey of the professional literature in the field of eating disorders evinces very little scholarly interest in the association between childhood sexual abuse and eating disorders and few explanations of it. A significant gap exists between studies that posit a lower level of association and clinical reports that indicate high levels and suggest potential reasons for the linkage. The latter remain isolated islands in the vast sea of eating disorder literature, failing to provide a full picture of the rate of association between the two phenomena or explain it.

Even the prominent feminist writers who deal with eating disorders, such as Susie Orbach, who link eating disorders with the inferiority and oppression of women in society, generally pay little direct attention to childhood abuse as a central aetiological in the development of eating disorders.

Note

1 Freud refers here to Katharina's *uncle*'s untoward advances towards her. Later publications make it clear, however, that she had been molested by her father not by her uncle.

References

Anderson, K. P., LaPorte, D. J., Brandt, H., & Crawford, S. (1997). Sexual abuse and bulimia: Response to treatment and preliminary outcome. *Journal of Psychiatric Research, 31*, 621–633.

Andrews, B. (1997). Bodily shame in relation to abuse in childhood and bulimia: A preliminary investigation. *British Journal of Clinical Psychology, 36*(1), 41–49.

Brewerton, T. D. (2004). Eating disorders, victimization and comorbidity: Principles of treatment. In T. D. Brewerton (Ed.), *Clinical handbook of eating disorders: An integrated approach* (pp. 509–545). New York, NY: Marcel Dekker, Inc.

Brewerton, T. D. (2007). Eating disorders, trauma, and comorbidity: Focus on PTSD. *Eating Disorders, 15*(4), 285–304.

Brewerton, T. D. (2011). Posttraumatic stress disorder and disordered eating: Food addiction as self-medication. *Journal of Women's Health, 20*(8), 1133–1134.

Brewerton, T. D. (2015). Stress, trauma, and adversity as risk factors in the development of eating disorders. In L. Smolak & M. Levine (Eds.), *Wiley handbook of eating disorders* (pp. 445–460). New York, NY: Guilford Press.

Carter, C. J., Beewell, C., Blackmore, E., & Woodside, D. B. (2006). The impact of childhood sexual abuse in anorexia nervosa. *Child Abuse & Neglect, 30*(3), 257–269.

Caslini, M., Bartoli, F., Crocamo, C., Dakanalis, A., Clerici, M., & Carrà, G. (2016). Disentangling the association between child abuse and eating disorders: A systematic review and meta-analysis. *Psychosomatic Medicine, 78*, 79–90.

Favaro, A., & Santonastaso, P. (2000). Self-injurious behavior in anorexia nervosa. *Journal of Nervous and Mental Disease, 188*, 537–543.

Finn, S., Hartman, M., Leon, G., & Lawson, L. (1986). Eating disorders and sexual abuse: Lack of confirmation for a clinical hypothesis. *International Journal of Eating Disorders, 5*, 1051–1060.

Freud, S., & Breuer, J. (1895). *Studies on hysteria*. Trans. J. Strachey. New York, NY: Basic Books. Retrieved October 22, 2017, from https://archive.org/stream/studiesonhysteri037649mbp/studiesonhysteri037649mbp_djvu.txt

Goldfarb, L. A. (1987). Sexual abuse antecedent to anorexia nervosa, bulimia, and compulsive overeating: Three case reports. *International Journal of Eating Disorders, 6*, 675–680.

Goodman, G., Bottoms, B. L., Rudy, L., Davis, S. L., & Schwartz-Kenney, B. M. (2001). Effects of past abuse experiences on children's eyewitness memory. *Law and Human Behavior, 25*, 269–298.

Guillaume, S., Jaussent, I., Maimoun, L., Ryst, A., Seneque, M., Villain, L., ... Courtet, P. (2016). Associations between adverse childhood experiences and clinical characteristics of eating disorders. *Scientific Reports, 6*. Retrieved October 22, 2017, from www.ncbi.nlm.nih.gov/pmc/articles/PMC5090200/

Hall, R. C., Tice, L., Beresford, T. P., Wooley, B., & Hall, A. K. (1989). Sexual abuse in patients in patients with anorexia nervosa and bulimia. *Psychosomatics, 30*, 73–79.

Herzog, D. B., Stoley, J. E., Carmody, S., Robbins, W. M., & van der Kolk, B. (1993). Childhood sexual abuse in anorexia nervosa and bulimia nervosa: A pilot study. *Journal of the American Academy of Child & Adolescent Psychiatry, 32*, 962–966.

Kearney-Cooke, A. (1988). Group treatment of sexual abuse among women with eating disorders. *Women and Therapy*, 7, 5–22.

Kearney-Cooke, A., Striegel-Moore, R. H. (1996). Treatment of childhood sexual abuse in anorexia nervosa and bulimia nervosa: a feminist psychodynamic approach. In M. F. Schwartz & L. Cohn (Eds.), *Sexual abuse and eating disorders* (pp. 155–175). Bristol, PA: Brunner/Mazel.

Lacey, J. H. (1990). Incest, incestuous fantasy and indecency: A clinical catchment area study of normal weight bulimic women. *British Journal of Psychiatry, 157*, 399–403.

McFarlane, A. C., McFarlane, C., & Gilchrist, P. N. (1988). Post-traumatic bulimia and anorexia nervosa. *International Journal of Eating Disorders*, 7, 705–708.

Miller, K. J. (1996). Prevalence and process of disclosure of childhood sexual abuse among eating disordered women. In M. F. Schwartz & L. Cohn (Eds.), *Sexual abuse and eating disorders* (pp. 36–51). Bristol, PA: Brunner/Mazel.

Molendijk, M. L., Hoek, H. W., Brewerton, T. D., & Elzinga, B. M. (2016). Childhood maltreatment and eating disorder pathology: A systematic review and dose-response meta-analysis. *Psychological Medicine, 49*(8), 1402–1416.

Nagata, T., Kiriike, T., Iketani, Y., Kawarada, Y., & Tanaka, H. (1999). History of childhood sexual or physical abuse in Japanese patients with eating disorders: Relationship with dissociation and impulsive behaviors. *Psychological Medicine, 29*, 935–942.

Oppenheimer, R., Howells, K., Palmer, L., & Chaloner, D. (1985). Adverse sexual experiences in childhood and clinical eating disorders: A preliminary description. *Journal of Psychiatric Research, 19*, 157–161.

Root, M. P., & Fallon, P. (1988). The incidence of victimization experience in a bulimic sample. *Journal of Interpersonal Violence, 3*, 161–173.

Rorty, M., & Yager, J. (1996). Speculations on the role of childhood abuse in the development of eating disorders among women. In M. F. Schwartz & L. Cohn (Eds.), *Sexual abuse and eating disorders* (pp. 21–35). Bristol, PA: Brunner/Mazel.

Schechter, I. D., Schwartz, H. P., & Greenfield, D. G. (1987). Sexual abuse and anorexia nervosa. *International Journal of Eating Disorders, 6*, 313–316.

Sloan, G., & Leichner, P. (1986). Is there a relationship between sexual abuse or incest and eating disorders? *Canadian Journal of Psychiatry, 31*, 656–660.

Smolak, L., & Murnen, S. K. (2002). A meta-analytic examination of the relationship between child sexual abuse and eating disorders. *International Journal of Eating Disorders, 31*, 136–150.

Tice, L., Hall, R. C. W., Beresford, T. P., Quinones, J., & Hall, A. K. (1989). Sexual abuse in eating disorders. *Psychiatric Medicine*, 7, 257–267.

Torem, M. S. (1986). Dissociative states presenting as an eating disorder. *American Journal of Clinical Hypnosis, 29*, 137–142.

van der Kolk, B. (1989). The compulsion to repeat the trauma. *Psychiatric Clinics of North America, 12*, 389–411.

Vanderlinden, J., & Vandereycken, W. (1996). Is sexual abuse a risk factor for developing an eating disorder? In M. F. Schwartz & L. Cohn (Eds.), *Sexual abuse and eating disorders* (pp. 17–35). Bristol, PA: Brunner/Mazel.

Waller, G. (1991). Sexual abuse as a factor in eating disorders. *British Journal of Psychiatry, 159*, 664–671.

Wonderlich, S. A., Brewerton, T. D., Joice, Z., Dansky B. S., & Abbott, D. W. (1997). Relationship of childhood sexual abuse and eating disorders. *Journal of the American Academy of Child & Adolescent Psychiatry, 36*(8), 1107–1115.

Wooley, S. C. (1994). Sexual abuse and eating disorders: The concealed debate. In P. Fallon, M. A. Katzman, & S. C. Wooley (Eds.), *Feminist perspectives on eating disorders* (pp. 171–211). New York, NY: Guilford Press.

Wooley, S. C., & Kearney-Cooke, A. (1986). Intensive treatment of bulimia and body-image disturbance. In K. D. Brownell & J. P. Foreyt (Eds.), *Handbook of eating disorders: Physiology, psychology, and treatment of obesity, anorexia and bulimia* (pp. 476–502). New York, NY: Basic Books.

Chapter 4

Women speak of the association between childhood sexual abuse and eating disorders

The narratives of women who suffer from eating disorders and were sexually abused as children demonstrate how their various forms of eating disorders form a vehicle for expressing, coping with, and reenacting the abuse – i.e., as ways to express the trauma that remains unspeakable and voiceless and cannot be mentalized.[1] They are uniquely suited to conveying physical and mental abuse; eradicating femininity; helping regain control over the invaded, exploited, and objectivized body; punishing the body that (was) betrayed and profaned; and the wish to forget the monstrous acts and struggle for self-healing.

By definition, trauma is an event so horrendous that it cannot be represented in words or other symbolic systems. At its heart lies an excess that evades all representation, leaving an empty space within the consciousness (LaCapra, 2001). When experienced as a lack or lacuna in consciousness, symptoms return and revisit the victim as they seek to fill it. Childhood sexual abuse is more traumatic than other traumatic experiences, lying beyond the vocabulary, comprehension, and conceptualization of the child victim. The young age at which the abuse is suffered prevents children from understanding and formulating the event because they do not comprehend the concepts of sex and sexuality. While children know that something dreadful has happened, they do not possess the tools to understand, conceptualize, or deal with sexual abuse.

By definition, the trauma of childhood sexual abuse is secret – frequently one that the victim hides even from herself. This accounts for the dissociative disorders that are so prevalent amongst childhood sexual abuse survivors, especially those abused by a family member or close relative. In the absence of words and mentalization, the child breaks down, splits, forgets, disappears, becomes mute. Words are replaced by symptoms. Because childhood sexual abuse takes place on/in the victim's body, even when it remains unspeakable it leaves a physical imprint via/in numerous somatic disorders.

In order to understand the link between childhood sexual abuse and eating disorders as described by abused women, the ways in which the two phenomena are associated can be divided into several categories. This division is, of course, arbitrary, adopted simply for the purpose of analysing and recognizing the impact of childhood sexual abuse on the development of eating disorders and understanding the way in which the latter help the adult survivor cope. Childhood sexual abuse creates a complex post-traumatic stress disorder characterized by multiple complex and interwoven symptoms. The separation between addictive behaviour and self-destructive behaviour, self-injury, revictimization, etc., for example, is arbitrary, all these being common symptoms of childhood sexual abuse. The tendency towards 'ordering' and classifying symptoms frequently means that the whole picture of the complex disorders that arise in consequence of complex traumas is lost. It is also important to understand the complex internal dynamic between diverse symptoms.

Most women who suffer from eating disorders assert that 'a link clearly exists' between childhood sexual abuse and eating disorders. This statement runs counter to the accepted discourse in the field of eating disorders, which still does not recognize any association between the two phenomena or address it within the treatment plan. Many women nonetheless find it difficult to conceptualize the interconnection. Knowledge of the correlation often appears to be intuitive and self-evident but word-less. This situation is consistent with the understanding that eating disorders are ways *unwittingly* chosen to express and deal with traumas that are unsymbolized, traumas that have not been mentalized and are only encoded by dissociative means.

The features of eating disorders that are associated with self-destruction, hurting the betrayed/betraying body (Zerbe, 1995), the eradication of femininity/removal of all signs of female sexuality, the need to regain control over and purge body and mind, and various avoidances and addictions attest to a clear and direct link with childhood sexual abuse. Eating disorders form a coping and survival strategy for post-traumatic existence. They are the ways in which many sexual abuse survivors choose – in most cases unconsciously – to give voice to the unspeakable trauma, constituting some of the ways in which dissociative states and non-mentalization take form. In eating disorders, the body serves as the arena for the emergence of a whole array of symptoms, generally in conjunction with a host of others – personality disorders, self-injury, suicide ideation/attempts, dissociative disorders, prostitution, addictions, etc.

The stories of women suffering from eating disorders shed light on the process whereby they 'choose' this or that particular form – commonly on the basis of trial and error. Some move from one type to another until they find the one that best suits their needs. Unlike the prevalent discourse in the field of eating disorders, in which efforts are made to separate eating disorders into clearly defined categories, the women's narratives reported in this study demonstrate that the whole spectrum comprises a single continuum along with the other severe symptoms the sufferers experience. All these form part of a range of symptoms that comprise the Complex PTSD from which childhood sexual abuse survivors suffer.[2] While the symbolism of the choice of a particular eating disorder is clear – thinness, for example, representing control and juvenility; fatness serving as a wall of defence, a kind of barrier between oneself and the world;

and vomiting a symbolic and concrete purging of the body from the pollution that has invaded it – it is also important to recognize that they all form part of the same matrix, together with other symptoms, all of which serve as coping strategies for dealing with childhood sexual abuse.

Eating disorders are an effective and socially acceptable way of expressing distress. As Susan Silverman eloquent observes:

> I don't mind having an eating disorder or a sexual addiction – that sounds all right. In fact, I'm very grateful for the label. The label allows me a definition – this is who I am. I have a disease I can work to control, not so different from being an alcoholic. My drug of choice is food; my drug of choice is sex. But I hate the word 'incest'.
>
> (1996, p. 192)

The ideal of thinness and obsessive preoccupation with the body and food are widespread in our culture, comprising an extensive social problem. Women who experienced childhood trauma and seek non-verbal ways to convey the damage it has caused them find eating disorders an easy and legitimate resort. As Shirley observed, 'Eating disorders are an accepted social tool laid in front of us so that we can voice our distress'. This discourse goes hand in hand with an understanding of the mental problems women have suffered throughout history as culturally dependent.

One of the most interesting findings that arose from the present study was that some of the women were unaware while suffering from eating disorders of having experienced any childhood sexual abuse. Most of them suffered from full or partial amnesia of the abuse and exhibited various dissociative disorders. The eating disorders themselves also served as a way of distracting them from the sexual abuse – a way of forgetting it and defending themselves against the knowledge of what had happened to them. Some – in particular those who were severely overweight – recounted that for long periods of time they had vehemently denied the possibility that their eating problems had any link with childhood sexual abuse. Any suggestion that they had been sexually abused as children enraged them. They employed their weight and fatness to suppress and repress the abuse and build a wall between themselves and what had happened, not being willing to recognize the severe effect the abuse had had on their lives and bodies. Others, suffering from anorexia and bulimia, described diverse levels of dissociation, including full or partial amnesia of the abuse. We may thus presume that if the interviews conducted with them had taken place while they were suffering from eating disorders, establishment of any link between childhood sexual abuse and eating disorders would not have been possible. The dissociation from the knowledge of the abuse during the period when they were suffering from acute eating disorders serves as one form of explanation for the disinterest prevalent amongst eating disorder experts in childhood sexual abuse.

Women talk about the association

When women suffering from eating disorders tell their stories, they describe a clear and direct link between their food issues and childhood sexual abuse. Their accounts reveal the various and complex ways in which the complex symptoms of eating disorders in their varied forms are connected to childhood sexual abuse. One of the most striking themes was 'Of course there's a link'. The women had a clear – if wordless – understanding that their eating disorders were associated with childhood abuse. When they attempted to articulate it, however, they did not always have an explanation. In some cases, they reported that in the past they had denied any possible connection because recognition of it also meant admission of the profound effect the childhood abuse had had on their lives – an acknowledgment that in their past, and often also in the present, they had sought to suppress and repress in every way possible.

In my conversations with the women, I was struck by the absence of language to describe the association between eating disorders and childhood sexual abuse. On many occasions, explanations remained within the silences, indicated in the transcripts by ellipses (. . .). Most of the women who found a way to articulate the link had undergone therapy, during which they had been able to work through the sexual trauma and conceptualize it for themselves. Sometimes, however, women in long-term therapy in which they had worked through the sexual abuse and gained an understanding of the link between it and their eating disorders still found it very difficult to articulate the connection.

One of the explanations for this fact is linked to the dissociative disorders from which many childhood sexual abuse survivors suffer. Most of the women whom I interviewed suffer or suffered from significant dissociative disorders. Many of them had no or only partial memories of the abuse during the period in which they suffered from eating disorders, only recalling it at a later stage in their lives. In such cases, the eating disorders appear to have served as an expression of the huge and inexplicable distress they experienced because the trauma that had created it was unavailable to memory. Here, eating disorders represent an unconscious language for describing unrecognized trauma. In some cases, even after the trauma was remembered the link between the two phenomena remained obscure to the women.

The women's stories reveal the way in which eating disorders function as a disguised language for conveying indescribable secrets – secrets they keep even from themselves via various dissociative mechanisms. The ability to clearly articulate the link between childhood sexual abuse and eating disorders verbally is the result of hard therapeutic work in which the women find ways to allow themselves to remember and conceptualize the sexual abuse they experienced and the effect it has had on their lives. Only after such working through can the words be found to describe the association between the abuse and the eating disorders.

Is there a link between childhood sexual abuse and eating disorders?

As we noted above, most of the women asserted that a clear association exists between the two phenomena. Some of them described the difficulty they had in the past in recognizing its existence, observing that for long periods of time they had denied such a possibility.

'Of course there's a connection'

Many of the women expressed certainty regarding the association between childhood sexual abuse and eating disorders. Vine, for example, stated that she never imagined that health-care professionals would not know and understand what she considered to be an obvious fact: 'Of course there's a connection, so like what? . . . I never thought for a moment that professionals in the field wouldn't connect them'. A social worker by profession, she related that she understood the link, *inter alia*, when she discovered that most of the women in the psychodrama group she participated in on an eating disorder ward had been sexually abused:

> There was someone who had been hospitalized almost at the same time as me and she told me that she in fact, I mean, she said lots about . . . symptoms, like post-trauma. She didn't sleep at night and all sorts of things like that and the minute she slept she had all sorts of nightmares and things like that. So then she told me that in fact her grandfather had abused her for many years. And I remember that there was a psychodrama group, that she made some sort of thing about . . . like it was really crazy and . . . and then at the end like, that . . . like at this stage when everyone had to say something, then lots of girls got up and said: 'Yes, X, Y, Z happened to me, too', like . . . I sat without saying anything, of course, because nothing had happened to me. But . . . but, I mean there was something . . . I don't know, that at least to me it was very clear.[3]

When asked, Karen also said: 'I'm sure they're linked'. Liora, who for many years denied any connect between the childhood abuse she had suffered and her weight, stated: 'Ok, you know that in my mind, from my perspective, it's clear that they're linked. Absolutely. Without any doubt'. Liliana, who had not been in therapy, associated her eating disorder with childhood sexual abuse: 'It's as clear as daylight'. She nevertheless found it difficult to verbalize it:

LILIANA: Yes, also, also, it's several things, it's several things. Your understanding too, the . . . with time, I think, it's precisely . . . I also think that . . . that . . . I'm wrong about connecting them? But really?

ANAT: Connecting what?

LILIANA: The abuse with, with the purging? I'm asking you, yes. Because for me it's . . . I don't know why, it's as clear as daylight.

Evelyne made a similar observation:

EVELYNE: Then I was aware that there's some link, to flashbacks, to everything . . . like, I mean, physically, even if I don't eat, I knew . . . I mean, it speaks a lot to me.
ANAT: What did you know?
EVELYNE: That . . . that it . . . I mean it's really connected with me that . . . whether it's something that happens at the same time, the abuse, or whether it's more during the period of memories, nightmares, and flashbacks. So the not eating really comes back to me and the purging really comes back to me, and they're not actually deliberate . . . the laxatives, everything, like. . .

According to women who had been in therapy at eating disorder centres, most of the women there had spoken during the treatment about childhood sexual abuse. Thyme, for example, observed: 'It's also something that's very, very clear, that most of the girls who were with me on the ward and others, almost all of them had been sexually abused'. Thyme adduces a very strong link between childhood sexual abuse and eating disorders – a connection she only understood after she herself became a mentor to other girls:

> The truth is that I spoke yesterday with a friend and I told her that you're coming and that . . . we talked about the subject and there really is a strong link between them. I only understood that after I begin to take care of youth.

Denial of the link

Some women described the difficulty in recognizing the association between their eating disorders and childhood sexual abuse. Even those who today are aware of the connection spoke of a period during which they had denied the possibility that they two might be linked. Naomi recounted how she had denied it because she was unwilling to recognize the effect the abuse had had on her life:

> For years I didn't want to believe that they were linked. Because from my perspective everything bad or good that happened to me afterwards, I didn't want to link it there. I didn't want things to be related to it. Like it's simple, it was really crying and shouting. If it had been at home, and it's in therapy, like, and . . . nothing in my life is linked to that, like. I was raped when I was 10 by that piece of s★★t, and it doesn't matter what, if it shaped my personality one way or another, like, because obviously if it hadn't happened today I would be a completely different person, I don't know what sort of person I was. So obviously it's somehow responsible for

> how my life was shaped. But I wasn't ready to accept that, that it somehow affected my life, somehow, something, something from that awful day in fact has stayed with already twenty years on. I mean, from my perspective, I think that I spent whole nights crying because of it, really, I wasn't willing to accept this fact.

Recognition of the link only came during therapy. Although Naomi described how she was still fighting it, she understood that understanding it would help her come to terms with the abuse:

> But it was only in retrospect that I could, like, see that the weight was linked to this. Like, maybe in the fact that suddenly someone put a mirror in front of you. Because I began to analyse, like, with my psychologist the whole thing of putting on weight . . . very unfortunately, at a certain stage I had to accept it, because if I didn't, it would have been like lying to myself and I had a lot of difficulty with that because . . . I found it very difficult to accept the fact that my weight was connected to that. Because if I fought it, like, I'm still fighting it. But today I know that it doesn't help to fight it – unless I work on myself psychologically and really find some sort of 'closure' [original English] for this whole subject, because it won't help.

Ruth described the process she underwent after being in a sexual abuse therapy group in which most of the participants were also struggling with eating disorders. She did not want to recognize the fact that the two were linked, even though unconsciously she was aware of the connection. Today, after therapy, she still finds it difficult to accept the connection:

> In the group, it was really the first time I'd connected the two things. First of all, I saw it but ignored it apparently, apparently I didn't attribute much importance to it. Apparently I knew unconsciously but not consciously. I knew there was a link. That because of these things I eat without knowing and throw up without knowing and all these things. The truth is that even today I'm not exactly sure where to put the finger. It's difficult for me to focus on things. Really difficult.

Orna, who has been in long-term therapy, still finds it difficult to recognize and conceptualize the link between her weight and the abuse she suffered:

> What's the link? Between eating and being fat and the sexual abuse I suffered. I've never understood this and I said, when I went to therapy, when I started talking about it, then I told her: There's this story of weight and there's this story and there's no connection between them. So today I can say, well and good, there's a link. To say yes, ok, but to what . . . how much I don't . . . I don't know. So, like, there are several links missing in the chain.

Orna recounted how even in her lengthy therapy the association between her eating disorder and the sexual abuse was still a topic that was taboo: 'I don't know how to say. Like, it's . . . my psychologist laughs at me a bit and says that it's the holy grail that can't be touched. Still. But it's not true. I mean, gradually it'll happen'. She refers to the dissociation that still marks her inability to connect her weight with the abuse: 'Like that . . . it's a place in which . . . every time we talk about it I . . . I don't have anything to say . . . I . . . disappear. Completely. And . . . I simply, really don't know what to say about it'.

Thyme similarly finds it difficult to conceptualize the link despite asserting it to be clear: 'I . . . it's like . . . to me it's self-evident but I . . . it's a bit difficult to explain'. Lane also spoke of a knowing that had no explanation: 'Are you familiar with this? That it's the sort of thing that you know, but you don't always have an explanation for it'. Liliana related how she intuitively understood the connection between childhood sexual abuse and eating disorders but had never bothered to put it into words:

> Personally, in relation to myself, I see a direct link. It's not that I see it, understand it here, I don't understand it intellectually. I – I like, I like feel it. Because I've not heard before that people have said it, ok? I mean, when you said it as well, it's not that I've heard someone say: 'It's linked'. I, it wasn't even related to putting it into words. I've always felt it was linked. But I didn't bother . . . yes, no, but I didn't bother . . . without words, it's like something you know. It's like I know that there are things that go with me, I know that I don't know how to explain them but I don't know, I really don't know. I don't know, I don't know beyond. . .

Lily stated that although today she understood the connection, in the past she saw no link:

> Look, then I didn't connect it to there. I mean, I didn't see any connection. Nor did I see any link between the . . . stopping eating. I mean, between the anorexia and this. What I can say, I mean, at that moment they weren't connected.

Debby likewise reported that in the past she could not recognize any link: 'I don't know if then I could have pointed to the fact that because my father touched me I started eating and throwing up. No'.

Eating disorders as a 'disguised language of secrets too terrible for words'

> It's like inventing new words that your body acts out.
>
> —Liliana

The women's narratives reveal that the absence of a language with which to describe and conceptualize the post-traumatic stress of childhood sexual abuse takes form in various eating disorders. By its very nature, childhood sexual abuse cannot be encoded in words, children not possessing the ability to understand or conceptualize what has happened to them. Symptoms are the only way in which survivors can give voice to the trauma. Eating disorders thus form, in Judith Herman's phrase, the 'disguised language of secrets' that conveys what is unspeakable (1997, p. 96). Through the symptoms of self-starvation, bingeing, and throwing up, eating disorders express what has happened to the body and soul. Frequently, survivors are not even aware of the fact, not having been able to conceptualize the sexual trauma and suffering from dissociation.

Although it was clear to the women that a link existed between childhood sexual abuse and their eating disorders, some found it difficult to put their experiences into words, in particular with respect to conceptualizing the link, meaning that it remained unverbalized. Liliana, who suffered from bulimia, well expressed the way in which eating disorders create a new language to convey what cannot be articulated in words:

> I think that it's interesting to check, that I assume that in most eating disorders it's children who've been abused. There's also the element of the distance from the abuse and the silencing . . . the need for this in order to speak about the abuse in other voices.

Thyme described her eating disorder as both hiding and conveying the abuse: 'I think that . . . that eating disorders come from sexual abuse. They damage a person's most precious possession. Her body . . . intimacy. All these things. And disorders . . . eating disorders are something that can really cover over the problem, create a certain roof'.

Shirley spoke of the desperate need for finding another language through which to describe the abuse, having attempted on several occasions to tell both her parents and therapists, neither of whom acknowledged the trauma. Molested as a child by her uncle, she told her parents as an adolescent. Not knowing how to cope with the information, they turned to a counsellor, who told them that they should do nothing. According to Shirley, the silence that prevailed after she told her parents of the abuse left her alone and defeated. Her attempt to give a voice and words to the trauma having failed, she was bereft of any coping tools to deal with the post-traumatic stress and unable to understand what had happened. She thus began to develop an AN-type eating disorder ('I fought for the status of the worst-case anorexic') and later bulimia. She was hospitalized several times for lengthy periods on an eating disorder ward, where she again told the therapists about the abuse. Here, too, the original trauma was ignored. The silence around the sexual abuse even after she had revealed it in therapy left her once again without words or tools to conceptualize the ordeal. For her, a 'disease' was the only concrete way she could find of conveying her distress:

> I think that through the eating disorder I created for myself . . . I mean, with respect to eating disorders and their affects or a disease, you can't dispute it. I had lots of different eating disorders that couldn't be argued. In contrast to the trauma, which wasn't concrete, the eating disorders were, I feel that. In this empty place, this dullness, this vagueness, I created for myself something that even I couldn't argue with.

She also described how the eating disorder formed a substitute for talking about the trauma, which was vague and unclear:

> With me, it was very there. I think that speaking through an eating disorder rather than speech about the trauma is . . . the trauma is in fact a sequence of minute pictures, of everything that happened after it, and the preoccupation with what it did to me, what it didn't do to me. I think that the fact that I wasn't very preoccupied with it, that I was preoccupied with food, that precisely what strengthens what preoccupation with food did for me: to deal with the trauma without dealing with it.

She recounted how the brown circle she made as a child in her diary in the absence of words and tools to deal with the sexual abuse turned into an eating disorder:

> The very fact that I addressed it. I remember that I wrote in my diary as a child, I think I was about 16, something like that, and every time I wrote something about my uncle I made a brown circle on the page in order to tell myself that I'd written about him. That he'd disturbed my peace, and like the more he disturbed my peace the more influence that brown mark had. And I think that this here, the eating disorder is here in order to tell myself that it had an effect.

The eating disorder turned into a way of dealing with the conspiracy of silence, functioning as a shout expressing the fact that something wrong had occurred:

> I think that the conspiracy of silence was so great that like the eating disorder for me was really some sort of way of shouting about it. Everyone at first thought that I was doing this, including my parents at the beginning, they thought I was doing this for attention . . . I think that I needed these symptoms not just for the surroundings, also for them, but I also needed them for me. In all that silence, it silenced in me everything that was already there and I needed another way of conveying what had happened.

Shirley described the eating disorder as proof of the existence of the trauma and its effects:

> The eating disorder was for me some sort of proof that the trauma had happened, because it doesn't happen without any reason, because there has to be some trigger for it. My need to harm myself comes from somewhere and it was proof for me. The greater the need I had to prove to myself that the trauma had affected me, the worse the eating disorder got.

In Shirley's mind, the eating disorder resembled a metastasis of the abuse. The fact that her therapists ignored the abuse even after she told them about it left her without tools with which to deal with it. She thus needed 'metastases', which have more 'meat' than the sexual abuse, to take its place. The treatment of her eating disorders rather than the childhood sexual abuse only addressed the spread of the cancer – not its root:

> I often said that it feels to me like cancer that begins very small and silently and the years go by and no one pays attention to it, and then it metastasizes. Suddenly, ten years later, you find a lump on the liver and they treat the lump but they don't know that in the meantime the cancer has metastasized throughout the whole body. It feels to me now that it's because it's so long ago, and certainly as a child I didn't know how to work through it. I got to 18 and no one had spoken to me about it, so I don't know how to cope with it and I don't have much meat there to deal with. And I think that most of the people I talk to about it don't understand the trauma. So the heart of the difficulty lies in the fact that there aren't many feeling, very few pictures, it's something that's not clear, the thing I'm addressing.

Sharon related how her eating disorder serves her simultaneously as a way of dissociating from the abuse and the only way in which she can convey her distress:

> It's also to put it out of mind and a way like for me to talk about it. I mean, that . . . that . . . that people will see that there's some sort of distress because . . . you can't show it any other way, at least that's the way I felt. I mean . . . how can they see that something's wrong? Only through the eating disorder, I didn't see any other way.

Thyme, who suffered from bulimia, also described how her eating disorder functioned as a kind of 'roof' or 'tent' covering the real problem – the abuse of the body:

> I mean the . . . the eating disorder is only a sort of tent that covers the . . . lots of things inside. And . . . it's really . . . the ward is called the 'psychosomatic

> ward'. It's really that, it's really the mind affecting . . . the body affecting . . . the mind affecting the body. Really like that. Things that have accumulated in the heart, the heart, the heart, the heart, burst out and they call it an eating disorder. And so I think it made it very easy for me that I managed to vomit. Because I found a way of expressing it in some form.

Debby perceived her eating disorder as a way of expressing her true hurt, one that could not be argued with and explained her inability to function – a sort of 'certificate of miserable':

> It seems to me as though . . . it sounds as if you . . . no . . . like you need the . . . the . . . difficulty, like it gives you some sort of recognition that what happened was awful and terrible. You like don't . . . you . . . That you can't heal yourself or learn or rehabilitate yourself it's because . . . because it may be that . . . it's like there's something that you like . . . need to be bad because that's proof that what happened was awful and terrible. It's really easy for you like to hold onto something, like . . . to hold onto it because it . . . because it's a certificate of miserable.

According to the women, eating disorders serve as a way of expressing the sexual trauma because of the social normativity of the preoccupation with thinness. They thus function as an effective cover story in social and personal terms. As Debby observed:

> Why this in particular? I think that this way I could obtain what I wanted without telling myself that it was what I wanted. I could tell myself that I was doing it because I wanted to be thin, because I wanted to look a certain way, and escape from the problem, the real thing. Another thing is that it made me feel good.

Dawn also regarded the 'normativity' of eating disorders as one of the reasons why she chose them as a way to convey the wound of the sexual trauma in the absence of a supportive environment or other tools, such as help centres for sexual abuse victims:

> I also understand that it's my way, that someone will look at me, will see what happened to me. Because in truth I didn't know anything else. Even today I can't see that I could have dealt with what I went through without the eating disorder. I mean, I don't see any other way of coping I could have chosen. There was no one else there. I didn't have a supportive environment, no one who understood, no one to talk to. I mean, I didn't hear about it at all. And the eating disorder was legitimate, it was legitimate to have it. I mean everyone has one.

Dawn recounted how she needed to exacerbate her eating disorder in order to draw attention to the fact that something was wrong with her and get help, when so many girls suffering from eating disorders:

> Most of the girls in my level at school had eating disorders, so in some place too . . . I had to get to the place in which mine would be sufficiently severe to get people's attention. Because at some stage too the eating disorder wasn't enough to get attention. Because everyone had one. Not everyone, but most of my group at school. And this was the only way I could get to someone, just to talk to them, to create some kind of contact. Because I couldn't come and say, 'This and this happened to me and I need help'.

Developing an eating disorder as a way of expressing her distress was also easier than confronting the trauma directly because she knew that there was treatment for eating disorders but not that there are help centres for sexual abuse victims:

> It's much easier to find treatment for eating disorders than for sexual abuse. Even today, I mean, apart from Shalom [a rape crisis centre] that treats the victims of sexual abuse, if it's not private therapy at my age I didn't know about help centres. So there was no one to talk to.

Debby told me how her eating disorder occurred when she was 15 because it was only then that she could first conceptualize for herself that what had happened to her was wrong:

> Then I understood that something was wrong, then I gave myself the right as it were to define the word, to define something. Before then, I didn't really have the . . . maybe a bit earlier, too, I felt that something wasn't right, but . . . maybe I simply couldn't define it. But I remember that at 15 it was really the place that that's it, that I felt and that's it, I could simply do something with it. That's not really any adult age, for then, but today girls are more developed, but like relatively speaking I see it as an age, a relatively good age, for understanding what happens. . .

Olivia similarly gave expression to the relief that the eating disorder brought her as a way of conveying the sexual abuse:

> And the . . . the . . . I don't know. Like the vomiting is me – I don't know how to explain it. It's like, it's the trauma. And that's why I think it really helped me, to be able to vomit. Because I was able to express it in some form.

Eating disorders as an expression of self-blame, self-destruction, and self-harm

Some of the severe damage caused by childhood sexual abuse is linked to the child's inability to understand that the person responsible for the act is the adult perpetrator rather than the child herself. The child victim feels as though she is to blame for the horrendous acts. This self-blame is sometimes reinforced by the perpetrator, who deliberately seeks to make the child think that she is bad, responsible for what happened, and deserving of punishment. His aim in doing so is to ensure that the child keeps the abuse a secret. Some of the interviews evinced that the mothers cooperated with the father during the abuse or after they were told about it, holding the child at fault. Feelings of guilt and responsibility are particularly strong when the abuse is committed by someone close to and loved by the child – a father, grandfather, brother, or close relative.

The child who feels that the abuse happened because she was bad, disgusting, or to blame develops numerous complex symptoms of self-punishment, self-destruction, self-harm, and not wanting to live. The women's narratives indicate a direct link between these symptoms and the various eating disorders, which serve as a means of self-destruction, self-harm, self-punishment, abuse of the guilty body, and even a slow form of suicide.

Eating disorders as a form of slow suicide and a way of being rid of the exploited body

One of the most severe and prevalent symptoms that develop in the wake of childhood sexual abuse is deep depression linked to the lack of a desire to live and suicide ideation/attempts. For many survivors of childhood sexual abuse, eating disorders serve as a way to express the will to die. Grace, for example, described the connection between the childhood sexual abuse she suffered at the hands of her brother and her eating disorder, which she portrayed as a 'slow suicide' deriving from an inability to find any worth in life and a wish to get rid of her contaminated body:

> And also a place of – of slow suicide, of being rid of . . . I didn't see any reason, like I didn't find any sort of spark that would tell me, ok, like, you, you have a place here. I didn't see any worth in life, I liked harming myself, like this was . . . it was fun. Look, in my feelings I already understood that I was fainting, that I was going to work and I was dizzy. Like, it's hard to stand up, there are things that are understandable. But . . . but to lose weight that was the most important thing, the surroundings didn't matter to me, I didn't . . . I don't know if I felt that like, I assume so, that I understood that I was endangering myself at some stage, but it wasn't – it didn't really matter to me . . . it's a matter of my body being used and so it's a way to

> hurt the body, through making it disappear, through slow suicide I call it . . . I feel dirty. And . . . I think that this link is specifically with the body, my body feels dirty and I need to – I have to be rid of it. . .

She described the perpetual desire to die:

> At Passover, two years ago, I think, that was a suicide attempt that like really I sat down, wrote letters to everyone . . . and just swallowed lots of pills . . . there wasn't a specific reason (laughs), it was everything, it was just . . . enough that I remembered the abuse, enough that I found it difficult with my feelings. Also, I didn't know how to express them properly, so every feeling I had would go, would raise a storm inside. So you know, the simplest thing, like, taking pills, done, and . . . it's something I've felt all my life, this worthlessness, the lack . . . this was something that was already enough . . . enough already of the routine.

Shirley also spoke of her lack of will to live, the eating disorder allowing her not to be alive:

> The lack of desire to live or be . . . the not living, the desire not to be alive, not to be. Not to live here. The eating disorder puts me in a place that I don't have to live because I'm sick. I can't live because I'm sick. So understand me: I can't be alive. It's like this identity allows me to be and not to be, to be . . . like to be alive but on the level of not being able to be.

She described the ability to decide to kill herself as a ray of light in the midst of her depression:

> I remember that I had went home for a weekend while I was on the ward and I was really, really depressed. I didn't want to be. Like to know for some really, really long time that I can die. And that's my ray of light. And every day when I woke up I felt awful but I knew: Shirley, you can kill yourself. That was a ray of light, the knowledge that I could.

Olivia, who stopped eating in sixth grade and became first anorexic and then bulimic, similarly referred to her wish to die:

> I wanted to die. I wanted like . . . I had a fantasy that I . . . first of all I wanted to faint. I wanted to get to a point where I would faint . . . But at the same time I really wanted to die. I was . . . I wrote a short book kind of thing about all sorts of things, how I would die, how I would kill myself and how then no one would notice that I'd disappeared from the house. I was really preoccupied with death, like . . . very . . . I didn't do anything about it . . . I really hated myself.

Sharon described the suicide risk that accompanied her anorexia and after her hospitalization on an eating disorder ward at the age of 15:

> I didn't want to get better, I wanted to die. Like, not really to die, that I was going to kill myself right now, but I did everything as though. I cut myself and I stored up the pills I was supposed to take, I didn't take them. I threatened to commit suicide.

Natasha told me of a painting in which she had given expression to who she was, harming her body through her eating disorder and her wish to bleed to death:

> I painted a black amorphous shape that resembled a stomach and in the middle I put an open wound through which streams of turbid liquid were flowing that resembled blood. The red colour of the blood, which was joined to the wound. Both together creating the deep pain that spreads all through the body. Both joining together into death, that was always in my thoughts during those years and in the years afterwards. My association of the wounded body is that it bleeds to death. I wounded my body by my eating disorder.

Eating disorders as self-destruction and self-punishment: 'To strike the sin I didn't commit'

Self-destruction, self-harm, and self-punishment are rituals typically practiced by survivors of childhood sexual abuse. All three are ways of punishing oneself that derive from feelings of guilt and responsibility for the abuse. They can also be understood as a way of dealing with dissociative disorders that cause scary and painful dissociation from the body and emotions/feelings. Entailing concrete pain and blood, self-hurting restores a feeling of being alive after the dissociative numbness and sense of being 'outside the body'.

Evelyne described her eating disorder as one of many layers of self-harm: 'The moment I feel weak or helpless, I immediately flee to not eating and to things that as it were give me power. All the levels of self-harm like, so the eating disorder is only one of them'. Karen spoke of vomiting as a way of harming herself because of her feelings of worthless and as a way of hurting herself before she could be harmed by others:

> Today I understand that this eating disorder – or the throwing up, primarily the throwing up – is in fact a way of hurting myself. So I see, I don't know if I read articles about this or something, but I see that there's a really strong tendency amongst survivors of sexual abuse to hurt themselves. For that reason I think there's a connection.

ANAT: Like how? You, if let's say we're talking about you, can you describe a little this wish to harm yourself? Where does it come from? Like, why do you want to hurt yourself?

KAREN: From a place that . . . that I'm already worthless. That . . . that sometimes I prefer to hurt myself than be hurt by other people.

Shirley perceived vomiting as a self-harming activity designed to express the feeling that something inside her was sick and that she was not yet ready for life:

> I would go and throw up and in this way I would also hurt myself. When I hurt myself I know that something inside me is sick. I strengthen this that I'm not well and I withdraw inside my world. I like say to myself: You see? You're not ready for the life that's outside, go back inside your shell.

She also described the role the vomiting played in giving expression to her anger at the people who had made her hurt herself: 'I could feel lots of times that when people upset me to say: See, look what you've made me do, like, to hurt myself. Like to feel the skin'. At one point in our conversation, she spoke of the need to feel her body – a need characteristic of women who feel dissociated from their bodies during childhood sexual abuse and hurt themselves in later years in order to feel that their body still exists: 'I remember that I had a time when I would do like this, push myself here or on this, like in order to feel my body, as well as to hurt it'.

Shirley spoke of various self-harming rituals via behaviours associated with her eating disorder, such as vomiting or taking laxatives, together with the desire to escape from being well or life:

> There was something that the more I harmed myself, the more I hurt myself I also reinforced my identity as a sick person. I also like punish myself. So I think that let's say, I remember that a certain stage I really saw, I mean I knew how to identify, when I choose to vomit, when I choose to take laxatives. It was always a sort of escape. It always represented an escape. An escape from being well, an escape . . . an escape from life, in my opinion.

Thyme described vomiting as a behaviour designed to 'strike myself' because she felt guilty for what had happened to her:

> I could say of myself that I was standing in front of a mirror, cursing myself, sometimes even beating myself. However much that sounds completely nuts. I knew that the vomiting wasn't doing me good and I deliberately did it in order to strike myself. In order . . . because I was to blame for what happened to me.

Eating disorders as an illusion of regaining control

> At the moment of trauma, the victim is rendered helpless by overwhelming force. When the force is that of other *human beings*, we speak of atrocities.
> (Herman, 1997, p. 33 [original italics])

The loss of control over one's body and one's self is one of the central traumatic factors in childhood sexual abuse. As Herman (1997, p. 33) notes, psychological trauma is an affliction of the powerless. *Traumatic events* overwhelm the ordinary systems of care that give people a sense of control, connection, and meaning. Traumatic events confront human beings with the extremities of helplessness and terror, and evoke the responses of catastrophe. The sense of utter helplessness children feel when they are abused frequently prompts them to avoid all experiences that trigger the same emotion. The desperate need for control takes the form of eating disorders, which become an illusionary expression of regaining control over one's body.

Poppy described how she controlled her body through bulimia after it had been a tool in the hands of others:

> First of all from my perspective is control, a form of control, I take control over this body. No one . . . because up to that moment, everyone had done with me what they wanted, my father beat me, my uncle touched me, everyone did what they wanted. And here I said: Now food will go in, now food will go out, I'll decide what goes in, what goes out, when it goes out, when it goes in. A form of control. Despite the fact that again, I know it's not control, but . . . it's . . . at that moment for me it was.

Evelyne also spoke of her eating disorder as allowing her to control what went into her body and what went out:

> An eating disorder is control. Control. The most, between us, control. It's absurd, like I'm 26 and I should be able to control via things other than eating or not eating, but yes . . . on the level of what goes into my body, what goes in, what goes out.

For her, it is also a form of prevention. Although she cannot stop the abuse, the eating disorder allows her to control the pain in her body: 'Yes, it's a matter of prevention. I mean, I can't stop what's happening to my body but I can control even the level of pain it feels, I mean at that level'.[4] She described food as the only area in her childhood that allowed her to feel victorious, feeling helpless in all the other significant parts of her life. Victory in the battle over food created a link between the eating disorder and control:

> So the child doesn't want to eat, so what? But . . . in these fights, there were lots of times I lost, lots of times I won. I mean, there were times when

> I would sit for hours in front of food and cry and then ultimately eat. And there were times when from my perspective I would win, I would go to bed hungry, so ... it was a form of a small victory of sorts. Somewhere along the line it became a connection. I mean, if at the beginning it was very ... I had to believe that it was so. I mean, that I could control only this. From force of circumstances that really ... that ... that really didn't allow me to take control over anything significant in my life. I mean, I couldn't choose not to go to school, I couldn't choose whether to go to places where I was abused. I couldn't ... it was things that today ... and ... between if I could or not, it was important to hold onto this.

To this day, she still escapes to not eating in order not to feel weak or helpless:

> The moment I feel weak or helpless I go straight to not eating and to the things that as it were give me some power. All the things of self-harm like, so the eating disorder is only one of them. I had about half a year of not eating anything at all like, to say something, to object. And then really I also went back ... it was a period when I really went back to not eating, like, and I lost a lot of weight then.

Liliana described her addiction to the sense of control her bulimia gave her:

> There's something in that. There's something very addictive about this control. That you're controlling everything ... that nothing from inside will do something to you that you don't want. You have a human need to eat, you'll eat, and when you want you get rid of it all and there won't be a crumb left. Nothing, to the last crumb. And the more completely the better.

Grace's weight loss served a similar function:

> But to lose weight was the biggest thing, the surroundings didn't interest me ... it was the feeling, every time I got on the scales and saw I'd lost weight, it was the greatest way in the world of inciting real feeling ... because I was in control, as it were. In control but losing control ... so thank God I'm in control, no one else is ... and that shows just how bad this need for control is ... so I rather associate it with anorexia as well, the need for control.

Lily referred to the sense of false control her anorexia gave her:

> In the anorexia I was very much in control, as it were, yes? No ... I wasn't in control. But I experienced it as control, and power. Until I eventually realized that I'd lost the power. But that was the experience much of the time ... in the context of control. It doesn't matter if it's realistic now or not. But in the context of control, of feeling in control, let's call it that. That

> there's something in an eating disorder, if it's anorexia, that gives you a very strong sense of being in control and it gives you power, as it were. I mean, now I have power.

When she related to the link between eating disorders and childhood sexual abuse, Shirley spoke of the need for control in order to guarantee that she would be able to cope with the bad things that were likely to happen to her:

> The other line in my view is the element of control. I remember that at a very, very young age I had a need as it were to see all the bad things that were happening before they happened, to know that I could, that 'I can handle it' [original English], to make sure that I would know how to cope with it. So I think that preoccupation with food for me was a microcosm that I knew what was happening in it.

The fact that the anxieties around thinness were familiar ones gave her a sense of being in control:

> Anxiety of another sort is not to eat too much. Another anxiety is that I'm not thin enough. But those are familiar anxieties, as it were, 'all [too] familiar' [Hebrew transliteration]. So I think that that's one axis, the axis of control.

She regarded the meaning of anorexia as being in control, the desire to be thin merely constituting a 'framing story' that disguises the real need: 'In anorexia there's something of control. I could control it. It's also a matter of thinness, that thin is beautiful. Like a sort of framing story that reinforces it'. She made a direct link between the loss of control during the sexual trauma and her feelings towards it and eating disorders, in which she had control:

> Apropos control – I didn't have any control in the trauma, over what I felt, what I feel towards it and what I don't. Like in the eating disorder I do, I know what it does, I know the implications. I feel it, it's tangible.

Sharon talked of the need to restore a sense of control over her body as the central link between abuse and eating disorders, describing the desperate need she had not to let anyone else decide 'what goes into her body' – even though during that period she did not remember the abuse:

> I think it's a type of . . . look, in an eating disorder you feel that you have control over your body. I mean, I put into it what I want and get rid of what I want, and I do what I want. It's completely a sense of control. And I think that if you compare this with sexual assault in fact, sexual abuse, then there you have no control, you really have no control at all. And in

> an eating disorder you can restore some control to yourself somewhere, so I think you can say that there's a very close link between them. . . . I don't know, I don't know at all. I mean I don't know why, I only knew that I felt that it was my body and I would do with it what I wanted. And it was also like that when . . . lots of times I said to my friends when they asked me why I was eating or why I went to the bathroom every time I ate, like no one thought anything of it at the time, so I told them: Because. I mean, like, I don't want to eat now, it's my body, what, are you going to tell me what to do? It was like that lots of times, around the subject of, really . . . I decide what I put into my body and no one else.

She also described the need to feel in control of her body in therapy and while hospitalized on an eating disorder ward:

> I felt I was in control, what I felt in the eating disorder was that I was in control, that I was doing what I wanted to do and I didn't care what anyone else said because it was my body and I was responsible for it, and those were the feelings I had then. That I was responsible for my body and that I would put into it what I wanted and would eat what I wanted and drink what I wanted and throw up what I wanted. . .

Natasha spoke of her strong need to control what went in and out of her body. In an email she sent me to round off the interview, she compared food to a foreign object that, as in the abuse, invaded her body:

> For me, food is very closely associated with the boundaries of the body and the need to protect them because they were invaded too often when I was a child and adolescent. I feel a strong need to control what comes within them and what goes outside them. Food feels like a foreign object to me that invades me. It's like a poison that spread everywhere inside, taking control and contaminating every part of my body. The moment I don't eat or throw up what I've eaten, I prevent or stop the invasion of the boundaries of my body.

Eating disorders as a way of 'self-medicating' the damage caused by the abuse

One of the significant themes that arose in some of the interviews was the perception of eating disorders as a way of healing the damage caused by the childhood sexual abuse. Noga, for example, compared her anorexia to chemotherapy, which although toxic, is used for purposes of medication:

> I tried to think of it as chemotherapy . . . toxic material is put into your body . . . that kills healthy cells . . . damages almost every good part of the

> body . . . destroys . . . hurts . . . ultimately leads to death in great pain. . . *but*, there's a good chance that despite all its bad aspects it will save the life of the person who's suffering . . . will heal the sick cells so that the person can survive . . . My anorexia was my chemotherapy.

In the absence of any other way of recovering, anorexia was her only option:

> Until I understand how they really do it . . . how people recover without chemotherapy . . . I don't have another option . . . that how the part that can be, the sick part, overcomes, that says it's great that the anorexia is here . . . that it's here to protect me, to defend . . . and maybe this sick part is in fact actually really healthy. . .

Maggie adduced the concept of 'self-medication' in describing her bingeing:

> I tell you, it sounds like some sort of 'self-medication' [English original]. Like some sort of self-medication. Yes, absolutely. It's calming. It's . . . there's nothing like chocolate when you're depressed. And when you're upset, when you're uptight, when you don't want to live, there's nothing like chocolate, like bread. Like cake. Like . . . from my perspective, it's very beneficial.

Food, eating, and sexual abuse

For some of the women, food is directly associated with the perpetrator and sexual abuse, leaving them in a perpetual fight with it. Olivia, for example, reported how the abuse she suffered at the hands of her father is related to the secrets she shared with him – the 'sin' of eating non-kosher food. Although for a long time she did not remember the abuse, she had the feeling that she had done something forbidden with her father, attributing this sense to the fact that they had eaten non-kosher food when her mother was out of the house:

> I always remembered that when Mum and Yaron [her younger brother] weren't in the country Dad and I would do something forbidden. But the answer to that something forbidden was that we ate lasagna at home. Because lasagna, because we never brought non-kosher food into the house. We only brought kosher food in. Outside it was ok to eat non-kosher food, but not in the house. Like, to bring non-kosher lasagna into the house was forbidden. And that night all the time I had a voice in my head that said: You're stupid, like, there was something completely different there and you simply don't remember it, and it has nothing to do with lasagna, that you like have just stuck that on without any reason.

In contrast to her mother, Olivia's father gave her large portions. Food thus formed a way of making her father feel good:

> There's something very calming about the very act of eating. 'til today, this picture of a large plate of pasta Dad used to give me . . . Mum always used to give me small portions. And like . . . this is me speaking again, from first, second, and third grades, like . . . and Dad was always like that, I don't know . . . perhaps it was because of this, like . . . I don't know what started what. If I felt a need to finish the plate only so that he would feel good, because it tasted good, and that . . . because I also had this thing, like, for him. Like so he wouldn't be hurt, wouldn't be sad . . . or from there, I don't know. But there's something very calming for me in food, like. . .

Natasha associated her eating disorder with her relationship with her father because it was he who cooked for and fed her in her childhood. Not eating was thus a way of protecting herself from her father and punishing him:

> Despite the fact that in the professional literature eating disorders are most often linked to the relationship with the mother, I feel that in my case they're much more closely linked to my father. It was he who crossed the boundaries when he hurt me physically and sexually and it's against him that I feel I have to defend myself. Most of my relationship with my father centred around food. He was always the one who did the cooking and feeding in the family. For him, cooking and feeding was a real ritual. Not to eat was like to resist him, to punish him, not to allow him to come near me, to protect myself against him. Even in my childhood, when I was angry with him and wanted to show my resistance, I would tell him that I didn't want to eat what he cooked and he would be deeply hurt.

The association between food and her father added another invasive and aspect to eating:

> Because food was so closely connected with me with my father the feeling is that if I put food inside me it's like having part of him inside me and then he can hurt me not just on the outside but on the inside as well. And then I'll have absolutely no way of protecting myself against him.

Evelyne told how her uncle's abuse of her was linked to the fight over food and a cruel ritual punishment in which she was left abandoned in an orchard in the dark when she refused to eat:

> We had a fight over supper, I refused to eat, and my aunt was also there that time. I think that my cousins had already finished eating or something like that, so I was there on my own. On my own, opposite the food and him.

> My aunt didn't really intervene, and at some stage he got so angry that he simply took me and went to . . . then I didn't live there but they had always lived in a village, like around it was full of orchards. And then he took me to a place like, at the end of the end of the village, which obviously as a kid I didn't know, and certainly didn't know where we were or how to get back from there to anywhere, and at night, like in the evening. And then he just left, like he left me there and went off. And I have no idea how long it was before he came back, but when he did, like, it was clear that when I got in the car . . . I go back and it really didn't matter what it was, like, I would do. I mean I'll eat, everything like that, it was clear that I'd lost my ability to resist even in the smallest thing, like. . .

Not eating as a way of recalling elements of the abuse

Some of the post-traumatic avoidances characteristic of the survivors of childhood sexual abuse are linked to triggers that recall colours, textures, or smells. Some of the women described avoidance of certain foods that reminded them of the texture or colour of semen. Olivia, for example, recounted:

> All of a sudden I understand, let's say a couple of days ago, I suddenly understood that I can't stand a huge number of foods. I wasn't aware of it until then. And all the foods are either white or (laughs) all sorts . . . and . . . I was completely unaware of it but. . .

While she is put off by certain foods she does not mind things most other people find disgusting:

> I have this thing that on the one hand I'm like really disgusted by . . . let's pickled cucumbers – I won't touch them in any way, shape, or form. Ketchup, if you put ketchup on me, I don't know what I would do. But, but, faeces, urine, vomit, and internal organs and . . . you know, I don't know why, dead insects, give me what you want, they doesn't faze me at all. . .

Arabella, whose father made her perform oral sex on him, described her sensitivity to various kinds of food, not eating some because they recall the abuse:

> I'm really, really sensitive about these things, 'til today. To how much things are seasoned, how they're arranged on the plate, what they look like, what they remind me of, what they resemble. If it's smooth, or sticky or . . . 'til

> today there are things that I won't eat, because of their texture in my throat, in my mouth. I think it started from everything my father did to me in my mouth. He did lots of things to me in my mouth, in my throat.

She also referred to her difficulty in putting things in her mouth, swallowing food, or eating in front of others, because this reminded her of the abuse:

> I don't remember myself feeling comfortable with the fact that my mouth moved and food would go in and people were sitting there, and . . . I find it very difficult. I often connect it to the fact that I eat alone, but I don't know if it's . . . that I'm used to eating alone, that I'm not used to talking while eating. It's connected for me also, because for lots of years, most of my meals I ate alone. But I think I also have a problem with this that . . . that there's something in my mouth and that my mouth moves. It's closely connected with me . . . to the things that my father did to me in my mouth and throat, from a very young age.

During the oral sex, she would not move so that she would not feel the texture or taste. Today, food and eating are linked in her mind with sexual abuse and she reenacts the fear of moving her mouth:

> I eat alone (cries). Most of the time I eat alone. People don't see how I eat. How I behave, how I behave with it . . . with food . . . my attitude towards food, my eating, my behaviour towards food, how I see it, what I think about it. How complex it is. Complexity, sensitivity, lots, but I have very clear memories, how the things he did to me in my throat. So only if I didn't move my mouth at all, if everything was . . . the more I didn't move, first of all my mouth, and then other places, the less I felt. I felt less, I was less afraid that . . . the taste, the texture of it.

Notes

1 Peter Fonagy coined the term 'mentalization' at the end of the 1990s in reference to the ability to interpret and give meaning to one's own and others' behaviour in the form of thoughts, emotions, and beliefs. Mentalization is of great importance in preserving emotional regulation in the context of early-childhood interpersonal relations that develop due to the proper responsiveness and optimal connection between the primary caregiver and the child. According to Fonagy, Gergely, Jurist, and Target (2002), this ability is impaired in people who suffer mental trauma and significant deficiencies in interpersonal relations in childhood.

2 See Chapter 9: Women, 'Madness', and a New Diagnosis.

3 Vine did not remember the childhood sexual abuse she had experienced at her father's hands during her adolescent hospitalization, only recalling it very recently.

4 Evelyne reported in the interview that she was still being raped (revictimization).

References

Fonagy, P., Gergely, G., Jurist, E. L., & Target, M. (2002). *Affect regulation, mentalization, and the development of the self.* New York, NY: Other.

Herman, J. L. (1997). *Trauma and recovery*. New York, NY: Basic Books.

LaCapra, D. (2001). *Writing history, writing trauma*. Baltimore: Johns Hopkins University Press.

Silverman, S.W. (1996). *Because I remember terror, father, I remember you*. Athens, GA: University of Georgia Press.

Zerbe, K. J. (1995). *The body betrayed: A deeper understanding of women, eating disorders, and treatment*. New York, NY: Gürze.

Chapter 5

Eating disorders in the service of dissociation

One of the key insights gained from the study of the link between eating disorders and childhood sexual abuse is the fact that eating disorders frequently appear when survivors dissociate and have no memories of the abuse. Without any recall of the traumatic events, eating disorders constitute a secret language the victims themselves are unable to decipher, serving as a way to express the awful events and their effects. While the body and soul remember, the women themselves are cut off from the events, not remembering what happened, not knowing how to conceptualize it or put it into words.

This chapter examines the contemporary theoretical and clinical knowledge regarding dissociative disorders and their link with childhood sexual abuse and eating disorders. Testimonies from eating disorder sufferers elucidate the way in which dissociative disorders form the link in the chain between childhood sexual abuse and eating disorders.

Dissociative disorders are strange and difficult to understand for those unfamiliar with the dynamics of childhood sexual abuse. Although they have been described by clinicians for centuries, mental healthcare professionals still do not properly comprehend them. Over the past thirty years, the huge developments in the treatment of trauma in general and sexual trauma in particular have led to greater knowledge regarding the close link between dissociative disorders and chronic childhood trauma. We now know that dissociative disorders constitute a central survival mechanism for children who suffer protracted abuse from close adults.

Many professionals still tend to regard dissociative disorders as genetic, remaining blind to their true source. The notion that eating disorders serve as a way of expressing a dissociated trauma challenges eating disorders therapists, and the lack of memories of the abuse also makes it difficult to address and treat the trauma. This fact may explain why eating disorder experts lag so far behind in keeping abreast with cutting-edge theories and treatment of childhood sexual abuse.

The understanding that eating and dissociative disorders are interlinked, both deriving from childhood sexual abuse, requires those working in the field of eating disorders to adopt the principles that guide treatment of complex childhood trauma. The clinical and research knowledge that evinces that eating disorders are a consequence of the dissociation through which childhood sexual abuse is encoded calls for eating disorders specialist to bring their premises and principles into line with those of CPSTD – even in those cases in which their clients have no memories of any abuse.

Dissociation and dissociative disorders

In her autobiography, Sylvia Fraser (1987) recounts how, as a result of being abused by her father, she created a 'secret accomplice' who could contain the experience and memories. Not being in touch with its existence, she could make her 'Other Self' the sole repository of the trauma:

> I did not remember my daddy ever having touched me sexually. I did not remember ever seeing my daddy naked. I did not remember my daddy ever seeing me naked. In the future, whenever my daddy approached me sexually I turned into My Other Self, and afterwards I did not remember anything that had happened
>
> (1987, p. 15)

Maya Reed (2002) gives a very similar account. She describes the first time her father abused her when she began school, dissociating – 'I was no longer there. I came back when it was all over'. Thenceforth, whenever the abuse took place, she disappeared, watching the scene from a distance without any feelings. She created 'Dina the N★★★★r' to feel and remember everything, not having any knowledge of this part of herself. She did not believe that she could have survived without Dina and this ability to dissociate. A social worker today, Reed recounts how she has lived her whole life in the shadow of the dissociative disorders from which she suffered, depicting how through the course of therapy she was able to accept and admire the survival strategy that enabled her as a child victim to bear the emotional and physical pain of the abuse.

These descriptions, given by two incest survivors, clearly demonstrate the ways in which severe dissociative disorders are created and the function they served. Both suffered from severe dissociative disorders such as amnesia (neither of them remembered the abuse until much later in life), depersonalization ('I saw far away what he was doing to his child'), and DID dissociative identity disorder ('My Other Self', 'Dina the N★★★★r') – a severe disorder that looks bizarre and arouses doubt and distrust even amongst mental healthcare professionals.

The clinical reports of dissociation are complex and not readily fathomable. The disorders we meet in our daily clinical lives are complex, difficult, and sometimes appear non-credible. An empathic response to a child whose father – frequently an otherwise respectable and 'ordinary' person – abuses her at night but returns to normal in the morning as though nothing had happened allows us to understand the function these severe disorders play, serving as a vital survival mechanism for children who feel abused, abandoned, and neglected by those supposed to take care of and protect them.

Many mental healthcare professionals are still unaware of the link between dissociative disorders and trauma, especially childhood sexual abuse. Many people who suffer from dissociative disorders are thus frequently misdiagnosed and receive the wrong treatment (Kluft, 2001). Most mental-care clinicians still lack any formal training in the treatment of dissociative disorders, directly adversely affecting the effectiveness of the treatment they provide to those whose history includes self-injury, addiction, eating disorders, childhood sexual abuse, physical abuse, neglect, chronic PTSD, borderline personality disorders, etc. (Chefetz, 2006).

Understanding that dissociative disorders serve as vital and normal coping strategies helps console victims, who feel blemished and sullied. These feelings are frequently reinforced by a diagnostic branding that, blind to the traumatic sources of the disorder, compounds the trauma of the original abuse, disregarding the courage they have summoned up to break the bonds of shame, guilt, and stigma and seek help.

Dissociation is a form of disconnection between normally interrelated things. Dissociative experiences are incommensurate with one's ordinary sense of self, causing a break in the continuity of consciousness. In severe cases, dissociation impairs the integration of consciousness, memory, personal identity, and perception. Dissociation may affect a person subjectively in the form of thoughts, feelings, and actions that seem to come out of nowhere – experienced as performed and controlled by an outside force. When normally related mental experiences and events are disconnected from one another, perception is distorted, exemplified in slight or severe changes in the significance and meaning given to personal or interpersonal events (Chefetz, 2006). Typically, dissociation makes a person feel 'taken over' by an emotion that seems to make no sense at the time – feeling unbearably sad without any apparent reason, a feeling that lifts as abruptly as it arrives, for example. The sense of doing something uncharacteristic but having no capacity to stop it is sometimes described as the experience of being a 'passenger' in one's body rather than the driver (ISSD, 2013).

Dissociative disorders are diagnosed on the basis of the presence of a significant number of dissociative symptoms. They are defined as disorders or lack of continuity in the normal personal integration of one or more aspects of psychological functioning, including (but not limited to) consciousness, memory, emotions, thought, body-representation, motor control, and behaviour – psychobiological functions designed to be anchored one within the other (Spiegel et al., 2011). Dissociative symptoms are experienced as an uncontrollable disturbance of consciousness and behaviour accompanied by a loss of continuity in subjective experience (for example, fragmented identity, depersonalization, and derealization) and/or a lack of access to information or control over normally controllable mental functions (for example, amnesia). The dissociative symptoms are related to trauma, many being accompanied by confusion and/or concealment due to their association with a trauma experienced as shameful. Although DSM-5 locates dissociative disorders within the spectrum of acute-stress and post-traumatic disorders in order to reflect their links with these diagnoses, they remain separate disorders. Both acute-stress and post-traumatic stress disorders include dissociative symptoms such as amnesia, flashbacks, emotional numbness, and depersonalization/derealization.

The DSM-5 (APA, 2013) identifies five dissociative disorders:

1) Dissociative Identity Disorder (DID): The most chronic and severe form of dissociation, known in the past as multiple personality disorder. This is characterized by multiple identities that control behaviour and thoughts accompanied by an inability to remember important personal information that cannot be attributed to normal forgetfulness. It involves a striking loss of continuity in the sense of self and feelings of being controlled and changes in emotion, behaviour, consciousness, memory, cognition, and intrusive thoughts. These signs and symptoms may be manifest to others or reported by the sufferer. Rather than constituting truly separate personalities they represent repressed experiences. The forgetting (amnesia) is commonly asymmetric, each dissociated state remembering different parts of the autobiographical information. Generally speaking, a central 'unifying' state exists that identifies with the client's real name. Typically, this state is not aware of the existence of the other identities. In most cases, the identities emerge in order to deal with threatening situations. These symptoms cause significant clinical distress or social, professional, and other forms of dysfunction. The disorder does not form part of a cultural or social practice, nor are the symptoms attributed to the influence of medical conditions or drugs.
2) Dissociative Amnesia: This is an inability to remember important autobiographical information, usually traumatic or stressful in nature. It constitutes a prolonged amnesia that cannot be explained as normal forgetfulness. Nor does it derive from organic disruptions such as blackouts following alcohol consumption or drug use. It can take the form of selective or local amnesia regarding a specific event(s) or general amnesia regarding one's whole personality or life-history. The novel aspect of this definition in DSM-5 lies in the claim that this disorder relates to the compartmentalization of traumatic memories rather than their forgetting. In other words, it consists of the inability to retrieve memories rather than their 'deletion'.
3) Depersonalization/Derealization Disorder: Depersonalization refers to a sense of a loss of reality (unrealness), disconnection, or observing one's body, thoughts, feelings, ideas, or acts from outside it (for example, changes in perception, a distorted sense of reality, a feeling that the self is not real or does not exist, emotional or physical numbness). Derealization is a feeling

of unreality or disconnection from the environment (for example, people or things appear unreal, imaginary, indistinct, lifeless, or distorted). During depersonalization/derealization, reality-testing remains intact.

4) Other Specified Dissociative Disorder: A chronic and repeated syndrome of various dissociative symptoms. This category includes identity disorders associated with loss of continuity in one's sense of self or agency, dissociative trances or episodes of possession amongst people who do not report amnesia. The disorder also includes identity disorders that arise as a result of prolonged and intense forced persuasion (e.g., brainwashing during captivity, torture, sects, etc.). It is manifested in long-term identity alterations.
5) Unspecified Dissociative Disorder: This relates to phenomena in which the characteristic symptoms of dissociative disorders interfere with social, professional, etc., functioning but are not fully consistent with the criteria of any of the other four dissociative-disorder categories. It serves as a diagnosis in cases in which information is lacking with which to determine a specific diagnosis.

Today, it is generally recognized that dissociation also includes physical elements, including loss of sense, perception, affective/motor functions, and sensomotoric and affective symptoms caused by a reliving of the trauma, such as distorted perception, pain, tics, and panic (van der Hart, Nijenhuis, Steele, & Brown, 2004).

Childhood sexual abuse and dissociation

The close link between dissociative disorders and childhood sexual abuse is well documented in the professional literature (Herman, 1997; Courtois, 1997; Briere, 1989; Chu & Dill, 1990). Dissociation is one of the central disorders that emerges in the wake of sexual and other forms of abuse in childhood and adolescence (Schwartz, 2000).

A child who is abused develops psychological adaptations to preserve her primary attachment to her parents in the face of daily evidence of their malice, helplessness, or indifference. These defences help her wall the trauma off from her conscious awareness and memory. Hereby, she is able to say that it did not really happen or minimize, rationalize, and excuse the behaviour. Because she is unable to escape or alter the unbearable reality, the child alters it in her mind through denial, suppressing the thoughts, etc. (Herman, 1997).

Although dissociative disorders are associated with all forms of childhood abuse, clinical experience demonstrates that sexual childhood abuse – in particular at a young age and perpetrated by people closely related to the child (e.g., father, grandfather, or brother) – is responsible for the most severe forms. In every case of dissociative identity disorder with which I have dealt, the abuse was at the hands of a father or grandfather, began at a very early age, and was particularly cruel and sadistic. Sexual abuse at the hands of a person whom one loves at a tender age is the severest of traumas, causing more shame and being harder to understand and conceptualize than physical or emotional trauma. It thus forces children to develop sophisticated dissociative mechanisms in order to survive.

It is thus no surprise that the study of dissociative disorders gained significant momentum with the development of the study of childhood sexual abuse. Psychiatrist Judith Herman, whose pioneering *Father-Daughter Incest* was published in 1981, wrote in the epilogue to the 2000 edition that one of the discoveries no one anticipated twenty years ago was the close link between trauma and altered states of consciousness. Despite the fact that dissociation was documented a century ago, its link with psychological trauma has only recently been noted (Herman, 2000). Herman also observes that we now have a better understanding of memory gaps amongst incest survivors and the delayed recall caused by childhood sexual abuse.

A 1987 study of fifty-three female clients (Herman & Schatzow, 1987) indicated that the severity of memory disorders was directly linked to the young age at which the abuse took place. In a study of childhood sexual abuse survivors conducted by the National Institute of Mental Health in the United States, psychiatrist Frank Putnam (Putnam, 1997 in Herman, 2000) found children who experience sexual abuse and employ dissociative mechanisms to survive are likely to develop a variety of physiological, psychiatric, and social disorders in adulthood. The severity is directly linked to the extent of the dissociative symptoms they exhibited in the wake of the abuse.

Numerous studies have evinced the extremely high rate – around 90 percent – of a history of trauma amongst dissociative disorders sufferers (Putnam, 1997). The renewed interest in the field of trauma and dissociation in the twentieth century based on accumulating clinical experience with childhood sexual abuse survivors has led to a clinical picture that includes extensive identification of disorders in personality structure and dissociative responses linked to chronic childhood abuse (Courtois, 1997). Traumatic memory and the disorders associated with it, such as amnesia and repressed/recovered memories of the abuse, are now gradually being more deeply understood, and a renewed interest is also being shown in dissociative disorders and dissociative identity disorders in particular.

The dissociation that serves as a primary defence mechanism during the abuse leads to the development of dissociative mechanisms in adulthood. In order to cope with feelings of fear, pain, and abandonment, children deny the traumatic reality they experience by dissociating it from consciousness (Sillon, 1992). Dissociation thus constitutes a desperate unconscious attempt to control and deal with frightening circumstances. The standard description of depersonalization – frequently described as watching the event from the ceiling or being a 'small bird on the windowsill' – is directly linked with childhood sexual abuse. When the body is invaded and sexually exploited, dissociation from it serves as a common and obvious survival mechanism. Many accounts of rape and sexual assault (including drawings made by victims) include the psyche leaving the body, as it were, the victim being portrayed from a viewpoint outside the body looking on.

> A standard – and sad – report of depersonalization is the recollection of floating on the ceiling watching as I was raped. The person below was me, sort of, but I wasn't there. But I was. It was all very confusing. I just feel numb about it now.
>
> (Chefetz, 2006, p. xvi)

Dissociative disorders help abused children preserve their lives and sanity by constructing an identity capable of coping with the pain, anxiety, threat, and shame attendant upon the horrors they experience. Creating alternative mental representations of the self and others that take the form of the negation of reality ('not me', 'not him', 'it didn't happen'), they identify solely with powerful objects that appear to offer a bond, defence, escape, or measure of relief from the pain. During and after the trauma, survivors dissociate from what happened by pretending or distracting themselves by entering other states of consciousness. When they become adolescents, they frequently avoid intimate relationships, which they have always experienced as abusive. As adults, they often engage in a variety of avoidance, addiction, and camouflage techniques (Schwartz, 2000). Other addictions may take the form of substance abuse (drugs, alcohol) or behavioural disorders – such as eating disorders. These strategies help conceal and distract them from the awful secret they keep inside themselves – frequently even hiding it from themselves.

Childhood sexual abuse is a chronic form of trauma in which the child is forced to adopt coping strategies in order to survive because she feels helpless and unable to cope with the abuse. When this exploitation is perpetrated by a family member, in particular a parent or another responsible and authoritative adult (teacher, priest, etc.), the child loses not only the ability to cope but also the capacity to rely on her parents' coping skills and help or that extended by other adults. From the small child's perspective, the abuse threatens her very existence. Dissociation thus serves as an adaptive tool (Davies & Frawley, 1994). In an effort to preserve the ability to trust adults, on whom they rely for their material and emotional needs, sexually abused children are forced to split the self into two (or more) states, one part representing the 'business as normal' of the day self, the other the nighttime nightmare, which is relegated to a dream-like or unreal existence.

Under more severe circumstances involving severe and prolonged early abuse, dissociation not only serves as an adaptive defence during the abuse but also becomes a central pillar of the organization of the self. One client, for example, 'invented' another girl who was abused while her father was molesting her and she herself had 'forgotten' what happened. Today, as an adult, she suffers from DID, exhibiting several identities of whose existence she is unaware. The origin of these self-fragments or other identities in childhood sexual abuse has been demonstrated in numerous studies. The multiple identities allow victims to cope with the abuse and preserve the memory of its perpetration while not being consciously aware of its existence (Herman, 1997).

Eating disorders and dissociation

In the last thirty years, the link between eating disorders and dissociative disorders has been established (Vanderlinden & Vandereycken, 1997), much higher rates of dissociation being reported by those suffering from eating disorders than control groups (Demitrack, Putnam, Brewerton, Brandt, & Gold, 1990). Several studies have found significantly high levels of dissociative experiences amongst participants with eating disorders and a history of sexual abuse, suggesting that dissociation originating in trauma plays a role in the development of bulimia (Vanderlinden & Vandereycken, 1993). Clinical descriptions of bingeing frequently include depersonalization, derealization, identity disorders, psycho-motoric numbness, and amnesia (McCallum, Lock, Kulla, Rorty, & Wetzel, 1992; Root, 1991; Sands, 1991; Torem, 1986). A long-term link exists between episodes of binge eating, purging, active dieting, reduced foot intake, and dissociative experiences (McCallum et al., 1992).

A study of 142 female students with eating disorders found a link between dissociation and eating disorders (Rosen & Petty, 1994). The authors thus suggested that elements whose goal is to teach clients to recognize their tendency to dissociate be incorporated into the framework of the treatment of eating disorders. A study conducted in Japan (Berger et al., 1995) of forty-one female eating disorder clients evinced that 22 percent of the participants met the criteria for multiple personality disorder, a further 15 percent demonstrating high levels of dissociation. A study of 103 female eating disorder clients (Dalle Garve, Rigamonti, & Todisco, 1995) found that dissociative symptoms were more prevalent amongst this group than the control group.

Women speak of eating disorders as a way of dissociating

The majority of the women I interviewed exhibited dissociative symptoms and disorders. Most suffered from full or partial amnesia of childhood sexual abuse, primarily during the period when their eating disorder was most acute. The women's reports included dissociative disorders ranging from full or partial amnesia of the abuse to depersonalization, emotional numbness, identity dissociative disorders, etc. Their accounts demonstrate how eating disorders serve to camouflage and repress childhood sexual abuse, playing a dual role – acting both as a distraction and detachment from the sexual abuse and as a way of unconsciously expressing the repressed, denied, and dissociated unmentalized trauma.

The nature of dissociation makes it difficult to conceptualize the significance of eating disorders as a form of disconnecting from childhood sexual abuse. The women's narratives indicate that they found it difficult to verbally formulate the diverse ways in which their eating disorders served as a way of disconnecting and denying what had happened to them, the obsessive preoccupation with eating and not eating disguising this inability.

Eating disorders and dissociative amnesia

Some of the women did not remember the childhood sexual abuse they had endured during the period they were suffering from their eating disorders. Those I interviewed conceptualized their eating disorders as a way of forgetting or not remembering the abusive events, many of their accounts evincing that their eating disorders 'suddenly' appeared without any apparent trigger.

Sharon – hospitalized at the age of 15 on an eating disorder ward for anorexia – stated that during this period she did not remember anything about the childhood sexual abuse she experienced, the memories only surfacing many years later when she went back to the place where it had occurred:

> The story began at 12, 14, when they found out I had an eating disorder in fact and . . . and . . . they tried to treat it in the community, but it didn't work, and they hospitalized me in Cedar Hills, after repeated suicide threats. It was only two years ago, really, after I'd mostly got out of it all, that I remembered . . . what had happened, the actual abuse.

Sharon was sexually abused by the son of family friends at whose house she used to sleep over regularly. She described the dynamic of the dissociation that occurred during the abuse, remembering the TV series being shown at the time but not the abuse itself:

> The parts I remember, that have . . . they're three brothers . . . the next thing I remember . . . is . . . I remember the TV, I mean, I don't remember . . . that . . . like, I focused on the TV and wasn't aware of what was happening to me at that moment. I, like, remember the series, what was on the TV, that's what I remember. The next thing I remember is getting up and going out of the room, and I went into the next room and hid under the blanket and cried, just like a little child. I *was* a little child. And . . . and then I remember I heard the door opening and I stopped crying, I wiped the tears away at that moment and he came close and took the blanket off and asked me if everything was alright, so I told him yes, 'Why shouldn't I be alright?' And he said to me: 'I thought you were crying and I didn't understand why you left'. Then I told him, 'No, it's nothing, I just didn't want to sleep on the floor'. Then he gave me back the blanket, went out, and I started crying again until I fell asleep. I thought maybe it was in his sleep. I mean, that

> he didn't know what he was doing, that it was in his sleep. That's . . . that's what I thought. But I just remember the series running in front of my eyes, that's the only thing, like, I was able to focus on, 'til today, when I try and remember, that . . . that really what comes to me, only these parts.[1]

Sharon experienced full amnesia of the abuse. In her interview, she related how, during the period in which she suffered from her eating disorder, she remembered nothing of it:

> I don't remember it, I don't . . . I really don't remember what happened, I remember parts and that's it. Today, I know in retrospect that . . . from the moment I was hospitalized they suspected that . . . sexual abuse in fact, that I'd undergone. But it's never come out, it's never been revealed in every possible way . . . because I didn't remember anything, I didn't remember anything until two years ago, really nothing.

She only remembered the abuse about two years before the interview took place:

> What caused me to remember was . . . two years ago, like, I discovered that with his father that it was like he was my father, really a father-figure for me, cancer. It was actually his birthday, so we went there and . . . and I always liked dressing up, putting make-up on, and looking nice and I came looking like I usually did, I didn't do anything special, and I remember that the first thing he said to Mum – the son, like, he told her that. . . 'Take care of your daughter that she doesn't turn into a slut'. And I remember that my first instinct was to shout at him in front of everyone not to come near me, that he should get away from me, and that I didn't want to hear him anymore. Even then I didn't understand where the reaction came from, I mean, everyone was shocked, including Mum, like she looked at me 'What's with you?' And I didn't – I didn't understand why I'd reacted like that. And then I just went around the house, where I'd spent time almost every day until I was 10 and . . . and went into the room it happened in and then I got it, in a boom! like.

Naomi was viciously raped by a neighbour at the age of 10 and immediately went home and then to bed, sleeping for three days claiming she was sick. When she woke up, she remembered nothing of what had occurred. Her bingeing and weight issues began straight afterwards:

> I don't think I understood what it was at all, really, like, I was a child of 10 and . . . no, the truth, I don't remember anything, no hesitation, like . . . I have no idea of what, what happened in my head. Like, there isn't, I simply went to sleep, I don't know . . . my whole body was painful, I don't know, from my perspective what happened at that moment was just to get into

> bed and to try and make it go away . . . so I don't know, like, I have no idea if I thought about it and decided not to, like, I don't think so. I slept for three days. I, like, I think that even on the morning I got up I didn't remember anything.

Her description of the emergence of her eating disorder as something 'very strange', developing 'suddenly' without any apparent reason in and of itself is representative of the dissociation she developed:

> Yes, it was for no reason. Because I simply, like, I can look at the album, like you know, turn the pages and suddenly I'm fat. You know, I wouldn't be photographed for a month, a month, if in a week I put on 10 kilos, like, during the *shiva* for my grandmother [after her death], so . . . it's, it's simply like that, like, in the album. I mean suddenly, there are pictures with me in undershirt and shorts, pictures of the next day, like, a page after, it's already . . . like, really, like, that, you look at it and it's very . . . very strange. Like, what's the issue with a page? That suddenly you see a big difference in weight.

Naomi only remembered the rape during a three-day workshop two years after having completed her army service:

> Some two years or something after I was released, in some workshop, an awareness workshop in the north, that was a couple of days, and there I remembered everything. I was at a workshop in the north with a friend. And it was a mixed workshop, men and women. And one of the exercises was to sit opposite a person of the opposite sex – men opposite women – and . . . to close your eyes, I don't remember what exactly it was. As fate would have it, I sat opposite someone whose eyes were exactly like his. Like, we were sitting eastern fashion, on the floor, and we had to look at one another and close our eyes. The second I closed mine, like, something pressed play in me. I told my friend I had to talk to her. I told her I'd remembered several things that had happened to me, that I don't know how to deal with them all in my head.

Olivia, who was abused by her father, also had no memories of the trauma. As an adolescent, she suffered from bingeing, then anorexia, then bulimia. During this period she also exhibited other symptoms of childhood sexual abuse, such as revictimization, self-injury, without remembering the actual events. She only recovered the memories at 28, in a group for rape victims in which she participated following several adolescent sexual assaults.[2] When I interviewed her, she was still in the very early stages of recalling what had happened:

> Well, I'll say first that I, only a year ago, something like that, did I remember, I began to remember what my father had done to me. With regard to it, it's

> hard for me to say much, like, I can . . . all my memory of my childhood is awfully confused, it's full of holes. And . . . I said that I think that . . . I think that that was what happened in Grade 6. It's like . . . I just . . . now I'm completely disconnected. But then I just knew it. Like, just, I don't know, I would sleep with my boyfriend and I would have all sorts of flashbacks. I don't know. But I don't know . . . like . . . you need to understand, I don't have, I don't have any clear pictures in my head. I don't, like, have things that I knew at the beginning . . . I don't have, I don't have any. I have flashbacks and that's it. I don't have . . . and like certain feelings, but I don't . . . I can't tell you at night he would come and do it, I don't know. I don't know.[3]

Olivia explained her inability to remember the abuse as due to the disparity between her father's normal, ordinary daytime behaviour and the 'something awful' that happened:

> It's something that I think that . . . like, that developed then, that I, like . . . like, I thought I understood something, and then suddenly something awful happened to me, and then after that Dad behaved as normal, and everything was fine, and it . . . and then, like . . . suddenly I don't know what I know and what I don't, and 'til today I'm always preoccupied with that.

She described her struggle between wanting to remember what had happened and the fear that she was crazy:

> I would do anything to remember, so that I would have something concrete . . . like, I wish I remembered. But it's not . . . dealing with it is s★★t in any case, but then at least I'd be sure, that I wouldn't have to doubt myself all the time. But the problem, that I'm always thinking I'm crazy, perhaps I'm a schizophrenic, perhaps I'm making things up. . .

Her dissociation took the form of the sudden and inexplicable development of an eating disorder in Grade 6:

> And I really, I have to say that I was a very cute child, and I wasn't . . . I wasn't fat like overmuch, really. And . . . and in Grade 6, like, all of a sudden, the first time I got some enjoyment out of not eating. Like, suddenly, I don't know. Like, this dizziness, and this tiredness, and this, it gave me some sort of satisfaction like that of . . . some sort of niceness. Like, finally I was doing something right.

Dawn – abused by her father from a very early age – described how vomiting helped her repress the memories of the trauma:

> When I started to throw up, I didn't see any connection. A child of 11. . . I decided that . . . I had to lose weight and I started throwing up. Over time,

every time I felt bad, I would throw up. And it was only after the hospitalization that the things started to come up and then I really understood that . . . that . . . that it was my way of . . . not letting them come up. I mean, every time I threw up I . . . repressed them a bit more and I . . . put it aside again and put it out of my mind.

Evelyne, abused by her uncle and then by numerous others, reported how she always knew 'something' had happened in the past but only remembered the abuse after she was released from the eating disorder ward on which she had been hospitalized:

ANAT: So, like, it's really, really difficult for you to talk about it. Despite the fact that you remember. Did you always remember?

EVELYNE: No.

ANAT: When did you remember?

EVELYNE: Specifically about him, somewhere I think I always knew on some level and I really, really suppressed it. Because to be afraid of him, I was always afraid, even as an adolescent. And there were lots of things that happened when I was already 21, 22. And, like, up until they really, really happened, and although there lots of things, until they really happened, I felt uncomfortable, or I had lots of red lights that I tried hard to avoid thinking about. I really, really took it in that it had happened, I mean in childhood, only when I was released. When I left the ward. And then I got home and . . . I knew about other things that happened with other people, I didn't know about him. Like, I sold myself the story of a very happy childhood until 7 and . . . everything began then.

Arabella, who was abused by her father, described her partial amnesia in relation to what he did to her and her inability to understand or conceptualize it:

ANAT: And in effect you kept it a secret, completely, until eight years ago?

ARABELLA: Yes. There were lots of years that . . . I really remembered it, on a physical level. On a physical level, on the level of the . . . nightmares, of awful things . . . really difficult things, in the intimate relations I had. Huge difficulties . . . but . . . those were years when I didn't know for certain it was him, and that that's what it was. My body behaved completely as though . . . behaved completely terrified, really terrified. In . . . it found expression in lots and lots of things. That I lived in terror, but not . . . and all sorts of therapists I went to asked me in a very . . . way . . . nothing. But there was one therapist, who works, and she worked with dance therapy. She asked me, she was convinced it had happened, she didn't have any doubt, and she asked me and I said no.

ANAT: Because you didn't remember or because you didn't want to say?

ARABELLA: Because I didn't understand what I remember. I was really terrified, and it. . .

ANAT: Like, you didn't conceptualize it as sexual abuse?

ARABELLA: Yes. And I didn't understand that it was really my father. Even though there were also things that really . . . that really, that I think if today I had such a nightmare I would be able . . . I had a recurrent nightmare for years and years . . . I remembered, like I told you. I remembered all sorts of feelings, I remembered states of assault on my body. But I didn't really understand what it was.

She described her eating disorder as a way of avoiding remembering or understanding the abuse:

> No, I didn't understand what was happening to me. And . . . even then I had food issues, and I didn't . . . yes, I had these states that . . . I would eat lots, in order not to remember what had happened, and afterwards I wouldn't eat . . . these states that I eat lots and then don't eat, sometimes I would continue to fight not to remember.

Yvonne arrived at her interview ready to speak about the link between childhood sexual abuse and eating disorders despite having no clear recollection of the abuse she had suffered. In the interview, she alluded indirectly and in fragmented form to the fact that she suspected that she had been abused by her father but did not know for certain or was not able to explicitly report what had happened. She described how the minute the subject of abuse arises she begins eating:

YVONNE: As I wrote you, I don't . . . I don't really remember anything related to it, but every time someone refers to this subject and . . . I feel that I'm paralyzed and silenced by fear. And it's not . . . I've been exposed to lots of difficult things in my life, like, also physical, like, I . . . just, we had a lecture not long ago, someone came to speak about how to treat victims of sexual assault, it was just so strange to me that I laughed and . . . I couldn't . . . I wrote you then that I remembered that something bothered me very much sexually at 12, I remembered it all the time, but suddenly when he showed us on the board all sorts of things that people say, it made me feel so awful and I began to be, like, manic laughter, like, and I started to eat, it was something that we didn't do. And I'm generally very compliant and obedient, and I caused somewhat of a furore around me, I really didn't want to hear what he was saying.

ANAT: What you're saying, in other words, is that you suspect because of these reactions, to which you paid attention, you suspect that it happened to you? That you don't remember it at all, like?

YVONNE: All the time I have something like this, and I feel that I'm getting closer to it in my memory, and like, all of a sudden, all of my thoughts burst out. This state, I'm always, what at 12 I always remembered . . . I don't know,

> but all . . . I really don't remember how it's linked, but every time I speak about . . . about such things . . . every time I feel that I'm scared I . . . I . . . this kind of picture comes to me that Dad was showering me, but I don't remember anything, like . . . more. . .

In a form characteristic of dissociation following childhood sexual abuse by a close family member, she also described how, despite her lack of real memories, she always remembered 'there was something':

> I don't know. And all the time I remembered this, but I never remembered how I was scared all the time, only recently it suddenly came together for me, and it's really powerful. And without any relation to this, I always remembered that there was something like this, that I don't remember.

Vine brought a dissociated story of childhood sexual abuse to the interview. At the beginning, she told me about the abuse perpetrated by her cousin. As we talked, however, it gradually became clear – albeit fragmentedly – that she also remembered being abused by her father, who started molesting her when she was 3 or 4. She had full amnesia of this trauma, which spread to everything that happened before she reached the age of 12:

> In fact, let's say I don't remember, until 12 I remember virtually nothing, nothing, nothing. I never knew why, even today I don't really know why, but up until 12 I remember virtually nothing of my life.

She told me how during therapy she had begun to remember her father's abuse:

> It's something that really from the moment I started therapy, even a bit before, from the moment the whole thing exploded with me. It's something that, like, exists inside me somewhere, you know, [in the] 'back of my mind' [English original]. I think that sometime around January, February, like, in terms of therapy I was pre-opening of these things, but they did begin to come up. I remember I came and said it explicitly, 'I feel that . . . I think, all sorts of things have begun to come up . . . I don't know if I can call them memories, suddenly I see a flash of something, I don't know. . .' Then, like, in May, like at the end of May, I simply said it, the first time I'd said it in therapy.

Like Yvonne, Vine also spoke of the fact that, despite the amnesia, she frequently felt that something had happened to her but this had always only been a vague feeling:

> There were lots of times that it was . . . like . . . something very vague, with question marks, and . . . like, I never really said. But really in May, like, I said, 'Ok, like . . . I think, I'm relatively sure that something happened'.

She reported that as an adolescent her eating disorder had taken control of her whole life, leaving no room for recollection of the worst thing of all:

> In short, it [the eating disorder] began to preoccupy me and as it did I was asking myself why it was. And then I remember, I don't remember precisely the . . . there's something that's really difficult, probably, when you lose control, to understand where exactly it falls through there. But . . . but I lost control of everything. I mean, it was something I was preoccupied with all day long, all the time. Like, how many calories is this, how many calories is that? How much I'm putting into my body now, and how much now.

She conjectured that she had developed an eating disorder because she could not cope with the memory of the abuse: 'But . . . I don't know, perhaps I just wasn't built for that at the time. Because if I could have dealt with it I probably wouldn't have turned to food, like, to not eating'. She described her preoccupation with food as allowing her not to remember what had happened:

> Just, instead of remembering everything, like, all of a sudden I began . . . when I started therapy, all of a sudden I began remembering things, so instead of that I began to think how many calories I'd eaten that day and what I would eat tomorrow and where I would throw it away and all sorts of things like that. Like, that's what filled my life all the time.

Although Naomi remembered the childhood sexual abuse, she also spoke of not remembering all the details and making attempts to remember: 'And sometimes there are parts of days I try and remember, remember . . . in order to know what happened there. And I just can't remember. I just get horrific headaches'.

Natasha, who was abused by her father at a young age and revictimized by other abusers, complete forgot all the trauma except for her father's mental and physical violence. Only when she was 19 did she partially remember the childhood abuse:

> No, I don't remember lots of years. I remembered the blows. I remembered the shouting. I didn't remember the sexual abuse and not . . . and I don't know . . . so . . . also the . . . like . . . the more covert abuse . . . and I didn't . . . I didn't know how to interpret it as something wrong. Because it was something that . . . it was the only thing I knew. Because that's . . . I knew that's how it was . . . that's how people behaved at home. And in general . . . until I was . . . 13, I think, I lo . . . ved him. Everything he said, it was the last word, that was what was right. And if someone else said something different and . . . I would say they weren't right because Dad had said that it was like this. And . . . like, he was the person I most admired, and most believed, and . . . when . . . and when I, like, had to listen to him, like, in effect to protect myself. . .

Natasha described various stages in her remembering and forgetting. After remembering the abuse when she was 19, she again forgot it. At around 22, she began therapy in the wake of a severe mental crisis, during which she remembered the sexual abuse perpetrated by her aunt's husband. Following that, she again remembered her father's sexual abuse of her when she was 6:

ANAT: So in effect, for many years you forgot the sexual abuse. When did you remember?

NATASHA: I remembered in stages. The first abuse I remembered when I was 19 or 20. And then I forgot it again, for some three years, and then I remembered again when I started therapy, after I'd completely collapsed, when I was at university, when I had a real, serious breakdown. And since then I've been trying to recover and recuperate. Then I remembered, like, this part, which was from age 6, then I remembered about two years ago. And several years ago I also fully remembered . . . what he . . . what happened to me with the . . . with my aunt's husband.

ANAT: How in fact did you remember: What . . . prompted you to remember?

(Long silence)

NATASHA: I don't know. It suddenly flooded into my head.

She told me how she had remembered the first abuse after seeing a film about rape:

> At the beginning I remembered the first time that I then forgot, I just remembered after some film that was . . . that . . . the . . . girl there was raped and . . . and then . . . and then, like, there was a story, around, like, around the . . . around the rape . . . and then I . . . like . . . suddenly remember that . . . I just thought about it that . . . wow, something like that happened to me, too, but ok, what happened, after all he didn't rape me, what happened, what I think of it generally, it's not the same thing. I remembered, like, for several days and then a week and then I forgot . . . and afterwards, afterwards, when I remember. I have flashes of memories. . .

Eating disorders and depersonalization

Another dissociative disorder characteristic of victims of childhood sexual abuse is depersonalization. This disorder, which – *inter alia* – takes the form of disconnection from the body, is directly associated with eating disorders. Vine described her traumatic memories as though they had happened to someone else, as though she had been outside her body and seen everything from outside:

ANAT: Do you have a specific memory? Like, when you say that you remember your father's hand, do you have a specific memory, what he did?

VINE: It's difficult for me to answer that as . . . I remember . . . something, ok, I don't know what, like, the memory, let's say my first memory was of something, that's like, my thought was there was a babysitter, who was actually the only unfamiliar person in the neighbourhood. That I'm sitting, like, on the chest of drawers without any clothes below and like he put his hands in. The next memory, I mean, that memory is a memory, and it's like split, you could say, because . . . like, on the one hand I'm there and on the other I'm also . . . like watching it from outside . . . like seeing it . . . like watching another Vine, like . . . that I'm watching it from the side.

Poppy, who did not forget the abuse she suffered at the hands of her uncle, described her disconnection from her body during the trauma:

> It's like when I was a child and I went through what I went through, I didn't experience it at all, I watched it somewhere from above, that's it, from my perspective that's where it ended. The same thing, my body is something, it's not part of me. But, but it's something that I . . . that I don't . . . I do it consciously, I mean, I separate it from myself. When I was small, I didn't do it consciously. When it happened, I remember the situation not like someone who experienced it but like someone who saw it. It might be dissociation.

She also described the emotional and affective detachment with which she remembers the abuse: 'I don't remember the physical contact, like, physically, I don't fe . . . don't fe . . . don't have any feelings . . . don't have experiences . . . my memory is not a physical experience, really not'. Up until today, she uses the same dissociative techniques that in the past served her as a way of protecting herself during the abuse:

> But today, and it was a sort of defence, I defended myself. Today, I separate myself from my body . . . it's not part of me, it's really not part of me. My body is something, it's not part of me and so I . . . and so I try as little as possible to interact with it. That's why I don't eat.

Naomi described the dissociation she experiences between her body and senses during intercourse and its link with eating:

NAOMI: There were times when I would sleep with someone and after he left I would immediately either stuff myself with loads and loads of food or after he went I would throw up all my soul.

ANAT: What are you referring to: where you are not exactly there?

NOFAR: It's not exactly that I wasn't there, it was sex for the body, not for the soul, not for being with someone.

ANAT: Like there was a disconnection between you and your body?

NAOMI: Exactly.

Eating disorders and identity confusion

Many eating disorder sufferers describe the symptoms of dissociative identity confusion – uncertainty, perplexity, or conflict regarding one's personal identity and the question of who one really is. In this state, it is difficult to preserve a sense of inner stability, coherence, and continuity (Chefetz, 2006). Here, too, it is important to go beyond the professional definition and extend empathy towards the small child who undergoes horrendous abuse at the hands of people near and dear to her at very early stages in her life that directly affect identity-formation. Trauma of this type impairs the ability to construct a defined, unified, positive identity. On occasion, a split occurs between the 'Daddy's bad nighttime child' and the 'good daytime girl', between 'Dina the N★★★★r' and 'Maya the pure white' (Reed, 2002), between the 'Egyptian princess who likes what Daddy does' and Sue (Silverman, 1996).

Olivia spoke of the splits that exist inside her and the obsessive compulsion to do shocking things not befitting the behaviour of an outstanding student:

> But this split, like, too, in university I think that it got to the most extreme state, I was in Haifa and studying and it and . . . like, I got really good marks in the first year and everything. But on the other hand I was like travelling, flying to Eilat and the north and doing all sorts of shocking things and taking part in all sorts of . . . like . . . like, on the one hand all the time in total control and on the other . . . like, really split, really strongly. It's really strange. . .

Orna, who was abused by her father and brother, had been in therapy for many years. Her identity confusion was evident both in her detailed description of the way in which she 'disappears' and does not know who she is and her fragmentary speech and lack of words in seeking to convey the difficulty in speaking about her obesity and the link between it and the abuse: 'It's the place in which. . . . Whenever people talk to me about it I . . . I don't have anything to say . . . I . . . disappear . . . completely . . . and . . . I . . . I simply truly don't know what to say about it. Like, I'm not me. I don't know who I am'.

Eating disorders and dissociative identity disorder

This disorder, defined as a chronic and severe form of dissociation, is not easy to diagnose because the women who suffer from it frequently do everything they can to hide their various identities. It is a direct and immediate result of childhood sexual abuse, which compels the child to develop other identities in order to forget what happened during the abuse and thereby survive. According to DSM-5, it manifests itself as separate identities that take control over behaviour and thought, the sufferer experiencing amnesia regarding important autobiographical information that is generally traumatic or stressful in nature – including (some of) the identities and their activities (Chefetz, 2006).

The first time I understood the developmental dynamic of dissociative identity disorder was when I watched the documentary film *Dialogues with Madwomen* (1994) directed by Allie Light. This tells the stories of seven mentally ill women. Katy tells how she was sexually abused by her father and his friends. A member of a group of paedophiles who believed that children must be sexually educated as part of their development, her father used to bring with him friends from the group who raped Katy in the basement of the house.

> You can't go through a ritual or be raped by your father and go to fifth grade the next day and have everything be ok. When traumatic events happen over a period of time, the child . . . develops ways of not remembering, very quickly. The way I developed was by creating other personalities that remembered for whoever was going to school.

Prior to our understanding of the traumatic dynamic that forces the abused child to develop various identities in order to survive, this disorder was known as multiple personality disorder. The term dissociative identity disorder is relatively new, being coined by the APA in 1994. Today, it covers five dissociative disorders in DSM-5, it now being known that 'the so-called different personalities are fragmented components of a single personality, abnormally personified and dissociated from each other', being experienced subjectively as operating autonomously or semi-autonomously (Ross, 1994, p. i). In simpler terms, the small child confronted with unbearable circumstances defends herself by creating identities that play different roles for her, such as remembering the trauma, thereby allowing her to forget what happened and go on living 'normally'.

Of the women I interviewed, only Evelyne said she had been diagnosed as suffering from dissociative identity disorder. It was thus not surprising that she dissociatively described her (partial) awareness of her dissociative disorder:

> When I began to lose control (laughs), I mean, there was a period that really, I think something like 23, something like that. So yes, there was a therapist that, like, told me about something that happened to me. I mean, in some group I was in. And I found it very difficult to hear it from her. I mean, she didn't tell me DID, but she told me like, I mean, my behaviour and all that, and there was a period when I accepted it from every direction . . . and I don't know, somewhere it all joined together, like. And then I went back again, and read again about DID really, and I had great difficulty with it . . . that there are lots of things, I mean, that really fitted, and precisely fitted, and like it was precisely what explains, and precisely . . . then it was very difficult.

Still suffering from the same symptoms today, she makes great efforts to prevent and control her dissociations:

> I mean, I have periods when I have lots of dissociations, and very dangerous, to myself, and as a result of that. And there are periods when I – I think that mostly in between, I just try, I mean . . . if it's really more to bring the things to mind, *a priori*, so that they won't need to come out in other places, like. Like . . . so, yes, I try to use reverse logic so that in fact it won't, it won't get to this state, but they still occur sometimes nevertheless. And like, you know, the smallest trigger is enough to make me go off somewhere and . . . like from there I never really know when I'll come out of it, and how I'll get out of it, and where I'll be, and what will happen, and what's happened up 'til then. . .

Eating disorders as addiction and distraction: 'It's instead of feeling'

Many of the women I interviewed described their eating disorders as an addiction, referring to them as calming down, distracting, etc. Like drugs and alcohol, the rituals of eating disorders – self-starvation, vomiting, bingeing, counting calories, etc. – serve as a means of disconnecting (dissociating) from the horrendous things experienced.

The question of whether it is possible to define eating disorders as an addiction is a matter of discussion in the field of eating disorders (Latzer, 2002). The link between childhood sexual abuse and addiction to various substances amongst women is well documented. Studies and clinical trials evince that most women who use drugs or alcohol were abused as children, the addiction serving them as a form of self-medication to deal with the effects of the trauma (Gur, 2008). Women suffering from eating disorders also exhibit relatively high rates of addiction to substances such as drugs and alcohol in addition to their eating disorder (Gadalla & Piran, 2007) – known in professional terms as 'comorbidity'. Drug addiction is also frequently described as 'chemical dissociation' because the addictive substances enable those taking them to cut themselves off from painful memories and ameliorate the severe post-traumatic symptoms.

Liliana referred to her bulimia as an addiction to control and the feeling of relief the vomiting gave her, together with the preoccupation with the throwing up:

> There's something very addictive about this control. That you're controlling everything . . . that you're looking for relief that you don't find there . . . you're standing at the entrance to the bathroom or you're planning the walk, and you're already collecting the hair and putting the ring next to the second one, and you're saying: Only this will bring relief.

Grace, who also has a gambling addiction, defined herself as an addict, describing her addiction to her eating disorder and gambling alike as a type of extreme feeling. Her addiction to gambling and eating disorder allow her to feel something despite the intolerable numbness:

GRACE: Because I'm an addict.

ANAT: Because what? What is it called? What does addiction give you? What role does it play?

GRACE: First of all, it gives me a strong feeling . . . today, I understand that it's a sort of feeling, like any sort of feeling, of lots of things, the feelings I had when I lost weight, when I feel that the feeling, I don't feel this feeling anywhere else. I want to feel it all the time.[4]

She described how the addiction also served to help repress the 'thing' that remained unspeakable: 'Every addiction helps, like . . . it's an escape, it's an escape, it's . . . it also has, the eating disorder as well, it's also in the gambling, it's all the addiction suppresses and makes me focus on something else, not on the thing that. . .'

Shirley spoke of her desire to be ill with an eating disorder as an addiction to 'patient identity'. Her need to be addicted to an eating disorder and the identity it gave her were the consequence of not being able to conceptualize the abuse she suffered at the hands of her uncle as traumatic. During adolescence, she found the courage to tell her parents about the abuse, but they chose to dismiss her. In the absence of any definition or conceptualization of the horrendous trauma, Shirley felt that the only way she could express the awful things she had endured was to adopt the identity of a sick person:

> I think there's something terribly addictive in the desire to be ill, in the desire to be identified as someone with a disease – it's addictive in terms of identity. It's really difficult, I found it really difficult to let go of that identity. That the disease is a very, it's a very central part of my life . . . and to go on throwing up and to continue not eating, it's something that preserves this.

She explained how her identity as suffering from an eating disorder helped her detach herself from reality:

> And I think that this identity is important in several respects. In my view, it's primarily important because I wasn't capable of connecting with what there was here and my way was simply not to be here . . . There was something in it that closed us up in this world of the eating disorder. All the time you have to weigh yourself, to weigh the food, to be preoccupied with weight, to focus on the disease. Each person with her own depression.

She explicitly noted that she chose to become addicted to an eating disorder rather than drugs or alcohol because eating 'was a great cover story':

> I think, why not drugs and why not alcohol or . . . an eating disorder is something that you can tell yourself you're doing for another reason. For instance, I just can't use drugs. It gives an element of escape, being preoccupied with something, the escaping from the present. That's what food gave me, it's a wonderful cover story. I can go on with it 'forever' [English original] because you can never get too thin. It's a sort of something that strengthens you every day, that allows you to focus on it more and more. . .

In contrast to drugs or alcohol, eating disorders are a socially acceptable form of addiction, the prevalent culture of thinness sanctioning an addictive preoccupation with food and weight – whose source in fact lies in an attempt to repress unbearable feelings:

> Just one more thing comes to mind that I had periods, I told this to my psychiatrist, too, fear of feeling, or not just fear but a feeling that my body had no filter. It's like a layer of material with holes and what goes through is swallowed up, like, it's, it really burns the skin. Like, that if I would feel something it would lead me to totally break down. Like, that if I'm not capable of filtering feelings and everything's too absorbed. Then all my preoccupation with food is a way of not dealing with feeling. Culture says: Choose – it's either drugs or alcohol or an eating disorder.

She described how in therapy she began to understand how the eating disorder prevented her from feeling the pain linked to the sexual abuse:

> I focus on the food and then I don't have to feel all sorts of other things. The eating disorder distracts me from feeling the things that I find hard to feel. It's difficult to feel because they threaten me, perhaps because I don't have enough flesh to feel it.

Lion similarly referred to her eating disorder as an addictive preoccupation with 'anorexia', serving as a substitute for dealing with the sexual abuse in order to prevent herself from 'going mad':

> She focuses so much on the anorexia, which she can't . . . she can't deal with anything else. It's huge, a person can go crazy from this. There are lots, you must know, lots of victims of sexual assault who . . . who go mad from it. Who get to closed wards, it's the greatest crossing of the boundaries that there can be.

Sharon also compared her eating disorder with drug addiction, describing how even when the eating disorder was not active she still had the feeling of being a 'clean addict':

> I can't say that I don't have an eating disorder or that I never will have. Because . . . I read a book about an addict once and in the university mentoring, too, we're always encountering this world of drugs and alcohol. It's something a bit stronger in adolescence and . . . I've heard lots and lots of people that . . . quoted something very true that . . . the very fact that they say of themselves 'I'm already a clean addict, cross wood' – it's that way with an eating disorder.[5]

Olivia, who did not remember the abuse she experienced at the hands of her father, observed how her obsession with her eating disorder had a calming effect that helped distract her from the memories and the need to deal with what had happened:

> It doesn't connect with me when people say, like, she eats in order to be fat, so that she won't be feminine and so no one will come close to her. I don't think that it's that in my case. I think it's like OCD, that you, like, focus on something obsessively because it calms you, because it stops you from thinking about the things that actually happened. And this preoccupation, like, I don't know, like a mathematical puzzle that I can worry away at and, like, it doesn't make you deal with what really is.

Vine, who was struggling with late memories of abuse at the hands of her father, explained her preoccupation with her eating disorder as allowing her to think about other things and not to feel:

> Because I, in recent years, have begun to understand how it began . . . in order, like, that I think about other things and not about what's really bothering me . . . but, but what's slightly different is that my eating disorder in fact, I've always defined it as something that comes so I don't have to feel . . . But in fact it comes in place of . . . I felt too much, I mean, at the beginning I . . . I felt all the time.

She described how the eating disorder served her wish not to feel or think about unpleasant things:

> Most clearly, when you think about it you can say that the eating disorder generally comes in order not to feel, and not to think about all sorts of things. It doesn't have to be all sorts of abuse, but with me, because it's narrative research, some sort of other preoccupation, rather than thinking, rather than feeling, in place of all these things. And I remember the first session with my therapist, who asked me: Why do you have an eating disorder? And I told her: It's instead of feeling – those were my words. It's simply instead of feeling.

Notes

1 This type of account is typical of trauma victims, who can report some of the details regarding the room in which the abuse took place even while dissociating from the trauma itself.
2 The repeated sexual traumas she suffered can be understood as revictimization, typical of those who experience childhood sexual abuse.
3 Around a year later, Orr participated in a group I led with Dr. Einat Zubery for women with eating disorders who had been sexually abused in childhood. Here, she said that she clearly remembered that her father had abused her.
4 Numbing is a disorder that causes great suffering, the desire not to feel negative feelings also leading to an inability to feel positive ones. It thus frequently also includes a need to create exaggerated 'feelings' in the desperate effort to feel something.
5 Deriving from Narcotics Anonymous philosophy, the idea of a 'clean addict' relates to addiction as a chronic disease of which the sufferer has to beware all his or her life. People who wean themselves off their addiction call themselves 'clean addicts', counting the number of days they have been clean in order to remind themselves that the addiction always lies in wait.

References

American Psychiatric Association (APA) (2013). *Diagnostic and statistical manual of mental disorders* (5th ed.). Arlington, VA: American Psychiatric Publishing.

Berger, D., Ono, Y., Saito, S., Tezuka, I., Takahashi, Y., Uno, M., . . . Suemastu, H. (1995). Relationship of parental bonding to child abuse and dissociation in eating disorders in Japan. *Acta Psychiatrica Scandinavica, 91*, 278–282.

Briere, J. (1989). *Therapy for adults molested as children*. New York, NY: Springer.

Chefetz, R. A. (2006). Preface: Why should you read these articles on dissociation processes? *Psychiatric Clinics of North America, 29*, xv–xxiii.

Chu, J. A., & Dill, D. L. (1990). Dissociative symptoms in relation to childhood physical and sexual abuse. *American Journal of Psychiatry, 147*, 887–892.

Courtois, C. A. (1997). Healing the incest wound: A treatment update with attention to recovered-memory issues. *American Journal of Psychotherapy, 51*(4), 464–496.

Dalle Garve, R., Rigamonti, R., & Todisco, P. (1995). *Trauma and dissociative experiences in eating disorders*. Paper presented at the Fifth Annual Spring Conference of the International Society for the Study of Dissociation, Amsterdam.

Davies, J., & Frawley, M. (1994). *Treating the adult survivor of childhood sexual abuse: A psychoanalytic perspective*. New York, NY: Basic Books.

Demitrack, M. A., Putnam, F. W., Brewerton, T. D., Brandt, H., & Gold, P. W. (1990). Relation of clinical variables to dissociative phenomena in eating disorders. *American Journal of Psychiatry, 147*, 1184–1188.

Dialogues with Madwomen. (1994). US film directed by Allie Light. Produced and edited by Irving Saraf. Light-Saraf Films.

Fraser, S. (1987). *My father's house: A memoir of incest and of healing*. New York, NY: Harper and Row.

Gadalla, T., & Piran, N. (2007). Eating disorders and substance abuse in Canadian men and women: A national study. *Eating Disorders: The Journal of Treatment and Prevention, 15*(3), 189–203.

Gur, A. (2008). [Women addicted to drugs: Characteristics and treatment]. In H. Mell, M. Hovav, & M. Golan (Eds.), *Addiction, violence and sexual offense: Mandatory treatment* (pp. 93–117). Jerusalem: Carmel.

Herman, J. L. (1997). *Trauma and recovery*. New York, NY: Basic Books.

Herman, J. L. (2000). *Father-daughter incest*. Cambridge, MA: Harvard University Press.

Herman, J. L., & Schatzow, E. (1987). Recovery and verification of memories of childhood sexual trauma. *Psychoanalytic Psychology*, *4*, 1–14.

ISSD (International Society for the Study of Dissociation). (2013). Retrieved July 16, 2017, from www.isst-d.org/default.asp?contentID=76#diss

Kluft, R. P. (2001). The difficult-to-treat patient with dissociative disorder. In M. J. Dewan & R. W. Pies (Eds.), *The difficult-to-treat patient* (pp. 209–242). Washington, DC: American Psychiatric Press.

Latzer, Y. (2002). Eating disorders as addiction. In H. Doitch (Ed.), *Adolescents and addiction* (pp. 29–41). Jerusalem: Association for Psychosocial Rehabilitation for Adolescent and Young Adults (Hebrew).

McCallum, K. E., Lock, J., Kulla, M., Rorty, M., & Wetzel, R. D. (1992). Dissociation symptoms and disorders in patients with eating disorders. *Dissociation*, *5*, 705–708.

Putnam, F. W. (1997). *Dissociation in children and adolescents: A developmental perspective*. New York, NY: Guilford Press.

Reed, M. (2002). *Shvuya: Kroniqa shel gilui arayot miqtzo'i – Sipur autobiografi* [*Captivity: A chronicle of professional incest – An autobiographical account*]. Tel Aviv: Tammuz (Hebrew).

Root, M. P. (1991). Persistent disordered eating as a gender-specific, post-traumatic stress response to sexual assault. *Psychotherapy*, *28*, 96–102.

Rosen, E. F., & Petty, L. C. (1994). Dissociative states and disordered eating. *American Journal of Clinical Hypnosis*, *36*, 266–275.

Ross, C. A. (1994). *The Osiris complex: Case studies in multiple personality disorder*. Toronto: University of Toronto Press.

Sands, S. (1991). Bulimia, dissociation, and empathy: A self-psychological view. In C. L. Johnson (Ed.), *Psychodynamic treatment of anorexia nervosa and bulimia* (pp. 34–50) New York, NY: Guilford Press.

Schwartz, H. (2000). *Dialogues with forgotten voices: Relational perspectives on child abuse trauma and treatment of dissociative disorders*. New York, NY: Basic Books.

Sillon, B. (1992). Dissociation: A symptom of incest. *Individual Psychology*, *48*, 155–164.

Silverman, S. W. (1996). *Because I remember terror, father, I remember you*. Athens, GA: University of Georgia Press.

Spiegel, D., Loewenstein, R. J., Lewis-Fernandez, J., Sar, V., Simeon, D., Vermetten, E., Carden, E., & Dell, P. F. (2011). Dissociative disorders in DSM-5. *Depression and Anxiety*, *28*, 824–852.

Torem, M. S. (1986). Dissociative states presenting as an eating disorder. *American Journal of Clinical Hypnosis*, *29*, 137–142.

van der Hart, O., Nijenhuis, E., Steele, K., & Brown, D. (2004). Trauma-related dissociation: Conceptual clarity lost and found. *Australian and New Zealand Journal of Psychiatry*, *38*(11–12), 906–914.

Vanderlinden, J., & Vandereycken, W. (1993). Dissociative experience and trauma in eating disorders. *International Journal of Eating Disorder*, *13*, 187-194.

Vanderlinden, J., & Vandereycken, W. (1997). *Trauma, dissociation, and impulse dyscontrol in eating disorders*. Bristol, PA: Brunner/Mazel.

Vanderlinden, J., & Vandereycken, W. (1996). Is sexual abuse a risk factor for developing an eating disorder? In M. F. Schwartz & L. Cohn (Eds.), *Sexual abuse and eating disorders* (pp. 17–35). Bristol, PA: Brunner/Mazel.

Chapter 6

The betrayed/betraying body

Eating disorders as ways of coping with the feminine body, sex, and sexuality in the wake of childhood sexual abuse

> I felt as though I was imprisoned inside myself, inside my body. This body that feels like a gaol doesn't belong to me and I want to get rid of it. It's a feeling that accompanies me everywhere. I feel like a child imprisoned in a woman's body. Someone has put this body on me which so much doesn't fit me, is too big for me, and I don't feel comfortable inside it. And so I'm also afraid to eat, because I'm afraid that this body will get even bigger, when all I want is to make it smaller, as small as possible.
>
> —Natasha

> We are starving the body who failed in its mission to protect the soul, or we over-feed him, being cruel to him, or just neglect him, or find it difficult to communicate with your body, let alone love him. To control of the body had been avoided from us by hitting us and we made ourselves the importance of controlling the body in every possible way. Forcibly occupy the place of the offender and take the reins into our hands – now I am. I'm the one who hurt, I'm the one who is bruising, I'm the one who is rewarding for punishing. Me.[1]
>
> —Roni Aloni Sadovnic

Eating disorders are directly linked to the female body, in many ways constituting an assault on the body and femininity. Contemporary eating disorders are a form of protest and rebellion in which women express the distress and oppression they experience through their bodies. They thus form another link in the chain of similar phenomena – accusations of witchcraft, demon possession, and hysteria – whose true causes have been repressed and suppressed in our patriarchal society. This chapter examines the significance of the oppression and politicization of the female body in a male-dominated society, the meaning eating disorders carry in the context of the female/feminine body, and the association between childhood sexual abuse and the female/feminine body and eating disorders.

The female body in patriarchal society

> The very fact of existence in a female body, with all its experiences along the axis of female time . . . awaits its own language. As [Virginia] Woolf says in *Professions for Women*, 'telling the truth about my own experiences as a body, I do not think I solved. I doubt that any woman has solved it yet. The obstacles against her are still immensely powerful – and yet they are very difficult to define'.
>
> (Halpern, 2012)

Feminism having placed the female body on the political agenda, women have begun to understand the complex messages they convey through their bodies. Western conceptual frameworks and the language in which they are formulated revolve around the male as model and norm, the female body only finding expression through the oppressive and dominating arbitrations in patriarchal terminology (Cixous & Clément, 1986). Simone de Beauvoir (1953/2010, pp. 25, 70) asserts that men consider women's body an obstacle, a prison, burdened by everything that particularizes it. It is one of the essential elements of the situation she occupies in this world.

As a characteristic product of the male genius (à la Karen Horney), psychoanalysis has shaped the perception of the female body as lacking and castrating. Freud (1932/1991) argued that women are ashamed of their bodies because, from the oedipal stage onwards, they experience it as castrating. The shame from which women typically suffer is thus due to the 'genital wound' that leads to 'penis envy'. Psychoanalysis and culture perceive the female body as a negation of the positivist essence of the male body, thus presenting it as lacking essential qualities and non-male.

Feminist analysis has demonstrated how women are oppressed within patriarchal society in various ways, including the objectification and degradation of the body (Wolf, 1991; Bordo, 1993). Women are frequently defined as their bodies, designed to give sexual pleasure to men. In Western culture, this objectification was created and perpetuated by images in the media and the male sexual gaze (Fredrickson & Roberts, 1997). All these phenomena encourage women to objectify themselves.

Feminist writers identified the attacks women make against the female body as a cry for help in the face of oppression (Cixous & Clément, 1986), linking female 'witches' with their later incarnation – hysterics – and interpreting these phenomena as demonstrative displays in which the female body assumes the right of speech in order to express in motion and mad rhetoric the desires and distresses of women silenced by patriarchal society. They contend that the 'treatment methods' practiced both by Christianity and Freudian psychoanalysis – the representatives of hegemonic patriarchalism in their day – reflect male anxieties and fantasies about the female body.

In order to break out of this trap, they argue, the boundaries of patriarchal language must be shattered by 'female writing'. French women psychoanalytical writers such as Kristeva, Irigaray, and Clément suggest that the perception of the female body can be changed by verbalizing its sexuality, desires, pleasures, and variable states – i.e., all the experiences that in the past could only be expressed in the form of hysterical demon possession (Ashur, 2006).[2] Giving a central place to the female body and its presence within language, they posit that psychoanalytic terminology prevents women from building positive relationships between their corporal existence and subjectivity. One of Irigaray's (1985) major goals, for example, was to create words for the female body in order to allow women to forge links between their existence as inhabiting a body and their status as thinking and acting subjects (Rozmarin, 2003).

It is thus not surprising that most women in Western society suffer from body anxiety and hatred (Orbach, 2015). According to Orbach, this problem is now so widespread that it is regarded as self-evident – an affliction from which millions of women suffer in silence. Body anxiety and hatred eat away at the self-security felt by girls and women. Every day, millions of women in the West get up in the morning, look at their stomachs, and wonder whether this is going to be a good or bad day with regard to food. They stand in front of the mirror and criticize themselves, setting off to exercise in order to keep their weight down. Rather than being something they love or embrace, their body is there to be argued and quarrelled with. They have grown up in a climate in which dissatisfaction with their body and the need to change it constitute the norm.

Women feel like this about their bodies because of the exaggerated preoccupation in Western culture with the female body image. Unrealistic visual images plastered across billboards and TV and computer screens encourage 'perfect(ed)' female images that have no connection with reality. Women are described as attractive, seductive, slender, possessing no body hair – 'tantalizingly untouchable, and yet, totally desirable' (Orbach, 2015). Habitually inspecting their bodies, they feel ashamed of them and put themselves at risk of developing eating disorders. This sense of disembodiment is reinforced and perpetuated by sexual harassment, sexual abuse, and rape (Murnen & Smolak, 2009).

The betrayed/betraying body: childhood sexual exploitation, the female/feminine body, and eating disorders

Childhood sexual exploitation represents a concretization of the attitude culture takes towards women. In male society, all women are objectified, the female body being viewed as a decorative object designed to provide male pleasure. In sexual molestation, the body forms the site where the abuse is performed. A child who is sexually exploited undergoes real, cruel objectification, becoming a sexual object. Her sole existence being to serve the needs of the male perpetrator, he uses her body for his sexual gratification. This objectification of the body has severe mental and somatic repercussions, survivors finding it difficult to develop a proper body image and regarding their bodies as a source of vulnerability, filth, contamination, shame, and guilt. Experiencing their bodies as having betrayed them (Zerbe, 1995), they regard them and femininity as a source of danger.[3]

In rape, the body is invaded and exploited to such an extent that the victim feels helpless and hopeless. She thus experiences a desperate need to regain control over her own physical existence. Although in most cases, sexual abuse is painful and unpleasant, in some cases some of the acts performed are arousing and stimulating, provoking unwanted sexual reactions. These make the child feel that her body has betrayed her (Zerbe, 1995).

Childhood sexual abuse is also directly associated with physical injury to the body, distorting the normal regulation of physical states (Herman, 1997). Many victims who cannot safely regulate basic biological functions develop chronic sleeping disorders, eating disorders, digestive problems, and numerous other symptoms of physical distress (Loewenstein, 1990). Repeated self-injury and other forms of attacks against the body are also very common amongst childhood sexual abuse survivors (Herman, 1997).

Childhood sexual abuse also leads to an array of health and psychophysiological problems in adolescence and adulthood (Arnold, Rogers, & Cook, 1990). Survivors exhibit a very high rate of somaticization problems and chronic syndromes that include physical symptoms that have no medical explanation. The range of medical problems found amongst this population is very broad (Padua, 2004).

Eating disorders – which are connected with a distorted body image, attacks on the body, femininity, and the need to regain control over the body – are associated with the trauma of the sexual abuse perpetrated on the body. They serve as a way of punishing the body by starving it, stuffing it, or torturing it by vomiting and purging. They function as a way of annihilating the feminine body, through the extremes of severe thinness or obesity that eradicate all signs of femininity – such as roundness, the menstrual cycle, and breasts. Hereby, they symbolize control over the body: 'I'm the only one who decides what goes in and out of this body'.

The link between the female/feminine body and eating disorders also runs through dissociative disorders (see Chapter 5). One of the common coping strategies rape victims adopt is depersonalization – disconnecting from the body. This strategy frequently turns into a full-blown disorder that is also tied to eating disorders, the abuse of the body, its starving, stuffing, and purging being perpetrated on a body from which the girl/woman is disconnected.

If the abuse continues on into adolescence, when girls begin to develop the first signs of female sexuality they frequently start fearing that they will become pregnant. In such cases, self-starvation, which delays the beginning of menstruation, forms a survival mechanism.

Childhood sexual abuse leads to feelings of shame and guilt in relation to the body that are also documented in studies and clinical models. These feelings cause a sense of revulsion and abhorrence towards the body that in many instances prompts the development of eating disorders (Kearney-Cooke & Striegel-Moore, 1994; Tripp & Petrie, 2001).

If we take into consideration the difficulties all women face in male, patriarchal society in feeling comfortable in their bodies and add sexual abuse to the mix, which leads to a particular sensitivity and vulnerability with regard to the body that has been abused, we can understand the epidemic of eating disorders as a contemporary feminine disease. Eating disorders form a way of punishing, hurting, cleansing, and purging the body, thereby giving expression to the horrendous nature of the abuse. Eating disorders exist at the junction between the attitude male culture holds towards the feminine body and childhood sexual abuse, which is a concretization of the objectification and misuse of the body. They thus function as an act of protest against the body's objectification and exploitation.

The body as a source of vulnerability, shame, guilt, and revulsion: 'Not dealing with the body is the eating disorder'

The women I interviewed described how they hate their bodies, their disconnection from them, and the desire to hurt and punish them. Poppy accused her body and beauty of overshadowing all the other aspects of her, causing her to hate it and deny it as a sort of defence and punishing it through her eating disorder:

> It really overshadows all the rest, and so lots of time I deliberately say: 'Ok, this is the body, I hate it, but it's not me'. I treat it as . . . as something that's not mine. It's a sort of, again, it's to punish the body. Because I really suffer when I throw up, really suffer when I don't eat a lot, enough, I really suffer, I punish it.

She described the disgust, hate, and alienation she developed towards her body because it had become an instrument in the hands of others:

> As far as I'm concerned, my connection is that from the day it happened, that what happened to me happened, my body became an instrument, and . . . I've used it that way, too. From the moment they taught me that my body is simply a pawn in some game, and . . . somehow a situation was created that everyone around me wanted first of all my body and only afterwards, perhaps, other things, even not all of them. I'm speaking of my best friend, including the teacher, including the family. I mean, it touched everything . . . everything. It's, I mean . . . from an emotional point of view, I knew, I understood, that my body is . . . is no more than an instrument, and that's how I started hating it. Disgust, hate. The disgust and hate towards my body and that it had become an instrument, that's the link. It's

> not 'Ok, he touched me, I'm going to throw up', it's not, it wasn't that, it was . . . it's something else. I mean, from where I am, hate, disgust for . . . for the body developed over the course of years, for what it represents for me.

Her ambivalent attitude towards her body – on the one hand blaming its external appearance for the abuse and on the other wanting to look good – caused her great confusion and difficulty:

> As far as I'm concerned, this body was an instrument, and probably if they chose it then there was a reason, and probably it was because of the way it looked, so that's the reason for the punishment. But that goes against, that contradicts, sorry, the fact that I *do* want to look good. I mean, there are lots and lots and lots of contradictions here. Everything that's happened to me in life is accompanied by lots of contradictions; I don't know how to explain it. I don't know why on the one hand I want to punish this body and hate it and on the other I want it to look good. I don't know, but I want it to look good, and as far as I'm concerned, it never does. So perhaps that's also a form of unconscious punishment.

She felt her body to be disconnected from her relationship with her partner:

> However awful it sounds, but the simplest things, like . . . my partner, I've lived with him for over three years and he still hasn't seen me, my body, I mean. I really, really, my body is something that's not connected to my relationship, as it were. Intellectually and emotionally and . . . I'm here, but physically I'm totally not here.

Olivia described how she uses her body as something that can help her find someone to protect her, together with her embarrassment and revulsion towards it:

> I think but that . . . like, like, on the one hand there's this matter of using my body and it's, and that way to find someone to protect me and all that. But at the same time, sure, like in high school and the army and that . . . I was totally disgusted by my body. Like, I felt really unattractive, I didn't feel I was sexy, I didn't . . . and I felt, like, I was really, really confused there.

She developed a special sensitivity to her body, accompanied by the sense that something was wrong with it so that it had to be hurt:

> And in the army, I began dancing. And . . . then for the first time I started connecting with my body. Today, let's say, I'm really, I feel my body, I really, like . . . I don't know how to explain it. I feel according to, where, can I say a bit tense or cramped or . . . the joints, what's released and what isn't, I can

> tell you. Like, I . . . I, like, am very connected to that. Today I'm also much more, like . . . I'm trying to learn how to take care of myself much more. I'm, let's say, trying, like, I perhaps hurt my face, but I'm trying to learn how to take care of it. You know, it's, like, to give back in some form, like, a bit of love. So today it's much, much better. I also, but . . . but I think that I have a long way to go in this respect because the basic feeling is still, like . . . it's something – something's wrong. Something . . . I don't know.

Evelyne made great efforts to not feel her body and to hide inside her clothes:

> I can, let's say, say something that's really new to me. Last Sunday, I got dressed. Walla, put on my trainers in this house and try the hardest not to feel my body, try the hardest to ignore it, and I tried, I have this thing, like, I often go against what I feel and against what I want to do. On the basis of the thought that I'm simply wrong (laughs). So, so really, instead of coming and . . . continuing to get dressed like that, like to hide.

Arabella described in great pain how she could not become a mother because her body did not heal:

> It's very, very, very painful for me, that in essence I didn't choose not to be a mother. My body still . . . my body and I weren't healthy or whole enough, or hale – from the word 'heal' – in order to choose, to say: 'I'm not going to bring a child into the world'.

The difficulty and pain of growing older crept up on her before she had had a chance to enjoy her body:

> And this feeling that . . . the stopping of menstruation, and all the changes in the body, that it was painful and bothered me ceaselessly. There's not a minute when I don't look at my skin and see how it's changing. And this feeling that . . . There was never a time in my life when I felt that my body was nice, good, happy, and wanted. . . (cries). I, there's never been a time when I had . . . there was never a time in my life when I felt good in my body. And this feeling, of so many years of feeling that it's disgusting, rotten, dirty, and to go from that into old age, to get older, it's awful (cries). I simply try, as much as I can, not to think about it, because it's sad. And . . . rather than thinking about it, it . . . I can be really depressed by it.

Ruth, who obviously neglected her body, told me how as an adolescent she had started ignoring it because she experienced herself as fat and ugly:

> I've never been happy with my body, never. Even today I can't look at myself in the mirror. Even today . . . because of this at home I never had any

> mirrors until recently. It's only recently that I've been able to get a mirror to see more or less what I look like before I go out. I simply never related to my body, simply.

Karen, who was sexually abused by her brother, described the disgust she feels towards her body when she showers: 'The truth is that I'm really disgusted by this body. Primarily when I'm in the shower. I . . . I forget myself in the bath. That's the way it's always been. I also always cry in the bath. I don't . . . I'm always disgusted'. She found it difficult to explain what she meant by 'I forget myself in the bath'. It is possible that she experienced dissociative episodes due to the difficulty of coming into direct contact with her body as she washed.

Yvonne related to the self-disgust that overwhelms her when she looks in the mirror because she is so thin and her poor body image:

> I looked at myself in the mirror a while ago and I was so disgusted by how I look so disgusting, like, thin, that I said that it's . . . I didn't understand, I, like, look and say: 'Now you know, you have this moment that you understand that you simply look disgusting, that's it, nothing nice can . . . nobody can see what you see now as beautiful'.

Thyme understood her eating disorder as being related to an inability to deal with her body after the sexual abuse, speaking of her disgust, guilt, and desire to hide her body. Here, the disconnection from the body and herself also took the form of referring to herself in the masculine:

> When someone hurts you in your body, afterwards you can't deal with your body. Not dealing with the body is the eating disorder. Like . . . it's not . . . I'm not just talking about looking in the mirror and feeling disgusted, and looking at yourself and feeling disgusted, and blaming yourself, and wearing large clothes because you're ashamed of yourself and . . . hiding from all the world and his wife.

Debby spoke of the disgust she felt towards herself and her body:

> I can't stand my body. I've got to the . . . there were days when . . . I had . . . I had a period when I got to 54 kilos. That I was . . . like sick and . . . I still didn't see myself that I wasn't . . . I was still disgusted by myself. It wasn't enough. To tell you that today I've had to work really hard to get to this day, and I'm still saying that I'm in a better situation now than before. Ichs. Ichs. Ichs . . . so I said it's clear . . . clear that no one can look at me. Like, I'm fat and I'm disgusting and ugly and I have . . . acne scars all over my face. Who's going to look at me, like?

Meggie reported that she was completely disconnected from her body: 'I and my body don't have a good connection . . . we're . . . it's two things . . . two different parts . . . that go together everywhere'.

Lily associated her feeling of disgust with the question of why her abuser chose her specifically, feeling that by being thin she would become less disgusting and thereby attract less abuse:

> Because there I felt it really strongly. Both the disgustingness and the wrongness and the fact that . . . what I said before, that he's coming for me and, like, he's like a mirror image, and he's, like, so ugly . . . I don't know if he's really ugly, but he's a monster as far as I'm concerned, so a monster is attracted to a monster . . . she's not . . . like, that was how it seemed to me. Like, and I looked, let's assume, around and said: 'Why isn't he going to her? For sure she's better than me, stronger than me . . . like I'm screwed up'. It was clear to me that I'm screwed up and because of that he's goes for me. And then if I'm thin . . . it's not connected, it wasn't connected to reality, but then I . . . if I'm thin . . . I'll be less disgusting, for sure, like.

Orna, a binge eater, described the feeling of disgust and smelling bad she felt as a child after being abused by her brother, still not feeling good about her body:

> As a child, I remember that I felt really, really neglected. Stinky. All the time I felt that I smelled really, really bad. He would always laugh at me, that I had a cold, I was disgusting, that I was smelly. And it was really . . . it really added to my self-image. I felt really, really bad about my body. And I felt all the time it was dirty and smelly, all the time. Really, the kids at school laughed at me so much. I was very . . . because I was fat. But I thought they were laughing at me not only because I was fat but because . . . but also because I was smelly. I felt smelly most of all.
>
> ANAT: How do you feel today about your body?
> ORNA: Today, I . . . don't know . . . what to say. It's too fat. Primarily that I'm too fat . . . I don't . . . I don't think I smell or something. But . . . I don't feel very attractive. I think.

Punishing the body: eating disorders as hurting the body on which the abuse was perpetrated

As the site of the sexual abuse, the body frequently becomes the object of hatred and punishment. As the interviews I conducted with the women in my study evinced, these attacks take diverse and varied forms, including self-starving, vomiting, neglecting one's appearance, self-harm, etc. The feeling that the body is to blame for what happened and must therefore be punished or made to disappear is shared by many women. Poppy, for example, told me:

> Lots of times I felt that my body was to blame for everything that happened to me . . . but for years I said: 'I'm to blame, this is my body, this is my chest', and like . . . yes, but it's a form of punishment. Again, I beat myself, I punish myself, punish this body.

Shirley wanted to make her body disappear, holding it to blame for the abuse she suffered at the hands of her uncle: 'I used to imagine that I had no body at all'.

Olivia spoke of being indifferent towards her body and the damage being inflicted at the same time as wanting to protect her brain from being injured as a result of her bulimia: 'I also have this thing that I'm really, really afraid of hurting my brain, because, like, my body as far as I'm concerned, you can do what you like with it, but don't touch my brain (laughs.)' Her body served her as an instrument with which to hurt herself, via the eating disorder and the wounding of her body and face that continues until today:

> Up until the army, and in university, it always served as an instrument, like, something . . . or as a way of hurting myself, also, I also . . . I was, once I cut myself, and then it made scars and then mess ups, it wasn't nice and then . . . and then at a certain point I got the idea that if I could perhaps beat myself, and it was blue, then no one would pay attention because you know, in the end it healed.

Evelyne sought to hurt her body to the point of death because everyone wanted it:

> Every time when the body was the top priority, I mean, also on the level of taking care of me like, it just did the opposite, it just made me to want to hurt it more. Like, because if it's just what's important to you [pl.], if it's what you [pl.] want, then I'll die.

Shirley felt that her body and its welfare were complete irrelevances:

> Something about the invasion of the body and its being hurt, like what people say about cigarettes, that they're bad for your health, but it doesn't make any difference to me. The body for me, or its welfare, it's something that's completely irrelevant to me.

Natasha described her battle with her body: 'I asked the amulet [part of one of her artworks] to help me connect to my body and find answers through it. As of today, I feel that it's light years away from me. In the meantime, I go on fighting my body'.

Thyme portrayed her vomiting as a way of punishing her body:

> It stems from two things. Both the thing of getting rid of it and the thing of . . . really self-guilt, and self-punishment, and self-destruction, and I'm to blame for this, and I'm disgusting, and all the . . . More links if I think about the fact that it's so awful, dealing with the body. Once again, it's the self-guilt, but it's terrible dealing with the body.

Shirley described vomiting as a way of feeling her body and hurting it:

> I think in the eating disorders themselves I really feel my body. I remember that when I threw up, the wound of the fingers, the thrusting of the fingers down the throat, to feel the throat afterwards, seared. Lots of time I could feel that when people get annoyed with me, let's say, to say, 'Look, see what you've made me do', like, to hurt myself. Like, to feel the skin. I remember I had a thing when I would do like this, I would punch myself here or there, like, in order to feel my body and hurt it.

Naomi observed how she was a thin, cute child until she began to put on weight after being raped, blaming her body for what happened to her and asserting that it was the 'mark of Cain' on her forehead that led her to hurt herself:

> For a long time I felt that my body was to blame for everything that happened to me. A really long time. And . . . there was also a period when I hurt myself, apart from the eating thing. This is a bit harder for me to talk about, but yes, I had a short period like that of . . . of 'I'm to blame' and everything, because of that. Like, I also didn't, we didn't talk about it at all, at home, like, it was really taboo, like, I walked on eggs. I felt guilty, I felt I had a mark of Cain on my forehead, and how could I beat my body? It's like being remorseful for a sin I didn't commit. . .

Eating disorders as purging the body and soul: 'To clean your insides out'

Many of the women reported feelings of dirtiness and contamination in the wake of the abuse, describing obsessive washing rituals to cleanse their bodies, souls, and surroundings. These reflect a desperate need to be purged and purified of the feelings of dirtiness and disgustingness the abuse has induced in them. The eating disorders serve as a way of scouring both the body and the soul.

Grace described the feeling of dirtiness with which she struggles, *inter alia* by means of her eating disorder. She began to understand the meaning of her brother's abuse of her at age 15, immediately after it stopped. She then developed severe feelings of dirtiness and the need to be cleansed: 'I think I began to understand that he'd done something wrong, that my body wasn't feeling right to me. It was with this, and it was other symptoms, what I told you, showers, all sorts of things. I felt dirty'.

Liora began to feel dirty after being abused as a child, trying to make her soiled body disappear by overeating and becoming obese:

> And, let's say, it was a thing also of eating, it was a thing of I would go to throw it in the bin, go home and have a shower because, because I'm dirty, because I touched the bin. And every little thing, I felt dirty. And . . . and I think that this link precisely with the body, my body feels dirty and I have to, I have to make it disappear, I have to cleanse it as much as possible.

Shirley related to her vomiting as a way of throwing up the 'disgustingness that's stuck to you': 'There's something here, you feel that something disgusting has stuck to you, really, you, like, feel the fat in your hands and the impulse to throw it up, simply in order to throw up the amounts of disgusting food'.

Grace described her eating disorders – anorexia and bulimia – as a way of cleansing herself:

> I see this as . . . as something I really hate my body, and I see, also from the need to cleanse it, to purify it, because I felt really, really clean when I didn't eat. And I think that it's also the bulimia, from one side this need to pull things in, and on the other, like, cleansing, simply to throw it all up.

Karen felt her vomiting helped her feel clean, although she had great difficulty in putting into words the thing that must be 'got out':

ANAT: What exactly does the vomiting do for you?

KAREN: To get it out. To get everything out that . . . all you can, all that you fee . . . it's a relief. To clean your insides out. I remember that I would throw up and then I would feel good about myself. Like, now I'm clean inside and everything.

Shirley felt that her anorexia helped her feel pure: 'Because anorexia is more something, more something that reflects something, a type of success, safety, pureness. Something that's pure'. Thyme tried to feel clean by taking showers and scrubbing, her inability to speak or write about the sexual trauma leading her to begin vomiting in order to cleanse her insides and get 'it' out:

> I was awfully depressed. I was showering more than ten times a day. I really scrubbed my body hard. Like, I was crazy to get it out somehow. Speaking didn't get it out. I would write lots. But there too . . . I couldn't recall the . . . this person, or what had happened. From there, I began in fact the . . . my

> eating disorder. The . . . the bulimia . . . I was showering lots in order to wash away the pain and it wasn't helping. It's also, like, in another way, a thing of disgustingness. Self-disgust. This thing of the showering and the thing of the . . . it's also something you find a lot in girls with eating disorders. The obsession with pureness. Like, to purge the . . . the . . . your insides. To get it all out by whatever means. It stems from two things. Both the thing of the getting it out and the thing of . . . really the . . . the . . . the self-guilt and self-punishment and self-destruction, and I'm to blame for it, and I'm disgusting.

Still speaking in the masculine, she also spoke of her need to get rid of the sexual abuse by vomiting, in the hope of washing away the pain:

> When you undergo something sexual, you really want to get it out and you don't know how. And the very fact that you, like, vomit every day . . . all this dealing with the . . . to get it out . . . I remember, in my first weeks, I was just really, drinking lots of water all the time, so as to vomit. Like to throw up the pain in . . . in a deeper way . . . but that didn't really help. I would shower lots of times to wash away this pain, but that didn't help.

Debby spoke of vomiting as a way of emptying out the body: 'The thing of emptying out drove me crazy. I really love the thing of emptying out'. Despite the throwing up, however, she was unable to empty out mentally in the same way as she could get rid of food she had ingested. She thus remained with the 'mental lousiness':

> Like, I wish I could empty out mentally, like I know how to do with food. I eat, eat, go and vomit like I've not eaten anything. My stomach goes in nicely. That's really good. It's finished. And so on. But at least you know how to . . . to (silence) . . . the . . . the lousy mind it doesn't work . . . no. I can't vomit. But it's clear that it comes from a bad place. I mean, it comes from the horribleness of self.

She described purifying her body of food by vomiting, this giving her a sense of repairing the damage done to it. Like the sexual abuse, food symbolizes a foreign body that penetrates the corpus. Throwing up thus helps create a feeling that the body has not been hurt:

> But because my father touched me . . . and because I was a fat child food compensated her, and I couldn't cope with my body's appearance, she . . . it's clear that . . . that . . . one thing leads to another. It comes from a place of . . . a place of disgust. It doesn't come from a good place. It's from a place of food and eating, and eating, and eating, and eating, and eating and then throwing everything up. Like . . . the . . . the . . . this purifying.

> It's something that does good. Like, now I'm pure. My body wasn't hurt. The food won't hurt it.

Debby related to vomiting as a way of expressing her anger at herself, explaining the ritual of eating and throwing up as a means of coping with her anger at others and herself – a ritual that helps her feel pure and new: 'It's to vomit on yourself, in effect, like . . . when I'm really angry or when I can't stand myself. The first thing I do is to eat and vomit. Then I'm new. Pure'.

The issue of disgustingness and the way in which eating and vomiting help her cope with it were prominent in Olivia's interview:

> Something in me from childhood, like, I've always been preoccupied with disgustingness. I'm very engrossed in that. There are things that today I associate with my father. Like lots . . . I always had a feeling that, like . . . I'm the most disgusting thing in the world and it's, like, it's . . . my destiny is to be a prostitute. Like, that's the experience. And I also think that there's something very closely linked to eating. The fact that I'm disgusting is something, like, that I don't know, like, I'm worthless, it's something that's always been there. I think that vomiting is closely related to that. That vomiting is . . . is really . . . I don't know, like what I throw up is me. It's just an expression of . . . Like, all this disgusting stuff, it's simply what I am.

Although she does not remember it explicitly, Olivia thinks that her father told her things that led her to feel that she is disgusting, encouraging her to behave in a sexual way inappropriate for her age and making her feel that she deserved to be humiliated and abused. For her, the vomit symbolized the trauma and the vomiting the possibility of getting rid of it:

> And what I am it's because . . . because of my father. Like, because, because . . . I don't know what he said to me to make me understand that I deserved it, but . . . like and already . . . when I was little, I was in Grade 1 or 2, something like that, I began to masturbate and . . . I remember my fantasies. And my fantasies were simply shocking. Like . . . always, I don't know. Like, some adult humiliating me and abusing me and explaining to me that that's what I deserved and things like that. And the . . . the . . . I don't know. Like, the vomit is what I am – I don't know how to explain it. It's like, it's the trauma. And . . . and because of this I think it really helped me that I could throw up. Because I could express it in some way.

Liliana referred to the feelings of disgust and the need to vomit she experienced after the abuse she suffered at the hands of her brother:

> I feel like throwing up, because I remember once I told him that it really wasn't right what he was doing. And he said to me: 'What nonsense you're

talking. I'll protect you'. And I felt the greatest disgust you can imagine. I mean, this feeling, this feeling, this disgust, no one can argue with it.

She described the feeling of the 's★★★ inside', the disgustingness, and the smells:

> It's precisely in the low place. From the low place, the most disgusting place, the place of smells, the place of the . . . yes, of this s★★★ inside. Yes, somehow . . . that it's strange that I say the s★★★ inside because the s★★★ with me can be seen, yes, really.

She felt relief after the vomiting, having succeeded in throwing up all the disgustingness and s★★★:

> It's . . . I don't have words for it, Anat. I'm not sure, I'm telling you, it's like s★★★ that has to come. Like, like something disgusting that has to come out. And this disgustingness comes out and you see it come out, and you know what, you also look at your vomit. I don't know if to check, if you check what comes out.

Lily used her thinness and vomiting as a way of getting rid of the self-disgust:

> It's not the fat . . . I looked fat to myself. But what I most had in my head was that I was disgusting to other people, and myself . . . and then if I'm thin . . . it's not connected, it wasn't connected to reality, but then . . . if I'm thin I'll be less disgusting. Yes. For sure. Like, it's . . . the disgustingness wasn't in my appearance now but it was . . . like, sorry for the expression, but it was through the food. I mean, through the vomiting. It was really disgusting. The disgustingness just began to come out. Like, instead of being between me and myself, it came out in the open. What was better than what, I don't know. It was . . . like, as far as I'm concerned, like, in terms of the experience, if to see myself as disgusting or to get it out. But . . . both are really disgusting experiences. And it's something that I wanted, I mean, that I remember myself, as something that I don't like, don't want, want to get out and can't.

Dawn described her throwing up as a way of dealing with the difficulty of containing awful feelings:

> And also the feeling of afterwards, it's just not to feel anything. It's to throw up everything that happens at that moment and not let anything stay inside. No feeling, nothing. Even today I only do it for that reason. I mean, I go home and it's too hard and I already can't contain anything. It's my way of coping.

Eating disorders as an expression of defending and protecting the body and soul after being abused

Childhood sexual abuse represents a radical breach of the boundaries of the victim's body and self. Sexuality becomes a 'weapon' the perpetrator uses to perform a violent act. It thus is not surprising that survivors expend great mental energy in trying to defend and protect the boundaries of the body and self against further penetration by avoiding anything to do with femininity and sexuality and any hints of sexual attractiveness.

The personality organizes itself to ward off anything regarded as invasive and penetrating in multiple ways. Eating disorders in their various forms are amongst the most central methods victims adopt to create the illusion of protecting/defending the body and soul against repeated abuse.[4] Frequently, survivors overeat as a way of eradicating their femininity and sexual attractiveness. In a society in which the latter is associated with slimness, obesity creates a kind of 'wall' that provides a sense of security. Many also go to the opposite extreme and become extremely thin and underweight. This, too, is a way of eradicating signs of femininity – roundness and menstruating (representing the transition from childhood to womanhood in puberty).

Obesity and fat as a defence against men and sexuality

Naomi, who was raped by a neighbour at the age of 10, avoids men and sexual relations at all costs, using her obesity as a defence:

> From the perspective of – of a man who looks at you because he's interested in you or just looks at you. And always, like, I don't know, let's say that as far as I'm concerned, it's a defence, like, the fat and . . . putting on weight, and food.

When she realized that some men are attracted to plump women, she understood that she would have to put on even more weight:

NAOMI: But bottom line, it's not . . . it doesn't do what it's supposed to, so for that reason it went up and up.

ANAT: What does that mean, it doesn't do what it's supposed to?

NAOMI: It doesn't do it because some men like plump women, and I've encountered more than one or two of those.

ANAT: Did it not keep men away from you altogether?

NAOMI: No, it didn't, like . . . so that's it, so all the things I tried, like . . . I tried to put on more, and I succeeded.

Meggie described her obesity as a way of hiding her sexuality:

> If you give me a choice between being fat and unsexual, which isn't legitimate because I'm fat, or . . . or thin and then people would relate to me as a

> sexual person, I would choose to be not legitimate, fat, over . . . I don't want my sexuality to be prominent, and if fatness allows . . . although I don't eat in order to get fat.

In periods of distress, Orna still puts on weight, her obesity and full stomach putting a barrier between her and her sexuality – and between her and her partner when they have sex:

> I don't quite understand why I have to preserve the . . . the fatness so much. Or why I don't lose weight. Because it's clear that being fat is a hindrance . . . perhaps . . . perhaps also the . . . really the need sometimes . . . when you eat a lot, then afterwards you can't have sex. Then . . . then or . . . it's possible, but you feel different, then it's also the . . . like to push him. Not in . . . in terms of weight or big body size, that . . . it's . . . I don't see the differences from today to tomorrow or next week. I mean, I . . . I, I, I'm here, but with my stomach, with a fully belly, then I feel that I'm . . . he's further away from me.

Liora described her obesity as a way of covering up and repressing her sexuality:

> Let's start with the fact that I think that girls who are fat, people who are fat, they're trying to cover something. And this trying to cover something, this to cover repressed feelings, this to cover . . . unconsummated love, it's a suppression of sexuality. I see this fatness as a repression.

The fatness around her thighs was meant to hide her genital region:

> Rather than repressing here as well, you put it on here (pointing to her thighs). I absolutely see a connection. I mean, from my perspective it's self-evident. I really . . . it's, you know . . . even though you see yourself like that, people see that here you're large, and here you're small. Then, like, I see the link here too, why here I want to cover up. It's the . . . it's my method. To cover up my thighs, the whole thing of the genitalia. I completely understand that. So as far as I'm concerned, there's absolutely a connection. Everything to do with fatness is linked to a lack of love.

She also referred to her fear of men, which began at a young age, and her need to defend her genital regions via her obesity:

> I was afraid of men from a very young age, which isn't supposed to be. At 6, 7, 8. You couldn't touch me. Just . . . you couldn't touch me. I was very closed off, without any contact at all with boys . . . there's nothing to talk about. Not a good experience. Not with my grandfather and not with my father. But . . . it's completely clear that there's a connection, without a doubt. I defend, defence, defence. All the time I'm defending this area.

> Now I'm sure that not everyone who's sexually abused has this thing with this region. But, like, my feeling, that generally women who are fatter here, it's a sexual and emotional matter, something that's linked to here. And whoever wants more to . . . to hide emotions, it's the stomach. That's my feeling, but . . . I don't know. And . . . it's not a theory, it's not something I've read.

Ruth described her unattractive appearance after having put on weight as a way of countering male interest centred upon her outward appearance:

> I'm so fat and ugly and who would want me at all. And my grandmother always, she always told me, you're fat and ugly and who'll want you, who'll want you? No one will take you, no one. That's why I don't make myself look nice, because I don't have energy for all these perverts. Maybe it gives something that whoever could really love me would love me for who I am, not because of my body. Because of what I have in my head, what I have in my soul. I don't know, it's a world of fat-hatters . . . probably there's a connection, probably that I eat a lot and try not to make myself look nice, the sentence: 'the person who'll love me will love me as I am'.

Naomi, who observed that she had been a beautiful child, felt the need to eradicate all signs of beauty, holding them responsible for the abuse she suffered:

> Like . . . because it's my defence. Like, everything I thought, it's ok, then I was thin as a child and everyone says that when I was a child I had the face of an angel and everything, I was also a bit developed, I had a chest and everything, I said: 'Ok, that's what must have got me there'. And I didn't want ever again to be in that, in that place, in that situation. And the only way to escape it was not to look the same . . . so they wouldn't say 'What a cute girl you are' and things like that. Because yes, you can say 'What a cute girl you are,' but you know, but then to whisper behind your back, 'But fat, too', like. . .

Thinness as a defence against men and sexuality

Many women directly link the sexual abuse they have suffered with their femininity. In not eating and becoming thin, they get rid of their female aspects, sexuality, and features – breasts, curves, menstruation – in order to protect themselves from a femininity they fear will invite more abuse. The struggle against femininity occurs during adolescence, as girls turn from children into women. In the wake of abuse, they are afraid of making this transition because they associate femininity with vulnerability. They thus seek to remove all signs of female development.

Shirley, who was anorexic, told me, for example: 'There's something in anorexia of being asexual'. Arabella linked her difficulty with any sign of fat on her body with her father's abuse, which began when she was very young. She regarded any sign of fat as dangerous because 'what is thick' is soft, weak, and vulnerable and 'can be entered':

> Let's say, to be fat or to be fat in certain places, that something that for me, I touch only those places in which I'm perhaps a little fuller, and it's not so much the form, like how I feel the form in my throat and inside my body. That which is thick is something that's soft, and then . . . what's soft is something that's weak and vulnerable, and can be entered. What's soft is something that isn't attached tightly enough . . . so also the matter of, of the thickness of the body, is closely connected to the fact that only . . . only the thin and skinny places, I feel that they're closed, that they're hard, and that they're strong, and that they're not . . . that they're attached to me.

She sought to remove all signs of femininity in her body because her father had exploited them, having an unconscious fear of everything 'feminine':

> So there's this . . . that it . . . and there's the . . . the things that are linked to all the feminine parts. Of . . . when I put on a bit of weight then my breasts get bigger. And the nightmares I have from this, that if my breasts are big and prominent then . . . then someone can get involved with them and . . . do things to my nipples. The . . . my father still. . . . He took me, did things, touched me, right at the beginning of my sexual development, and I really . . . I have a fee . . . memory, a very clear feeling and knowledge that I felt that my breasts were growing for him. Because he was there all the time with his mouth and with . . . with . . . fee . . . with his desires and lusts. Really, when my nipples began to hurt. So – so that's my difficulty with food. I can't stand it. But what I'm trying to explain, and I really want you to understand, is that . . . it's first and foremost this fear, it's not on a conscious level, that it's feminine, it's on the most existential level for me.

She was afraid of her 'soft' body because she experienced it as a source of danger: 'My difficulty with food is completely associated with the thickness of my body. The fact that . . . my body will be soft, and that's dangerous (cries)'. She described her need to tighten and close her body up as a defence and survival mechanism she still employs today:

> When my father used to do things to me, then all my body tightened up and shrank into itself, and only that way did I have a feeling that . . . I had a feeling that . . . and I, it's something that still happens to me. When I'm sitting on the bus and people touch me, my body knows to contract

> in millimetres. So that my skin tightens and closes up and then I won't feel that they're touching me. It's closely related to this tightening up that I need, that . . . my body feels that it has to tighten up all the time to save itself.

She has particular difficulty with the region around her waist and downwards, which she has sought to deal with with the help of a therapist who works with the body: 'I felt I was ready to do some work with . . . with what happens with my waist downwards, with . . . my pelvis and genitalia. The place most . . . one of the most wounded places with me'.

Lily, who was abused as a child by her uncle and became anorexic in her adolescence, described how being thin served her as a way of repressing the abuse:

> There's something in my adolescence that . . . with all the eating disorders, with the anorexia, I didn't have any periods, I looked like I don't know what. And I felt that, like, this way I'm more able to drive off the abuser, like, that he would no longer want me, in the sense that I'm now not really . . . look like. . .

Natasha, who suffers from anorexia, was abused by her father. She spoke of living in the perpetual shadow of the threat of abuse by men and the need to rid herself of her female body in order to protect herself against the expected abuse:

> Among other things, femininity and the feminine aspects of my body threaten me, because to be feminine means to be wanted by men, and for me that means they'll hurt me again. Sexual attraction equals abuse. For men, this feminine body I've been put in is like a red rag to a bull. It invites assault and abuse. For this reason, I want to get rid of it so that I can protect myself against men and against the abuse that awaits me around the corner.

Natasha hated her mother's body, a fact she attributed to her 'fear of femininity':

NATASHA: I hated her body. I remember that . . . it's still difficult for me today . . . I find it hard to look at her . . . if, let's say, she changes her clothes and I'm with her in the same room, I find it difficult to look at the female body. And I remember that she was once naked in a room when I was young and I remember how I looked at her and was just revolted.

ANAT: Why?

NATASHA: I don't know. Perhaps . . . perhaps it's . . . perhaps by . . . what . . . this fear of femininity. Like I look at my body and I'm revolted by it.

Evelyne, who was severely abused by her uncle and then others, including a teacher at school and her army commander, suffered from anorexia and vomiting. Her eating disorders perpetuate her difficulty in maturing, which stems from her problems with dealing with femininity:

> From wearing trainers at home, which is an attempt to do the most, the most not to feel my body, and the most, the most to ignore it. Like, it's a form of . . . I don't know, a girl, retarded, let's say, that somewhere her vision and thought is that of a child, and the body can be really developed and, like, I don't see myself as my chronological age, and don't accept it. And . . . on the contrary, if there's any way, I think, that I can deny it . . . And yes, lots of time I had a lot of 'impact' [English original] that really . . . and . . . I don't know, it's, like, to perpetuate the fact that I'm a long way off from being an adult, a long way off from being big, and like, somewhere the . . . yes, it's a bit like that, it serves a purpose, that's all, no doubt.

Grace described the 'absurdity' of wishing to avoid being feminine and her wish to feel like a child because her abuser had hurt her even though she was a child:

> It's a matter of, like, to feel that no one will be attracted to me, to feel like a child. Which is absurd, no? Because they were attracted to me when I was a child, in quotation marks. And it was always my thing . . . as long as I could hold something in my flesh, as long as I had flesh on my body, so yes I'm fat, I can still take some weight off.

Yvonne had a breast reduction in an attempt to remove all signs of femininity because she was ashamed of her body. She described her discomfort and wish to disappear, finding it difficult to give words to these feminine aspects:

> It didn't develop normally with me, adolescence, body-image, all my peers like that, I'm like this . . . I never had a problem with the . . . I don't know, I never attached much importance to it, I was busy with other things, apart from the fact that I had a really large bust, and I had a breast-reduction operation. And also . . . I always tried to get rid of everything that . . . you know, every development, all these things, I was always ashamed of them, so perhaps with me it was an experience that everything you see, and you start being different from others, then I was really ashamed of it. It really seemed to me that it . . . like saying to someone to take off their clothes, with me it's like something you see and I don't want anyone to see it, especially when you've got a large bust, developed . . . I remember it was very difficult for me during this time. And when I got my period and all that, it was . . . I didn't know where to put myself. But the . . . how I experienced myself that . . . that I don't want there to be any signs like that . . . that I'll be different, that I'll . . . something like that that I want to disappear, so perhaps it's . . . accept now some expression, also some discomfort with who I am, and want to disappear.

The women objected to the prevalent view that eating disorders are linked to the desire to look good and slim, asserting that it derives from the need to not look good and thus avoid any signs of femininity. For them, the common understanding of eating disorders refuses to recognize the suffering behind them and the role they play in the lives of the survivors of childhood sexual abuse.

Arabella spoke with great pain of her difficulties with her feminine body and the fear of being fat. Experiencing it as something that made her body weak and vulnerable and easily entered, she protested against the idea that the goal of eating disorders is to look better:

> I know how much my feeling about my body isn't connected to how others look. It's not connected to how models look or what's beautiful and what isn't, that has no connection to what this is in the eyes of others. It's absolutely linked to my difficulty with the abuse.

Lily also expressed her anger over the view that anorexia is a function of looking thin and sculpted, asserting that it is rather a way in which she protects herself:

> I'm so fed up with hearing the prevalent view, that's so stupid, that most women with eating disorders 'do it in order to be thin and sculpted, good-looking, models'. If that were the case . . . everyone would agree that 38 kilos is too low in everyone's opinion.

Fear of menstruation and the attempt to prevent it by self-starvation

The desire to prevent menstruation is commonly adduced by anorexic clients, being linked to childhood sexual abuse via the fact that menstruating is a symbol of the femininity they associate with abuse and rape. Signifying the ability to become pregnant, many girls starve themselves so that they will not start menstruating and run the risk of becoming pregnant at the hands of their abusers. Joy, who was abused by her grandfather, could tolerate any form of blood but menstrual:

> I'm willing to cut myself and to see blood flowing from every place in my body, but there's no way I'm going to put up with blood in this place . . . no way. I'll starve myself to death rather than have any blood from there. When I was a child and he used to rape me, I don't remember exactly when, perhaps age 9, I suddenly understood . . . I think my grandmother explained it to me, that when I got my period I would be able to get pregnant. And I got so scared that I might get pregnant by him. Up to this day, I can't stand this blood. I'd rather die. . .

Evelyne starved herself in order to stop menstruating:

> One of the things I found most difficult was my period, which at the time was traumatic, really (laughs). So yes, somewhere, like, it's the power to stop it as well. The thought was that, 'What, my period has come? I have to stop eating again'. Like, there's nothing like this.

Lily spoke of using her anorexia to stop her menstrual cycle and thus protect herself against her uncle's abuse: 'Like, I'm disgusting, I'm revolting, I'm not a woman. Like, I don't have any periods, I don't have anything, so, like, what . . . what it . . . it doesn't have any reason to come to me. It's, like, a protection in other words'.

Vine wished her period would stop, still today fearing it might return, because she does not want to be a woman. Her wish is to remain a small child so that no one will seek to hurt her:

> In effect, the anorexia took from me a very significant feminine aspect from me, and that's my period. I remember that I hoped and prayed it would disappear, when I was at the beginning of the disease. Today, I'm really afraid that it'll come back, because it makes me a woman and I don't want to be a woman. I want to be a little girl. That way perhaps no one will want to hurt me.

Notes

1 Aloni-Sadovnic, R. (2010). Life after death: The first manifesto of childhood sexual assault victims. www.alonilaw.com/138627/Victims-of-sexual-assault-s-Manifesto

2 These writers were influenced by Simone de Beauvoir, who identified the way in which woman are perceived as object vs. male subjectivity, and Lacan, who argues that the social, linguistic, and interpersonal space is structured by the symbolic order – language. French feminist psychoanalysts hold that language is a male linguistic structure, femininity thus being driven into the subconscious already in the pre-verbal stages of development. In order to free it, history must be therefore challenged and a new language introduced.

3 Zerbe does not associate the 'betrayed body' with childhood sexual abuse, however.

4 The illusion lies in the fact that the defence is ineffective, both because on many occasions it does not prevent revictimization and because the eating disorder damages the body, thus not protecting it.

References

Arnold, R. P., Rogers, D., & Cook, D. A. (1990). Medical problems of adults who were sexually abused in childhood. *British Medical Journal, 300*, 705–708.

Ashur, D. (2006). Haqdama [Preface]. In H. Cixous & C. Clément (Eds.), *The newly-born woman* (pp. 7–23). Tel Aviv: Resling (Hebrew).

Beauvoir, S. de. (1953/2010). *The second sex*. Trans. C. Borde & S. Malovany-Chevalier. New York, NY: Vintage.

Bordo, S. (1993). *Unbearable weight: Feminism, western culture and the body*. Berkeley: University of California Press.

Cixous, H., & Clément, C. (1986). *The newly-born woman*. Trans. B. Wing. Minneapolis, MN: University of Minnesota Press.

Fredrickson, B. L., & Roberts, R. A. (1997). Objectification theory: Toward understanding women's lived experiences and mental health risks. *Psychology of Women Quarterly, 21*, 173–206.

Freud, S. (1932). Femininity. In *New introductory lectures on psycho-analysis*. Harmondsworth: Penguin, 1991.

Halpern, R. (2012). *The body and its discontents: Israeli women's fiction 1985–2005*. Tel Aviv: Hakibbutz Hameuchad (Hebrew).

Herman, J. L. (1997). *Trauma and recovery*. New York, NY: Basic Books.

Irigaray, L. (1985). *This sex which is not one*. Trans. C. Porter. Ithaca, NY: Cornell University Press.

Kearney-Cooke, A., & Striegel-Moore, R. H. (1994). Treatment of childhood sexual abuse in anorexia nervosa and bulimia nervosa: A feminist psychodynamic approach. In M. F. Schwartz & L. Cohn (Eds.), *Sexual abuse and eating disorders* (pp. 155–175). Bristol, PA: Brunner/Mazel.

Loewenstein, R. (1990). Somatoform disorders in victims of incest and child abuse. In R. Kluft (Ed.), *Incest-related syndromes of adult psychopathology* (pp. 75–111). Washington, DC: American Psychiatric Press.

Murnen, S. K., & Smolak, H. W. (2009). Are feminist women protected from body image problems? A meta-analytic review of relevant research. *Sex Roles, 60*, 186–197.

Orbach, S. (2015). Give us back our bodies. *Huffington Post*, May 22, 2015. Retrieved October 22, 2017, from www.huffingtonpost.co.uk/2011/03/08/give-us-back-our-bodies_n_7411178.html

Padua, A. (2004). The body can tell: Issues in the medical treatment of survivors of childhood sexual abuse. In Z. Seligman & Z. Solomon (Eds.), *Critical and clinical perspectives on incest* (pp. 483–497). Tel Aviv: Hakibbutz Hameuchad and Tel Aviv University Publishing House (Hebrew).

Rozmarin, M. (2003). Epilogue: From being a man to becoming a woman – Luce Irigaray's theory of the inter-sex difference. In L. Irigaray (Ed.), *This sex which is not one* (pp. 81–93). Tel Aviv: Resling.

Tripp, M. M., & Petrie, T. A. (2001). Sexual abuse and eating disorders: A test of a conceptual model. *Sex Roles, 44*, 17–32.

Wolf, N. (1991). *The beauty myth: How images of beauty are used against women*. London: Vintage.

Zerbe, K. J. (1995). *The body betrayed: A deeper understanding of women, eating disorders, and treatment*. New York, NY: Gürze.

Part II

Treatment of eating disorders and childhood sexual abuse

Introduction

> The eating disorder makes it so that the worse state you're in, the less they are ready to treat you.
>
> —Noga

My research has raised serious questions regarding the treatment methods customarily employed in eating disorder centres in relation to childhood sexual abuse. These revolve primarily around the widespread tendency to ignore women's traumatic history, exemplified both in labelling diagnoses and inappropriate forms of treatment that frequently directly counter the principles of the treatment of complex childhood trauma. The women's voices in this context are clear and lucid, surprising in their ability to precisely identify those elements that, rather than being therapeutic, reenact the abuse and their capacity to describe those forms of treatment that were helpful. Despite the close links between the two fields, until recently they appear to have developed along parallel lines, almost never intersecting.

Eating disorders only entered DSM-III in 1980 – the same edition that first included a definition of PTSD. The field largely developed within the medical-psychiatric establishment – in contrast to childhood sexual abuse treatment, which evolved in feminist therapeutic circles. Expertise in treating childhood sexual abuse was garnered primarily in the framework of rape crisis centres, being largely due to pioneering professional women who laid out the fundamental principles and methods of treatment appropriate to sexually abused women. The field was also heavily influenced by the emergence of treatment methods for PSTD and dissociative disorders.

Women sexually abused in childhood suffer from a wide range of symptoms, including eating disorders. Only some of those with eating disorders seek treatment at eating disorder facilities. Others go to sexual abuse centres, addiction-treatment centres, general psychiatric wards, or non-specialist therapists. Both childhood sexual abuse and eating disorders being characterized by secrecy, shame, and concealment, many survivors do not seek treatment of their own accord.

This section traces the development of eating disorder and childhood sexual abuse treatment methods, examining whether those conventionally employed in the former field are appropriate for women, most of whom are known to have been sexually abused as children. We shall hear the stories of women about the treatment they received and critically summarize the problematic as it arises from them in the context of the treatment of childhood sexual abuse in the framework of eating disorders and general psychiatric hospitalization. We shall hear the accounts of women suffering from eating disorders who underwent treatment in sexual abuse centres and analyse the advantages and difficulties of treating clients who suffer from eating disorders in these settings.

Chapter 7

Treating eating disorders

> I can't bear the way in which eating disorders are treated in the hospital. So when I read about your research I decided to participate in it. I said that from lots of perspectives I don't like it. First of all, I don't like the violence, the lack of respect for boundaries. The hospital is difficult for me in general. You're walking a fine line when facing another person's body. It's difficult for me that the measure for treatment success is a physical one: weight, appearance, eating. I mean, precisely the same thing they [the perpetrators] saw in the abuse. Only the body . . . as if there's no person inside. That's very difficult for me. The whole thing of forced eating is impossible in my opinion. But that's really from my corner, that forcing things into the mouth . . . and it's . . . like, for me it's. . . . it's really hard. And that's not even getting to the restraint and instances that are really extreme, not just in eating disorders. It's hard for me, it's hard for me that they do that at all. Like, any physical constraint is really difficult for me in general. So I agreed to talk about it. It's important to me that this voice somehow be heard when we face the therapists. The truth is that they're exhausted. Primarily by the anorexics. Really battered, like extremely tired, exhausted. And that's one of the more difficult cases, to be the one monitoring an anorexic patient at lunchtime. One of the ways in which the nurse can be punished is to finish lunch with all the anorexics. It's the worst thing. But still, the whole approach, I've always been driven mad by the . . . I really don't see how you can treat it with something technical. There has to be why and what.
>
> —Maggie, a hospital nurse, abused by her father

Clients with eating disorders challenge those who treat them because they are frequently at high risk of significantly damaging their health or facing death. Many have seriously distorted views of reality, are extremely defiant, and find it difficult to cooperate with the treatment plan. Authoritarian medical forms for treating eating disorders thus developed that revolve around coercion, punishment, invasiveness, and rigid boundaries. These methods are employed in crisis situations when clients are unwilling to collaborate and must be protected against themselves. In the field of eating disorders, these modes of treatment include a treatment contract that includes the client's agreement to gain weight as a prerequisite for continued treatment, the exclusion of those who do not comply with the regulations, monitoring after meals, supervision in the bathroom to prevent them from throwing up, restraint, and forced eating on the ward.

Authoritarian, invasive, and forced methods of intervention are utterly inappropriate forms of treatment for survivors of childhood sexual abuse because they reenact the original trauma, in which the responsible, loved adult exploited his authority and wielded power over the helpless child. Authoritarian and coercive forms of treatment repeat the abuse eating disorder clients suffered as children. The damage caused by violence cannot be treated by methods employing the same means as the original trauma. Those abused by the exploitation of adult power and authority need a therapeutic relationship that will act as a corrective experience to the abuse – a relationship based on mutual respect and equality that shuns power, coercion, and authoritarian control.

Childhood sexual abuse is also characterized by neglect, abandonment, and opposition. The invasiveness and violence of the perpetrator are compounded by the denial, disavowal, and disregard of caregiving figures who, while not actively participating in the abuse, stood on the sidelines and did nothing to stop it. The therapeutic relationship must therefore be active, caring, and concerned. A punitive form of treatment that refuses to accept clients who do not comply with the rules and regulations reenacts for them the denial, indifference, abandonment, and neglect they experienced as part of the abuse.

The survivors of childhood sexual abuse suffer from functional lacunae that make them predisposed to revictimization – even within the therapeutic setting. Women who have been exploited by loved authority figures frequently confuse love with submission to authority. Their low self-image prompts them to regard themselves as weak and undeserving of good relationships. Never having learnt the safe boundaries of human relations, dominance and control often seem appropriate forms of treating clients who 'respond well' to punitive and aggressive authoritarianism. Treatment methods that reenact the power and coercion exploited by the perpetrator on the one hand and the neglect, abandonment, and denial they experienced from those around them can never repair the damages caused by abuse.

Women molested in childhood frequently find it difficult to accept authority, resisting rules and regulations even when outwardly appearing to be submissive and cooperative. Such women need a therapeutic relationship that is compassionate, empowering, mutual, and egalitarian in order to heal their relations with others and their own selves. They experience authoritarian and coercive treatment as a reenactment of the perpetrator's intransigence and arbitrariness and thus as untherapeutic – even when it seems to alleviate some of their symptoms.

As we shall see below, assessment studies conducted in recent years from the perspective of women treated for eating disorders demonstrate their dissatisfaction with the treatment they received and a tendency not to seek help. The findings of these studies are consistent with my own, indicating a clear discrepancy between clients' needs and the treatment they actually receive.

The stories of the women I interviewed graphically illustrate the fact that the prevalent forms of the treatment of eating disorders do not meet the needs of the victims of childhood sexual abuse. The women clearly identified the central points at issue in the conventional methods of treating eating disorders, as well as the elements they regard as necessary for effective treatment. These accounts are strikingly commensurate with the fundamental principles established in recent years for the treatment of complex trauma.

Eating disorder treatment methods: a review of the literature

Due to the complexity of eating disorders and the severe and chronic health problem attendant upon them, treatment guidelines stress the need for medical treatment and follow-up, together with psychosocial intervention, nutritional advice, and pharmaceutical treatment where appropriate (NIMH, 2008). The professional literature regarding the treatment of eating disorders is extensive, covering various forms ranging from psychodynamic psychotherapy to behavioural therapy, cognitive-behavioural therapy, interpersonal therapy, family therapy, hospitalization, and pharmaceutical therapy (Gore, Vander Wal, & Thelen, 2001).

Recent years have witnessed increased attempts to identify and assess the effectiveness of the prevalent treatment methods. The fact that only a limited number of studies have been conducted in this regard and the use of small, selective samples have both been criticized. The argument is made that little knowledge is available regarding the ways in which eating disorders are treated and their respective effectiveness (Woodside, 2005). The majority of studies were based either on analysis of case studies or small samples (de la Rie, Noordenbos, Donker, & van Furth, 2006). The majority of these were also conducted from the perspective of the therapist rather than the client.

Studies evaluating eating disorder treatment from the client's perspective

The views of clients suffering from eating disorders regarding the effectiveness of the treatment provided have now begun attracting increasing attention (Gulliksen et al., 2012). Although qualitative studies that give room to the voices of clients still remain few and far between (Rance et al., 2017), more are now being conducted. Their findings point to treatment experiences very similar to those reported by the women I interviewed for my research (for example: Rance et al., 2017).

A study carried out in Britain (Newton, Robinson, & Hartley, 1993) found a mean delay of five years between the appearance of an eating disorder and the appeal for help. The majority of participants in counselling and self-help groups regarded these as effective forms of intervention, behavioural therapy not being experienced as helpful. A Norwegian study (Rosenvinge & Klusmeier, 2000) found a similar delay, the most effective forms of treatment being individual and group therapy in a community setting and self-help groups. Over half the participants regarded family therapy as unbeneficial.[1]

A study evaluating treatment at a specialist eating disorder centre from the perspective of the women being treated (Swain-Campbell, Surgenor, & Snell, 2001) evinced that the clients' primary source of dissatisfaction lay with the emphasis placed on gaining weight or the cessation of binge eating or vomiting and the pressure for change. The clients frequently reported that the therapeutic alliance played an important role – citing, for example, the helpfulness of a sense of connection and trust, collaboration, and shared commitment.

A meta-analysis of twenty-three qualitative studies relating to the assessment of treatment from the perspective of eating disorder clients (Bell, 2003) found that the participants cited therapist support and understanding as central factors contributing to improvement and recovery. 'Medical interventions' were regarded as unbeneficial, the majority of participants relating negatively to interventions that focused exclusively on weight. The importance of addressing broader issues than food and weight was also noted.

A qualitative study of the evaluation of eating disorder treatments from a client perspective (de la Rie et al., 2006) indicated similar findings, a long delay occurring between the onset of the disorder and receipt of treatment, due both to the system and the sufferers. This also observed that the treatments given at specialist eating disorder centres and self-help groups were regarded as the most effective, the most significant elements being a connection with the therapist, the quality of the therapeutic alliance, a sense of peer-group equality, and treatment of related problems in addition to the eating disorder symptoms themselves.

The importance attached by clients to treatment offered by understanding and supportive therapists in an environment that allows honesty and candour is highlighted by another qualitative study (Tierney, 2008). This examined the assessment of treatment by women who had been anorexic and were treated in a hospital framework. The clients objected to the focus on physical aspects – which, while alleviating physical symptoms and accelerating their release from the ward, often led to an immediate regression after their release. Many maintained that they needed more psychological forms of intervention. They also expressed a need for help in developing relationships with groups of equals within their communities, appreciating treatment offered by therapists with whom they developed a sense of connection and who treated them with respect.

Poor success rates and high levels of dropout are common features in the treatment of anorexia nervosa. We elicited the views of 12 women who were recovered, or in recovery, for anorexia nervosa and had received treatment. Results revealed the women's high degree of dissatisfaction with treatment and their perception that the treatment system is overly focused on, and driven by, food and weight. In contrast, what the women really wanted was to be seen and treated as a 'whole person' and to have a 'real' relationship with their therapist (Rance et al., 2017).

As these various studies demonstrate, dissatisfaction with the prevalent forms of treatment is directed primarily towards an overemphasis on eating disorder symptoms and behavioural therapy – rigid regulations, competition for 'prizes', focus on the pathology of the eating disorders, and insufficient attention to profound psychological problems.

The feminist critique of eating disorder treatment

The treatment methods adopted in specialist eating disorder centres have long been criticized by feminist therapists, who maintain that they focus on weight gain, weight stabilization, and the normalization of eating habits. They argue that most of the programmes employ cognitive-behavioural approaches directed at controlling the eating disorder rather than the psychological problems that lie at their base (Sesan, 1994; Orbach, 1986). In their opinion, these methods fail to help women understand how their thought processes impede improvement and recovery. Hilda Bruch (1974, 1982) and Susan Wooley (1990) thus caution therapists against the exclusive use of cognitive-behavioural therapy in treating women suffering from eating disorders. Not only does CBT on its own not cure, especially when employed simply to control the eating disorder symptoms, but it can also do actual damage, prompting women to repress emotions that lie at the heart of their problems (Wooley, 1990).

Orbach (1986) also points to the disregard of the sources of the disorders, arguing that it is easy to understand why anorexics draw so much attention from the mental healthcare and medical establishments. While she notes the therapists' desire to help women stop starving themselves and alleviate their symptoms, she also calls for recognition of the mental aspect of anorexia and the need to make it part of the therapeutic framework, above and beyond the symptomatic level. In her view, when this approach is adopted we quickly realize that the routine treatment offered by most hospitals and clinics must be dramatically revised.

The treatment of childhood sexual abuse within the field of eating disorders

Very little has been written in the eating disorders field about treating sexual abuse (Kearney-Cooke & Striegel-Moore, 1996). Feminist eating disorder clinicians contend that, despite the controversy over the role sexual abuse plays in the development of eating disorders, many women suffering from eating disorders were sexually abused as children. The task is thus to promote ways to encourage its disclosure and methods to treat its consequences (Wooley, 1994).

Kearney-Cooke and Striegel-Moore (1994) suggest a treatment model based on the principles for treating adult survivors of childhood sexual abuse – i.e., the three-stage treatment plan set out by Herman (1997). These include healing relationships, fostering the ability to self-calm, teaching techniques for recovering memories, finding strategies for coping with reenactment, developing ways to deal with the shame, and halting the cycle of revictimization.

Women talk about treatment in eating disorder frameworks

Women's experiences of treatment within eating disorder contexts range from good and healing to hard, unsuitable, and unhelpful. In some instances, the treatment is even regarded as harmful, reenacting past traumas. In most of the cases where the experience has been positive, the success of the treatment is linked to the warm and caring relationship developed with the therapist. Analysis of the elements of effective treatment evinces that even if she did not deliberately address the sexual abuse the therapy was nonetheless based on the guiding principles of the treatment of sexual abuse. These include the cultivation of a therapeutic alliance characterized by a sense of mutuality and equality between client and therapist, client empowerment, addressing of past sexual traumas, caring, warmth, and support.

The reports given by the women I interviewed for my study indicate that while the topic of sexual abuse was raised by the survivors in eating disorder treatment frameworks, it never took centre stage. They attributed the low rate of success to this factor, the treatment not getting to the root of the forms of distress, and the eating disorder not being recognized as a way to cope with their distress. Treatment rather focused primarily on alleviating their eating disorder symptoms. Some women related that although after treatment they had in fact managed to reduce their eating disorder symptoms, in the lack of any treatment of the childhood sexual abuse they developed other symptoms – substance abuse, gambling, prostitution, suicide attempts, etc. In many cases, the clients' secrecy, dissociation (e.g., amnesia of the sexual abuse), and difficulty in talking about the abuse reinforced the eating disorder therapists' tendency towards focusing on the eating disorder symptoms and making no room for working through the sexual trauma. The following accounts address some of the central themes that arose in my interviews with women who had been abused as children and were being treated in eating disorder frameworks.

Focus on the body and diet: 'They only deal with food and . . . the body and not with the person inside'

One of the prominent themes raised by women who had been treated in eating disorder frameworks was their perception that the therapeutic approach these adopted placed too much emphasis on the body and diet, gaining weight, and stopping vomiting. They complained that too little attention was paid to the psyche and the distress their eating disorders served to express, thus reenacting the way in which the perpetrator had related to their body as an object. Perceiving their eating disorders as a symptom conveying what they could not put into words, they felt the treatment ignored the roots of the problem. The tendency towards focusing on the eating disorders without addressing where they came from prevented them from relinquishing the symptoms and recovering.

Sharon, who was hospitalized at the age of 16 for nine months on an eating disorders ward, expressed her feeling that the therapists did not offer her the help she needed, only succeeding in making her put on weight:

> I didn't feel they understood me, I didn't feel they knew what . . . what I was going through, that they could succeed, that they could really help

> me. I mean, I wanted the help, I was there for a specific reason, but . . . but I didn't feel they could really help, apart from getting me to put on more weight.

Shirley described her frustration with the eating disorder ward on which she spent many months and the overemphasis it placed on diet and learning a healthy lifestyle. She felt the whole focus laid on the eating disorder symptoms, which camouflaged the real problem – the sexual abuse. She only understood that the eating disorder was a disguise rather than the root of the problem later when treated by a sexual abuse specialist:

> I think that understanding that the eating disorder was a disguise was one of the most significant factors in my process. What the hospital does only reinforces the fact that it's the problem, that it's the fault, it's what needs to be fixed. Everything revolves around weigh this, do that. It only reinforces all the time that that's the problem. That you need to learn a healthy lifestyle. I don't care s*** about a healthy lifestyle, that's not my problem! My problem is not a healthy lifestyle. My problem is why am I doing this? What does it do for me? I think it's not a coincidence that lots of women go back there. It's not because they haven't learnt how to live a healthy lifestyle.

Evelyne, who spent frequent spells on eating disorder wards, also described what she experienced as a focus on the body to the exclusion of the psyche and the traumas she had suffered, believing that the patients themselves collaborated in this ruse:

> You can't come and relate only to the body when there's a soul inside that's so often ignored. The person frequently ignores it, too. So when you come and only perpetuate it, and focus solely on the body, that's the only thing that matters, and only . . . like, actually, you, like, take care of the body. But there's a person inside, who sits and objects to this, feels, and reenacts, and . . . in effect, if you don't relate to this and everything the person underwent.

Some of the women explicitly adduced the fact that this exclusive focus on the body reenacts what they had experienced during the sexual trauma. The perpetrator using the victim's body for his own needs, ignoring her and her humanity, one of the most severe consequences is dissociation from the body both during and after the abuse. Treatment that focuses solely on the body is thus experienced as a reenactment of the trauma. Evelyne, for example, alleged that the treatment had only compounded her eating disorder and urge to self-harm:

> If you only relate or take care of the body, and insist that that's the only important thing, and that's in fact the only thing that's seen, it reenacts it.

> I mean, it aggravates the eating disorder, in my opinion, and the self-harm in general. Because ultimately, if it's only legitimate to hurt when you start bleeding then the blood will keep flowing.

She also addressed the lack of treatment of the sexual abuse and the overemphasis on getting clients to eat:

> So somewhere, it's as though you have to work with the person not for them – certainly not against them . . . they don't provide any tools for treating the abuse. It's as though there they make you eat, ultimately, I mean, it's a form of fattening. Get to a certain weight or eat a certain menu and everything will be ok, like, you need to keep doing this.

Maggie also noted that eating disorder therapists who relate solely to food and the body reenact the sexual abuse that had used the body and ignored the person inside:

> There's some story [i.e., the sexual abuse], but it's not relevant at present, and they only deal with food and the . . . again, only with the body and not with the person inside. In the abuse the central thing is our body. Which was used, that was the only thing they saw, not us or our souls. So if the treatment focuses on the body, appearance, weight, etc., and they don't see what's happening to us inside, they miss the whole thing.

For Evelyne, any form of treatment that focused on taking care of her body without relating to the soul is doomed to fail from the start, even if the client has gained the 'right' weight:

> So it doesn't matter and the treatment will fail. I mean, that person, that girl, may now put on the 20 kilos she needs to. But in another week, when she leaves the ward, she'll go back to there. And that's actually what happens most times. I mean, I've seen it enough with girls, and I've seen it with girls who were with me on the ward.

Yvonne, who works in a care-giving profession, related to the difficulty eating disorder treatment finds in addressing the source of the problems rather than the symptoms:

> I think that people, even mental health and eating disorder professionals, have no understanding of this at all, like . . . don't know, perhaps what the source of the problem is, or even . . . between us, there's no sensitivity to . . . don't know, perhaps it was me, that I was sensitive to this, so it seems to me that people don't relate to it. In short, there's no answer, even today I'm not getting treatment.

Grace, who received treatment for her eating disorder in various eating disorder frameworks, including hospitalization and community centres, maintained that it was better to attend to the problem rather than focusing solely on food:

> I'm not sure that even in the hospital they really get to grips with it. I mean, the issue of focusing more on food, and the food isn't the problem, it's a symptom. I think that there has to be – the problem itself has to be addressed. Why do I think I have an eating disorder? Actually to understand the meaning, to understand that the eating disorder is a symptom, not the problem. And to try and get a bit deeper, to people's feelings.

Sharon stated that the psychologist who treated her on an adolescent eating disorder ward did not make her feel that she was really interested in listening to her, her sole focus lying on getting her to put on weight:

> I didn't talk because I didn't . . . I never talked. I never felt that anyone wanted to listen to me, because I would sit and do other things. So . . . it's not . . . like . . . they didn't give me the feeling. They gave me the feeling that I had to get fatter, like, to put on weight, and then everything would be fine.

She spoke of how the sole concern on the ward centred around food:

> It always comes back to the same thing, food, I mean, because the subject's always food. Like, you don't put on half a kilo then you don't go home or you don't get certain privileges. So if you lose weight or you don't put on the half kilo, you get a feeding tube and Ensure [nutritional shake] or all the things that go on there. So, like, the subject's always food, like.

The fact that she did not eat, she maintained, attested to her distress. Rather than her feelings being addressed, however, she was given a feeding tube:

> So . . . again it was, it revolved around food, like, if I don't eat then . . . there's something bothering me, like, I'm not not eating for no reason, it's because . . . that's difficult for me, because I feel bad, but . . . if I didn't eat I got a feeding tube.

Coercive and punitive methods: 'Force is not the way, not with girls like us'

> Physical and psychiatric acuity in the framework of eating disorder treatment constitutes a great 'temptation' to engage in interaction and intervention that takes power away from the client. Often, it can reenact, via projective

> identification, the core of the traumatic experience by being too authoritarian. The client actually unconsciously 'drives' the staff in this direction.
>
> —Dr. Einat Zubery, Head of the Eating Disorder Treatment Unit, Notrim Clinic, Ra'anana[2]

The women I interviewed asserted that the coercive and punitive methods commonly adopted by eating disorder treatment centres were unsuitable and inappropriate, despite understanding that they are intended to cope with the disruptive and even life-threatening situations typical of clients with eating disorders. This type of approach is prevalent on eating disorder wards that house women and girls in acute physical and emotional states and/or in danger of dying. Other treatment frameworks also engage in invasive forms of treatment, such as mass intake interviews or forced participation in certain types of treatment (e.g., family therapy or dietetic treatment). The women described how this form of 'treatment' destructively reenacted the severe abuse they have suffered.

Grace associated 'coercive' and 'aggressive' forms of treatment with the low rates of success hospitals have in treating eating disorder clients, asserting that women who have been abused and been made to feel helpless cannot recover when the treatment includes coercive tactics:

> And I see the success in hospitals, it's not great, it's not great, and often it's coercive. And of course I'm a person who's been abused and lost control over my life, I don't need any more of that, I don't need another place that's coercive – that's not going to help me. So it's – it's something I think is very, very important, to get the message across. As far as what they do is concerned, how they force people there, with respect to food and everything, not sure that's the right way. This force is not the way, not with girls like us, and I assume lots of other girls who have eating disorders have been abused.

Maggie, who like many others had been forced to give her father oral sex, explicitly linked forced eating and everything related to it to this form of abuse: 'With me, the abuse was oral sex, so that anything that has to do with forced eating directly reenacts the abuse and makes me disconnect and disappear. It's enough to see my effort to cope with dental treatment to understand'. She also related to the restraint commonly used with disruptive clients in the context of the sexual abuse she had suffered:

> Restraint is violence. And I'm completely opposed to it. But the person who suffered abuse that included physical restraint, then in any situation in which my hands aren't free I dissociate. So if they restrain me physically they don't get anything from me.

Evelyne similarly addressed the restraints commonly imposed in order to make girls eat when in danger of dying, observing that they should never form part of treatment. Despite seeking to avoid such situations, the very fact of witnessing them was enough to make her dissociate:

> You can go on saying to a girl who weighs 30 kilos that if she doesn't eat she'll die. That might be precisely what she wants, so it has absolutely no effect on her. But even if she doesn't want to [die], and really wants help, you have to understand that restraint, even if it's for a 'good' reason, to help the body recover, as it were, it's not an option. I mean, because in my opinion, and again, I've done everything to avoid this situation, but even to see it pushed me into rewinding it over and over in my mind.

For Evelyne, feeding tubes and restraint touched a very traumatic spot, prompting flashbacks of the sexual abuse. Such procedures take away clients' control over their bodies, thereby reenacting the sexual trauma when they felt and were helpless, she argued:

> Because I can give you an example of something that's very, very hard for me, and as far as I'm concerned, I was prepared to do everything not to get into such a situation. . . . There were situations in which girls were restrained so as to leave the feeding tube in. And as far as I'm concerned, it was simply . . . it wasn't connected to me at all, and even if we're not talking, say, about a friend or someone like that, and I would break down. Because to see something like that, it was the most traumatic thing. It touched precisely on that spot that . . . that . . . it's absolutely, to take control over a person's body away from them and to say: 'I decide, I know best, I decide'. And done with the ostensible purpose of saving that girl, because obviously, if she continued not to eat and to spit out the feeding tube, then death's around the corner. But . . . like somewhere, as if as far as they're concerned the ends justify the means, but . . . the humanitarianism is immaterial, and what it does to her, and what flashbacks it causes her and all of us. So like somewhere, yes, it immediately touches for me precisely on the sore spot of the abuse.

Sharon suffered greatly from the coercive and punitive treatment methods employed on the eating disorder ward. During her first week on the ward, she witnessed the forced insertion of a feeding tube into one of the girls' mouths, an event she interpreted as a power struggle between the girl and a member of staff. From that moment on, she lost all trust in the latter, perceiving them in frightening terms:

> I saw them as intimidating figures, I saw them as figures who didn't really care. And it was like that virtually from my first week. Because it was my

> first week, the first weekend I spent there, there was a critical moment as far as I was concerned, in which everyone became bad, no one was caring, no one interested. It was an incident with one of the girls, a completely unjustified incident. She had to take a feeding tube and she was arguing with one of the therapists, that, like, it wasn't ok, that she didn't need to take it, and she really didn't have to take it according to the rules. And the therapist insisted, 'Because I said so and that's it', and called Dr. Palmer in fact, who was the doctor on duty, and the girl fainted. I spoke to my mother on the phone, and began crying, and told her that I didn't want to be here, that they're bad and that they're . . . they do things by force, and they don't care about us, and all they're interested in is getting us to put on weight. And then they forced me to put the phone down and I got hyperventilated, and then they put me in the same room with her, and I remember that I saw her lying on the floor, like, and like no one cared, and eventually she got out of the treatment room with a feeding tube. Like, it didn't matter what happened, and how bad she felt before she fainted, and that she cried in there, and lay on the floor like I don't know what, ultimately she took the feeding tube, like . . . And it was Dr. Palmer who gave her the feeding tube, so I never saw him after that as someone whom I could trust.

Sharon movingly described her pleas to leave control over her body in her own hands and cries to the staff that she did not like being forced to eat:

> And it all began, this whole game with food, like . . . I'm sitting in front of the plate and I'm not eating, like, I don't feel like eating, who's going to tell me otherwise? And on my second day, they already wanted to give me a feeding tube, because I wouldn't eat, so I told them: 'Why do you think that you're going to put a feeding tube into me?' Lots of times I told them, like, we would be sitting in the weighing sessions, on weighing days, and I would say to them: 'Like, what do you want from me? I don't want to eat, it's my decision, I mean it's my body and I'll decide what I want to put into it'. I would cry to them about this, I really remember one weighing session when I really cried to them that I would decide what I wanted to do and they forced me, and I told them I didn't like them forcing me.

Maggie maintained that the reward and punishment system only made her more defiant. She also described the difficulties in trust characteristic of girls abused by close relatives and her dissociation:

> Promises of rewards and presents only bring out the child-rebel in me. I don't believe in promises and don't need rewards. You have to remember that someone who's been abused at a young age by someone who was

> supposed to protect her doesn't trust easily, at least that's true for me. Use of threats and punishment for me only make me resist more. And if the punishment's too severe, then I disconnect, and then let them try and find me.

Sharon talked of the difficult feelings of attachment to the feeding tube and the invasion of her privacy even when she went to the bathroom:

> All the ... going around with a pillar, it had there, like, because it was such a good friend ... so you're just going around with a pillar, and you're sleeping opposite . . . all day long you're under surveillance, you don't have a minute alone. It's like saying two hours after food surveillance, so between lunchtime and the four-o'clock snack you have an hour . . . everyday in front of the attendants, you can't do anything. You can't leave the pillar outside when you go to the bathroom, you can't even go into the loo with it, you can't close the door completely, so ... Lots of times still today I feel the feeding tube in my throat and nose. I mean, really . . . but often it was much easier than to deal with the food.

In the power struggle, she felt it was better to accept the feeding tube than to cope with the fights and threats. For her, this way of solving the problem was inappropriate, ignoring the reasons behind her refusal to eat:

> Because then it was simple: 'Okay, we'll give you a feeding tube and finish the whole thing', like. . . 'We shouldn't need to fight with her to get her to eat', I don't need to fight with myself to eat and I don't need to fight with the attendants, and I don't need to fight with anyone, and I don't need them to threaten me with a feeding tube. So 'Good, give me a feeding tube', like. . . 'I don't have a problem with that, that's the way you solve things' . . . I mean, if I don't want to eat it's a sign that something's bothering me, like. . . 'So good, let's give her a feeding tube and if she doesn't drink it, then another one', so it's again, it all revolves around food.

Yvonne, who is studying to become a health-care worker, told me how she was forced to undergo the intake interview in the presence of students, comparing it to rape and describing her humiliation:

> It's something I'm sensitive about, I don't want to be in this place. And they forced me, they didn't tell the students observing the interview to leave the room, they just forced me, that if I want to enter, I have to do it with them. And it was so ... like ... like someone crumpled me ... and then trampled on me, to show me that there's no. . . 'You see? Here, we decide what happens to you and what's said to you, and what. . .' And I found it . . . don't

> know, like how can you talk next to someone, it's like someone who raped you saying things, not next to someone I want. And I just . . . I was humiliated, and since then every time I've seen them somewhere in the corridor, I just had an awful experience.

Evelyne spoke of how the fight over food and what she experienced as submission to the therapists reactivated the sexual abuse:

> Somewhere I felt that the place itself aroused lots of things in me, which was much worse, I mean, if I had been at home . . . ah, the fights with them as well, whether to eat or not eat. It's somewhere . . . it was a lost battle. Because obviously you're there so you have to eat what you're given, you have to eat. I didn't really have a choice of saying no. I mean, I could have said no but that has . . . I can't back it up. I mean, I can't really get up and leave or not eat, so . . . I mean, there are implications, so somewhere it straightjacketed me. Like . . . it put me into a place where I had to submit to them.

Sexual abuse in the framework of eating disorders

Many women reported in the interviews I conducted with them that the subject of sexual abuse arose during their treatment in special eating disorder frameworks – primarily hospital wards and group therapy, many of the participants reporting having been abused as children. In some cases, their disclosures were completely ignored. The women's accounts thus reflect the way in which their reluctance and inability to talk about such awful secrets – sometimes due to amnesia – is met by many eating disorder therapists' incapacity to deal with the issue. Some of the examples demonstrate a lack of training and understanding of the dynamics of childhood sexual abuse.

The ignoring of sexual abuse

Clients treated in the various frameworks of eating disorder treatment reported that the treatment did not address the sexual abuse despite the prevalence of the discourse. Dawn was hospitalized for eight months on an adolescent eating disorder ward, later also being treated for several years in an outpatient eating disorder unit. She described her feeling that, focusing on the stopping of the vomiting, these frameworks discouraged talk about the sexual abuse. This disregard dovetailed with her reluctance to talk about it:

> I don't think they would have dealt with it. I mean . . . they were preoccupied with making me stop throwing up. I mean, but again, it didn't get

> to that place . . . because in order for it to get to that place I would have had to talk – and I didn't'

Her unwillingness to talk about the abuse she suffered at the hands of her father was matched, she felt, by the lack of room given to it within the eating disorder treatment:

> The eating disorder treatment – for me, it didn't help. Not the hospitalization and not the clinic. But again, probably because I was in such a different place. I mean, the eating disorder was the symptom of something completely different that just didn't . . . didn't have a place. True, I didn't say anything about it either, but the feeling was also that this wasn't the place to talk about it. I went to be treated for the eating disorder, not for that. But it suited me, because I didn't want to deal with the abuse. 'Til today I haven't been able to deal with it.

On the adolescent eating disorder ward, she had to tell the staff about the abuse in order to forestall family therapy that meant facing her father. Her parents had divorced by that time and she had had no contact with her father since. She described the anger she felt when, even after she had spoken of the abuse and the family therapy had been halted, no one then related to the abuse. This allowed her to be subsequently revictimized: 'The terrible anger because they knew and didn't do anything. Because I'd told them that my father had abused me and then nothing else was said about it. And the revictimization wasn't delayed in coming after the hospitalization'.

Thyme also talked of her feeling that there had been no room for talking about the abuse on the eating disorder ward on which she had been hospitalized, which fed into her unwillingness to address it:

THYME: With the . . . the sexual assaults there wasn't . . . they weren't dealt with at all.

ANAT: Because you didn't want to? Or because they didn't make it a safe enough place to do so?

THYME: I think both . . . I didn't want to at all. But also no one else . . . no one suggested something that was. . .

Evelyne reported that most of the women hospitalized with her on the eating disorder ward had been abused and that this should have been the most important and real focus of treatment as long as the eating disorder was not life-threatening: 'Considering the fact that I think some 80 percent, if not 90 percent of the girls there had been abused, then it's pretty significant. And if you're not in an acute state of 30 kilos, then somewhere, like, the thought is – treat what's real'.

The ignoring of the sexual abuse stemmed from the fact that the treatment focused on the eating disorder and weight levels – despite the other problems clearly lying behind these:

> But it's not . . . you can't really . . . I mean, don't know, it's . . . because the stress is so much on the food, so even when it does come up, when things like the abuse come up and . . . it's very difficult, because somewhere they're trained to treat you for the weight, dieticians, and nurses, and all that. The person who leads the group is also usually a nurse or a team of social workers, or . . . even if it's art therapy, or anything else, I mean, the direction is . . . I mean, it's clear that . . . in most cases there, if not all, they have other problems that led to . . . the eating disorder, but. . .

She suggested that the acute condition of many of those hospitalized precludes any discussion of their traumatic history:

> I think that the staff, too, somewhere. Like, it's not that they're 'Only talk about food' and all that. It's clear that that's not, that's not the 'issue' [English original] for all of them. But yes, I think that as far as emergency situations are concerned, then obviously a girl who weighs 30 kilos won't start talking about flashbacks and her history and what made her stop eating. It's more acute.

Childhood sexual abuse treatment in eating disorder frameworks

The women who found a way to talk about the childhood sexual abuse during their eating disorder treatment described feeling that the eating disorder therapists were not sexual abuse specialists. This fact was exemplified in several central ways – ignoring the revelation of the secret of the abuse, relating to revictimization as 'relationships', stopping treatment even once the clients had built trust and shared the secret on the grounds that they required specialized sexual abuse treatment, and ambivalence towards any discussion of the abuse.

Dawn was molested at a very young age by her father and then in adolescence by her mother's partner. Continued sexual exploitation during adolescence of women abused as children is a common feature of childhood sexual abuse, known as in the literature as revictimization. Women abused in childhood – generally by close and loved figures in their lives – fail to develop safe boundaries in relation to their bodies and psyches, confusing love with exploitation. They are thus likely to find themselves again in abusive relationships. While sexual abuse specialists are well aware of this phenomenon, those without any knowledge of the mental dynamics characteristic of childhood sexual abuse survivors frequently find it difficult to understand. Often, they are confounded by what they perceive as the 'choice' of abusive relationships. Dawn, for example, described how, when she summoned up the courage to tell her eating disorder therapist about her mother's partner's ongoing abuse, she spoke of it as a 'relationship':

> I think I found it very difficult to define it because I really liked and was really close to my therapist. But . . . she didn't know how . . . to talk to me about it. I mean, she used the wrong words. They really shut me down. She related to one of the abuses, which happened while I was with her, as a relationship. Up until today, I mean, I never corrected her. I never told her how it made me feel when she said it.

After she began talking in treatment about the sexual abuse, she was told she could not continue being treated at the eating disorder centre because she needed sexual abuse rather than eating disorder treatment:

> After five years, they told me . . . that . . . the clinic in fact told me that I couldn't go on being treated there. After five years, they've finally understood that the problem isn't the eating disorder. That I don't need treatment for that, that that's been the easy thing all these years. They've referred me to a sexual abuse treatment centre and told me if after I finish treatment there I still feel I need them, then I can go back. But there's no longer any point in persevering with the eating disorder treatment.

Evelyne, who began remembering the abuse she suffered at the hands of her father during her eating disorder treatment, described the dilemma the head of the clinic faced in working through the sexual trauma:

> He suggested that we stop talking about it. He started with that and told me: 'You know that there are all sorts of treatment methods for trauma, of talking and not talking about it'. And then we [she and her therapist] began saying that it's no longer possible not to talk about it, because it's a gathering snowball, and it can't be stopped.

She also spoke of the change that took place in her therapist's attitude, from initially thinking that the sexual abuse should not be talked about to realizing that the process could not be stopped:

> My therapist as well, if you ask me in February, she explicitly told me that there's no point talking about the abuse. But . . . but it's not like, that doesn't mean that she doesn't think there's a link, she just thinks that I'm not ready to make it yet. . .

She told me how, as could have been expected, the memories caused her to regress, manifested in an exacerbation of her eating disorder. She was thus advised to focus on stabilizing the eating disorder rather than deal with the memories:

> Because the moment the things began to come up, even before I'd admitted it, I knew, really . . . so again, like, I stopped eating, I lost weight, so they told me: 'Forget about that now, don't deal with it, eat, focus on eating'. And probably, like, they . . . because even before, I know that before I began to open up those things, they sat together and thought about whether it was right or not. And then the moment they saw that I was opening them up and the first thing I did was to stop eating, just like I did when I was 16, when I developed the things, they told me: 'Forget about it'.

Evelyne felt forced to fight in order to get the traumatic memories back. Although her therapists advised her not to talk about them in order not to regress further, she needed to 'find the lost ends':

> No, it doesn't happen like that today, because it's not like if I remembered something and was also willing to bring it to therapy, then I wouldn't bring this to therapy because Dr. Severn [the head of the eating disorder clinic] told me not to. No, (laughs), with all due respect to Dr. Severn, that's not what happened . . . like, if I didn't talk about it then I was still not eating, and if did talk about it I wasn't eating either. So if already. . . . But I really feel as though, recently, whether it's difficult or not I have to do it! It's like I – I have to because it's as though I'm trying to find all sorts of lost ends.

Wanting to remember what had happened so that she could integrate her past, Evelyne spoke of how this strong desire convinced her therapists to allow her to talk about the abuse in parallel to the treatment for the eating disorder:

> Like, I do want to remember what I can, of course, and to talk about things in order to make some integration of sorts of my past and as it were to go forward. But actually what they're telling me, that if, if this talking is what's causing me to stop eating, then perhaps I shouldn't do it now. That's what they're . . . not, that's what they told me . . . say it was February, today they're no longer telling me that. They're . . . there's nothing to do about that issue, but just to talk about things, and to eat while doing it (laughs), which sounds completely wacko to me.

While they remained ambivalent about talking about the sexual abuse at a time when the eating disorder was still unstabilized, one at least took her side in a discussion over whether it was right to talk about the abuse or not in light of her regression:

> I've been with her almost four years, like from the moment I entered the clinic. I think she'll say that yes, because just like she told the head of the clinic yesterday in my presence, she told him that perhaps . . . because he said, like, once more, we're talking about this and I'm not eating. So she told him that perhaps if we put eating aside for a moment and work on that, because you can't stop working through it right now, 'too late' [English original], then something in the food will move already, of its own accord.

Even here, however, the therapist was very cautious about working on recovering the traumatic memories. Feeling that she was afraid of how she might cope with them, she was uncertain whether to encourage Evelyne to continue to talk about the sexual abuse. Evelyne thus had to 'educate' her therapist in this regard:

> I can tell you that I feel that my therapist was very, very cautious, very cautious, and, like, a bit afraid. Not, I don't think that she couldn't contain me, no, really not. But as though she was uncertain in herself, what was the right thing. And if I don't talk about it, I mean if she sees that I'm finding too difficult to talk, does she encourage me to? Or to let me, like, to let me stay silent, to remain in my silence. That's how I felt at the beginning, at least, that she wouldn't raise the subject of her own accord, really not. Today, I think something's changed, I think I've educated her. Yes, absolutely.[3]

Another theme that arose in the interviews was that of therapist uncertainty regarding the question of whether they should start addressing the abuse when the eating disorder treatment was about to end. Evelyne spoke of the fact that her therapists had told her that since she was nearing the end of her treatment it was perhaps better not to bring up the abuse:

> And then, like, in this time, more or less, a bit afterwards, she told me: 'Perhaps you don't need to talk about this, we're nearly at the end of the treatment. And you have to start bringing things to a close and think about how you're challenged, like, now, by a life without treatment'.

Hospitalization for eating disorders

Up until the mid-1970s, hospitalization for eating disorders was regarded as a last resort, the majority of clients being anorexics placed on general wards with the goal of raising their weight levels. As with suicidal clients, hospitalization was perceived as a way of saving lives, the intervention methods – including feeding and medication – being primarily medical. Since then, however, the increasing awareness of the integration of medical and psychological factors in the aetiology of eating disorders has led to a shift towards hospitalization on psychiatric wards (Bruch, 1974, 1982). Although these continue to emphasize weight gain, they also address the psychological aspects of treatment (Vandereycken,

1985). In the United States, for example, specialist wards and programmes offering accommodation for eating disorder clients have been established, many of which integrate behavioural control of eating disorder symptomology with a range of individual, group, and family therapies (Sesan, 1994).

Researchers and clinicians are trying to improve the high rates of premature dropout from treatment. There is evidence that provision of personal choice at the beginning of hospitalization, enhancing patients' autonomy and volition, significantly reduced dropout during the first weeks of inpatient treatment. These new therapeutic interventions and other treatment strategies designed to increase patients' autonomous motivation and to reduce resistance to change could achieve higher rates of treatment completion (Vandereycken & Vansteenkiste 2009).

Feminist therapists criticize the basic nature of hospital care, arguing that it tends to preserve oppressive tendencies via its unnecessary control of the women's behaviour. These methods 'silence' women all over again (Kearney-Cooke, 1996). While the procedures prevalent on these wards – denial of access to the bathroom after mealtimes in order to prevent vomiting, forced feeding, exclusion from certain activities for clients whose weight is low, and withholding privileges for not complying with the regulations – may be helpful to a certain degree, they also perpetuate the objectification of the 'female body' – the woman as simply her body – that is so widespread in society (Sesan, 1994). The treatment setting in most hospitals is hierarchic and controlled by men, exemplified in power gaps between patients and staff and within the department members themselves. Although, as feminist writers note, more and more women are choosing to specialize in eating disorders, today constituting the majority of therapists in this field, most of the heads of unit remain men trained in accordance with the traditional male medical model (Greenspan, 1983; Sesan, 1994).

Stories of hospitalization on eating disorder wards

For most of the women I interviewed, hospitalization was a bad experience. Some also described it as a safe haven from outside life, however, returning time and again. The majority objected to the aggressive procedures – forced eating and punishment followed. The theme of 'coerced collaboration' was also prominent – the system of immediate removal from the ward for non-'voluntary' cooperation with forced feeding or continued self-harming. In such cases, the clients were transferred to adolescent psychiatric wards – which they experienced as even worse than the eating disorder wards.

Thyme spoke of the difficulty of entering the dining room, this prompting her not to talk about her problems:

> When they put me on the eating disorder ward, I went into panic mode, seeing how they . . . that they shouted in the dining room that . . . because they didn't want to eat and . . . one of them even threw a knife at an attendant. And you can't do anything, the dining room of the ward, it's something . . . it's the worst part of the whole place, because of the difficulty in

> coping with food. And I decided that I wasn't going to talk about anything and would keep silent. And really, I ate almost nothing. I preferred not to eat so as not to be stopped from throwing up.

Sharon shared how her treatment focused on weight gain but was otherwise of no benefit to her:

> Let's say it didn't help me. I mean, that's not the way . . . like how it helped was really to gain weight, it got my weight up, but they didn't make progress with me anywhere, they never made any progress . . . I don't think that . . . I didn't feel they understood me, didn't feel they knew what I was going through, that they could succeed, that they could really help me. I mean, I wanted the help, I was there for a reason, but . . . but I didn't feel that they really offered me any help apart from gaining weight.

She reported the 'threats of infusions for not eating and of the feeding tube', the lack of privacy – '24-hour a day monitoring and being escorted to the showers and bathrooms'.

Thyme similarly described the difficult two hours after mealtimes, during which the bulimic girls were watched to ensure that they did not vomit, citing these as some of the most difficult cases:

> First of all, it's . . . it's . . . it's the most difficult thing to cope with, I think, with the food. That hour, that two hours. I was monitored the whole time. The anorexics were monitored for one hour. The bulimics or anorexics of the 'purging type' [English original] are monitored for two hours after meal times. And these two hours, they're like an eternity. To think that the food is sitting in my stomach and is making me fat and I'm to blame, and I have to find a hiding place. I have so many reels in my head, but those minutes, of after meal times, that's the worst thing for a girl.

She recounted that the counsellors who supervised the girls during these hours kept their distance and did not relate sympathetically to the clients' obvious distress: 'And, like, what did the counsellors do? I only blamed myself, so why have you come to work here? For what? And even if they did keep some sort of distance or didn't make too much contact. I don't really believe that, to tell the truth'. She also objected to the rules on the ward, maintaining that the counsellors were preoccupied with making sure they were kept and failed to show any sensitivity to the girls' afflictions:

> Like everything was rules and regulations, rules, rules, rules. You couldn't sit on the floor. And that was really difficult for me, I was nervous. I cried. The first thing I did was to go and sit on the floor in the corner. On the floor. With my legs crossed. And the counsellor: 'Thyme, get up, Thyme, get

> up, Thyme, get up, Thyme, get up'. But you see I'm crying, so why don't you come and ask what's happened? Why not come and say something to me? Nothing. That was the attitude there. The whole time, I felt that way.

She related that while the ward had no isolation room as on the adolescent psychiatric ward and no aggressive measures were implemented, there was a 'calming-down room'. When a client refused to cooperate with the treatment, she was also immediately transferred to the adolescent psychiatric ward:

> No. At Cedar Hills there's no isolation room. It's called a 'calming-down room'. To the extent that a girl really does go wild on the level of hurting herself and things like that, then they put her in there. But probably after several hours she'll go to Superb Heights [a psychiatric hospital]. She won't stay at Cedar Hills.

Sharon spoke of being dragged by guards to the calming-down room, where she spent long periods of her hospitalization. Although today she doesn't experience herself as a rebellious or disruptive, she was very defiant at that point in her life:

> Because I really . . . like, I don't know, I'm not that sort of person. I mean, I just – I remember lots of times I was in the calming-down room with an SOS injection, lots of times. Half of my stay at Cedar Hills I was in the calming-down room, in effect. They also dragged me several times into it with the help of the guards.

Dawn similarly described the traumatic experience of being put into the calming-down room, which reenacted the feeling of being controlled and of no escape. She reported the flashbacks of the abuse that arose when she was inside and the loss of trust in the therapists after being released from confinement:

> On the ward I was on, the old one, there was one calming-down room, small, without any windows. I remember the first time they put me in there. How they dragged me there, how I pleaded with them not to put me in it, I couldn't promise I would behave properly or not escape to throw up. But I never went wild, never screamed . . . remember being afraid of it . . . the calming-down room, being dragged there, the crying after I'd been locked in, the difficulty in someone controlling me and not having any means of escape. And the more I cried the chances of getting out of the room diminished. And eventually, after I fell asleep because of all the crying and pressure and pain, only then was there any possibility of getting out. And the getting out was even more frightening, going out into a place where you know you don't feel protected or safe, where no one understands you and no one knows.

The women I interviewed spoke of the feeling of being abandoned and 'thrown out' when they were removed from the eating disorder ward. Evelyne reported how they 'threw her off' the ward after she cut herself: 'Then I escaped back to the ward. And after six weeks they threw me off, because I'd cut myself'. Sharon told me how she was transferred to a psychiatric ward because she was told that her eating disorder was under control and they did not know what else they could do for her:

> And that was it, I was hospitalized for ninth months at Cedar Hills, and then they released me and transferred me to psychiatry, and told me that the eating disorder was under control but that I had behavioural problems. They found it difficult with me. And then I was three months on psychiatry and it was really lucky I left after three months . . . At Cedar Hills they told me that my eating disorder was under control and it was no longer the issue and that they couldn't, they didn't know how to take care of me . . . I was cutting myself, I mean, I was cutting myself on a regular basis.

She described the regression she fell into due to her desperate attempt to convey her distress and her fear of going home. Rather than being treated, however, she was transferred to the psychiatric ward:

> I think I was in some sort of place of showing them that I wasn't ok so they wouldn't release me, so I did everything. If it was cutting myself or if it was stealing the nurse's keys, without doing anything with them, just to . . . to show them. And if it was monitoring, say the supervision we had after meals, then to . . . deliberately go back to vomiting, and just not listen to the counsellors, like, to do what exactly the opposite of what they told me to do on purpose. Because I didn't want them to send me back home. And then they transferred me to psychiatry.

Although Thyme referred to the close and warm relationship she developed with her psychiatrist on the adolescent eating disorder ward, she also spoke of her as a 'hard type', recounting the abusive and humiliating rituals she endured at her hands:

> She really hurt me. She used to tell me . . . I had a problem, I don't remember what they call it in psychological terms, that I thought all the world was against me all the time. Now Dr. Ormond is a much harder type. She doesn't speak gently, like I'm talking now. Several times despite needing to bring an eating diary I didn't bring one, because what am I going to write there? That I'm vomiting every day? Now, I'm not going to sit and lie. And there were lots of girls who did. But I'm not like that. I just told her: 'Listen, I haven't brought the diary and I've lost four kilos this week'. And she just laughed at me at levels that . . . there aren't things like. And she told me:

> 'You're just crazy, crazy, where do you want to get to?' It's really insulting to tell someone who's hospitalized that they're crazy.

Thyme related that she was already scared of becoming mad, a fear compounded by being sent to the psychiatric ward whenever she refused to cooperate on the eating disorder ward. The symptoms of CPTSD following childhood sexual abuse are severe and complex, including dissociation disorders that frequently resemble psychotic episodes. Not only do survivors often feel themselves to be 'crazy' and abnormal but they are also misdiagnosed by mental healthcare professionals. Thyme spoke of her identity disorders and the not knowing 'Who and what am I?' characteristic of victims and the significant damage done to her self-image as an adolescent: 'Because anyway you . . . especially after I was at Superb Heights. There were times when I really thought – perhaps you really are like them? Perhaps I'm . . . like, it really undermines the . . . the . . . what I am and who I am'.

Sharon described how she was diagnosed during hospitalization for her eating disorder as suffering from 'borderline personality disorder' – a diagnosis that meant she was not drafted into the army. These disorders – characterized by problems of identity and relations with others, emotional dysregulation, and a tendency towards anger attacks, typically exhibited by childhood sexual abuse survivors – are frequently diagnosed as borderline personality disorders. This diagnosis carries a serious social stigma (Herman, 1997, p. 123). Branding adolescent girls at a critical stage of identity-formation with such a diagnosis without helping them to understand the roots of the trauma from which they are suffering causes great developmental damage, perpetuating the abuse:

> They told me that I had 'borderline personality disorder' and that's why I wasn't accepted by the army. And that's the diagnosis that's not letting me go now. Because they can't actually let me . . . what they told me in the army is that when you have such a diagnosis they can't know what I might do. As though I go and up and down and they don't know what I'll do, so they can't let me go through basic training. They told me, 'You can volunteer [like other girls, women not being enlisted]', but they also gave me a profile of 64, so it's like what can I do, be a clerk? I'm really not cut out for that sort of job.

Up until today, Sharon finds it difficult to know whether the diagnosis was correct. While exhibiting some of the symptoms, she is functioning well, working as a mentor in a girls' boarding school. She thus wondered how the diagnosis she received as an adolescent has affected her self-image:

> If I compare the borderline personality disorder features with how I really was at Cedar Hills and what I still am sometime today, then I can say yes.

I mean, you know, it's a changing self-image, in relationships with people and . . . moods, and all sorts of things like that. So it's like . . . I can say that it's part of me. But I can say that that's what they told me then at Cedar Hills and because of that I think that it's . . . like, that it's like that.

Hospitalization on eating disorder wards as a haven

The women's stories as they recounted them in my interviews with them demonstrated how hospitalization on an eating disorder ward could serve as a refuge in the midst of their horrendous distress – an 'asylum' that allowed them some respite from dealing with their lives. Phyllis Chesler notes how it can serve as a type of the 'bell jar' of which Sylvia Plath speaks so movingly:

> Perhaps one of the reasons women embark and re-embark on 'psychiatric careers' more than men do is because they are, quite horribly, at 'home' within them. Also, to the extent to which *all* women have been poorly nurtured as female children, and are refused 'mothering' by men as female adults, they might be eager for, or at least willing to settle for, periodic bouts of ersatz 'mothering', which they receive as 'patients' . . . There [in the mental asylum], as 'helpless' and 'self-destructive' children, they were superficially freed from the female roles as private social losers, as wives and mothers. However, neither 'madness' nor mental asylums offered them 'asylum' or 'freedom' . . . . All . . . existed under a 'bell jar' – both inside and outside the asylum.
>
> (1972, pp. 35, 15 [original italics])

Hospitals can provide a form of relief from living with severe problems within male-dominated patriarchal society. Prison also has some of these same qualities (Ajzenstadt, Soffer, & Steinberg, 2010). My clinical work with women prisoners has made me well acquainted with the need women plunged into severe mental crises have for a refuge from life. This need is particularly characteristic of women who were abused as children and thus have first-hand experience of sitting under the 'bell jar' that separates them from the 'normal' world.[4]

Shirley recounted that her hospitalization on an eating disorder ward was one of the best periods in her life because it allowed her to feel as though she was separated from the outside world by a glass partition, bestowing upon her a 'patient identity':

> And I'm like stuck with the disease. And I remember that then I understood . . . I think that the pressures of society were precisely the pressures I didn't have to deal with. You don't want to have to deal with your

> boyfriend and studies and all that. There's something very addictive about the disorder. The hospitalization was one of the best times of my life. I think that every time things became a bit much for me, I felt as though a bell jar was coming between me and them. And I see you, but I'm not really connected to it. I'm cut off from the world. For me, the hospitalization was a desert island: I got up in the morning and I had the ward. It's the not being, as Tamir said in the film ['Metamorphosis', directed by Natalie Brown, which tells the stories of sexually abused women]: 'To be a post-person'. That's something I very much connect with. It's not to be here.

Women who have been abused in childhood feel tainted and flawed, the silence imposed on the subject not allowing them to express their distress. Being hospitalized gives them a recognized identity as a 'patient', enabling them to convey what they cannot talk about. This brings them some relief from the need to cope with the 'freedom' of being outside the ward:

> We were only patients there, nothing more than that. There's something about that in my view that really, really preserves the illness. It's a sort of really necessarily 'refuge' [English transliteration]. But it's also very . . . and I saw, most of the women with me went 'back and forth' [English transliteration]. They were hospitalized, they went in, they got out, they went back. I think it's very hard to adjust. I remember when I left the ward for freedom outside, I was extremely depressed, I didn't want to be.

She related to the need to escape from life on the outside during periods when the outside did not correspond to her inner feelings:

> I think that part of my attachment to the hospital is that it's far more in line with my perception of reality. For example, it's very hard for me when I feel that there's a huge gap between the perception of outsideness and the flow of life in summer. Winter's far easier for me. In winter, there's a balance between my inside and the outside.

Dawn described her hospitalization on an eating ward in terms of a summer camp:

> I treated the hospitalization like a summer camp. Really like that. I mean, at first, it was really hard. For the first month, I thought for sure it would take six weeks, because that's the minimum you have to be there, and then I would be released. And then when I understood that it was good for me to be there, then I already didn't . . . didn't . . . no longer. . .

She described how her symptoms got worse and she started acting out in order to show that she did not want to go home, telling me how as a child, when she had no 'home', the ward became her home.[5] Although it was a bad place for her, she was also treated badly at home:

> The feeling of the . . . not belonging there, to home. I didn't belong there. And at Cedar Hills you find yourself like . . . you get used to it, you find yourself your own corner on the ward, like . . . and . . . you find yourself the most amazing friends in the world on the ward and it's difficult, it's difficult, because you have your own corner there, and it becomes home, it becomes home. You reside there, you live there, you eat there, six meals a day, even though they treat you badly, at home I was also treated badly, it becomes home, I mean, in every respect.

In contrast to the emptiness and not-belonging she felt after her release, the ward allowed her to feel things and become attached to friends:

> At that moment I remember I'd been released and I'd gone to school, that I was supposed to go the day after to get released and go directly to school, and everyone's looking at me as though I'm an alien, a different kind of person than them, and you're not . . . not the same person. And I felt, don't know what I felt, I mean, I'm trying to remember the feeling. And I felt I didn't belong, and I felt odd, and I felt that I didn't feel anything. Like, no . . . a sort of emptiness like, I had at that moment. At Cedar Hills it was true . . . like it was, it was bad, but I had my friends and I didn't feel completely empty, I could feel things. And even at home I didn't have a sense of belonging.

Evelyne described how she decided to be hospitalized on the eating disorder ward in order to escape from the pressures at home, the situation there being far more difficult than the freedom she had on the ward:

> And somewhere, like I had to make this surrender of whether I want to or not, I'll placate them, and in fact go onto the ward. Primarily so that I'll have somewhere to be and so they'll get off my back. So at the time I went in and then I left, like, I released myself after a month. And after several weeks I went back again, because the situation at home was far worse than on the ward. In the hospital at least I had a certain measure of freedom from them.

When after three months on the adolescent psychiatric ward, the staff wished to transfer Thyme to an open ward, she resisted because the closed ward was a safe haven from reality. Despite its hardships, she needed to stay there in order to deal with the sexual abuse and eating disorder:

> After three months they wanted to transfer me to the open ward as a sign of progress . . . as a sign . . . and that. I really suffered there, but . . . I was also really scared of returning to that normality, of dealing with all the fears,

> because in fact, still, no one knew anything. Not the abuse nor the eating disorder. No one knew anything. As far as they were concerned, I went back because I'd swallowed thirty paracetamol.

Evelyne referred to the holding function the hospitalization served and the difficulty of leaving to return to life. It exerted a strange pull on her, allowing her to shrug off the existential problems of life:

> I mean, it's much harder to leave the ward after you're there. I mean, also because it's a sort of 'holder' [English original], all of life. Because you're there 24/7, and it's for a period and you're as though immersed in treatment. But then, it's really, really difficult to leave and go back to life. And somewhere it draws you back. Like, the smallest difficulties, suddenly you say: 'Ah, it's best to be on the ward'. And it's not true, and you need a bit of distance to understand that.

Psychiatric hospitalization

The women's stories evince that their experiences on the psychiatric wards were difficult, depressing, and disturbing. The way in which girls and women are 'treated' in them immediately calls to mind the 'treatment' 'hysterics' received in the nineteenth century – punishment, coercion, and violence. In general, they experienced the psychiatric hospitalization as far more difficult than the eating disorder wards. Many felt it to be a form of punishment, being frequently transferred from eating disorder wards when they harmed themselves or refused to cooperate.

Thyme recounted, for example, how she was shunted to and fro between the adolescent eating disorder ward and a psychiatric ward in another hospital because she was meant to be learning how not to vomit. The isolation in which she was kept all day made her feel like a caged animal:

> And then they transferred me to Superb Heights. There they put me on a rehab programme. I felt like an animal. I was isolated all day. Sometimes when I was with . . . screaming, because . . . because . . . because I didn't like it. Because I'm not an animal and because no one has the right to treat me like that . . . I personally don't believe much in this system of isolating people. I don't really think it helps.

Sharon, who was moved from an adolescent eating disorder ward to a psychiatric ward, told me that 'psychiatry was scary'. The staff not addressing her eating disorder, she did not understand why she had been sent there and sought to escape:

> I remember that my food thing didn't really interest them, I mean, really didn't interest them. Like, no one checked on it. The truth is that I haven't

> a clue what I did there, don't know why they transferred me. There was the thing of the suicide, I suppose, the self-harming. And once I escaped from there, I got out through the bars, me and another friend.

Thyme was sent to an adolescent psychiatric ward after a chain of events beginning with being brutally raped on a day trip on the eating disorder ward. When she told the therapist there about the rape, she was transferred from outpatient care to full-time hospitalization:

> She just came into the room and told me: 'Thyme, if you don't undress right now, I'll send you straight back to Superb Heights'. And of course that was my worst nightmare, to go back to Superb Heights. So I undressed and gradually she saw a mark and then another and blood here and blood there, everything was still so . . . just . . . just starting crying. I didn't have . . . and . . . she . . . hugged me, and from there I went back for another two months at Cedar Hills.

Her condition not improving and even deteriorating, she was then transferred to the adolescent psychiatric ward. There, she was regularly restrained despite the trauma she had experienced. Losing trust in the therapists, she regretted having told the psychiatrist on the eating ward about the rape:

> Then they used to restrain me. Like . . . from the frying pan into the fire. Like . . . then I felt . . . and just lost all trust as well. So I said to myself, Why did you tell? Why did you tell? Like it helps . . . Why did you tell, ultimately to be restrained in isolation at Superb Heights?

The nurses on the adolescent psychiatric ward adopted an authoritarian approach: 'At Superb Heights, the person who decides there is the male nurse . . . and the nurses at Superb Heights are really, really hard. They don't treat you as a person'. She described herself as an 'impudent' child ready to criticize the way in which the ward was run, giving a chilling account of how she was given pharmacological psychiatric treatment in order to shut her up:

> There are both male and female nurses. I don't know which is worse any longer, but lots of times . . . I was a spirited child . . . really sharp. I could never see something that was . . . I was really sanctimonious. I saw something that wasn't right, always, never was shy but went and told the person to their face: 'It's not right what you're doing'. . . . But they put me, they gave me Atomin to sedate me, which is really strong, and knocks you out. Mum would come and visit me and I would fall asleep in front of her. I just couldn't help myself. It was so painful, and so painful for Mum, but the psychiatrist wouldn't listen at all.

Thyme described the aggressive nature of the treatment, the regular use of isolation and restraint, and the physical violence towards the adolescents typical of the ward:

> Anything that wasn't right, straight to isolation. Anything that wasn't right . . . in isolation itself, straight to restraint . . . with them there wasn't any 'If not by force then by reason'. With them, it was. . . 'If not by force then by greater force'. At Superb Heights, they used an awful lot of force. Lots of force. I saw a lot there of . . . the patients and girls who suffered . . . they got blows, but . . . not always justified.

On one occasion, not wanting to eat because she was trying to stop vomiting, she went wild and was grabbed by several male nurses, who left blue marks all over her body. They completely disregarded the huge anxiety and distress food aroused in her because of the fear she would not be able to vomit it back up:

> In my opinion, there there's lots and lots of . . . like, they would call me . . . every time anyone went wild, they would call the guys, like. Exactly like the mad people in films. I didn't believe it would be like that. But as far as I'm concerned, I remember they grabbed me once, and just because I didn't want to eat, when I was trying to stop vomiting. They grabbed me and left so many blue marks on my body . . . they really struggled with me. And like . . . where's the consideration? Where's the knowledge? The experience? A girl suffering from bulimia for five years, struggling with something really hard, each time anew, with the food. And when she knows ahead of time she won't be able to throw it up . . . the meal, because she's monitored 24/7.

Thyme spoke of the lack of warmth and support and her need for love rather than the strictness and boundaries ostensibly designed to create strong psyches:

> Where's a little support? You know, today I take care of girls, also with eating disorders. I'm not involved in giving treatment but I'm very supportive . . . I know that in detox institutes this strictness and boundaries are something that really help. . . . But I didn't need it. I needed love.

For her, the coercion and restraint reenacted the sexual abuse, particularly in light of the fact that it was men who grabbed her by force:

> I, it was very, very difficult for me to deal with this, precisely because of this. Because first of all, I oppose violence anyway. I've always been like that. But it really hurt me, like, in my heart. Even if I was a bit disruptive, like, that two guys, too, it's not the girls, it's two guys, who grab me with force, all

> of a suddenly taking me to the isolation room. First all of, it immediately aroused a flashback, awful.

The damage caused by the violence and use of force reinforced her already low self-image and feeling of worthlessness, prompting her to make a suicide attempt:

> Second of all, that, like, instead of lifting a person up it brings you down even more. You feel worthless in the first place. I felt worthless. I didn't just try to commit suicide for no reason. I didn't just give up on my life for no reason . . . the second time I swallowed pills. Or . . . I felt minus.

She summed up her experience on the psychiatric ward as horrific: 'The truth is that it was shocking at Superb Heights. There, the . . . awful, I think, the way they abused the adolescents there'.

Family therapy and mother/daughter-relations treatment

Some eating disorder treatment frameworks use family therapy as the preferred form of treatment, requiring all clients to participate in it. This approach reflects the way in which those within the eating disorder field ignore the traumatic history of the women being treated. Family therapy as the default approach is inconsistent with the understanding that many, if not most eating disorder clients, have a history of childhood sexual abuse – so often committed by primary caregivers. Girls are sexually exploited by adult perpetrators, in most cases a close family relative or other responsible adult with whom the child is familiar. The trauma of childhood sexual abuse is also associated with feelings of abandonment, neglect, and denial/looking away/indifference by the other responsible family members who do not see, hear, acknowledge, object to, or prevent the abuse.

Family therapy in situations in which it is known or suspected that the client was abused by a family member must be adapted to the survivor's needs (Goldstein & Katz-Charny, 2004). It cannot be mandatorily and unilaterally imposed on all eating disorder clients. Sexual exploitation within the family is based on the power possessed by fathers in patriarchal families – power that in the case of childhood sexual abuse is directed against the weakest members. Family therapy as the preferred mode of treatment reinforces the message that the family is more important than the individual. Hereby, it strengthens the decree of silence, emphasizing the supremacy and exclusivity of the family and treating insensitively those for whom it became a web of violence and destruction.

Employing a single treatment method for all clients and forcing a certain type of treatment upon everyone, including those who manage to protest against family therapy, is contrary to the guiding principles for treating people suffering from CPTSD. These focus on recognizing the individuality of each client and personalizing treatment to their specific needs (Courtois & Ford, 2009).

In their interviews with me, the women spoke of the difficulty family therapy caused them when it formed an integral part of the eating disorder treatment, and its unsuitability to their circumstances. One of the key problems that arose was the fear that the perpetrator of the abuse would be present. Clients with an unreported history of abuse within the family – particularly father-daughter incest – were forced to confront the perpetrator in the family-therapy sessions at a stage when they were still unready to reveal the awful secret.

Other difficulties related to the focus on the clients' relationship with their mother when they felt the central problem to be the abuse committed by the father. In most cases in which the father was the perpetrator, the clients also exhibited great anger towards their mothers, who did not see or protest against the abuse or protect them against it. The complex relationship with the mother in cases of father-daughter incest is an important issue in treating childhood sexual abuse. Family therapy that focuses on the anger in mother-daughter relations without recognizing the possibility of abuse by the father by its very nature exposes stores of anger against the mother. It also tends to shift the focus away from blaming the perpetrator towards blaming the mother. It thus makes it difficult for clients to identify the source of the problem and receive treatment for it.

Dawn was abused by her father, never telling anyone of the fact. When she was 11, her parents divorced and her father left home. At this point, the abuse stopped. As an adolescent, she was hospitalized on an eating disorder ward. The treatment included family therapy, to which her father was invited despite having had no contact with her for several years. Only after a month or so of family therapy did she summon up the courage to tell her therapist of the abuse in order to ensure that her father stopped coming. Although the therapist ended the family therapy with the father, even telling Dawn's mother of the abuse, the subject of the abuse was never addressed in the therapeutic setting. The family therapy forced Dawn to reveal the awful secret before she was ready to do so. Worse, after she had done so, the ward therapist – and Dawn's mother – never referred to it again:

> Actually, I didn't really have any contact with him, until the hospitalization, and I actually never said anything. So obviously they invited Mum and Dad. And only when after a month I asked them to stop, like, bringing them, did they understand that something wasn't right. And then I did say that there'd been something. And they told Mum, and I remember that then just, from that minute onward there was no more family therapy. But we also didn't . . . didn't . . . didn't talk about it. I mean, I was released from the . . . it was said once and then they never talked to me about it again.

Yvonne, a social worker from an Orthodox Jewish family, described her difficulty with the fact that the treatment at the eating disorder clinic was conditional upon her agreement to participate in family therapy:

> I told her: 'My family don't know anything, they never knew anything'. She said: 'No, without your family you can't'. I told her: 'Ok, if it's not possible it's not possible'. She told me: 'You have to understand, treating eating disorders is done in the context of the family framework, and can't be done without that. And there's no other option, only with the parents. Do your parents beat you?' I said: 'No'. She said: 'No, because if they beat you, then you can do it without them'. I told her: 'Listen, this is my reality and they don't know, as far as I'm concerned, imagine they don't exist in this world, as far as I'm concerned right now. . . . I want to be healthy, you want . . . ok'.

Her fierce resistance to letting her mother take part in the family therapy led her to drop out of programmes in frameworks in which family involvement was a prerequisite:

> But . . . apparently in eating disorder treatment it's unforgivable that your mother isn't in the picture, which made me drop out apparently from several other places, because I'm not ready to listen to the suggestion that she'll be part of . . . that she'll be part of this story, even if only because I think that she doesn't deserve to be a part of my world.

Her opposition to making her parents part of the treatment stemmed from her wish not to let them know about her eating disorder. Her destructive symbiotic relationship with her mother made her unwilling to let her into her emotional world:

> When they hear that it's that kind of argument, then there's no choice, the family has to be in the picture. And they won't be, even if I have be sick for the rest of my life or die. So that's what will be. Every time I say that, if I'm involved in a terror attack, in some place where I'm not supposed to be, and I come back to life, then my mother will kill me for being there. So ok. So I say that if she knows I have an eating disorder, it's not that I'll die from it, I'll die from her, from what she'll broadcast to me. It won't help if you teach her how to see me eating and not say anything, or how to encourage me to put on weight, it won't help, she won't last with it. There's something in her, in what passes between us, in the air, like, that I can't . . . I can't, I can't let her into my emotional world.

During the course of her interview, it became clear that Yvonne suspected that her father had abused her, a fear that well explains her strong antipathy to family therapy.

Olivia reported that her relationship with her mother was a central issue in the explanation of her eating disorder in the group therapy at an eating disorder centre: 'The link was the eating disorder with Mum who was very, very hard, and very demanding, and very, lots of cursing and abuse . . . like . . . like, that was the link'. In the absence of any memories of abuse by her father, she connected with a narrative of an abusive mother. Only later did she begin to associate her eating disorder with the abuse she suffered from her father:

ANAT: And you connected with this narrative of an abusive mother? Of the mother. . .

OLIVIA: Yes, yes. Because Mum was very, very hard. Today, I'm beginning to see the story a bit differently, but in my experience I had a mother who cursed me and hated me, and criticized me all the time. And . . . in parentheses, I might tell you that she was very, very unkind to Dad, and I felt a need to comfort him and that. And to protect him against her. Despite the fact that he never protected me against her. And because she was always, you know, so preoccupied with my weight and that and outward appearance, and it was important to her that I be thin . . . so, like, from there it . . . I think but that . . . like . . . don't know.

'Not in our school': transfer to other frameworks due to lack of specialization

One of the disturbing themes that arose in the interviews was the fact that clients were transferred from one treatment framework to another due to the lack of specialization with regard to some of the CPTSD symptoms from which childhood sexual abuse survivors suffer. Because such victims frequently exhibit a range of complex symptoms in addition to their eating disorder, the treating of an eating disorder as a disease in and of itself may lead to fragmentary approaches to treatment and referral of clients to other specialist centres. This reenacts the feeling of abandonment and betrayal that accompanied the trauma. In the absence of a diagnosis that covers all their symptoms, specialization is built around a specific symptom. Clients are thus frequently transferred to other frameworks at particularly critical stages in their treatment.

After a period of treatment in which the childhood sexual abuse survivor fails to adapt to the framework of the eating disorder centre and shows no signs of improvement, she is often referred to another treatment centre. The new environment also frequently refuses to accept her because it is not equipped to deal with her eating disorder. Thus eating disorder centres send clients to psychiatric wards or refer them to treatment at sexual abuse or detox centres, sexual abuse centres in turn referring them to eating disorder clinics. In most cases, the transfer to another framework is or is experienced as a form of punishment, abandonment, or rejection.

After developing a basic trust in their therapist and sharing the awful secret of the abuse they suffered as a child, many clients are told that their problem is not an eating disorder but sexual trauma. Precisely at this critical point, at which the survivor has shared the horrendous secret for the first time, her fears relating to its exposure are realized and she is told she cannot be treated and is transferred to a specialized sexual abuse programme. Girls who have been abused feel damaged, ostracized, and unworthy, living in the fear that no one in the world will accept them, take care of them, or love them if they know about their awful secret. Their removal from treatment and transfer to other settings perpetuates and reinforces this feeling, reenacting the elements of the original abuse.

Specialist sexual abuse treatments also transfer clients who have severe eating disorders – despite the fact that the eating disorder is a well-known symptom of childhood sexual abuse. Evelyne, for example, recounted how the head of the ward on which she was hospitalized told her that she needed treatment for sexual abuse. Although she experienced this as being 'thrown out', today she is grateful to him, because she then found her way to 'A Place of Her Own'. This was far more suited to her needs:

> But if there's something else that I think that I can be grateful to the ward for it's that Dr. Pinel in fact told me nicely: 'Take care of. . . *the* problem you have. It's not an eating disorder. Take care of the abuse'. It was very painful at the time he said it, because it was a sort of being thrown out of there. But there was a lot of power in it, because in fact, it just reminded me that in fact the roots of this are not whether I can eat or not eat.

Sharon related how she was transferred from an adolescent eating disorder ward to a psychiatric ward: 'I didn't know why they were transferring me there. They said I had behavioural problems, and the eating disorder was under control, and they couldn't do any more for me on the ward. Apart from weighing me once a week'.

Thyme spoke of how she was shunted back and forth between the eating disorder ward, the closed psychiatric ward, the detox centre to wean her off vomiting, and the open psychiatric ward. Her account reflects the damage and injustice done to her every time she moved from place to place. Her first hospitalization on the adolescent eating disorder ward was at the age of 15, after a suicide attempt:

> And I was really eating almost nothing, I preferred not to eat so that they wouldn't catch me throwing up. And then after four days he simply asked me: 'Do you want to die or live?' Dr. Palmer. I told him: 'To die'. He immediately sent me to Superb Heights, to . . . the psychiatric ward there, for adolescents. I was there four months. After three months, they wanted to transfer me to the open ward, as a sign of progress . . . as a sign of that and, and I got really nervous.

After she returned to the eating disorder ward, she was told they could no longer help her:

> After stopping the vomiting at Superb Heights I went back to Cedar Hills, but at Cedar Hills they told me that they couldn't help me any longer. They . . . if I gave them tools to help me, then they would know how to help. But they still haven't found me after three years.

Her self-harming led the eating disorder ward to seek to 'shunt her off' to the adolescent psychiatric ward: 'I cut myself a lot at Superb Heights. A lot. Even when I was at Cedar Hills a bit. But at Cedar Hills, if they saw it just once they would shunt me off to Superb Heights'. When her physical and emotional state started seriously deteriorating, the eating disorder ward decided to transfer her to a rehab programme in an adolescent detox treatment community. She experienced the best eating disorder ward in the country as 'despairing' of her:

> Again, another month here and another month here, and another month at Superb Heights, and another month at Cedar Hills and all the time from here to there, from here to there, until it got to the point that my eating disorder destroyed lots of things . . . I had lots of heart problems, I had a real problem with my hair falling out. Serious weight loss in a very short time period. I would faint several times a day. I was very weak. My face was pale. My teeth were decaying. Like, my situation wasn't good at all health-wise. I'm not talking about mentally. And just, Cedar Hills, however good a ward it is for eating disorders and actually the best place in the whole country, they just despaired of me and sent me to stop the vomiting. Then they wanted to transfer me to Ranges [a detox centre for adolescent drug addicts [where I'd do rehab for everything, because the eating disorder is an addiction to everything.

Forcibly transferred to a youth rehab centre, from which she immediately escaped after a couple of days, she was then hospitalized for rehab on a closed adolescent psychiatric ward: 'I didn't agree to go to Ranges. And again, no one really asked me. I escaped from Ranges after a few days and then they transferred me to Superb Heights. At Superb Heights, they made me a rehab programme. I felt like an animal'. In her experience, although she wanted 'to be healthy and good', no place wanted her:

> They wouldn't take me at the boarding place and told me simply that I was a girl who was endangering herself and society, so they didn't want me. They weren't ready to take responsibility for me, despite the fact that I'd already had all those hospitalizations and really wanted to be healthy and good and didn't have any suicidal signs of any form. And that's it, and from

> there I heard all the time like, no, no, no, no, no. We don't want you, don't want you, don't want you, don't want you.

'The operation was a success but the patient died': How getting rid of symptoms can interfere with vital survival strategies

Like the range of other complex symptoms caused by childhood sexual abuse, eating disorder symptoms serve as a survival mechanism and way of coping with complex traumas. Frequently, they form a dissociative way of dealing with the abuse at stages when no other constructive modes are available. As dangerous and destructive as they are, they are still vital for survival in the absence of other, safer coping strategies to deal with traumas that threaten to overwhelm and obliterate the victims.

The centres designed to treat destructive symptoms such as eating disorders or addictions seek to get rid of them. But the only way to relinquish symptoms that, however awful they may be, serve as coping and survival strategies, alternative safe ones must be found. This can only take place after a healing process that takes time and demands patience, sensitivity, compassionate acceptance of the severe symptoms, and recognition of the role they play as coping strategies.

In many frameworks that deal with clients with destructive and dangerous symptoms – such as eating disorders, addictions, self-harming, and suicidal attempts – the therapeutic contract involves an agreement to quit them immediately. This assaults vital coping strategies at a stage when clients do not yet possess alternatives for coping with the trauma, causing them to feel that their needs are being ignored and something that protects them is being denied them – even when on the conscious level they are ostensibly dedicated to getting rid of the symptoms.

The consequences of the loss of survival mechanisms without replacement by other safer and healthier ones may be devastating, leaving clients without any of the defences or coping strategies they have used for many years. Although this type of treatment is insensitive and ignorant of the role the symptoms play in survival, it is very common in eating disorder treatment centres.

The stories of the women I interviewed indicate the role the eating disorder symptoms play, demonstrating the meaning of the 'war' in which they engage with the staff over getting rid of them. Shirley, for example, described how her symptoms served as a vital survival mechanism:

> And that's the eating disorder: it stops me from feeling the things it's hard for me to feel. Hard for me to feel perhaps because they're threatening, perhaps because I don't have enough meat to feel them . . . it doesn't matter any longer where or why they appeared. I mean, except for the reason why it appeared or didn't appear, today all of us have developed for ourselves

> some sort of pattern that's destructive, that has to be dealt with, behavioural or whatever, but has to be dealt with. But yes, but they must be seen as the symptom.

Evelyne felt that control over eating was the only place in which she felt safe, having great difficulty with what she experienced as her therapists' wish to deny her something that, while hurting her, also gave her a sense of safety. In her view, she needed to be in a better emotional state before she could let her eating disorder symptoms go:

> And then when the therapist said, 'You need to stop not eating', it sounded the most absurd thing in the world to me. What on earth? I'm willing to stop the cutting and the self-harming, but . . . like, to stop not eating? Like, it was really, like, it's still really difficult for me to do, and it was also very hard to hear it. I mean, because on the one hand I know that it hurts me, but on the other it really gives me a sense of safety. That there's one thing that's certain. I mean, when it's really, really hard for me, and everything's collapsing around me, it's the place I escape to. Like it's 'safer' [English original]. Like, I know what's happening, I know what will happen if I eat a lot, I know what will happen if I don't eat, I know. . . . I mean, I know where it leads to, I understand the . . . where it ends up. And . . . and somewhere it's much harder to give up on that, and much harder . . . I mean, it's really something, if you take that away from me, like, don't know, I would need to be in a really, really good place emotionally to agree to give that up. And don't know, then, like, somewhere there are fights, like, really on the one hand I understand that I have to give it up. On the other, I try to fight people who try and take it away from me. And . . . out of the thought that it's not, that it's not right to give it up, out of the thought that I don't have anything else.

Dawn described how her eating disorder serves her even today as a way of coping, years after the treatment, because she still has not dealt with the sexual abuse:

> Because if not, because if it wasn't for this [the eating disorder], I couldn't contain it and I don't have any other way to cope with it. Talking doesn't help – and there's no one to talk to anyway, because no one knows. So the eating disorder's the only thing where I'm with myself, without the help of anyone else on the outside, can help myself. Yes.

Sharon reported how her eating disorder helped her – and her ambivalence towards giving it up:

> The problem here with the eating disorder, is the problem that it's ambivalent. I'm, like, working on it, I really don't want to be sick, but it's one day this and the next day like . . . like one day I said to myself: 'What, you're normal? You'll give up the eating disorder? Then what will happen?' I said:

> 'If I don't have the disease? What will I do?' It's, like, something very concrete, I attribute things to it, I project onto it anything I want, it's hard for me – I vomit, what more do I need? It solves my problems. If I didn't have it I'd have to deal with all these problems.

Consistent with other clients, Grace's eating disorder treatment focused on food and was of little help. For her, the attempt to 'get it rid of it by force' was not a useful approach. She wanted specialized sexual abuse therapy – such as that she had received at a sexual abuse treatment centre:

> When I was ill, it was one of the really good places I experienced. I think that the disease . . . like, the eating disorder is a very difficult disease, on the one hand you have to get rid of it by force, like, because it's really difficult to get out of. On the other, I'm not sure that that's the solution, because the proofs of the disease aren't . . . the recovery [rate] isn't high amongst the girls. I was regarded there [on an eating disorder hospital ward] as a success story, there's not much recovery. And when there's not much recovery and they . . . they check, then you have to check whether something's wrong there. In my opinion, the issue focuses more on the food, and the food isn't the problem, it's a symptom. So I think you need more psychological treatment, more professional, like, let's say, where I am now [a regional sexual abuse treatment centre], to bring something more professional into the hospital, and I see the success [rate] in the hospital, it's not great, it's not great.

Describing the difficulty in focusing on her acute physical state without treating her inner state – which was much worse – in parallel, Evelyne asserted that while treatment designed to cope with severe external symptoms might stop anorexics from dying, it does not prevent another sort of death:

> To link the body and myself, because there's no connection between them . . . and this link has to be, and the very fact that the therapists often tend not to, I mean, they collaborate with the lack of connection, only makes it worse . . . Sometimes people say, like: 'Ok, the situation is very acute'. But inside it's even worse. So if the situation outside is acute, imagine what it's like inside, and . . . if they don't take care of it, then there won't be anything to take care of. Because then if she doesn't die from anorexia she'll die from . . . cutting, or something else.

The women's stories prove the truth of the maxim 'The operation was a success but the patient died' – i.e., the very success in getting rid of the symptoms leads to more dangerous threats, including suicide. As Dawn observed:

> The eating disorder treatment – for me, it didn't help. Not the hospitalization and not Sinai Clinic. But again, probably because I was in such a

different place. I mean, the eating disorder was the symptom of something completely different that just didn't . . . didn't have a place. After I was released, as far as they were concerned I was healthy. I don't think that they would have dealt with it. I mean, they were only concerned with getting me to stop vomiting. Because of that, after I was released from the ward I made a serious suicide attempt. I really wanted to die.

Optimal treatment: 'If there are monsters, then he's the fairy godmother'

The treatment regarded as most effective for eating disorders was that which reduced the symptoms and allowed clients to develop good relations with their therapists. For some of the women, the treatment helped them control their symptoms – not eating and vomiting. Olivia, for example, underwent treatment in a private facility for eating disorders while she was in the army. This helped her stop throwing up and allowed her to understand she was not alone:

OLIVIA: Like, where the eating disorder itself was concerned, it was relatively good treatment, but as far as the other things were concerned, it was a beginning to understand, like, the rest, like, to see that there are other girls who are going through it.

ANAT: Ok, as far as the progress of the disease was concerned, like, of the eating disorder, you're saying that you turned to the army, you were treated at Allan [a specialist eating disorder facility] for about how long? Half a year?

OLIVIA: Between half a year and a year, something like that.

ANAT: And they really helped you, and that actually you succeeded in stopping the. . .

OLIVIA: Yes, yes, yes. I got to the place that I, that I didn't need to vomit anymore and that I . . . you know, there are periods, there are periods when I eat more, there are periods when I eat less. But I no longer . . . the obsession I had, it was, like, no longer . . . like, all this ritual, all the need to do it, all this . . . and it became, like, something that I could control. To some degree.

Lily recounted how she received very good treatment from an eating disorder therapist after having a very bad experience with a previous therapist. She attributed the success of the former to the fact that the therapist accepted her as she was, reinforcing her strengths rather than focusing on the pathology of the eating disorder:

> Two things were really significant for me there. First of all, the person himself, that, like, didn't have – ah – warmth, and he *was* warm, but let's say the previous therapist was really warm and caring and like towards me. And Ian

> was ordinary, like, I [don't] know what to call it, kind. And even when I was silent, he didn't bother me. Like, there was something very unbothersome. Very accepting. Very strengthening. He reinforced me the whole way with my own strengths, like, I worked a lot on my own strengths and not with the . . . my scary things. Because I had, like, some scary parts. But he reinforced my strengths all the time, like, all these things that were also there.

The support she received from her therapist helped her overcome the feelings of guilt, self-anger, and self-disgust she developed as a result of internalizing the sexual abuse:

> Like, all the time he reinforced me from this place. And it was something that did me a lot of good, like, that I'm not a beast, I mean, another thing that was good for me, because I was awfully angry at myself. All the time I was angry with myself, blamed myself, was upset with myself, what not with myself, disgusted with myself, everything. Don't like myself.

Another contributing factor to the success of the treatment, she felt, was that rather than pressing her to recover from the eating disorder her therapist suggested she try and 'befriend' it:

> He didn't tell me that I had to get out of this story of the eating disorder, but what he did tell me was . . . like, he went in another direction. He told me that if I'm doing it and I need it, that's ok, it helps me, and I have to think about how it helps me, and why it does me good, like. 'Don't fight it now', really from another direction. 'Cooperate with it, get to know it, be friends with it', I don't know what to call it. But he wasn't . . . he wasn't fighting me. And that was something that really, really helped me, without question.

The support and acceptance she received from her therapist enabled her to build a relationship of trust with him and talk for the first time about the sexual abuse:

> I mean, at first I didn't understand what he wanted from me at all, like, how not to be angry with myself when I do things that are so disgusting. And what's good about that. Like, there wasn't anything good about it. But, like, with him, I managed to find a way to actually see what was good about it. And then I opened up the subject of the sexual abuse. I mean, like, there the link was created. Like, I needed to feel really, really safe and that when I told it to someone they wouldn't blame me, wouldn't get angry at me.

For Lily, this therapist was the 'fairy godmother' who aided her in recovering from her eating disorder: 'It really, really helped me. 'Til today I'm still enormously grateful to him for this change. It's . . . it's . . . really. As far as I'm concerned, it's, you know, if there are monsters then he's the good beauty, he's really amazing'. Talking about the sexual trauma helped her recover in a relatively short time after years of suffering:

LILY: It was just . . . it amazes me, like, how it's possible to recover in such a relatively short time . . . true, I'd had years and years of suffering before then, but relatively speaking in a short period of time. And I really got out of this madness of all the time thinking that it would never stop. For sure, I'll have it to some degree or other, or this or this . . . nothing, like, nothing. And it seemed to me, like, that could never be.

ANAT: So in that period you stopped vomiting and all the symptoms disappeared?

LILY: All of them. Like . . . the vomiting as well, and . . . but also the way of thinking, I mean, what to eat, how to eat, if I'll vomit afterwards. Like, all this focus around this just wasn't there. Not just, but it wasn't.

Orna similarly spoke of having had a good treatment experience – which has lasted until today – with the psychologist who treated her on a hospital eating disorder ward and then outside that framework. The good relationship was created in the first session when she said that there was 'something' she wanted to talk about and the therapist found a way of dealing with it without pressuring her:

> That, like . . . at the beginning . . . the first session, when I met her I said to her there was something I wanted to talk about. I told her that there's something and she was actually very smart, she said, 'Ok, let's see'. I asked if the treatment could succeed if we didn't talk about something that I . . . she said she didn't know, we'd have to wait and see. That was a very inviting answer, because on one hand she didn't say no, absolutely not, but on the other she didn't say yes, and she like gave me a very true answer. And so that made an opening, like. She was actually the first person I ever talked to about it.

Dawn regarded the therapist who treated her eating disorder as wonderful, both thanks to the specialized eating disorder treatment and to her good relationship with him:

> And really Dr. Palmer's amazing. I mean, I can say. I've had a number of therapists in my life and really he's a great therapist. He's a great eating disorder therapist. In the way he treats it. I mean, that today I understand that it's more 'CBT' [English original] treatment, that then simply didn't have a definition. But generally in the relationship with him, he was the closest to a good substitute father figure.

Thyme related to the fact that the head of the eating ward she was on was a good listener, always ready to talk and give support:

> At Cedar Hills, if you [m.] saw Dr. Palmer in the corridor and said to him: 'Dr. Palmer, I'm sad, my heart hurts, I want to talk with you a bit', he would never push you away. He would also stay until 10 o'clock at night on the ward if necessary. I had much more access to Dr. Palmer. I liked . . . I used to like talking to him. He would also tell me things straight to my face, everything.

Summary: childhood sexual abuse, eating disorders, and appropriate eating disorder treatment

The stories of the women I interviewed and their insights into the treatment they received are important and moving because they accurately describe both its deficiencies and healing aspects. They demonstrate from practical experience the need to adapt eating disorder treatment to the principles guiding the treatment of Complex PTSD? in the wake of childhood abuse. The central points that arose are conceptualized below in light of the professional knowledge we have now accrued in treating survivors of childhood sexual abuse.

Focus on the eating disorder symptoms

One of the significant criticisms is focusing on the eating disorder symptoms rather than on their origin. The blindness prevalent in relation to the traumatic origins of eating disorders impedes treatment because it collaborates with the role played by the eating disorders. Eating disorders are dangerous and destructive coping mechanisms created in the absence of mentalization processes and the presence of dissociative mechanisms. Survivors use them as a way to 'escape' from addressing the abuse – which is secret, nameless, and unspeakable – because thinness, diets, vomiting, etc., are regarded as socially legitimate.

The dissociation even within the therapy frequently perpetuates the need to hold onto the symptoms, thereby interfering with the healing process. In order to alleviate the symptoms, the trauma which gave rise to them must be acknowledged. In the absence of a safe place in which to talk about the abuse and tools with which to give it words, clients feel that no constructive way of bringing up the subject exists. They are thus condemned to employing indirect, largely destructive, ways of coping with their distress.

Forms of treatment that focus on the symptoms and view them as the problem perpetuate this pathology. As indicated in many of the interviews, when the origin of the problem is not addressed even when the symptoms may be alleviated, clients continue to search for other, often destructive, ways of dealing with and making it known – such as addiction to gambling, self-harming, protracted self-destruction, etc. This finding is consistent with the results from studies of treatment assessment from the perspective of the clients. Herein, one of the primary complaints relates to the tendency amongst therapists to focus on the eating disorder symptoms rather than the root of the problem (e.g., Swain-Campbell et al., 2001; Rance et al., 2017).

Getting rid of the symptoms without providing safe alternative coping strategies: 'My anorexia is my chemotherapy'

The criticism voiced regarding the focus on getting rid of the eating disorder symptoms is associated with the understanding that they act as a vital survival mechanism when sexual abuse survivors are still not ready to directly confront the original trauma. This approach must take into account the defence role the symptoms play. In order to eradicate destructive symptoms that serve as coping strategies, treatment must be trauma-oriented. This recognizes the traumatic sources of the symptoms, making room for them within the treatment and helping clients gradually develop safe alternatives. This method demands deep empathic understanding and compassion towards the survivor-victim and the recognition that getting rid of the eating disorder symptoms leaves them, at the beginning of treatment, bereft of defence mechanisms.

Focus on the body and neglect of the psyche

Forms of treatment that focus on weight and food reenact the abuser's use of the victims' bodies for his pleasure, at his whim. This reenacts one of the most traumatic elements of the original trauma. Hereby, he makes them into objects of sexual gratification and dehumanizes them. The women treated in eating disorder frameworks objected to the approach that centred on the body and a virtually exclusive focus on losing/putting on weight or the stopping of vomiting. This criticism is also in line with the feminist critique voiced within the eating disorder field (e.g., Sesan, 1994) regarding the danger of objectification and perception of the woman as her body – an ever-present danger on hospital eating disorder wards.

Reenactment of the misuse of power, authority, and specialist status

Sexual abuse is an exploitation of power, the victims being helpless in the face of the strength and power of the adult perpetrator. Any intervention that takes power away from the hands of the survivors is thus ineffective in effecting any change for good. The women who participated in this study clearly and unambiguously objected to all forms of coercion, punishment, and expulsion, experiencing them as a reenactment of the abuse. Not only do they not heal, but they are frequently harmful and dangerous.

The women described a series of authoritarian procedures and approaches – from rigid admission criteria (such as agreement to family therapy, minimum initial weight, etc.), non-empowering treatment that gave no room to their strengths through to punitive and autocratic steps such as being thrown off the programme/ward/centre for not abiding by the regulations, detention in a calming-down room, restraint, and forced feeding. From the minute they became candidates for treatment, they experienced an inappropriate use of power and authority. This not only reenacted the sexual abuse setting but also on occasion constituted a form of revictimization.

The need to deal with women and girls who harm themselves in dangerous ways poses a real challenge to eating disorder therapists. While some aggressive interventions may be necessary in order to save lives, it remains important to revisit such procedures in order to find ways that are more sensitive to the danger of reenactment to which abuse survivors are so exposed.

Invasiveness and lack of respect for privacy

In the wake of childhood sexual abuse, survivors fail to develop normative physical and identity boundaries, the violence invasion of the body and soul causing serious mental damage. One of the consequences is oversensitivity to any form of procedure that reminds them of the invasive abuse. These processes – lack of privacy in the bathroom, for example – are experienced by clients as traumatic and injurious, reenacting the original trauma. On some wards, the lack of respect for privacy also takes the form of mass intake interviews at which clients are forced to reveal intimate personal details to therapists from various units, including psychiatrists, psychologists, social workers, occupational therapists, etc., and students from diverse caring-profession fields. The message they receive is clear: 'Even here there's no respect for your privacy. Even here, we possess the authority, on the basis of our (professional) status, not to respect the boundaries of your privacy'.

Focus on pathology rather than the survivor's personal strengths

Treatment methods that focus on the pathology of the eating disorder and the other self-destructive forms of behaviour characteristic of those sexually abused as children cause great damage and perpetuate clients' already low self-image. In several of the interviews, this focus even encouraged suicidal attempts. The women also voiced their yearning for a treatment that would empower them – despite their destructive symptoms – and give them strength, love, support, and attention. Those defined as good treatments prominently featured a focus on strengths rather than pathology.

Survivors of childhood sexual abuse frequently come to therapy with a 'shopping list' of severe and complex symptoms and diagnostic labels. Their serious and complex conditions and the difficulty of treating these with conventional methods prompt therapists into branding them with diagnostic labels. These often predict a poor prognosis and focus on their pathology. In such cases, it is very tempting to give up and despair of any form of recovery. One of the guiding principles for treating CPTSD thus stresses the importance of recognizing strengths and recovery even with clients suffering from severe trauma. This principle constitutes the basis for creating a therapeutic alliance with clients in extreme conditions caused by early relational trauma (Herman, 2009).

'Nodding therapists'

Another recurring theme was the clients' experience of their therapists as indifferent, uncaring, and passive. The traditional psychodynamic methods of treatment are based on opacity and client distance in order to allow for transference that gives the therapists a better understanding of their clients' inner worlds and unconscious early relations. In psychoanalysis, transference and projection play a central role in the therapeutic process, enabling identification of unconscious conflicts, memories, and feelings which can then be treated.

Today, we now know that these forms of treatment are unsuitable for treating childhood sexual abuse survivors, this kind of trauma by definition including an environment they experience as indifferent, disbelieving, disavowing, and disregarding. Therapists in this tradition are thus experienced by clients as uninterested in their fate. The professional literature regarding treatment of childhood sexual abuse highlights the central role played by the therapeutic alliance as providing a corrective experience by abjuring aggressive and authoritarian on the one hand and neutral and distancing attitudes on the other.

An understanding of the dynamics of childhood abuse indicates that if the victim is a child and the perpetrator, as is most commonly the case, is a parent, a close family member, or a primary role model such as a teacher, coach, or religious leader, the absence of a protective parent or the presence of a passive bystander is felt palpably as the presence of the perpetrator. Abuse is compounded by neglect when others fail to notice or intervene (Herman, 2009, p. xiv). Women who have experienced indifference and disregard on the part of central primary-caretaker figures in their lives require active, engaged, involved, and caring therapists.

'Not in our school': transfer of clients from one framework to another

One of the disturbing phenomena that arose in some of the women's stories was their transfer from treatment framework to another after being diagnosed with problems in whose treatment the facility did not specialize. This theme recurred in the context of both eating disorder and sexual abuse treatment centres. Some of the women had been transferred several times from eating disorder frameworks to psychiatric wards or rape crisis centres. Clients suffering from eating disorders were not accepted by rape crisis centres because the latter had no experience in treating eating disorders or sent to rape crisis centres because the eating disorder clinic could not treat the sexual abuse trauma. This removal from treatment perpetuated their sense of worthlessness and blame, rejection, and neglect caused by the original trauma.

Eating disorders are among the well-known consequences of childhood sexual abuse. The specialized treatment of both must therefore be integrated and made available at the same time. In the current situation, in which two separate fields of expertise exist that do not seek to integrate, clients suffer serious damage that reenacts elements of the early trauma. Ignoring the complexity of the symptoms and the close link between them, the unintegrated approaches taken today tend to reinforce the accepted classifications of independent disorders and comorbidity rather than regarding and treating them as a single cluster.

The rationale behind transferring clients from one centre to another is based on the claim that each lacks the specialized knowledge necessary to deal with certain symptoms. This attitude reenacts splits and dissociation in clients, reinforcing their sense of rejection and lack of worth. As we shall see in Chapters 9 and 11, CPTSD treatment based on expertise in treating the whole range of symptoms is thus the most effective approach.

Conclusion

In light of the findings of this study – which joins an expanding and growing body of knowledge relating to the association between childhood sexual abuse and eating disorders – the great challenge the latter field faces is the proper way to treat clients at serious risk in such a way as not to reenact the original trauma. The questions that must be addressed are: Do emergency situations justify the use of aggressive and authoritarian approaches? How can treatment methods be democratized and humanized so as to approximate the guidelines recommended for working with clients sexually abused in their childhood (Davies & Frawley, 1994; Courtois, 1997; Herman, 1997)? To what extent should life-threatening situations influence the treatment spectrum? How can we integrate both specialized sexual abuse and eating disorder treatments?

Notes

1 The difficulties attendant upon family therapy may be attributed to childhood sexual abuse perpetrated by family members: see section 'Family therapy and mother/daughter-relations treatment'.
2 Personal communication, 2.9.2010.
3 For vicarious trauma, see Chapter 10.

4 My clinical work with childhood sexual abuse victims also frequently brings me into contact with their 'bell jar', whose sensing requires skill and empathic understanding due to its transparency.
5 Many childhood sexual abuse survivors suffer from a sense of inner 'homelessness', the home being the site of the abuse and thus a dangerous rather than a safe place.

References

Ajzenstadt, M., Soffer, M., & Steinberg, O. (2010). *In prison I rest: Women prisoners beyond the walls*. Bnei Brak: Hakibbutz Hameuchad (Hebrew).

Bell, L. (2003). What we can learn from consumer studies and qualitative research in the treatment of eating disorders? *Eating and Weight Disorders*, *8*(3), 181–187.

Bruch, H. (1974). The perils of behavior modification in treatment of anorexia nervosa. *Journal of the American Medical Association*, *230*, 1419–1422.

Bruch, H. (1982). Anorexia nervosa: Therapy and theory. *American Journal of Psychiatry*, *139*, 1531–1538.

Chesler, P. (1972). *Women and madness*. New York, NY: Avon.

Courtois, C. A. (1997). Healing the incest wound: A treatment update with attention to recovered-memory issues. *American Journal of Psychotherapy*, *51*(4), 464–496.

Courtois, C. A., & Ford, J. D. (2009). *Treating complex stress disorders*. New York, NY: Guilford Press.

Davies, J., & Frawley, M. (1994). *Treating the adult survivor of childhood sexual abuse: A psychoanalytic perspective*. New York, NY: Basic Books.

de la Rie, S., Noordenbos, G., Donker, M., & van Furth, E. (2006). Evaluating the treatment of eating disorders from the patient's perspective. *International Journal of Eating Disorders*, *39*(8), 667–676.

Goldstein, A., & Katz-Charny, J. (2004). Therapy with families that have experienced sexual abuse. In Z. Seligman & Z. Solomon (Eds.), *Critical and clinical perspectives on incest* (pp. 278–301). Tel Aviv: Hakibbutz Hameuchad and Tel Aviv University Publishing House (Hebrew).

Gore, S. A., Vander Wal, J. S., & Thelen, M. H. (2001). Treatment of eating disorders in children and adolescents. In J. K. Thompson & L. Smolak (Eds.), *Body image, eating disorders, and obesity in youth* (pp. 293–311). Washington, DC: American Psychological Association.

Greenspan, M. (1983). *A new approach to women and therapy*. New York: McGraw-Hill.

Gulliksen, K. S., Espeset, E., Nordbø, R. H., Skårderud, F., Geller, J., & Holte, A. (2012). Preferred therapist characteristics in treatment of anorexia nervosa: The patient's perspective. *International Journal of Eating Disorders*, *45*(8), 932–941.

Herman, J. L. (1997). *Trauma and recovery*. New York, NY: Basic Books.

Herman, J. L. (2009). Foreword. In C. A. Courtois & J. D. Ford (Eds.), *Treating complex traumatic stress disorders* (pp. xiii–xvii). New York, NY: Guildford Press.

Kearney-Cooke, A., & Striegel-Moore, R. H. (1996). Treatment of childhood sexual abuse in anorexia nervosa and bulimia nervosa: A feminist psychodynamic approach. In M. F. Schwartz & L. Cohn (Eds.), *Sexual abuse and eating disorders* (pp. 155–175). Bristol, PA: Brunner/Mazel.

Newton, T., Robinson, P., & Hartley, P. (1993). Treatment for eating disorders in the United Kingdom, Part 2: Experience of treatment: A survey of numbers of the eating disorders association. *Eating Disorders Review*, *1*, 11–21.

NIMH (National Institute of Mental Health). (2008). *What are eating disorders?* Retrieved October 22, 2017, from www.nimh.nih/health/topics/eating disorders?/index.shtml

Orbach, S. (1986). *Hunger strike: The anorectic's struggle as a metaphor for our age*. Harmondsworth: Penguin.

Rance, N., Moller, N. P., & Clarke, V. (2017). 'Eating disorders are not about food, they're about life': Client perspectives on anorexia nervosa treatment, *Journal of Health Psychology, 22*(5), 582–594.

Rosenvinge, J. H., & Klusmeier, A. K. (2000). Treatment for eating disorders from a patient-satisfaction perspective: A Norwegian replication of a British study. *European Eating Disorders Review, 8*, 293–300.

Sesan, R. (1994). Feminist inpatient treatment for eating disorders: An oxymoron? In P. Fallon, M. A. Katzman, & S. C. Wooley (Eds.), *Feminist perspectives of eating disorders* (pp. 251–271). New York, NY: Guilford Press.

Swain-Campbell, N. R., Surgenor, L. J., & Snell, D. L. (2001). An analysis of consumer perspectives following contact with an eating disorder service. *Australian and New Zealand Journal of Psychiatry, 35*, 99–103.

Tierney, S. (2008). The individual within a condition: A qualitative study of young people's reflecting on being treated for anorexia nervosa. *Journal of the American Psychiatric Nurses' Association, 13*, 368–375.

Vandereycken, W. (1985). Inpatient treatment of anorexia nervosa: Some research-guided changes. *Journal of Psychiatric Research, 19*, 413–422.

Vandereycken, W., & Vansteenkiste, M. (2009). Let eating disorder patients decide: Providing choice may reduce early drop-out from inpatient treatment. *European Eating Disorders Review, 17*, 177–183.

Woodside, B. D. (2005). Treatment of anorexia nervosa: More questions than answers. *International Journal of Eating Disorders, 37*, 541–542.

Wooley, S. C. (1994). Sexual abuse and eating disorders: The concealed debate. In P. Fallon., M. A. Katzman., & S. C. Wooley (Eds.), *Feminist perspectives on eating disorders* (pp. 171–211). New York, NY: Guilford Press.

Chapter 8

Specialist sexual abuse treatment

In recent years, specialist treatment of the survivors of childhood sexual abuse has begun to be offered in centres devoted to treating this population. Eating disorders constituting one of the most prominent symptoms of childhood sexual abuse, some of the women and girls who suffer from them seek help at these facilities rather than at specialist eating disorder clinics.

Several of the women I interviewed for my study having been treated in both frameworks, they were able to compare them. Their accounts clearly demonstrate that they found the specialized sexual abuse treatment more beneficial and effective. This chapter reviews the principles of childhood sexual abuse treatment and examines client experiences in childhood sexual abuse centres.

Childhood sexual abuse treatment

Models for treating childhood sexual trauma began emerging in the 1980s in the wake of the rise in public and professional awareness of the problem due to exposure of the epidemic and documentation of the severe mental and social damages it causes (Courtois, 1997). Between the mid-1980s and early 1990s, several models were proposed, constituting the 'first generation' of childhood sexual abuse treatment programmes (e.g., Courtois, 1988; Herman, 1997; Briere, 1989, 1992). These highlighted the treatment of the effects of trauma, making the abuse a significant – if not exclusive – focus. This approach sharply contrasted with the prevalent method during this period, which ignored or dismissed reports of abuse as wishful thinking or childish fantasies (Courtois, 1997).

Significant progress has occurred since then, accelerated by accumulating clinical experience in treating survivors, more sophisticated diagnostic classifications (including a broader identification of personality-structure disorders, and dissociative responses linked to ongoing childhood trauma), and the incorporation of additional approaches. Today, we already have a 'second generation' model (Courtois, 1997) for treating survivors of childhood sexual abuse. While this largely preserves the original focus on post-traumatic symptoms, its horizons are broader, addressing other life-events, object relations, and personality structure and more clearly defining treatment stages. It also takes into account the issues of recovered vs. unbroken memories and suspected vs. certain abuse (e.g., Herman, 1997; Courtois, 1997; Davies & Frawley, 1994; Putnam, 1989). Although acknowledging the need to work through the trauma, this model also pays attention to self-development and identity-formation, object relations, attachment style, and cognitive and emotional schema, seeking to stabilize moods and symptoms and encourage the development of self-management skills (Courtois, 1997). Themes and questions associated with the abuse, its destructive dynamics, and impact are treated throughout the process in parallel with other issues, the abuse only being directly addressed after clients have achieved a sufficient degree of stability and gained skills and ego strengths (Courtois, 1997).

This collaborative form of treatment seeks to empower the client (Courtois, 1997) in the wake of the feeling of helplessness and disconnection from the abuse. Its goal is to help survivors regain control and create new, healthy relationships. It is thus based on the principles of restoring power to the victims, reducing isolation, diminishing helplessness by increasing range of choice, and countering the dynamics of dominance (Herman, 1997).

The professional literature stresses the importance of developing a therapeutic alliance. Childhood sexual abuse survivors lack a basic trust in people and themselves and any belief that relationships can be supportive rather than exploitative. They fear intimacy, closeness, warmth, human contact, and intrusion. They possess a significantly distorted view of love relations, finding difficulty with boundaries and identifying with the abuser. They are also the subject of anger attacks, aggressive behaviour, and violence, repeatedly finding themselves in the role of victim (Schwartz, 2000). Therapists must therefore nurture a therapeutic alliance based on collaboration, persuasion vs. coercion, ideas vs. force, mutuality vs. authoritarianism. They must only use the power that lies in their hands to foster the client's recovery, resisting any temptation to misuse it. These principles – which are applicable to every therapeutic setting – are of particular significance when dealing with clients suffering from the effects of arbitrary and exploitative power (Schwartz, 2000). Survivors of childhood sexual abuse were the object of the misuse of power and control and were betrayed by those closest to them. Experiencing an authority figure who is humane, generous, non-retributive and non-punitive, open to feedback and interested in change can thus in and of itself be of great comfort and deeply healing (Schwartz, 2000). Therapists must thus endeavour to create an environment of joint investigation, equality, and mutual influence. At the same time, this must not impinge on the asymmetric aspects of the therapeutic relationship. In order to challenge old attachment styles and forge new ones, they must strive towards democratizing and humanizing the therapy rather than pulling rank by wielding sovereign authority or appealing to professional expertise.

The stories of women treated in sexual abuse centres

> . . . a corrective, like . . . for all the things I'd always looked for and didn't have.
>
> —Evelyne

The most prominent theme in the accounts of the women I interviewed was their belief that the sexual abuse treatment was most appropriate to their needs, addressing the root of the problem rather than merely the symptoms. The women described the treatment approach taken in sexual abuse centres as more empowering and mutual than what they received in eating disorder or other treatment frameworks.The flexible boundaries herein enabled them to deal with the past trauma, mobilizing their cooperation in facing their self-destructive tendencies. Several of the women had previously been treated at eating disorder centres or received general forms of treatment, only later seeking help at sexual abuse specialist centres. Many of these described the treatment at sexual abuse centres as constituting a corrective experience to what they endured in other treatment settings. In their opinion, the abuse constituting the root of their problems, treatment of the trauma itself was far more significant than treatment of the symptoms. The feeling of being related to on a more equal and mutual basis also directly contributed to the success and effectiveness of the treatment.

Another central theme that arose was the feeling of being better understood and less scared of being judged for their dangerous or destructive behaviour in sexual abuse centres. One of the recurrent motifs was the feeling of being at 'home'.[1] Evelyne, for example, who had experience on eating disorder wards, said that, being in a bad state and wanting help, she sought a framework that would not focus on her eating disorder:

> Precisely in the last year, I mean, a year and a half ago, I began going to A Home of Your Own. When I got there I was already feeling that I was falling, I mean, physically as well. And somewhere, like, yes, I wanted treatment, but I didn't want treatment for the eating disorder.

The progress she made during the year she was at A Home of Your Own included both an increased capacity to trust people and a greater ability to talk about the abuse:

> Yes, in lots of way this was the right place for me. In this year, I've done lots of things that I hadn't dared to before. And who knows how many more years it'll take me to do them. Both with regard to trusting people and with regard to opening up things. That's still difficult, but, like, it's much better than it was before I got to A Home of Your Own.

She attributed this progress to the fact that her therapists were attentive, caring, and willing to give her space. Reading between the lines, it is clear that the treatment was marked by mutuality, equality, and empowerment, the therapists adjusting themselves to her needs and willing to acknowledge mistakes and seek to emend them. This allowed Evelyne to experience the treatment as corrective:

ANAT: What, what enabled you, like? What allowed you to open up, to trust?

EVELYNE: Really, when I got to A Home of Your Own, I was more able lots of times to say what I needed. Which is also something I never dared to do before. And the fact that lots of times they actually listened to me. I mean, their ability, but listening, caring, and trying to be where I was, even when they made mistakes, they really tried to go back and understand what had been wrong, what they could correct, what they could change, what could help. And I think that that's something I just never had with other people, like . . . so it really helped me to trust. And the place itself was very, I mean, a very calming environment isn't the word for it, but very supportive, and very protective, and it was something of a corrective, like . . . for all the things I'd always looked for and didn't have.

Although A Home of Your Own did not tolerate self-destructive and dangerous behaviour, unlike during her eating disorder treatment Evelyne felt the boundaries there were flexible. This allowed her to relinquish some of her worst symptoms without feeling any coercion:

> So as far as I'm concerned now, to give up and cut without restraint or not eat to the point of weighing nothing, is not an option. Because I know that then I'll have to give this place up, I mean, I'll be forced to relinquish it, because if I'm in an acute state physically they'll hospitalize me. And I'm not ready for that. Like, I'm not ready to give up on that, because right now it's working for me. So even if that sometimes means surrendering something, not necessarily from a place of submission. That's really something that's changed.

Today, she has more freedom of movement to cope with the eating disorder, the therapists at A Home of Your Own knowing that if they push her she becomes stubborn and eats less:

> I mean, because at A Home of Your Own, if today I choose to eat, then it's me choosing to eat. I mean, they really try right now to give me the . . . the space, like, they don't push me too much. Because they know that only makes me worse. Like, I'll go and eat less. And so yes, there're lots of times that I chose to come and be part of it, because I understand that it's good to let others be in peace in order to preserve the. . . (laughs) to preserve my

> right to come here. And as far as I'm concerned it is a right, so I'm going to exercise it.

Naomi, who was treated by a therapist at a sexual abuse clinic after treatment by a non-sexual abuse specialist therapist, described the difference between the two:

> Like, I was in treatment with two therapists. One was for three months, the other for 2½ years, something like that, no . . . and with the first, it was very much a system of, like, we'd sit facing one another and until I opened my mouth nothing would happen . . . and with the second, she was someone I got to through the [rape crisis] centre, an amazing woman. And at the first session, she said to me: 'So tell me why you're here'. I just shot it all out, the hour was over, and I went home.

Poppy underwent numerous forms of psychological treatment from a young age, finally ending up at a sexual abuse centre. Here, in contrast to her previous experiences, the therapists had specialist training in treatment childhood sexual abuse. At the time of the interview, she was being treated by the head of the sexual abuse centre. Neither the abuse nor the eating disorder ever came up in her previous treatments. Today, she is beginning to talk about both, although still finding it difficult:

> I was in treatment, but we never . . . nothing ever opened up, I never talked about the abuse, I never talked about the . . . about the . . . about the . . . eating disorder, I only talked with Doreen at Roods [a sexual abuse treatment centre]. So today I'm being treated there, I think a year or something, but it's treatment that, every time we touch on something small and I, there's a sort of regression on my part, because I go backwards, because it scares me, because I feel it's not the right thing at the moment.

Never turning for help to any eating disorder centre because of her trust issues, she had no faith in the establishment or therapists, all of which had let her down:

ANAT: I mean, you didn't think to go to an eating disorder specialist?

POPPY: No, I don't trust the establishment, I don't trust therapists, I don't trust . . . I mean, until I got to Doreen, as far as I was concerned, they'd all let me down.

She regarded her present treatment as a 'last resort' in the light of her despair and disappointment and feeling that no one up to that point had really cared about her. She thus understood women who do not seek treatment because of their deep distrust of therapists stemming from self-harm on the one hand and a sense of being let down by professionals on the other:

> There was never anyone who really cared enough about me to do something with it, so ... no, to turn to them? I won't do that ... really not. And even when I got to Doreen, it was, I was simply in despair, it was a period when I was simply in despair, I got to her when I was already really tired. And it was, it was a sort of 'Ok, this is the last chance'. Fortunately, it turned out well ... yes, but ... but ... I can understand girls who ... women who don't, who don't get treatment, like my sister.

Her present treatment, which she experienced as supportive and good, was helping her work through the sexual abuse for the first time, despite her difficulty in talking about it:

> However much I say that I don't talk about it, but Doreen ... when I do talk about it with her, she's always telling me that it's amazing how much I remember. I mean, that I told her about the first time, I told her details even about what I was wearing, I remember everything ... and maybe again, I remember what it's convenient to remember, parts. In this year, since I've been with Doreen, I've talked about it more than ever before. True, I don't go into ... still can't really open everything up, but I at least ... talk. Before then ... before then I was silent.

Before this therapy, she had suffered from severe physical symptoms, being hospitalized on numerous occasions. Today, her physical and mental state have both greatly improved due to the treatment:

> Really, at the beginning, I was always in hospital. And today, I really ... even if I'm sick, I'm sick for a day, two, and then I get over it. I'm much stronger physically, mentally. And lots of time, I do see the good in myself, which is something that's very ... it's not, not ... not trivial. This year, I've come a way, a really good and long way, with Doreen's help, it's been simply amazing.

For the first time in her life, she felt someone truly understood her and was not judging her, even when she spoke about very bad behaviours. The sexual abuse specialist conceptualized the symptoms characteristic of childhood sexual abuse that Poppy exhibited, such as promiscuity, thereby helping her feel less blemished and more understandable to herself. This was the first time she had felt at 'home':

> Who really understands me. Because when I talk about things, she really, really gets me. And when I ... sometimes I'm afraid of telling her something,

> for example when I was with lots of men, that she'll say I'm a prostitute, as others did. But . . . she really saw it from the other side, that my body simply became an instrument. And it's amazing that I have this place. The very fact that I have this home. This place, to come and tell her this. I've never told anyone what I feel or what I think, because what I felt or thought was never important enough.

Ruth had never sought treatment, only going to a rape crisis centre several years after being raped – an event that may be perceived as revictimization. She was afraid she would be judged for not having escaped from the abuse. This fear was assuaged in a session with the person in charge of accompanying victims to trial hearings, which she experienced as positive: 'With Rina, I felt, like, with her, she wasn't judging me'. This contact with the rape crisis centre led to her participation in a support group for sexual assault victims, which helped her understand her self-destructive behaviour:

> I went to a rape crisis centre because I wanted to understand things about myself better, why I do certain things, why I don't do certain things today . . . unhealthy sex, ah, all sorts of things, why I'm self-destructive. I'm really self-destructive.

She found the group to be a very positive experience, helping her to know she was not alone. She also spoke of the feeling of being at 'home' as a corrective experience:

> I feel that it's not enough, that I want more . . . that I've not yet dealt with everything enough. The group gave me a whole lot. To know I'm not alone. To know that there are other girls like me. Just I know that to hear, to accept another direction, to leave stronger, to know that I have another home.

Grace, who was treated for many years in an eating disorder framework, was prompted by a friend who had also been abused to go a sexual abuse centre. She experienced this as a very different type of therapy to than she had had in the past:

> So I started to talk and here and there she suddenly told me about the abuse, and ok, like, I was also abused, and so she told me about her treatment there. I never even knew it existed. And so she told me, like, 'You have to go, like, there's nothing like it, like, it's different from all the other places I've been to . . .' I told her: 'But I'm in therapy, I've had treatments'. 'No, it's different, it's different'. And it sounded, like, ok, you know, there's the natural thing of being in love with therapy, and getting attached. The moment you're in therapy, you're sure it's the best and your therapist is the

> best. But I tried it. I said, I'm going to try. And today I can say that it really is different to anything else I'd tried, because they focus on this specific thing. So their tools are much more . . . the treatment is easier.

Through this treatment, she was able to work through the sexual abuse and find confidence as a person, despite her initial difficulty in developing a relationship of trust. She felt that the therapist invested a great effort in building a relationship that would allow her to talk about the abuse:

> Both working through the abuse and finding confidence as a person, because of the boundaries there. I think it's meant to begin with trust in the relationship, like all relationships. And for her, too, she made a great effort. I mean, I couldn't look her in the eyes, couldn't . . . lots of things. I mean, a whole year we were a chair, back to back, because . . . because there was something in her gaze, or how she walked, or something made me . . . or in the need not to be seen, my truth, don't know what.

This therapist sought to accommodate herself to Grace and her resistance to therapy, on occasion taking unusual steps such as sitting in the garden with her:

> She had huge amounts of patience with me. And again, I'm not sure that anyone else would have . . . she told me, like, that there was some situation in which they sat in a staff meeting and someone said: 'What, I wouldn't do that, let's say, sit with her in the garden, and I'm not someone who . . .' and she decided that she would. At a later stage, she told me that she'd gained from it, like, she'd gained and I'd gained. It showed me with respect to my progress that I feel a huge amount of progress and development.

In contrast to previous therapists, she also felt that this one was invested in her – thereby helping her to invest in herself: 'She didn't give up on me, and I, it made me not give up on myself. Because – because people have given up on me all my life. So this is something that you see in retrospect and you say, wow, she did something!'

Analysing the reasons why this therapy had been successful, she adduced first of all the feeling that the therapist was willing to accept her where others had not because she understood the symptoms of the abuse: 'I assume that . . . that she could take me differently, from the moment she understood the symptoms, the . . . I'm not sure that a therapist outside really knows how to take things like this'. She experienced the sexual abuse centre as a place that exhibited sensitivity to the abuse and knew how to approach and understand it: 'So I assume that there are lots of things there, that they know how to approach better, there's the, more sensitivity, more sensitivity to me, more understanding of me'.

Note

1 This is associated with the feeling of homelessness characteristic of childhood sexual abuse survivors, who were victimized precisely in a place supposed to be warm and protective – within the bosom of the family home.

References

Briere, J. (1989). *Therapy for adults molested as children*. New York, NY: Springer.

Briere, J. (1992). *Child abuse trauma: Theory and treatment of the lasting effects*. Newbury Park, CA: Sage Publications.

Courtois, C. A. (1988). *Healing the incest wound: Adult survivors in therapy*. New York, NY: W.W. Norton.

Courtois, C. A. (1997). Healing the incest wound: A treatment update with attention to recovered-memory issues. *American Journal of Psychotherapy, 51*(4), 464–496.

Davies, J., & Frawley, M. (1994). *Treating the adult survivor of childhood sexual abuse: A psychoanalytic perspective*. New York, NY: Basic Books.

Herman, J. L. (1997). *Trauma and recovery*. New York, NY: Basic Books.

Putnam, F. W. (1989). *Diagnosis and treatment of multiple personality disorder*. New York, NY: Guilford Press.

Schwartz, H. (2000). *Dialogues with forgotten voices: Relational perspectives on child abuse trauma and treatment of dissociative disorders*. New York, NY: Basic Books.

Part III

A new diagnosis and treatment proposal

Introduction

Although many women who suffer from severe eating disorders were sexually abused as children, the eating disorder field has been very slow to recognize the traumatic history of such clients. This fact is evidenced by the diagnoses given, which brand women as ill without acknowledging that their 'disease' is an expression of post-traumatic distress. The forms of treatment offered thus not only are not commensurate with but frequently conflict with the principles of the treatment of childhood sexual abuse.

Eating disorders are an expression of the post-traumatic distress caused by childhood sexual abuse, developing hand in hand with numerous other symptoms of childhood sexual trauma – identity disorders, attachment/relational disorders, personality disorders, dissociative disorders, addictions, self-destructive behaviour, etc. These function as survival and coping strategies for the survivors of childhood sexual abuse. The following chapter examines the way in which these mechanisms have changed form down the generations, reflecting the 'diagnosis' and 'treatment' women receive in hegemonic patriarchal society.

The accounts of the women I interviewed indicate that the diagnosis and treatment of eating disorders without reference to the traumatic sources of the problem exacerbate their condition, perpetuating the camouflaging of its roots. The women with whom I talked felt that the diagnosis of eating disorder distracted attention from the childhood sexual abuse that lay at its root, thereby turning the symptom into the problem. The fact that the disease was placed at the centre of the diagnostic and therapeutic discourses prompted them to further dissociate themselves from the abuse. This interfered with their recovery process. As Shirley noted, 'It's like liver cancer that's not treated, only the metastases being treated rather than the cancer itself'. This type of diagnosis collaborates with the disavowing and dissociative parts of the victim's mind. Although research demonstrates that the majority of psychiatric inpatients have a history of molestation, abuse, or abandonment by a caregiver, the consequences of adverse childhood experiences constituting the single largest public-health problem in the United States (Fellitti et al., 1998) and likely worldwide, vastly more funding is available for studying the genetic components of mental illness than preventing and treating the long-term effects of child abuse and neglect (van der Kolk, 2009).

The question that thus arises is whether it is right to classify women abused in childhood as suffering from eating disorders when they exhibit symptoms characteristic of a severe, protracted, chronic trauma that occurred at a decisive developmental stage in their lives. Eating disorders are one component of a vast array of complex symptoms that must be diagnosed and treated as a single entity. The very fact of diagnosing eating disorders as an independent disease – a separate mental disorder – is problematic, forming just one more example of the 'Latin names' (Appignanesi, 2008) given to female 'madness'. Distancing and disguising the traumatic sources of the problem, these dictate forms of treatment that perpetuate the social control and oppression of women.

When the aetiology of the trauma is neither diagnosed nor treated, survivors receive diverse diagnoses due to the complex problems from which they suffer. When their various symptoms are not understood as 'a coherent formulation of the consequence of child sexual abuse', in Herman's definition of CPTSD, they tend to be sent for eating disorder treatment as anorexics, bulimics, binge-eaters, etc. Here, they are diagnosed as suffering from 'comorbid' symptoms due to their accompanying symptoms – the well-known and predictable effects of childhood sexual abuse. In the absence of a proper and comprehensive diagnosis of complex trauma, many are given false and stigmatizing diagnoses, leading to inappropriate and at times even detrimental treatment.

This part of the book examines the link between women, madness, and childhood sexual abuse, demonstrating the way in which diverse manifestations of 'madness' amongst women are in fact the characteristic symptoms of childhood sexual abuse. I suggest that Complex PTSD (CPTSD) is the best and most appropriate diagnosis for such women and should replace branding diagnoses that ignore their traumatic history. One of the latter is eating disorders, which is defined as a separate, independent disorder rather than as one symptom along the spectrum of Complex Post-Traumatic Stress Disorder. A CPTSD diagnosis also leads to better, more appropriate, and more effective forms of treatment for survivors of childhood sexual abuse. Reviewing specialized forms of CPTSD treatment, this part also analyses the impact of hard and challenging treatments on therapists and offers a trauma-oriented model for the treatment of CPTSD.

References

Appignanesi, L. (2008). *Mad, bad and sad: A history of women and the mind doctors from 1800 to the present*. Londen: Virago.

Fellitti, V. J., Anda, R. F., Nordenberg, D., Williamson, D. F., Spitz, A. M., Edwards, V. et al. (1998). Relationship of childhood abuse and household dysfunction to many of the leading causes of death in adults: The Adverse Childhood Experiences (ACE) study. *American Journal of Preventive Medicine, 14*(4), 245–258.

van der Kolk, B. (2009). Afterword. In C.A. Courtois & J. D. Ford (Eds.), *Treating complex stress disorders* (pp. 455–466). New York, NY: Guilford Press.

Chapter 9

Women, 'madness', and a new diagnosis

As we have seen in the preceding chapters, the perception of the current epidemic of childhood sexual abuse is the latest episode in the ongoing story of female madness. Beginning with witches and demon-possessed women in the Middle Ages, this shifted to female hysterics during the Victorian era and has now become borderline personality disorder, anorexia nervosa, bulimia nervosa, etc.[1] Mania, melancholy, neuroticism, delusions, aberrant acts, visual and auditory hallucinations, phobias, fears, sleep disorders, dissociation, communication with spirits and imaginary friends, addictions, self-harm, and self-starvation are all characters in this drama of female mental health. In their Latin and Greek forms, these became diagnoses such as melancholy, hysteria, anorexia, etc. – frequently shortened into scientific abbreviations: AN, BN, BPD, DID, ADHD, OCD, etc. (Appignanesi, 2008). Our narrative has encompassed all these terms and their link with childhood sexual abuse.

Allie Light, who directed the film *Dialogues with Madwomen* (1994), interviewed seven women diagnosed as mentally ill and hospitalized on psychiatric wards. Having spent time on one for post-partum depression herself, she added her voice to those who spoke of the sexual abuse they had suffered in childhood, painting a dark picture of the attitude the psychiatric establishment takes towards mentally ill women. When she told her psychiatrist that, none of the women in her family ever having attended college, her dream was to be the first in the family to do so, he burst out laughing and told her that she would have to learn to cook a turkey before dreaming of going to college. 'One weekend he told me I could go home if I promised to bake a turkey. The next weekend I could go home if I promised to mop all the floors'. Despite his predictions, Light attended college, lecturing for many years in the Department of Women's Studies. In her view, fluent women public speakers in the 1950s – not to speak of those who were sexually active – were frequently labelled as mad.

The mental health field is strewn with examples of stigmatization, discrimination, and double standards in clinical practice (Chesler, 1972). Early on, feminist critics of the mental health system revealed how diagnoses serve as a means of punishing and tainting women who do not conform to male interest. In the 1960s and '70s, the feminist movement helped raise awareness in the Western world of the frightening scale of childhood sexual exploitation and the mental damage it causes. Feminist theoreticians have also demonstrated the way in which women use their bodies to protest against female oppression. Phyllis Chesler's (1972) remark that much of the 'insane' female behaviour manifested today represents an attempt by socially powerless individuals to unify the body and emotions remains true today.

The degree to which the fact that traumatic history is characteristic of most psychiatric patients – particularly women – is ignored today is nonetheless quite astonishing. Childhood exposure to interpersonal traumatic stressors such as childhood sexual abuse is so prevalent that it has been labelled the 'silent epidemic' (Kaffman, 2009). A third of all children across the globe are estimated to have been abused physically, one in every four girls and one of every five boys being sexually abused (United Nations, 2006). In the United States, the damage childhood abuse causes is considered to be the most significant and pressing current public-health problem of the day (D'Andrea, Ford, Stolbach, Spinazzola, & van der Kolk, 2012).

According to the most up-do-date professional literature on trauma, interpersonal childhood trauma gives rise to a range of symptoms, including co-existing severe and chronic disorders – emotional dysregulation, drive-control disorders, attention and cognitive disorders, dissociative disorders, conduct disorders, and interpersonal-relationship disorders. This spectrum of symptoms has yet to be defined in the DSM.

The findings of this study, which examined the link between childhood sexual abuse and eating disorders from the perspective of the women themselves, join the growing protest from various directions against 'establishment' psychiatric diagnoses and the feminist literature addressing the politics of diagnosis.[2] The stories of the women I interviewed closely correspond to Freud's patients, suggesting – as Freud initially concluded – that the link between childhood sexual abuse and mental disorders in adulthood is tantamount to the 'discovery of a *caput Nili* in neuropathology' (1995, p. 103). The severe post-traumatic symptoms to which sexual abuse gives rise have taken various forms throughout history in line with the sociocultural norms of the period. In this chapter, we shall see how the view of contemporary eating disorders as a 'female mental disease' constitutes another link in the long chain of branding diagnoses attached by the male hegemonic establishment to symptoms caused by childhood sexual trauma. I thus suggest that CPTSD is a much more appropriate diagnosis than the stigma of female 'madness' and the best prognosis for successful and effective integrative treatment and recovery.

Eating disorders, hysteria, and 'madness' in women

> There's also the matter of thinness, thin is beautiful. Like, a sort of framing story that nourishes it . . . Food is a great cover story. You can go on with it forever, because there's no such thing as too thin . . . so I think that we're talking about the link between culture and anorexia, culture only makes it possible, it's not the

> cause. The cause precedes culture. Culture says: choose between drugs or alcohol or eating disorders . . . I think that food is somehow a cultural tool we've been given to realize all our inner needs. I think that somewhere the fact that culture says that you have to be thin, it's a sort of thing that gives me and others like me our cover story. A cover for the real reason for why we're doing it.
>
> —Shirley

As many convincingly argue, eating disorders are a cultural disease. When we examine the way in which diseases respond to the cultural framework, we must thus look beyond the doctors, diagnoses, and therapies and listen to the voices of the women themselves (Bromberg, 1998). This is precisely what I have done, allowing the women I interviewed to speak and recount their own stories and experiences, giving expression to their understanding of the link between childhood sexual abuse and their eating disorders and their response to the treatment they received.

Their narratives are difficult, moving, painful, and very disturbing. They demonstrate how the women 'chose' their eating disorders from the cultural repertoire on offer in order to try and convey the distress caused by rape. By not allowing the trauma of rape to be spoken of, patriarchal society delegitimizes it. In a continuation of the secrecy that pervades the abuse, survivors are given a stigmatizing medicalized diagnosis that ignores the traumatic sources of their distress. Some of the women's narratives are disturbingly reminiscent of ancient 'treatments', calling to mind the 'hysterics' locked up in psychiatric hospitals at the end of the nineteenth century. 'The cruelest treatment was developed in hospitals, which included forced hospitalization in inhumane conditions. Hysterics were restrained, made to go naked, tied down with splints, and treated with devices and heavy streams of water' (Levy, 2009, p. 262).

Eating disorders and CPTSD caused by childhood sexual abuse are two relatively new areas of professional knowledge. Although both have long histories, they were only structured as psychiatric disorders in the 1970s and '80s. The professional discourse relating to the association between them is of even briefer duration – and littered with controversy. As we have seen, professional and clinical circles define eating disorders as a 'female disease', the psychiatric establishment ignoring and lagging behind in the recognition of their traumatic origins. This fact has serious consequences for proper diagnosis and appropriate and effective treatment. The analysis of the link between childhood sexual abuse and eating disorders and the multiple examples cited evince how women abused as children unconsciously 'choose' various types of eating disorders – together with a broad range of other symptoms – as a way of expressing the unspeakable, inexpressible, unsymbolized, and unmentalized horror of rape. Where words fail and in the absence of any ways in which the trauma can be worked through, eating disorders serve as survival mechanisms. As Noga observed: 'My anorexia is my chemotherapy'.

The rape of a child by a loved adult supposed to take care of and protect her is something not even the devil could have devised. Survivors of childhood sexual abuse thus create an 'arsenal' of bizarre and serious symptoms representatives of the patriarchal hegemonic establishment, religious authorities, and the medical world diagnose and 'treat' in line with the spirit of the times. Mental diseases take different forms in accordance with social norms. People in different cultures express their distress in many and varied ways commensurate with their gender, age, social class, ethnic background, and worldview. Physical symptoms and mental afflictions are adopted unconsciously from the repertoire available in the culture in which they live (Bromberg, 1998). Because food and the body become the arena in which women are allowed to express themselves, they become a language through which to communicate. As we decode them, we see how intimately linked they are to the psychological conditions created by our present social climate (Orbach, 2006). Contemporary culture celebrates body shape and slenderness. In its preoccupation with women's body image the 'choice' of an eating disorder is, as Shirley observes, 'a sort of social tool given to us in order to meet our inner needs'.

Contemporary culture is dominated by a form of medicalization whereby the language and ideology of medical knowledge controls the way in which people express their physical and mental pain (Brumberg, 1988). A byproduct of the process of secularization, this has come to govern the way in which human behaviours are defined and the classification of some of these as mental illnesses. The religious conceptualizations of previous centuries have simply been replaced by scientific medicalization.

The ignoring and silencing of sexual trauma that is so common in the eating disorder field belies the fact that the history of the perception of the link between eating disorders and childhood sexual abuse goes back to the very beginnings of psychoanalysis. In his late-nineteenth-century account of his treatment of Katharina, Freud understood her vomiting as a 'substitute for moral and physical disgust . . . the memory of the attempt on her at night when she had "felt her uncle's body"' (1995, p. 131).[3] The majority of eating disorder clinicians and researchers deny and disregard this statement, continuing the long tradition begun by the '*fathers* of psychoanalysis' – Freud, Jung, Breuer, etc. (some of whom continued the sexual abuse their patients had already suffered).[4] A long line of clinicians in their wake have continued to ignore, cast doubt on, or suppress the existence of survivors of childhood sexual abuse, labelling them with stigmatizing diagnoses and treating them in inappropriate ways (Herman, 1997).[5]

Although the professional literature relating to childhood sexual abuse recognizes that eating disorders form an integral part of the symptoms exhibited by survivors, reports of the association in eating disorder literature only began appearing at a relatively late stage in the development of knowledge about childhood abuse and dissociative disorders. Nor has it yet become well known and accepted therein, fierce controversy still existing with respect to the role of childhood sexual abuse in the formation of eating disorders (Wooley, 1994).

Central feminist writers in the eating disorder field also attribute no role to sexual trauma in the aetiology of eating disorders. They rather argue that the latter are a function of female existence in male-dominated patriarchal society, constituting an expression of anger and protest against female oppression. Believing the latter to underlie the emergence and dictating the treatment of eating disorders alike, they rarely directly adduce the close association between childhood sexual abuse and eating disorders. Although the discourse relating to the oppression of women in our culture encompasses the discourse of childhood sexual abuse, feminist theoreticians such as Catharine MacKinnon (2005) identifying sexual assault as the primary weapon through which patriarchal society ensures and preserves male superiority, dominance, and female oppression. Few feminist eating disorders specialists directly acknowledge childhood sexual abuse to be a central aetiological factor in the development of eating disorders.[6]

According to the World Health Organization (2017), gender-based violence is the number one public-health problem today, constituting a violation of human rights. Childhood sexual abuse is an extensive and traumagenic aspect of this phenomenon that takes a heavy mental toll on survivors and society. As Judith Herman (1997) noted early on, the history of the psychiatric establishment is littered with victims of 'combat neurosis' induced by the 'war of the sexes'. Gender-based violence of this type exacts a high price in terms of mental health and public-health expenditure.

All this takes us back to the story of female madness and the various ways in which it had been defined throughout history by the representatives of patriarchal hegemony. I suggest that in many cases, the 'madness' was in fact a severe and complex – but eminently understandable and natural – set of post-traumatic symptoms brought on by the cruel rituals involved in the sexual abuse of girls. The present study evinces that eating disorders are amongst the most common manifestations today of the unspeakable and unutterable trauma of childhood sexual abuse.[7]

A new diagnostic definition

The understanding that most women develop severe eating disorders in the wake of being abused as children challenges the very classification of eating disorders as an independent diagnosis. Eating disorders are in fact but one in a cluster of complex symptoms caused by childhood sexual abuse. In many instances, women suffering from eating disorders also exhibit other complex symptoms – such as dissociative disorders, personality disorders, addictions, self-harming, PSTD, depression, anxiety, hypervigilance, sleep problems, flashbacks, etc. Many are diagnosed as suffering from comorbidity – a psychiatric term that refers to the existence of another mental disorder(s) in addition to the primary diagnosis or the effect of secondary diseases/disorders on the principal diagnosis.

The lack of an accurate and comprehensive diagnostic concept has serious consequences for treatment, because the connection between the patient's present symptoms and the traumatic experience is frequently lost. Attempts to fit the patient into the mould of existing diagnostic constructs generally result, at best, in a partial understanding of the problem and a fragmented approach to treatment (Herman, 1997).

I suggest that eating disorders in fact constitute a direct and integral symptom of complex trauma. Diagnosis playing a major role in the way illnesses are treated, traditional definitions must be replaced, allowing eating disorders to be depathologized and new treatment methods developed. Recognizing trauma as an aetiological factor in the formation of eating disorders will pave the way for a new understanding of treatment and recovery, one that fosters a new conceptual framework for the psychological treatment of trauma survivors (Herman, 1997).

Women with eating disorders frequently receive deficient and fragmentary treatment that focuses on alleviating their eating disorder symptoms rather than addressing all the others they exhibit. They are also often thrown out of treatment programmes and transferred to other settings because of their complex symptoms – childhood sexual abuse PTSD, personality disorders, addictions, suicide attempts, etc. In the absence of an integrative form of treatment, they suffer significant damage. Specialist treatments designed to treat only some of a range of severe symptoms reenact the rejection, neglect, and splits that formed part of the original abuse dynamic, perpetuating survivors' feelings of being worthless and rejected, their inability to form close relationships, and status as defenceless, homeless, and blemished.

Complex Post-Traumatic Stress Disorder

CPTSD is an integrative diagnosis that avoids labelling or branding those to whom it is given. It includes an understanding of the role trauma plays in the severe symptoms survivors exhibit and offers appropriate and integrative forms of treatment based on a diagnosis that focuses on comprehending the complex traumas responsible for the severe disorders clients display, addressing all rather than merely some of the symptoms. Its strength lies in its integrative nature. Rather than a simple list of symptoms, it coherently formulates the consequences of prolonged and repeated trauma (Herman, 2009).

Complex psychological trauma is the result of exposure to severe long-term, repeated stress that causes damage at a crucial stage of development (Ford & Courtois, 2009). Expanding the notion of PTSD, it was developed in order to distinguish one-off traumas from protracted, chronic trauma characterized by ongoing contact with the perpetrator and constant expectation of further abuse (Courtois, 2008; Courtois, Ford, & Cloitre, 2009;Courtois & Ford, 2013).

Children who endure trauma suffer from significant developmental damage. Advances in neuroscience demonstrate that those who are raised by hostile, abusive, or neglective primary caregivers suffer from brain-development damage that interferes with their ability to focus, think, and self-regulate (van der Kolk, 2009).

CPTSD symptoms are more diffuse and severe than those of PTSD, victims of protracted trauma exhibiting personality changes that include attachment and identity problems. They are also at high risk of revictimization both at their own hands and those of others (Herman, 1992). Customarily, they display alterations in consciousness and corporal, emotional, and relational difficulties, including severe symptoms – such as dissociation, emotional dysregulation, somatic disorders, and relational and spiritual alienation (Ford & Courtois, 2009). These symptoms form part of the sets belonging to borderline personality disorder, a significant overlapping being documented today between childhood sexual abuse and borderline personality disorder diagnoses (Herman, Perry, & van der Kolk, 1989; Briere, 1989).

CPTSD does not relate solely to childhood sexual abuse but pertains more generally to situations of ongoing, chronic trauma in which the victim is held captive by the abuser. Childhood sexual abuse is one of the commonest and cruellest of ongoing traumas in contemporary culture, meeting all the criteria for a CPTSD diagnosis. Our understanding of the latter derives in large part in fact from research into and treatment of the victims of childhood sexual abuse.

One of the advantages of the concept of CPTSD lies in the fact that is integrative, Rather than a simple list of symptoms, it is a coherent formulation of the consequences of prolonged and repeated trauma (Herman, 2009). Neutralizing branding and pathological diagnoses, it paves the way for understanding the traumatic origins of diverse disorders and the development of appropriate methods of treatment (Herman, 2009). The new classification of CPTSD is very useful as a conceptual model for gaining a picture of the complex symptoms exhibited by those exposed to ongoing trauma (Courtois, 2008).

A controversial diagnostic concept

CPTSD was first coined in 1992 by Judith Herman (1992) with the aim of creating order amongst the confusion of syndromes exhibited by the survivors of extended abuse – primarily in childhood – by people close to them or authority figures. According to Herman (2009), it aids clients in giving meaning to what they experience, thereby paving the way for appropriate forms of treatment. Recent years have witnessed a real development in its use as a diagnostic tool. Although relegated to the 'Associated Features of PTSD' in DSM-IV, it has taken on a life of its own. The World Health Organization included it in the eleventh edition of the International Classification of Diseases (ICD-11 Alpha Draft, 2012). DSM-5 followed suit, making it a dissociative subtype of

PTSD (APA, 2013). Basic guidelines for treating CPTSD were published in the International Society for Traumatic Stress Studies (ISTSS, 2012) and the APA (2013) in conjunction with the International Society for the Study of Trauma and Dissociation (ISSTD, 2013).

A glance at the history of the identification of trauma as an aetiological factor in the development of mental disorders reveals that PTSD only gained recognition after a long and tempestuous battle. Although the term is well known and common amongst professionals and the public at large alike today, its entry into DSM-III in 1980 was fiercely fought: trauma as a factor in the development of mental disorders had been ignored from the end of the Second World War through the Vietnam War. Its importance lies in the understanding that particularly horrendous events that lie outside the scope of human experience destroy ordinary coping mechanisms, creating psychological havoc.

Rather than arising from the mental health establishment, the initiative for including PTSD in psychiatric diagnostic manuals was triggered by two political movements. The first was the anti-war faction in the United States, which reached its peak in the wake of the Vietnam War, bringing to public and professional awareness the imprint that war experiences stamp on returning soldiers' mental lives. PTSD was promoted as a way of uniting all the psychopathological effects of the traumatization diagnosed amongst thousands of Vietnam veterans under one banner (van der Kolk, 2001). The second was the feminist movement that emerged in Western Europe and the United States. This brought the public's attention to the prevalence and damage caused by sexual and domestic violence against women and children. This in turn led to the recognition that the most common post-traumatic stress disorders were not those suffered by returning soldiers but those to which women and children were exposed in civilian life (Herman, 1997).

In the wake of these breakthroughs, it became evident that most of those suffering from the effects of trauma who sought clinical treatment also exhibited a range of other psychological symptoms not currently recognized as part of PTSD – depression, self-hatred, dissociation, depersonalization, aggression towards the self and others, and intimacy, pleasure, and gratification problems. Many of these – which were not included in the current diagnosis of PTSD – were frequently classified as comorbid symptoms. Not falling under the category of traumatic symptoms, they reflected the developmental damage caused by ongoing trauma, the relationship between victim and perpetrator, and the lack of social support system (van der Kolk, 2001).

In 1992, Judith Herman thus proposed the term CPTSD as an answer to this need. Since then, it has gained widespread recognition, being the subject of a plethora of studies. One of the members of the working group of DSM-IV (APA, 1994) who sought to examine whether it should be accepted as a psychiatric diagnosis, Herman recounts that the term was subjected to a field trial. Its findings corroborated the existence of somaticization, dissociation, and affect dysregulation – three cardinal symptoms of CPTSD – particularly in survivors of childhood abuse. It occurs less commonly in those abused in adolescence or adulthood and more rarely in people who have endured a single acute trauma 'not of human design' (Herman, 2009). These three symptoms also proved themselves to be correlated (van der Kolk, Weisaeth, & van der Hart, 1996).

Researchers assumed that the demonstration of the prevalence and internal consistency of the CPTSD diagnosis would constitute strong grounds for its inclusion in DSM-IV. Although the PTSD working group concurred with this view, the move encountered stiff opposition from top-ranking psychiatrists. Arguing that it should not form part of the trauma spectrum because it does not fit neatly under the category of an anxiety disorders, they proposed that it be included under dissociative disorders or somaticization – or even personality disorders. These categories not acknowledging the traumatic sources of the disorder, this move would have perpetuated the very situation the concept sought to address, branding victims by refusing to recognize the root of their problems. In the end, CPTSD was relegated to 'associated features' of PTSD in DSM-IV.

The arguments and controversies surrounding the inclusion of CPTSD in the DSM were reignited by the publication of DSM-5 in 2013. Studies nonetheless demonstrate that only 20 percent of people with a history of trauma are diagnosed as suffering from PTSD, 34 percent being diagnosed as suffering from CPTSD due to comorbidity with PTSD (van der Kolk, Roth, Pelcovitz, Sunday, & Spinazzola, 2005). The diagnosis was further entrenched when dissociation was included as a dissociative subtype of PTSD in DSM-5. At this point, the term became part of the spectrum of post-traumatic disorders.

The failure to include CPTSD as a distinct subtype in DSM-5 leaves us – well into the early stages of the twenty-first century – without an accurate or comprehensive term for clients who have undergone extreme and protracted traumatic experiences (Herman, 2009). This circumstance has serious clinical implications, therapists frequently making no connection between client symptoms and the traumatic event that gave rise to them. Today, extensive documentation attests to the fact that CPSTD symptoms are responsible for far more than the disorders attributed to a PTSD diagnosis (Cloitre et al., 2010). Treatments that have proved effective in cases of PTSD (e.g., Hembree, Street, Riggs, & Foa, 2004) are not always appropriate to CPTSD sufferers, even being harmful and deleterious in some cases (Herman, 2012).[8]

Today, numerous studies indicate that relating to CPTSD as an independent diagnosis has led to substantial clinical progress in the treatment of broad populations. As Herman notes, CPTSD is 'more parsimonious' than the concept of multiple comorbidities. Although CPTSD shares some features with several other psychiatric disorders, it is not congruent with any one alone. The alternative is multiple comorbidity diagnoses and overlapping treatment protocols. These lead to polypharmacy and inefficient, poorly tailored psychotherapy. 'To suggest that this problem would be solved by better training for clinicians is to miss the point entirely' (Herman, 2012, p. 257). Over the past two decades, we have accumulated extensive knowledge about 'complex trauma', a psychiatric condition which possibly constitutes the most common set of psychological problems to drive human beings into psychiatric care (van der Kolk, 2009).

The stories of the women I interviewed for this study similarly illustrate the way in which the lack of a comprehensive diagnosis that identifies the traumatic aetiology of symptoms leads to the diagnosis of clients with eating disorders as suffering from (multiple) comorbidity – complex symptoms all of which form part of CPTSD. Clients are thus branded with stigmatizing diagnoses and prevented from receiving appropriate treatment, only being treated fragmentarily or partially. Focusing on removing the eating disorder symptoms does not treat or heal the cluster of symptoms created by CPTSD.

Notes

1 Orbach (1986), for example, notes the 'problematic use of the word anorexia – which literally means loss of appetite – to describe a syndrome that is about the denial and overriding of hunger and appetite' (1986, p. xi).

2 The first time in which women participated in producing the canonic list of psychiatric disorders was during the preparations for the publication of the revised DSM-IIIR in the 1980s. A group of male psychoanalysts suggested that 'masochistic personality disorder' be included. Several women's groups protested, demanding to be allowed to take part in the process – up to that point confined to small male groups – on the grounds that such a definition ignored knowledge regarding the psychological states of victims. The psychiatric establishment, which acknowledged its lack of familiarity with the extensive literature on psychic trauma that had arisen in the 1980s, stood firm. Eventually, the name was changed to 'self-defeating personality disorder', appearing only in an appendix to DSM-IIIR and not being included in DSM-IV (Herman, 1997). Today, diagnoses are regularly entered and removed from the DSM on the basis of political considerations and pressure from power and interest groups – such as pharmaceutical companies. Recently, top-ranking officials within the psychiatric establishment have added their voices to the dissatisfaction with later versions of DSM, however, the most prominent being Allen Frances, who headed the team responsible for publishing DSM-IV (Frances, 2013).

3 In the original 1895 version, Freud refers to Katharina's uncle rather than her father and sexual harassment, only adding a footnote 'to reveal the fact that Katharina was not the niece but the daughter of the landlady. The girl fell ill, therefore, as a result of sexual attempts on the part of her own father' in 1924 (Grubrich-Simitis, 1997, p. 26). In a video work entitled 'The Father not the Uncle', Michal Heiman (2008) reads Freud's case description of Katharina, creating a new visual text and seeking to correct the power relations created by 'spaces without witnesses'. Hereby, she gives voice to those who have been abused by their fathers, exposing Freud's attempt to disguise this type of molestation.

4 Jung, for example, was unable to resist attractive clients, crossing the therapist-client boundary on several occasions. One of those with whom he became involved was the young Sabina Spielrein, whom he treated between 1905 and 1909. Spielrein wrote Freud telling him of her relationship with Jung and asking his advice. Freud replied that that Jung could not possibly have acted as she suggested and asked her to suppress her emotions and keep the relationship secret. Breuer similarly became involved with 'Anna O.' (Bertha Pappenheim).

5 Reviewing the history of research into mental trauma, Herman argues that the field suffers from episodic amnesia and fierce controversy, suggesting that preserving traumatic reality in one's consciousness requires a social context that confirms the statements made by survivors and protects the victims. The latest trauma to have arisen in public consciousness is sexual and domestic violence against women, the political context in which this won recognition being the rise of the feminist movement.

6 Two prominent exceptions are Kearney-Cooke and Striegel-Moore (1994) and Wooley (1994).
7 See Natalie Brown's film 'Metamorphosis'. In Ovid's original, fifty of the 250 metamorphoses describe those of women who were raped and silenced into objects, plants, animals, rivers – one having her tongue cut out to prevent her from relating the crime.
8 These include exposure to traumatic elements without a sufficiently stable and safe basis having been established, an ability to regulate emotions having been developed, or a relationship of trust formed between client and therapist.

References

APA (American Psychiatric Association). (1994). *Diagnostic and statistical manual of mental disorders* (4th ed.). Washington, DC: American Psychological Association.

APA (American Psychiatric Association). (2013). *Diagnostic and statistical manual of mental disorders* (5th ed.). Washington, DC: American Psychological Association.

Appignanesi, L. (2008). *Mad, bad and sad: A history of women and the mind doctors from 1800 to the present.* Londen: Virago.

Briere, J. (1989). *Therapy for adults molested as children.* New York, NY: Springer.

Bromberg, P. (1998). *Standing in the spaces: Essays on clinical process, trauma, and dissociation.* London and New York, NY: Routledge.

Brumberg, J. J. (1988). *Fasting girls: The emergence of anorexia nervosa as a disease.* Cambridge, MA: Harvard University Press.

Chesler, P. (1972). *Women and madness.* New York, NY: Avon.

Cloitre, M., Stovall-McClough, K. C., Nooner, K., Zorbas, P., Cherry, S., Jackson, C. L., Gan, W., & Petkova, E. (2010). Treatment for PTSD related to childhood abuse: A randomized controlled trial. *American Journal of Psychiatry, 167*(8), 915–924.

Courtois, C. A. (2008). Complex trauma, complex reactions: Assessment and treatment. *Psychological Trauma: Theory, Research, Practice, and Policy, S1*, 86–100.

Courtois, C. A., & Ford, J. D. (2013). *Treatment of complex trauma: A sequenced, relationship-based approach.* New York, NY: Guilford Press.

Courtois, C. A., Ford, J. D., & Cloitre, M. (2009). Best practices in psychotherapy for adults. In C. A. Courtois & J. D. Ford (Eds.), *Treating complex traumatic stress disorders: An evidence-based guide* (pp. 82–103). New York, NY: Guilford Press.

D'Andrea, W., Ford, J., Stolbach, B., Spinazzola, J., & van der Kolk, B. (2012). Understanding interpersonal trauma in children: Why we need a developmentally appropriate trauma diagnosis. *American Journal of Orthopsychiatry, 82*(2), 187–200.

Dialogues with Madwomen. (1994). US film directed by Allie Light. Produced and edited by Irving Saraf. Light-Saraf Films.

Ford, J. D., & Courtois, C. A. (2009). Defining and understanding complex trauma and complex traumatic stress disorder. In C. A. Courtois & J. D. Ford (Eds.), *Treating complex traumatic stress disorders* (pp. 13–30). New York, NY: Guilford Press.

Frances, A. (2013). *Saving normal: An insider's revolt against out-of-control psychiatric diagnosis, DSM-5, Big Pharma, and the medicalization of ordinary life.* New York, NY: HarperCollins.

Freud, S. (1995). The aetiology of hysteria. In P. Gay (Ed.), *The Freud reader* (pp. 96–111). New York, NY: W.W. Norton.

Grubrich-Simitis, I. (1997). *Early Freud and late Freud: Reading anew* Studies on Hysteria *and* Moses and Monotheism. Trans. P. Slotkin. London and New York, NY: Routledge.

Hieman, M. (2008). *Attacks on linking.* Tel Aviv: Museum of Art.

Hembree, E. A., Street, G. P., Riggs, D. S., & Foa, E. B. (2004). Do assault-related variables predict response to cognitive behavioral treatment for PTSD? *Journal of Consulting and Clinical Psychology, 72*(3), 531–534.

Herman, J. L. (1992). Complex PTSD: A syndrome in survivors of prolonged and repeated trauma. *Journal of Traumatic Stress, 5*, 377–391.

Herman, J. L. (1997). *Trauma and recovery*. New York, NY: Basic Books.

Herman, J. L. (2009). Foreword. In C. A. Courtois & J. D. Ford (Eds.), *Treating complex traumatic stress disorders* (pp. xiii–xvii). New York, NY: Guildford Press.

Herman, J. L. (2012). CPTSD is a distinct entity: Comment on Resick et al. *Journal of Traumatic Stress, 25*, 256–257.

Herman, J. L., Perry, J. C., & van der Kolk, B. (1989). Childhood trauma in borderline personality disorder. *American Journal of Psychiatry, 146*, 490–495.

ISSTD. (International Society for the Study of Trauma and Dissociation) (2013). *Adult treatment guidelines*. Retrieved from www.isst-d.org/default.asp?contentID=49

ISTSS (International Society for Traumatic Stress Studies). (2012). *ISTSS expert consensus guidelines for complex PTSD*. Retrieved February 15, 2017, from www.istss.org/ISTSS_Main/media/Documents/ISTSS-Expert-Concesnsus-Guidelines-for-Complex-PTSD-Updated-060315.pdf

Kaffman, A. (2009). The silent epidemic of neurodevelopmental injuries. *Biological Psychiatry, 66*, 624–626.

Kearney-Cooke, A., & Striegel-Moore, R. H. (1994). Treatment of childhood sexual abuse in anorexia nervosa and bulimia nervosa: A feminist psychodynamic approach. In M. F. Schwartz & L. Cohn (Eds.), *Sexual abuse and eating disorders* (pp. 155–175). Bristol, PA: Brunner/Mazel.

Levy, I. (2009). Afterward. In C. Bollas (Ed.), *Hysteria* (p. 262). Tel Aviv: Tola'at (Hebrew).

Light, A. (2008). Dialogues with madwomen: Allie Light. In G. Morris (Ed.), *In action! Interviews with directors from classical Hollywood to contemporary Iran* (pp. 227–234). London: Anthem.

MacKinnon, C. (2005). Difference and dominance: On sex discrimination. In A. E. Cudd & R. O. Andreasen (Eds.), *Feminist theory: A philosophical anthology* (pp. 392–402). Oxford: Wiley-Blackwell.

Orbach, S. (1986). *Hunger strike: The anorectic's struggle as a metaphor for our age*. Harmondsworth: Penguin.

Orbach, S. (2006). *Fat is a feminist issue: The anti-diet guide*. London: Arrow.

United Nations. (2006). *UN Secretary-General's study on violence against children*. Retrieved from www.unviolencestudy.org/

van der Kolk, B. (2001). The assessment and treatment of CPTSD. In R. Yehuda (Ed.), *Traumatic stress* (pp. 1–29). Washington, DC: American Psychiatric Press.

van der Kolk, B. (2009). Afterword. In C. A. Courtois & J. D. Ford (Eds.), *Treating complex stress disorders* (pp. 455–466). New York, NY: Guilford Press.

van der Kolk, B. Roth, S., Pelcovitz, D., Sunday, S., & Spinazzola, J. (2005). Disorders of extreme stress: The empirical foundation of a complex adaptation to trauma. *Journal of Trauma Stress, 18*(5), 389–399.

van der Kolk, B. Weisaeth, L., & van der Hart, O. (1996). History of trauma in psychiatry. In B. van der Kolk, A. C. McFarlane, & L. Weisaeth (Eds.), *Traumatic stress: The overwhelming experience on mind, body, and society* (pp. 47–76). New York, NY: Guilford Press.

Wooley, S. C. (1994). Sexual abuse and eating disorders: The concealed debate. In P. Fallon, M. A. Katzman, & S. C. Wooley (Eds.), *Feminist perspectives on eating disorders* (pp. 171–211). New York, NY: Guilford Press.

World Health Organization. (2017). *Violence against women*. Retrieved February 15, 2017, from www.who.int/mediacentre/factsheets/fs239/en/

Chapter 10

Treating CPTSD

The change in diagnostic terms and shift from a diagnosis of eating disorders to CPTSD have opened up the way for better and more effective forms of treatment. Over the past decade, numerous treatment models meeting the needs of the new diagnosis have been proposed in the field of psychotherapy.

The CPTSD treatment model

The complexity of treating clients suffering from CPTSD requires that therapists be willing to adopt multiple treatment models (Ford & Courtois, 2009). The broad range of symptoms and comorbidities frequently demands work on several therapeutic fronts and the use of a variety of intervention approaches. The challenges of treating the effects of complex trauma demand the creative and sensitive application of clinical concepts and techniques tailored to the needs of the individual client (Courtois & Ford, 2009, 2013).

It is important to ensure that the diverse forms of treatment are integrated rather than separated in order to prevent reenactment of the splits characteristic of the dynamic of the original trauma. The treatment must be accommodated to each individual client and her capacities, being flexible and capable of changing in accordance with her needs. It must be based on a systematic plan that employs effective therapeutic practices, organizing itself around cautious assessment of the client and following a series of well-thought out, graduated stages. The steps themselves must be adjustable, based on the recognition that regression is an ever-present threat and that issues and stages may need to be worked through several times as the client seeks to construct safer and more effective coping strategies.

In recent years, an extensive body of scholarly literature has outlined clear guidelines for treating CPTSD (Courtois & Ford, 2009, 2013). Many studies demonstrate that interpersonal elements play a central role in effective treatment, highlighting the importance of a positive therapeutic relationship, a caring, empathic psychotherapist, and attention to the ebb and flow of the therapy session – including client-therapist attunement and connection, transference, and countertransference, boundary negotiations, and attachment-level response.

Studies evince that supportive and caring treatment is significantly more successful (Briere, 2013).

Three stages of recovery

The meta-model – extensively employed in the treatment of CPTSD and dissociative disorders – consists of three stages. These seek to stabilize the client's condition before beginning work on the trauma itself (Courtois & Ford, 2013).[1] The phases are organized in such a way as to provide a gradual response to specific issues and develop skills along a continuum (Herman, 1997). Treatment actions and assignments must be carefully graded, initial emphasis being laid upon creating a sense of safety and security and establishing emotional stability. The difficulty survivors of extreme trauma experience in self-regulation is much better understood today, in part due to developments in neuroscience that indicate that emotional regulation is related to brain development (see 'Neurobiological and developmental implications for treatment').

Clients being vulnerable at critical points in treatment – exposure to traumatic memories at the beginning, for example, and when the end of the therapy is in sight – therapists must keep a close watch out for signs of deterioration. They need to collaborate with clients in order to help them regulate the power of their emotional responses, encouraging them to find supportive and safe relationships beyond the therapeutic alliance. The task in the first stage is to establish safety, security, and trust. In the second stage, the task is to come to terms with the trauma story. The third sets out to repair and enlarge the survivor's social connections (Herman, 2009). One of the most important aspects of this model lies in the fact that in the first stage it avoids all forms of exposure. Clients can only engage with their traumatic narrative when they have created a safe basis in the present. The steps and techniques of each stage are organized on the basis of several elements. These relate primarily to the client's clinical state – her ability to regulate her emotions, motivation, and responses to the treatment. It is important to assess each client's mental strength and recovery capacities, adapting the therapeutic process to her specific state.

Although the three-stage model is presented as linear, the three phases do not always follow the same order. Although security and self-caring issues are always given preference at the outset, this does not mean that the trauma must be ignored. Clients benefit significantly from trauma-informed treatment at the beginning of therapy. Making space for the trauma and naming its effects helps them give meaning to their experiences, enabling them to recognize – often for the first time in their lives – that their symptoms are intelligible in the context of aggressive and dominant relationships. This understanding acts as a healing antidote to the feelings of stigma and shame that blight their lives (Herman, 2009).

Many clients finding it difficult to learn and apply new skills, therapists must anticipate backtrackings and regressions as an integral part of the therapy. Rather than viewing them as signs of failure, they indicate the client's need to work through a particular issue once again, honing and polishing her newly acquired skills. In this sense, the model can be conceptualized as an ascending spiral: while the therapeutic steps are completed and new skills attained in progressive fashion, clients also return again and again to earlier learning stages. The skills they have mastered are challenged and reexamined, re-learnt and entrenched progressively throughout the three stages. Although progress is always 'two steps forward, one step backwards', the direction is always forward-looking, seeking to help the client acquire skills, regulate her emotions, and find stability in the safe space of the therapeutic room and alliance. As gains are made and the client starts regaining control over her life, the steps forward gradually begin to overtake those going backward (Courtois & Ford, 2013).

Neurobiological and developmental implications for treatment

Recent decades have witnessed a sharp growth in our understanding of the way in which childhood trauma affects brain development and self-perception. New disciplines such as neuroscience, developmental psychopathology and interpersonal neurobiology has revealed that trauma produces actual physiological changes in the brain (van der Kolk, 2014). Today, we know that being dependent upon a malignant or severely misattuned caregiver interferes with brain development, impairing growth as a focused, thoughtful, and well-regulated human being. Early exposure to danger trains the brain to be vulnerable, making people more irritable, impulsive, suspicious, and compelled to engage in fight-or-flight reactions. Abuse and neglect programme the brain to make defensive adaptations. While these help people survive in the world of constant danger, they come at a terrible cost (van der Kolk, 2009, p. 456).

One of the key concepts for understanding the consequences and implications of neurological conditions in the diagnosis and treatment of CPTSD is self-regulation. Enhancing a client's core ability to engage in reflective self-awareness in the service of consciously regulating emotions and processing information helps create a framework for guiding clinical conceptualization and engagement. It also aids in client education, treatment planning, and the monitoring of therapeutic progress and outcomes (Courtois & Ford, 2013, p. 49).

The three-stage model of recovery takes into account the fact that inappropriate or too-early talk about traumatic memories frequently leads to hypervigilance and a feeling of insecurity. Treatment must serve as a safe haven for those who live in constant anxiety and a sense of ineffectiveness rather than as a place in which they feel they must confront their traumatic experiences without regard to the cost. Learning to autonomously modulate one's arousal level is essential for overcoming the passivity and dependency associated with the fear of reliving the trauma (van der Kolk, 2009, 2014).

The sociocultural context of extreme trauma and clinical practices

CPTSD is a function of clinical intrapsychic, interpersonal, and sociopolitical factors, the trauma-related symptoms developing and existing due to interpersonal and cultural non-recognition and an absence of appropriate reparation mechanisms. It also forms part of intrapsychic coping strategies. Today, we know that the severest symptoms – such as dissociation – are mediated by the close link between the intrapsychic and sociocultural elements of trauma: the denial of the violence perpetrated against women and children and the failure to recognize and diagnose the traumatic origins of mental disorders. These circumstances are of significant clinical import for both diagnosis and treatment, recovery most frequently occurring in healing relationships that include social awareness (Schwartz, 2000).

As Herman (2009) notes, it is important to recognize the social ecology of prolonged and repeated interpersonal trauma. Firstly, it is always embedded in a social structure that permits the abuse and exploitation of a subordinate group. The predominance of women among clients who meet the criteria is explained by the 'insidious pervasiveness of violence against women and girls'. Secondly, such trauma is always relational, occurring when the victim is captive and under the perpetrator's control and domination.

Social and political denial of extreme trauma is a widespread phenomenon, ranging from Holocaust denial to the effects of prostitution and domestic violence. People who suffer forms of trauma that are not socially or politically recognized not only have to deal with the traumatic events themselves but also with the fact that the latter are neither validated nor legitimized by those around them. The victims of socially recognized traumas – war or car accidents, for example – enjoy a socially sanctioned identity, the traumatic events they experience possessing a social and legal status. Childhood sexual abuse, in contrast, is regularly denied, suppressed, or explained away. Not only are the victims themselves frequently held responsible for it but it is then compounded by social norms that deny its existence and delegitimize it.

Victims thus face an incredibly difficult task in attempting to conceptualize the abuse and start on the road to healing and recovery. Sexual traumas also induce strong feelings of guilt and shame because the survivors so often feel to blame. Trauma that is insufficiently worked through is condemned to recur and express itself through acting out. In the absence of any appropriate working through and corrective processes, those who have suffered socially non-recognized trauma must employ defensive mechanisms such as amnesia, dissociation, eating disorders, addictions, etc.

Girls and women are at particular risk of falling victim to violent interpersonal crimes – rape, childhood sexual abuse, and battering – at the hands of male perpetrators. Most victims are abused by people close to them – a family member or other intimate whom they trust in their daily environment. Violence is a pervasive, tenacious, and frequently occurring event. A worldwide phenomenon, it crosses the lines of race, ethnicity, nationality/national origin, class, religion, age, and sexual orientation (Mendelsohn et al., 2011).

Treatment models for female victims of interpersonal violence are grounded in the feminist analysis of gender-based violence. This indicates that rape, childhood sexual abuse, sexual harassment, and wife battering are not isolated acts performed by disturbed individuals but frequent expressions that reflect the power men hold and wield in order to perpetuate their superiority and dominance over women. Deeply embedded within the psychology and structure of patriarchy, these abuses are sanctioned by custom and tradition. Sometimes they are of a ritual nature – as in gang rape. Only rarely addressed as crimes, they are thus often concealed, excused, or even condoned, the victims being silenced, blamed, and made to feel ashamed (Mendelsohn et al., 2011).

Recognition of violence against women and children as a broad and widespread social phenomenon has significant clinical implications. Guilt and shame, for example, are prevalent and long lasting emotions amongst CPTSD victims. A therapeutic orientation that includes awareness of the social context of interpersonal trauma helps women who have been assaulted or abused to understand that this is a common social phenomenon rather than taking personal responsibility for it. Recognition of the broad social context of trauma helps reduce feelings of guilt, blame, isolation, and stigma, allowing them to work through the trauma rather than remaining trapped within the secrecy and denial – and thus forced to express their suffering by acting out (Mendelsohn et al., 2011).

The best prognosis for healing and recovery is predicated on healing relationships that take account of intra-psychic processes and sociocultural contexts alike. It is thus vitally important to create therapeutic interactions based on mutuality and equality that abjure all forms of hierarchical control. This task is far from easy, contemporary culture being riddled with practices based on chains of command, control, and the authority of the 'father'. These are so accepted they are very difficult to identify. As a profession, psychotherapy is based on Western medical methods in which therapists and specialists always hold the upper hand, the voices of clients – all the more so when these are women – being regarded as insignificant and inconsequential.

The treatment of women abused through the exploitation of male power in contemporary society requires therapists to challenge these common forms of relationship and forge new ones. The therapeutic alliance must be humanized and democratized instead of dominated by the invoking of higher authority and professional expertise (Schwartz, 2000). In this context, psychotherapists and the other mental health professionals face a 'real mandate to challenge rather than reinforce conventional social arrangements and to reenvision social justice' (Schwartz, 2000, p. xvi).

Recognition of the primacy and uniqueness of each client

The CPSTD treatment model is structured around the recognition of the primacy and uniqueness of the individual and a commitment to work towards her welfare. Every client must be assessed individually and treatment planned differentially in line with her specific needs. Treatment must be based on a phenomenological approach that sees her as she is. Although the symptoms, deficits, and distresses from which she suffers are largely responsible for prompting her to seek help and are often the goal of the interventions, it is important to identify and strengthen her personal resources, capacity for recovery, and personal needs, making room for and respecting her values and personal context (Courtois, Ford, & Cloitre, 2009).

Personal empowerment

The CPTSD treatment model is based on the principle of personal empowerment and self-definition, recognizing the client's mental strengths and powers. It encourages survivors to understand their particular experiences in the context of the symptoms and stresses from which they suffer and determine personalized treatment goals. Clients must be given the final say in the meanings and interpretations given to their personal history, identification of their needs and present priorities, and goals for the future. As Herman (1997) observes, the core experiences of psychological trauma are disempowerment and disconnection from others. The first principle of recovery is the empowerment of the survivor. She must be the author and arbiter of her own recovery.

Therapists must be empathic, active, and responsive listeners, guiding clients in such a way as to enable them to speak as openly as possible, examine, and work through the feelings they have suppressed or felt are forbidden. They must create relational conditions in which their clients feel seen, appreciated, and validated. The goal must be to establish a corrective experience of the invalidation characteristic of the original abuse.

Therapists must also aspire to create a state of mutuality as far as possible in order to encourage their clients' collaboration and empower them. The inherent power discrepancies in the therapist–client relationship should be related to explicitly. Therapists must also take responsibility for using the power they hold, employing it for their clients' good while simultaneously fostering their autonomy. They must exhibit an openness to questions relating to authority, including their own, and support the client's authority over her life, memories, the therapeutic alliance, and the treatment's progress.

Therapists must also scrupulously maintain appropriate boundaries within the therapeutic alliance and the necessary restrictions, taking responsibility for avoiding dual relationships – i.e., multiple roles between therapists/mental health practitioners and clients prior to, during, or after the treatment. Therapists must also avoid making their clients feel pressurized, coerced, or exploited – wittingly or unwittingly (Somer & Saadon, 1999).

Recognition of clients' strengths and resilience

However severe the trauma a person has experienced, the basis on which the therapeutic alliance must be established remains the same: encouraging and cultivating their strengths and capacity to recover. Such an approach provides clients with a unique opportunity to exhibit their ability to build a healthy relationship, offering them a new model for developing trust and a sense of safety in their relationship with others. This principle is of note in light of the fact that CPTSD clients frequently seek help because they are suffering from a range of complex and severe symptoms from which they have little belief or hope that they can recover. In the face of such symptoms, therapists tend to lift up their hands and despair of the possibility of being able to help, becoming increasingly tempted to apply pejorative diagnostic labels to them and forecast bad prognoses. The search for points of strength and focusing attention on these and the ability to recover rather than targeting the severe and threatening symptoms is central for treating women sexually abused in childhood.[2]

Creation of a therapeutic alliance characterized by trust, collaboration, mutuality, and non-authoritarianism

> The people who work in this profession must really come with their heart, from their soul. They don't need to go through things in order to be therapists but first of all I think that can help, but also if not, then I think that really they must come from a place of 'I work in a place like this because I want to do good. Because I want to give love, because I want to strengthen people, to fill them with strength so that when they leave the hospital they'll be better able to deal with things'.
>
> —Thyme[3]

The therapeutic alliance – a human relationship built between client and therapist – forms the essential basis on which recovery from interpersonal trauma is predicated. Complex trauma is an atrocity committed by one human being upon another. In many instances, the perpetrators are close loved ones in positions of authority, responsible for caring for and protecting the victims. Survivors thus have great difficulty with interpersonal relationships, placing trust in people, or believing that relationships can be safe, supportive, non-exploitative, and non-authoritarian.

Establishing a relationship with clients abused at a young age by close relatives is a particularly challenging task for the therapist in light of the tendency many survivors exhibit towards ensnaring therapists into reenacting the traumatic relationship. Clients bring central themes from the trauma into the therapy setting – abuse, cruelty, victimization, helplessness, indifference, denial, abandonment, and neglect. These are likely to form an integral part of the therapeutic relationship, making the work difficult, complex, and arduous. Creating a warm, caring, supportive therapeutic alliance is difficult in the face of the expectation of behaviour similar to that demonstrated by the perpetrator – betrayal, abuse, neglect, or abandonment. Forming a therapeutic alliance becomes somewhat easier if the clinician understands at the outset why the client might be unable to imagine a relationship that is genuinely caring, freely chosen, fair to both parties, mutually attuned, and mutually rewarding. It becomes the therapist's task, then, to model, explain, and engage the client in such a relationship, knowing that initially the client will perceive this as another likely set up for betrayal (Herman, 2009).

An empathic understanding of the deep – and justified – lack of trust displayed by clients, their great suspicion of interpersonal relations (particularly caretaking figures), and their immense difficulty in accepting anything that reminds them of the original trauma requires great investment of time and effort into establishing the therapeutic alliance and creating a safe and healing relationship. If successfully established, however, this allows clients to internalize a new, positive relational experience free of any of the elements that reenact the original trauma for them – exploitation, over/abuse of power and authority, indifference, denial, isolation, abandonment, and neglect. In order to find an effective way of coping with their understandable difficulty in committing themselves to therapy, therapists must devote themselves to gradually developing a relationship of trust. At all costs, they must avoid abandoning their clients if and when they 'disappoint' or are uncooperative.

In her renewed connections with other people, the survivor recreates the psychological faculties damaged or deformed by the traumatic experience. The therapist's responsibility is to use the power conferred upon her to foster the client's recovery, resisting all temptations to abuse. This promise – central to the integrity of any therapeutic relationship – is of special importance to clients who are already suffering as the result of another's arbitrary and exploitative exercise of power (Herman, 1997).

The traditional diagnostic methods, which disregard the trauma, brand CPTSD victims with pejorative and humiliating labels because of their failure to develop healthy relationships and appropriate therapeutic relations. One of the most striking examples is the 'borderline-personality disorder' diagnosis, which blames and brands victims who display a 'pattern of unstable and intense interpersonal relationships characterized by alternating between extremes of idealization and devaluation'. Such diagnoses fail to recognize the fact that such reactions are natural under the circumstances of the original relational trauma. Nor do they acknowledge the personal and social responsibility imposed upon mental healthcare professionals to help heal the victims of traumas caused by a social structure that permits the exploitation and subjugation of the weak. The treatment methods based on these stigmatizing diagnoses frequently brand clients' difficulties in developing trust in the therapist as 'personality disorders'. Little consideration is thus given to their enormous fear of dependence and emotional contact with caregiving authority figures.

Another challenge derives from the difficulty in bearing witness to the traumatic narratives. It is all too easy to fall into the trap of thinking that clients are making things up. Frequently, the truth of what happened to them is too difficult to accept emotionally. Therapists who commit themselves to treating the victims of human barbarity must deal empathetically with such inevitable relational difficulties, taking responsibility for helping their clients overcome their difficulties in trusting others.

Safe boundaries

The arbitrary and cruel violation of boundaries and infliction of extreme chaos by responsible adults upon children prevents the latter from erecting safe boundaries in relation to themselves, their bodies, and others. This fact has serious ramifications for the establishment of the therapeutic alliance, clients frequently struggling with the boundaries of therapy and the therapeutic relationship. They are also at high risk of revictimization, both at their own hand and that of others. Not knowing how to protect themselves from invasive behaviour or revictimization by others, they often confuse abuse with love. Therapeutic relations should serve as a corrective experience in this regard, helping victims to learn and rebuild safe and salubrious personal boundaries.

Clients' inability to preserve safe boundaries and their tendency to violate them – symptoms that form part of the identity and personality disorders from which they suffer – frequently cause treatment frameworks to introduce rigid boundaries and punish or even throw clients off the programme. In earlier chapters, we saw how this is exemplified on eating disorder wards, where uncooperative clients and those who act out are often immediately told they can no longer be treated. Treatment and rehab centres for victims of childhood sexual abuse also frequently employ the same policy.

It is vitally important that therapists clearly understand the dynamic of the violation of boundaries within the traumatic experience so that they can establish a therapeutic relationship that will form a corrective experience and help rebuild safe boundaries. Childhood sexual abuse is characterized by arbitrary, intransigent, and aggressive behaviour on the part of the perpetrators, who exploit their power in such a way as to make the victims feel they are unpredictable, capricious, and cruel. Boundaries and rules thus often remind them of the abuse. This understanding demands that the therapeutic framework be experienced as sensitive and compassionate towards the violation of boundaries while safeguarding necessary borders. Clients must therefore be allowed to participate in the determining of rules and boundaries and their negotiation, the reason for them and their justification always being clearly explained. My experience in treating former female prisoners – who frequently violate boundaries due to their traumatic past – indicates that it is possible to maintain flexible and continually negotiable borders even when treating the most 'difficult' of clients.

Clients who have been betrayed and abandoned by responsible adults find it difficult to believe that therapists truly care about them and have their welfare at heart. The very nature of the abuse they have suffered makes it difficult for them to trust. They thus continually test others to see how they will respond. The therapist and therapeutic alliance are no exceptions to this rule, clients consistently checking to see whether they are trustworthy. These tests frequently find expression in untoward behaviour, such as violating boundaries and rules. Often feeling helpless against this onslaught, therapists tend to start acting out as well in order to counter the assaults, acting punitively, reenacting the original trauma, and stopping therapy. Such responses reenact, vindicate, and perpetuate their clients' belief that people cannot be trusted. This creates a vicious circle, clients acting destructively towards themselves and others because they cannot trust them, those seeking to help them in turn feeling helpless and thus being driven to punish or abandon them.

In order to break the cycle, therapists must find ways of coping with the challenges such clients pose. They must thus constantly look actively and creatively for ways to deal with their clients' behaviour, always being motivated by kindness and compassion in order to ensure that they represent a model of beneficent relations characterized by clear but flexible boundaries that respect the individuality and needs of each client.

A fine line exists between maintaining clear and safe boundaries and avoiding the erection of arbitrary borders and engaging in harsh punishment. Therapists must exhibit an empathic understanding of the difficulty clients experience in learning to recognize safe boundaries. Hereby, they can prevent any recurrence of the feeling of arbitrariness that characterized the abuse, letting the client know that the boundaries are both clear/safe and reasonable (in both senses of the word). The boundaries must be established gradually in order to ensure flexibility, always being clearly explained – both in terms of why they are necessary and their importance for relationships. Rather than creating intractable rules and punishing clients when these are violated, boundaries should be constantly negotiable. This is the only way in which the therapy can become a good model for healing, safe, supportive, non-exploitative, non-abandonment, and non-hierarchical human relationships.

Encouraging a support system outside the therapy

Therapists must encourage clients to develop support systems outside the clinical setting to supplement the therapeutic alliance and relationship. Most clients looking for help believe that no one can be trusted or relied upon because their experience is precisely the opposite. Therapists must therefore help them correct their distorted perceptions while respecting and empathizing with the experience that induced them. They must present clients with a good model of human connection, teaching them to develop social skills in order to encourage the building up of outside support systems in various areas of life – work, studies, romantic relationships, etc.

The hazards of listening: the challenge of treating childhood sexual abuse survivors

Therapists must understand the degree of difficulty and danger that awaits them during the arduous process of bearing witness to the trauma and developing a healing relationship with their clients. Only when they do so can they take responsibility for their reactions and develop a healing and reparative relationship with their clients.

Even when the listener – in his capacity as psychoanalyst – is trained by discipline and by profession to treat trauma and to be its witness, the experience of the witnessing – of the listening to extreme-limit experiences – entails its hazards and might equally shake up one's whole grip on one's experience and one's life. The professionally trained receivers of the testimonies cannot fulfil their task without, in turn, passing through the crisis of experiencing their boundaries, their separateness, their functionality, and indeed their sanity, at risk [*sic*]. They have to learn how to recognize these hazards, how to integrate these pitfalls of the witnessing into the fulfilment of their professional and human task (Felman & Laub, 1992).

While extreme forms of trauma are by definition horrendous and inconceivable, shocking, and heartbreaking, filled with examples of human cruelty, evil, ignorance, denial, and indifference, the treatment of childhood sexual abuse poses particular challenges. These include listening to the stories of the abuse and betrayal of helpless children by those meant to take care of them. The desire not to listen, hear, or be exposed to such stories prompts a universal response to shut one's ears and turn away. Frequently, *contra* popular myth, the perpetrators are not disturbed paedophiles or mentally ill but normative, ordinary people whom it is difficult to believe capable of committing such acts against children. They are often people in positions of educational or spiritual authority, members of respected professions, and prominent members of society.

The victim, by the same token, is customarily regarded as unreliable, 'disturbed', a 'pathological liar', 'borderline', etc. The unique forms in which childhood sexual abuse is encoded also make it difficult to believe the horrendous stories, particular for those unfamiliar with the specific dynamics of traumatic memories and dissociation. Claims of 'she's making it up', 'it never happened', 'she brought it on herself', and 'she didn't resist' are common. It is thus important for the therapeutic setting to include social awareness of the significance of these forms of abuse – i.e., that they constitute part of a widespread social phenomenon rather than being specialized clinical cases or tragic personal circumstances. Such awareness is still unfortunately not prevalent amongst mental healthcare professionals.

Transference and countertransference

Clients sexually abused as children by people supposed to take care of them exhibit a particular form of transference towards the therapist that is a function of the human cruelty they have suffered. Traumatic transference includes a number of human-relation themes that were distorted by the abuse – a sense of threat, experience of helplessness, an inability to trust people in general and therapists in particular, sexual transference, etc. (Herman, 1997). Because of the number and complexity of their symptoms, their (survivors of childhood abuse) treatment is often fragmented and incomplete. Because of their characteristic difficulties in close relationships, they are particularly vulnerable to revictimization by caregivers. They may become engaged in ongoing, destructive interactions, in which the medical or mental health system replicates the behaviour of the abusive family (Herman, 1997).

Therapists can be overwhelmed by the need to become witnesses to stories of horrendous events, reacting instinctively in ways that may put the therapeutic alliance at risk. Traumatic countertransference includes the whole range of therapists' emotional responses towards the victims and the trauma itself. If they cannot self-regulate, they may confuse or alter the specific themes characteristic of trauma that arise in the treatment setting, thereby threatening the therapeutic work.

Therapists may give in to the temptation to label their clients with pejorative diagnoses that lead to bad prognoses, ignoring the sources of the trauma. This trap has been described in relation to therapists working with women diagnosed as suffering from borderline personality disorder. Their difficulties in therapy and the therapeutic alliance are often attributed to disturbed personalities rather than the trauma. The chances of effective treatment – the prognosis – in working with women diagnosed with a personality disorder being regarded as very slim, therapists tend to lay the blame for the failure of the therapy at their clients' feet. They thus seek to evade taking responsibility for the need to deal with the challenges attendant upon healing the severe damage caused by people whom society respects.

Traumatic transference and countertransference are an integral part of working with women who have experienced human cruelty (Davies & Frawley, 1994; Kinsler et al., 2009). Therapists must therefore be familiar with the roadmap of treatment relations with clients who have suffered extreme trauma, learning to navigate them without falling into common and foreseeable traps. Today, we know that transference and countertransference are coloured by the abusers' aggressiveness and cruelty and the victims' sense of helplessness, lack of trust, and anger. The trauma the victims experienced being relational – i.e., one that happened within a set of relations – it is inevitably reenacted within the therapeutic setting. Therapists must thus find a way to successfully deal with such scenarios.

Dissociative disorders are also typical of those who suffer from eating disorders. Many survivors thus come to therapy cut off in various ways from the trauma they endured. Within the therapeutic space, their traumatic history takes diverse, disguised forms. The unmentalizable representations of the parent as simultaneously abuser and caregiver, as well as the polarized experience of the self that develops around inconceivable object representations, can only be tolerated and internalized by children via the defence mechanism of dissociation (Davies & Frawley, 1994). The abused child cannot properly mentalize relationships or develop a positive sense of herself within a relational context. She thus dissociates, forgets, suppresses, or represses the experience, the dissociated parts manifesting themselves in the therapeutic setting in the form of an unconscious transference of the original feelings linked to the trauma onto the therapist.

This reenactment of unconscious elements of the trauma can form a useful tool in working with survivors of childhood sexual abuse. Identification and understanding of these unconscious behaviours can help clients integrate the previously inaccessible images that arise in the therapeutic relationship, thereby helping them to cope in the world. Davies and Frawley (1994) identify eight relational positions in this regard: the unseeing, uninvolved parent and the unseen, neglected child; the sadistic abuser and the helpless, impotently enraged victim; the idealized, omnipotent rescuer and the entitled child; and the seducer and seduced. In order to successfully cope with these complex challenges, therapists must ensure that they engage responsibly with their clients' transferences and their own countertransferences, being aware of the former and effectively managing the countertransference and vicarious trauma effects.

Vicarious trauma

Once the prolonged damage caused by traumatic events was conceptualized and the diagnosis of PTSD became part of the DSM-III in 1980, clinicians began understanding and recognizing the risks attendant upon listening to traumatic narratives. It gradually became clear that even second-hand exposure to traumatic events has an inevitable and irreversible effect. The long-term psychological effect of paying close and protracted attention to traumatic stories and reenactments has now become known as 'vicarious' or 'secondary' trauma. People who work with trauma victims can be deeply and seriously affected by the disclosure of their experiences, the effects sometimes lasting months or years (McKann & Pearlman, 1990). Vicarious trauma can cause severe mental, psychological, and spiritual damage. Its most significant aspect may be the loss of hope and meaning.

Vicarious trauma relates to an inner transformation caused by empathic involvement with clients who have suffered horrendous forms of trauma and the traumatic content itself. Therapists who are exposed to accounts and reenactments of abuse perpetrated by human beings on others – in particular, acts of cruelty committed by responsible adults against innocent children – on an ongoing basis become secondary victims, as it were. The trauma experienced by their clients becomes part of theirs – with similar results. Although the transformation is not necessarily negative, the concept of vicarious trauma refers solely to adverse consequences.

The cognitive schemes of therapists who work with trauma survivors constantly undergo change, affecting their emotions, relationships, and lives. Working with people who have suffered cruelty, betrayal, and aggression is a difficult task. Vicarious trauma is thus most common amongst therapists treating CPTSD clients abused by adults as children.

The extent of the destructiveness of the changes therapists experience depends on the degree to which they integrate and assimilate the traumatic narrative. Their life experience also affects their response to the victim and the trauma she has suffered. Therapists must understand that strong emotions constitute an inevitable part of working with trauma clients. They must also be ready for the possibility that they may lose their balance from time to time. No therapist is immune from the dangers of vicarious trauma.

The professional theoretical and clinical literature suggests various ways of dealing with vicarious trauma and the dangers attendant upon listening and witnessing. The goal is to support therapists and encourage them to protect themselves in such a way as to enable them to provide better service to CPTSD clients. Four aspects are emphasized: professional supervision, social support, spiritual renewal, and radical self-care (see below).

Therapists must take responsibility for protecting themselves, acknowledging the dangers of vicarious trauma and the difficulties involved in the type of transference and countertransference that occurs in the treatment with trauma survivors. It is important to be in touch with one's personal senses and the emotions that arise in the treatment framework. Knowledge of one's personal and professional limitations is also imperative. The damage caused by complex trauma not being easily healed, it is important to focus on processes rather than results and positive behaviours and achievements rather than difficulties and disappointments.

In order to deal effectively with the challenges of transference and countertransference, therapists must ensure that they remain authentic and emotionally accessible and honest. Authenticity entails understanding the source of one's emotions and needs and using them to better comprehend and help one's clients. Emotional accessibility pertains to maintaining openness and transparency with respect to one's motives and the treatment goals – answering honestly but sensitively when the client asks how we are feeling, for example. At the same time, however, it is also important not to confuse authenticity and openness with inappropriate self-disclosure of personal information or involvement in parallel relations (Pearlman & Courtois, 2005).

No one is immune from countertransference, making mistakes, or suffering vicarious trauma when treating CPTSD clients. Even highly qualified and trained therapists thus need trauma-informed consultation when working in this field (Pearlman & Courtois, 2009). Today, we know that the difficulties attendant upon maintaining a therapeutic framework of good connections, the transference and countertransference characteristic of working with CPTSD clients, and the dangers of vicarious trauma all demand that therapists invest in self-care and self-transparency (Pearlman & Caringi, 2009).

Supporting the recovery of people who have been affected by severe, prolonged, or early violence, neglect, or abuse is an honour and a challenge. It is an honour because it requires earning the trust of those whose trust has been compromised in other relationships. It is also a challenge because it requires the therapist to maintain self-awareness and attention to emotional reactions and behaviours while remaining attuned to the client's needs. (Pearlman & Caringi, 2009, p. 202).

The ABC Model – awareness, balance, and connection

Most of the therapists who deal with CPTSD do so in the framework of public-health services. Their welfare is thus largely governed by the policy of the body that employs them. Frequently, those on the front lines of client care are para-professionals, such as advisors. These spend long hours with people suffering from eating disorders on eating disorder or psychiatric wards. When the service provider is not built to meet the needs of CPTSD, these caregivers do not always receive the necessary training, support, advice, or professional guidance they need. This inevitably puts them at risk of vicarious trauma, burnout, wrong judgement calls, and violation of boundaries. Service-provider policies must therefore be carefully examined and revised to ensure that their employees are properly qualified for the work they do.

The ABC Model (Pearlman & Caringi, 2009) – Awareness, Balance, and Connection – was developed as a coping framework in order to help service providers avert, prevent, and deal with such problems. Driven by a desire to create a balance for therapists and establish supportive networks both within and outside the field, it focuses on the need to raise systemic awareness and provide coping tools. Therapists must know that the difficult nature of their work is recognized and make sure they are given the proper training to meet its demands. Service providers must also adopt a policy of helping therapists meet the challenge of working with CPTSD clients by creating a balance between their work and personal lives.

The key factors here are managing the number and type of clients and the accessibility of professional supervision. The employing body's policy must be to give therapists the opportunity to rest, recover, and regroup. Not only should they allow them breaks and permit flexible work schedules but they should also encourage them to take holidays in order to achieve the necessary balance. Connections and relations within the work setting and outside of it are vital for breaking the feelings of isolation and loneliness that are characteristic of working with severe trauma. Teams that provide peer support being the first frontline of defence, they must be established, encouraged, and provided with administrative and professional support.

When building a support system for therapists working with CPTSD clients, the four following aspects must also be addressed:

a) Ongoing informed professional training and supervision: Therapy for CPTSD survivors must be based on proper training, appropriate skills, emotional maturity, and competency. Unfortunately, interpersonal violence, and traumatization are still neglected issues in most mental health programmes (van der Kolk, 2009). Therapists must demonstrate emotional maturity in order to be able to deal constructively with the emotional toll exposure to trauma exacts and the relational dynamics characteristic of trauma survivors. They must also be able to cope with the severe symptoms and comorbidities their clients exhibit – including addiction and serious mental illnesses.

   Therapists who lack the necessary training and professional supervision to help them deal with such issues may well encounter serious difficulties in coping with transference, countertransference, and vicarious trauma. This is likely to cause them to make therapeutic errors that might otherwise have been avoided or become frustrated and stressed, thereby unwittingly reinforcing their clients' sense of stigmatization, reactivating the trauma, or aggravating their symptoms.

   The intensity and complexity of the transference and countertransference in CPTSD therapy demands professional supervision to enable and ensure that therapists recognize and understand the two processes. Examination of one's personal responses within a framework of professional, safe, and trauma-informed supervision can be a great help in identifying and coping with the damages of vicarious trauma. Trauma-informed professional supervision also provides a framework in which therapists can cultivate empathic responses and reduce personal pressures.

b) Social support: Therapists must develop a professional and personal network of support and emotional and practical help. The presence of supportive and meaningful communities serves to expand one's identity beyond that of 'trauma therapist', promoting therapist welfare on both the personal and professional level.
c) Spiritual renewal: CPTSD therapists must seek ways of renewing themselves spiritually. Religious traditions, attachment to nature and/or aesthetics, and finding joy and ways to laugh are significant resources in this respect. The exposure to human evil and the horrors people perpetrate against one another, in particular those weaker and more vulnerable than themselves, calls upon therapists to find ways of understanding human behaviour and the dynamics of human evil.[4]

d) Radical self-care: CPTSD therapists must actively seek to balance the horror stories to which they are exposed with rest and recuperation – sports, enjoyment, relaxation, etc. It is important to pay attention to and avoid empty activities and relationships and cultivate energizing, supportive, and meaningful ones.

Notes

1 Herman presented the model in *Trauma and Recovery* as a revision of that proposed by Pierre Janet a century ago.
2 Lily's story of a therapist committed to strengthening her provides a striking example of the importance of this principle: 'He reinforced me the whole way with my own strengths, like, I worked a lot on my own strengths and not on the . . . my scary things. Because I had, like, some scary parts. But he reinforced my strengths all the time, like, all these things that were also there'.
3 Hospitalized on adolescent eating disorder and adolescent psychiatric wards, Thyme is now working as a mentor for at-risk adolescent girls.
4 Hannah Arendt's concept of the 'banality of evil' or Primo Levi's books, for example.

References

Briere, J. (2013). Foreword. In C. A. Courtois & J. D. Ford (Eds.), *Treatment of complex trauma: A sequenced, relationship-based approach* (pp. vi–x). New York, NY: Guilford Press.

Courtois, C. A., & Ford, J. D. (2009). *Treating complex stress disorders*. New York, NY: Guilford Press.Courtois, C. A., & Ford, J. D. (2013). *Treatment of complex trauma: A sequenced, relationship-based approach*. New York, NY: Guilford Press.

Courtois, C. A., Ford, J. D., & Cloitre, M. (2009). Best practices in psychotherapy for adults. In C. A. Courtois & J. D. Ford (Eds.), *Treating complex traumatic stress disorders: An evidence-based guide* (pp. 82–103). New York, NY: Guilford Press.

Davies, J., & Frawley, M. (1994). *Treating the adult survivor of childhood sexual abuse: A psychoanalytic perspective*. New York, NY: Basic Books.

Felman, S., & Laub, D. (1992). Foreword. In S. Felman & D. Lab (Eds.), *Testimony: Crises of witnessing in literature, psychoanalysis, and history* (pp. xiii–xix). New York, NY: Routledge.

Herman, J. L. (1997). *Trauma and recovery*. New York, NY: Basic Books.

Herman, J. L. (2009). Foreword. In C. A. Courtois & J. D. Ford (Eds.), *Treating complex traumatic stress disorders* (pp. xiii–xvii). New York, NY: Guildford Press.

Kinsler, P. J., Courtois, C. A., & Frankel, A. S. (2009). Therapeutic alliance and risk management. In C. A. Courtois & J. D. Ford (Eds.), *Treating complex stress disorders* (pp. 183–201). New York, NY: Guilford Press.

McKann, I. L., & Pearlman, L. A. (1990). Vicarious traumatization: A framework for understanding the psychological effects of working with victims. *Journal of Traumatic Stress, 3*(1), 131–149.

Mendelsohn, M., Herman, J. L., Schatzow, E., Coco, M., Kallivayalil, D., & Levitan, J. (2011). *The trauma recovery group*. New York, NY: Guilford Press.

Pearlman, L. A., & Caringi, J. (2009). Living and working self-reflecting to address vicarious trauma. In C. A. Courtois & J. D. Ford (Eds.), *Treating complex traumatic stress disorders* (pp. 202–224). New York, NY: Guilford Press.

Pearlman, L.A., & Courtois, C.A. (2005). Clinical applications of the attachment framework: Relational treatment of complex trauma. *Journal of Traumatic Stress, 18*(5), 449–459.

Schwartz, H. (2000). *Dialogues with forgotten voices: Relational perspectives on child abuse trauma and treatment of dissociative disorders*. New York, NY: Basic Books.

Somer, E., & Saadon, M. (1999). Therapist-client sex: Clients' retrospective reports. *Professional Psychology: Research and Practice, 30*(5), 504–509.

van der Kolk, B. (2009). Afterword. In C. A. Courtois & J. D. Ford (Eds.), *Treating complex stress disorders* (pp. 455–466). New York, NY: Guilford Press.

van der Kolk, B. (2014). *The body keeps the score: Brain, mind, and body in the healing of trauma*. New York, NY: Penguin Books.

Chapter 11

Eating disorders, CPTSD, and appropriate treatment

We cannot solve our problems with the same thinking we used when we created them.

Albert Einstein

Understanding the close association between eating disorders and childhood sexual abuse leads to the need for a new way of thinking about the therapeutic services women receive in the eating disorder clinics and other frameworks to which they turn for help for their severe CPTSD symptoms. Sexual trauma is the result of the abuse of power and authority wielded by adults against defenceless children. Therapeutic services must therefore provide a corrective and healing experience of equality, mutuality, and compassion at the heart of which lies the recognition of the client's autonomy within the process of recovery.

The women I interviewed for this study who suffer(ed) from eating disorders and were abused in childhood reported that their most positive treatment experiences were at centres specializing in sexual assault/abuse. While these thus appear to be best suited to treating CPTSD clients with a history of childhood sexual abuse, they do not provide an integrative treatment that addresses all the aspects of CPTSD. They do not treat severe eating disorders, addictions, and the like that form part of the complex symptoms caused by childhood sexual abuse. In the absence of centres that deal with the whole range of CPSTD symptoms, the treatment women currently receive is partial, fragmentary, and deficient.

One of the questions that arises is whether separate treatment frameworks focusing on particular symptoms should continue to exist in the light of the current knowledge that these symptoms form part of CPSTD. Eating disorders, addictions, prostitution, juvenile delinquency/crime, etc., are all individual symptoms of the overall effects of childhood sexual abuse and thus CPTSD. Would it not be better to set up specialist CPTSD centres that can address the range of CPTSD symptoms – including eating disorders? Treatment under the definition of CPTSD would prevent a fragmentary approach that ignores the range of CPTSD symptoms that merely seeks to eliminate a particular symptom (the eating disorder or addiction, for example). In providing an integrative response to all the symptoms and sources of the problem, it would also obviate the need to transfer clients from centre to centre or ward to ward due to lack of expertise in one area or another.

As we have seen in earlier chapters, the division of treatment options is frequently arbitrary. Many clients arrive at centres with symptoms of one kind or another only to discover that treating these does nothing to help their underlying cause. If they succeed in getting rid of their original symptoms, they thus frequently develop new ones. Existing centres must therefore recognize the traumatic origins of the disorders and the complexity of the symptoms. They should be prepared to offer integrative treatment of the symptoms and their origin alike.

The understanding that many women suffering from severe eating disorders were sexually abused in childhood joins the knowledge that many women with mental disorders are the victims of complex interpersonal trauma. Many women do not report such events due to shame, dissociation, or even full or partial amnesia of what happened. These circumstances indicate that the treatment of women suffering from eating disorders must become trauma-informed (Elliot, Bjelajac, Fallot, Markoff, & Reed, 2005).

The development of knowledge concerning the severe effects of childhood sexual abuse has stamped its imprint on numerous areas of the treatment of girls and women in distress. Today, high numbers of women addicted to drugs (Gur, 2008), runaways and homeless girls (Chesney-Lind, 1989), women exploited in prostitution (Gur, 2008), female delinquents (Gur, 2004), women hospitalized in psychiatric institutions (Yen et al., 2002), women suffering from dissociative disorders (Somer, 2004; Putnam, 1997; Ross et al., 1991), women diagnosed with borderline personality disorder (McLean & Gallop, 2003), and women with eating disorders are thought to be survivors of childhood sexual abuse.

Turning eating disorder services into trauma-informed services

Recognition of the fact that most women who suffer from severe eating disorders were sexually abused in childhood suggests that eating disorder services should become trauma-informed. This view has developed in recent years following the growing realization of the high rates of childhood sexual abuse amongst clients receiving treatment for various types of frameworks. Trauma-informed services correspond to current knowledge regarding the effects of violence and victimization on the lives of women and their development. This affects all areas of treatment, from administrative procedures to the instructions given to the staff – directors, secretaries, admission officers, counsellors, etc. – that all interactions with clients must be beneficial and healing and seek to avoid reenacting the trauma. Trauma-informed services provide a warm, inviting, and safe place in which clients are respected, their specific needs addressed, all their symptoms acknowledged, and help given them to overcome the obstacles they face in reaching out for treatment.

Trauma-informed treatment is constructed in such a way as to minimize reenactment or reactivation of elements of the original trauma and provide clients with a supportive, democratic, and egalitarian environment in which they have the final say in their treatment and therapist choice. The guidelines for treating trauma outlined in Chapter 10 can serve as the framework for developing such an approach:

- Recognition of the effects of violence and victimization on development and coping strategies: The experience of victimization must be validated and clients' difficulty in looking for help be recognized from a place of compassion and understanding of their coping strategies and adjustment and in such a way as to increase their sense of security and hope of survival.
- Use of the empowerment model: This integrates elements that can increase clients' power in personal, interpersonal, and political spaces, enabling them to take responsibility for and control over their lives. The goal is to develop a form of mutual cooperation that will help them feel that their experiences and choices are validated.
- Giving clients full choice and control over the recovery process: Working towards client autonomy enables them to take responsibility for the healing process rather than remaining rebellious and resistant. If clients make bad choices, these can be discussed with them, helping them to understand why they made them. This helps them achieve joint, mutual treatment goals.
- Relational collaboration: Interpersonal violence being predicated upon power disparities, the trauma of experiencing overwhelming force can only be healed when clients are exposed to relationships in which they feel they are equal and respected. Therapists must therefore be aware of the inherent discrepancy in power in caregiving/client relations and do everything they can to minimize it. In order to reduce the pressure women feel to comply with authority, the service must be structured in such a way as to ensure that clients have the explicit right to direct and guide the treatment – including refusing to answer questions, declining a particular form of therapy, asking for an alternative form or another therapist, and changing the services they receive (where and when such resources are available).
- Honouring clients' need for safety, security, respect, and acceptance: The service must create a safe and welcoming atmosphere. This includes sufficient space for comfort and privacy and the avoidance of exposure to violent or sexual material. Staff should ensure that client confidentiality and privacy is respected, giving clear information and consistent explanations regarding what clients can expect to occur. Clear boundaries and well-defined rules are also vital for creating a safe environment.

- Reinforcing clients' strengths and adaptive capacities vs. focusing on symptoms and ability to recover vs. pathology: Trauma-informed practices perceive symptoms as the consequence of the need to adapt to traumatic circumstances rather than as pathology. They validate the client's capacity to recover and focus on her strengths, even when the coping strategies she has adopted in the past cause problems in the present. In this way, they reinforce her self-image and open up avenues for developing new skills and finding new resources that enable better, more effective, and safer ways of adapting to present-day situations.
- Minimizing the likelihood of revictimization: When service providers understand the potential for revictimization that exists due to the power they hold and the survivors' fear – or even expectation – of being hurt again, they can explicitly commit themselves to protecting those who turn to them for help. Invasive and insensitive procedures must be avoided, clients being given concrete information relating to the models of recovery. Above all, staff must be sensitive and do their best to avoid creating situations clients experience as reenacting elements of the original trauma.
- Involving clients in planning and assessment: Clients must be involved at all stages in the planning and assessment of the services, participating in target groups or routine feedback forums designed to assess the services and help improve them.
- Mentoring services: It is important to place clients who have recovered on the staff, where they can serve as mentors for new clients. Clients just beginning treatment who find it difficult to believe in caregiving figures can build a basis of trust with mentors. Representing a model of success, mentors can offer hope and the possibility of change and recovery. Their personal example can demonstrate to current clients that it is possible to overcome even the worst forms of trauma.

The treatment milieu must provide a corrective experience to all aspects of trauma – both the damage inflicted by the perpetrator and that caused by bystanders who ignored, neglected, or abandoned the victims. It is thus important to avoid interventions that clients may experience as invasive, rigid, or arbitrary. Neutrality and distance can also be experienced as neglect or an unwillingness to engage. On occasion, therapists must walk a very fine line between showing an interest, which the client may experience as intrusion, and caution in asking questions, vagueness, and ambiguity – which may be felt as bystanding or turning a blind eye. Therapists must be aware of this challenge and the ever-present danger of making clients feel as though the original trauma is being reenacted. Such awareness is the cornerstone of creating trust and a healing relationship with clients, ensuring that therapists understand their clients' severe reactions and their difficulty in persisting with the treatment. It also enables therapists to deal with such challenges in a way that exhibits their self-transparency and willingness to receive feedback. The stories of the women in my study evince that therapists who are prepared to receive criticism and admit mistakes reinforce client motivation to continue with treatment.[1]

An appropriate and integrative eating disorder treatment approach

> I think the message I want to convey to Dr. Palmer is to try and dig under the surface, not to look at it as an eating disorder and address the subject of the food and how to get people to put on weight and then release them. It's more really to examine what . . . what distress we're actually exhibiting. Because otherwise it's never going to go away, it'll always be there.
>
> —Sharon

> Because I assume that many girls who have eating disorders have been sexually abused, so in fact to introduce there something more focused of – in this field, and then simply to develop it.
>
> —Grace

It is important to integrate existing knowledge in the eating disorder field with the existing knowledge of how to treat survivors of childhood sexual abuse. Development of appropriate treatment for trauma victims requires a fundamental revision of the treatment of eating disorders – mass intake, forced feeding, restraint and/or isolation, removal from treatment for "non-cooperation" etc In line with Ford and Courtois' (2009) principles of CPTSD treatment we discussed in the previous chapter, an integrative model for treating childhood sexual abuse victims in the eating disorders field should include:

- Educating professionals to understand the meaning of the high rates of childhood sexual abuse amongst eating disorder clients. In light of the prevalence of a history of childhood sexual abuse amongst eating disorder clients, eating disorder professionals must overcome their resistance and opposition to treating clients sexually abused as children.
- Reexamining the aetiology and diagnosis of eating disorders and comorbidity. The recognition that most women with eating disorders – especially those with severe disorders and comorbidities – have experienced extreme trauma (including childhood sexual abuse) challenges the aetiology and diagnoses prevalent within the eating disorder field. It is important to make room for a history of trauma – whether remembered or not. Diagnoses must similarly correspond to the developing body of knowledge relating to CTPSD. Diagnoses of eating disorder with comorbidity that do not take the complex trauma that lies at the basis of the aetiology into account lead to the pathologization of clients and inappropriate forms of treatment.

- Developing specialization in CPTSD treatment within the eating disorder field. Eating disorder facilities must be equipped to treat CPTSD and all its symptoms. These include the whole range of symptoms that occur as a result of childhood sexual abuse. This comprehensive and integrative form of treatment can help prevent the phenomenon of 'Not in our school' that occurs today when specialist treatment centres focus on single symptoms rather than the disorder as a whole. It can also avert situations in which while the symptoms of eating disorders are alleviated clients develop other destructive ones to replace them – prostitution, substance abuse, suicide attempts, etc. – because the root of the problem has not been addressed and is forced to manifest itself in other ways.
- Increasing knowledge of dissociative disorders. Dissociation is a common defence mechanism for coping with childhood sexual abuse. Eating disorders themselves act in the service of dissociation, helping women cut themselves off from (the memory of the) sexual abuse they have suffered. An understanding of the internal logic and structure of dissociation are vital for the effective treatment of women suffering from eating disorders. Some dissociative symptoms – in particular those related to dissociative identity disorders – are very difficult to treat (Kluft, 2001). Such clients are thus frequently misdiagnosed and receive inappropriate treatment in mental health facilities (Chefetz, 2006).

The incorporation of eating disorder treatment within sexual assault centres

The understanding that eating disorders form an integral part of the spectrum of CPTSD symptoms of childhood sexual abuse demands that special sexual assault centres be equipped to deal with eating disorders. The present study demonstrates that, due to the lack of expertise in eating disorder treatment, women sexually abused in childhood who suffer from eating disorders find it difficult to get treatment at sexual assault centres. It is important that such specialist centres relate to eating disorders as part of the range of complex symptoms exhibited by those sexually abused as children and develop methods to cope with the severe eating disorders from which their clients suffer. In this way, the prevalent current phenomenon of turning away clients with severe eating disorders and referring them to eating disorder frameworks can be prevented.

The incorporation of eating disorder treatment within centres for at-risk women

Today, extensive evidence attests to the fact that high numbers of at-risk women – drug addicts, those exploited in prostitution, delinquents, at-risk youth, etc. – were sexually abused as children. Childhood sexual abuse being one of the primary reasons for the various distresses women and girls suffer, it is unsurprising that many of them develop eating disorders alongside other symptoms – addictions, delinquency, prostitution, running away from home, etc. All these form part of the matrix of CPTSD symptoms. It is thus important that centres for at-risk women are equipped to deal with eating disorders as an integral part of their treatment programmes.

Note

1 See, for example, Evelyne's comments regarding the difference between A Room of Your Own – a facility for treating young victims of childhood sexual abuse – and the eating disorder wards on which she was hospitalized: 'Really, when I got to A Room of Your Own, I was more able lots of times to say what I needed. Which is also something I never dared do before. And the fact that lots of times they actually listened to me. I mean, their ability, but listening, caring, and trying to be where I was, even when they made mistakes, they really tried to go back and understand what had been wrong, what they could correct, what they could change, what could help.'

References

Chefetz, R. A. (2006). Preface: Why should you read these articles on dissociation processes? *Psychiatric Clinics of North America, 29*, xv–xxiii.

Chesney-Lind, M. (1989). Girls' crime and women's place: Toward a feminist model of delinquency. *Crime & Delinquency, 35*(1), 5–29.

Elliot, D. E., Bjelajac, P., Fallot, R. D., Markoff, L. S., & Reed, G. B. (2005). Trauma-informed or trauma denied: Principles and implementation of trauma-informed services for women. *Journal of Community Psychology, 33*(4), 461–477.

Ford, J. D., & Courtois, C. A. (2009). Defining and understanding complex trauma and complex traumatic stress disorder. In C. A. Courtois & J. D. Ford (Eds.), *Treating complex traumatic stress disorders* (pp. 13–30). New York, NY: Guilford Press.

Gur, A. (2004). *The experience of prostitution among women who involved in street prostitutions in Israel* (MA thesis). Tel Aviv University Publishing House (Hebrew), Tel Aviv.

Gur, A. (2008). Women addicted to drugs: Characteristics and treatment. In H. Mell, M. Hovav, & M. Golan (Eds.), *Addiction, violence and sexual offense: Mandatory treatment* (pp. 93–117). Jerusalem: Carmel.

Kluft, R. P. (2001). The difficult-to-treat patient with dissociative disorder. In M. J. Dewan & R. W. Pies (Eds.), *The difficult-to-treat patient* (pp. 209–242). Washington, DC: American Psychiatric Press.

McLean, L. M., & Gallop, R. (2003). Implications of childhood sexual abuse for adult borderline personality disorder and complex posttraumatic stress disorder. *American Journal of Psychiatry, 160*(2), 369–372.

Putnam, F. W. (1997). *Dissociation in children and adolescents: A developmental perspective*. New York, NY: Guilford Press.

Ross, C. A., Miller, S. D., Bjornson, L., Reavor, P., Fraser, G. A., & Anderson, G. (1991). Abuse histories in 102 cases of multiple personality disorder. *Canadian Journal of Psychiatry, 36*, 97–101.

Somer, E. (2004). To be or not to be: Childhood trauma and dissociative disorders. In Z. Seligman & Z. Solomon (Eds.), *Critical and clinical perspectives on incest* (pp. 164–192). Tel Aviv: Hakibbutz Hameuchad and Tel Aviv University Publishing House (Hebrew).

Yen, S., Shea, M. T., Battle, C. L., Johnson, D. M., Zlotnick, C., Dolan-Sewell, R. et al. (2002). Traumatic exposure and PTSD in borderline, schizotypal, avoidant, and obsessive-compulsive personality disorders. *Journal of Nervous and Mental Disease, 190*, 510–518.

Epilogue

> What I would like to do is scream: and in that scream I would have the screams of the raped, and the sobs of the battered; and even worse, in the center of that scream I would have the deafening sound of women's silence, that silence into which we are born because we are women and in which most of us die. (Dworkin, 1983, p. 163)

Writing this book aroused in me mixed, ambivalent feelings. On the one hand, I felt a duty and drive to publish it in the hope and belief that my voice – that of someone who specializes in complex traumas in general and childhood sexual abuse in particular, seeking to enhance the treatment survivors of childhood sexual abuse receive within the mental health service in general and the framework of eating disorders in particular – could be a channel through which women can make themselves heard. On the other, time and again I found myself reluctant to publish a critical book that might be interpreted as dismissing all the important work eating disorder experts have been doing. On several occasions, I put the manuscript away. Each time I did, however, something happened to make me feel that it was important, giving me renewed energy to return to it.

As I analysed the data I gathered for my doctoral dissertation, I gradually became aware that contemporary eating disorders are the direct successors of the 'madness' attributed to women, the modern diagnosis of 'eating disorders' being both arbitrary and fragmented and contributing to the silencing and muting of the trauma that lies at their basis. My personal resistance to psychiatric classifications began much earlier, in the context of my work with female prisoners and drug addicts. Over thirty years ago, when I began working in a female gaol, I saw how the writing on the wall was ignored – the horrendous abuse the inmates had suffered as children. Rather than recognizing this background, other diagnoses were always made – borderline personality disorder, antisocial personality disorder, etc. These labels not only brand and humiliate women but also indicate a bad prognosis.

As a therapist, I understood that another conceptual diagnostic framework was necessary to give visibility to the severe trauma the women had experienced in childhood, one capable of identifying their acute symptoms and disturbed behavioural and relational patterns (including those with themselves) as coping strategies and offering alternative ways of coping that are safe rather than destructive. At that time, the only available diagnosis was PTSD. This primarily relating to single-event traumas occurring in adulthood, it does not fit all the complex symptoms attendant upon childhood maltreatment. The conceptual framework I found was the developing field of feminist treatment of women and the treatment of women survivors of childhood sexual abuse. This change in diagnostic definitions and the new approach to treatment that followed in its wake have brought about a dramatic revolution in the rehabilitation of women offenders, prisoners, drug addicts, and those exploited by prostitution – a high percentage of whom also suffer from severe eating disorders.

The field of eating disorders, in contrast, developed within the psychiatric establishment. Taking on the very psychiatric diagnosis of 'eating disorders' seemed to me like being the child who points out the emperor's nakedness. To my great surprise, as I finished writing the book – coincidently coinciding with the publication of DSM-5 – prominent psychiatrists across the globe, headed by Allan Frances, chair of the task force that produced DSM-IV, began questioning this key diagnostic tool. In *Saving Normal* (2013), he argues that the 'psychiatric Bible' will hyper-inflate the already existing plethora of psychiatric diagnoses in DSM-IV, warning that millions of 'normal' people are thereby likely to become psychiatric patients. This phenomenon can only play into the hands of the Big Pharma.

Therapists who have undertaken to treat people suffering from mental health issues daily face the question of how human beings cope with the atrocities we commit against one another. Today, the epidemic of childhood abuse is the most widespread global health problem, it being estimated that around a third of all children are abused. We now know that most psychiatric patients have a history of childhood abuse. As Bessel van der Kolk observes, however, 'It is ironic that, despite the fact that people with complex trauma histories probably make up the bulk of patients seen in mental health centers, they remain nameless and homeless' (2009, p. 464).

One of the central pillars of my work today is the attempt to improve the way in which populations known to contain survivors of complex traumatic childhood history are treated. For some years, I have taught a course on 'CPTSD and dissociative disorders – diagnosis and treatment' in the framework of the MSW clinical treatment of trauma track in the School of Social Work at Tel Aviv University. I also teach courses on transforming treatment services into trauma-informed services in a broad range of frameworks. I meet with top-ranking officials from the Welfare Ministry and give presentations on the subject in numerous services. As part of my previous work as head of the female prisoners' rehabilitation programme, I made protracted efforts over many years to turn it into a trauma-informed programme. These efforts were far from simple, the examples cited in the book demonstrating that many treatment procedures revolve around the therapist's expertise. They are thus frequently punitive and authoritarian. Many therapeutic staff resist the democratization and humanization of the treatment process, the idea that the final authority must lie with the patients requiring them to thoroughly revise the way they think. In my experience, when therapists receive the proper training – including knowledge of interpersonal trauma, an understanding of its dynamics, and appropriate treatment tools – patients diagnosed with severe disorders and refractory symptoms exhibit real, even miraculous, signs of improvement.

At the basis of this book lies the courage the women whom I interviewed found to speak about the most awful thing of all in the hope of bringing about a change in the way women suffering from severe eating disorders are treated. It reflects my commitment to give them a platform and utilize the professional tools at my disposal to work on their behalf. The treatment of women who have suffered human cruelty requires us as therapists to take upon ourselves the difficult – at times Sisyphean – task of creating a therapeutic alliance based on mutual respect, compassion, love, and empathy. My hope is that this book can sow some seeds of humanity, healing, and mutual responsibility in the soil that has been scorched by the betrayal of the social agents of the society in which we live.

References

Dworkin, A. (1983). *I want a twenty-four hour truce during which there is no rape: Letters from a war zone*. Retrieved from http://www.nostatusquo.com/ACLU/dworkin/WarZoneChaptIIIE.html.

Frances, A. (2013). *Saving normal*. New York, NY: William Morrow.

van der Kolk, B. (2009). Afterword. In C. A. Courtois & J. D. Ford (Eds.), *Treating complex stress disorders* (pp. 455–466). New York, NY: Guilford Press.

Appendix

Dawn's story

Prologue

Dawn is 25, a social worker, bright, ambitious, and pretty. During our interview, I asked her if she would be willing to tell me about the abuse she suffered at the hands of her father. Although she was unable to give me an account of it immediately following the interview, on her way home she wrote to tell me on the first computer she could find that she had spent her whole life waiting for someone to ask her: 'What exactly happened?' She said she would write down her story and send it to me.

It is a perfect example of what this book has set out to address: the horrendous nature of incest, the way no one around took notice or cared, dissociation as a vital survival mechanism, the dynamics and role played by her eating disorder, the hospitalizations on eating disorder wings during her adolescence, the routine family therapy on the ward, to which her father was also asked to participate, her resistance, the way in which her therapists paid no attention to the sexual abuse even after she had told them about it, and her tragic revictimization. Above all, however, it demonstrates Dawn's astonishing will and ability to survive. Today, she is in a much better place than she was when I interviewed her. She has completed her Masters in Social Work, is working, and is in a positive and safe long-term relationship.

She chose to write her personal story in order to help women and girls caught in the circles of abuse and severe eating disorders. It is told here in her own words, both from her written account and the interview.

A girl in a prison: childhood, sexual abuse, and dissociation

I was born on a kibbutz to parents who didn't particular love one another. They got married at a really, really young age, when they were nineteen. It's only recently that I discovered that they didn't really want to get married but because my mother got pregnant, my father's parents forced them to get married because they were religious. And then my sister was born, and two years later I was born. My father immigrated to Israel when he was one year old and lived all the time in the south. My mother is a kibbutz child. They met in the army and went to live on the kibbutz.

We lived on the kibbutz until I was seven and then we moved to the city. My parents' relations were never good, they never got on. There was always shouting at home, quarrels, curses, and even physical violence. Life under the shadow of fear of what would happen. What would cause my father to lose his patience again? What smallest thing would set him off? Inside the house he was one person and outside he was someone completely different. At home, there was shouting, anger, blows, and later abuse as well. Outside, there were smiles, goodheartedness, and rather strangely even shyness – an attempt to appease everyone around him. An educated man trying to build himself.

My mother couldn't do anything. My father didn't let her go out to work. He was always suspicious of her. He was always sure that she was doing things behind his back. Always when she went out, even if we went with her, when she got back he would interrogate her about where she'd been and everything.

Ever since I remember myself I've tried to be a perfect child, the one who's good at school, quiet, organized, the best at rhythmic gymnastics, the one everyone only had good things to say about. When I was seven, something broke. I continued to be the perfect child outwardly, and really ever since, up to today, but inside everything was broken, shattered, broke down.

I remember the first time as if it were yesterday, but I'm not always sure that that was the first time. And perhaps there were times before then and it's hard to accept the fact that I can't remember.

My mother and sister went shopping. Mum always liked my sister better, because she was prettier than me. She was prettier than me, much prettier. And it was obvious that Mum liked her better. When we were small, she would take her with her mostly and I would stay at home. I always had the feeling that they took her out because they could boast about her, how pretty she was. The pretty girl that everyone looked at and complimented her and my mother. My mother's pride and joy.

Being pretty was always the most important thing in the house, the outward appearance. Marks were important but not enough to get encouragement or love for. My sister was always also the more disturbed one, so she got more attention. I always saw her as the bad child. The one who didn't go to school, who got bad marks, who hated me, who shouted at me and beat me up.

And so from about six I started staying alone a lot with my father in the house, because my mother would try as much as possible not to be at home, and she would take my sister with her. That time I got out of the shower and Mum and my sister had already gone out. I could see my room from the bathroom and I saw my father looking at me. I went into my room and saw my father coming towards it. I remember he came in, close the door, and I was still undressed. I wondered if I should start looking for my clothes in the wardrobe and what he was waiting for. I remember that I was frightened and afterwards

I wondered why. Because I was just a seven-year-old, but already then I felt something wasn't right, something forbidden. I wondered what Dad could do and what he shouldn't do. I felt it was forbidden but I still wasn't sure.

Remember that I felt confused, walking round with my back to my father behind the bookcase to look for clothes, and a second later remember him close to me from behind, touching me under the towel and putting his fingers into my genitals. Gradually it got more painful and he got stronger. He didn't say a word and that only made more frightened of him. Dad was always strong, when he beat me it hurt. I was always afraid of him. Remember that I was dumbstruck, don't remember crying, don't remember feeling anything – remember it as though something very technical. But today when I think about it, I'm on the verge of tears, and it's really hard to go back to those moments. A small child, so small, and Dad hot-tempered, touching his little girl, and Mum not doing anything.

I think that already at that age I understood that if I wanted a parental figure in my life I would have to look elsewhere, because at home there was nobody who would protect me, who would look after me. I think that already then I understood that it wasn't right, but I didn't understand the enormity of the awful act.

At the same moment all these feeling just welled up. I was frightened to cry, I was frightened to move, I was frightened that I might set him off, and I wasn't sure what would happen I did. I felt so small. I remember that I felt on that occasion something inside me go dumb. A part of me was silenced. For five years, not a week passed without it happening.

My second memory is of Mum again taking my older sister shopping. I remember my father seconds afterwards in my room, I even remember the pyjamas I was wearing. I remember it was winter and remember being disconnected – remember being there and not being there – doing what Dad asked – knowing how it hurt when he beat me and doing everything not to get beaten.

Remember that in those years Dad got into the shower with me and Mum was at home. Remember Dad looking at me undressing and asking me to look at him. Remember him enjoying the showering and me being crushed again every time. Doing everything so that the walls I'd built around myself wouldn't fall down, that I wouldn't feel anything. Dad would get in the shower, and look at me angrily so that I'd understand I had to take my clothes off. At first, he would keep his clothes on, turn the tap, look at me, and then touch me, soap me, sometimes he'd ask me to close my eyes. And then he'd get in as well. And in minutes his male organ would be inside me. I remember it was much easier because then there was no need to hide the blood. He didn't get angry with me because I'd made more work for him. The shower was the place it hurt less, where he was less angry, where it was quieter.

And Mum was there! Downstairs, and nothing! I can't understand that. When I write this now I can hardly move, the tears are streaming without end, want to scream. But then nothing came out of me. I remember being there, but I don't have any feelings, nothing! I was completely disconnected from myself. Gradually, I simply wasn't there. Or I was but I could only see what was happening, I wasn't in my body, I didn't feel anything – nothing.

Lots of times by underwear had blood stains on it and I did everything I could to hide them. I was afraid that Mum would get angry, I was afraid that Dad would get angry, I was afraid that something would happen to me if somebody knew. I didn't know how to understand what was happening. I was afraid to speak, so I shut up and I hid it. At home, I didn't want anyone else to know, outside I hoped that someone would realize that something was wrong. I was ashamed of my body. I'm still ashamed of it today, hate it, loathe it. When I was putting on weight, I used to do everything to get it off, so I could disappear.

From Grade 1, I would go off to school before the sun rose. My sister and I were began school at the same time but I would leave much earlier. The first child at school. Lots of things that happened then I didn't understand why I was doing them as I do now. I would leave for school so early, even before the gate was open, and would get to the classroom and it would be empty. I would do this almost every day. My mother never asked me why I was leaving so early. I wanted not to be at home. I would also always try to stay after school. I mean, if the teacher need volunteers for something, or other things. Probably during this time I was still totally in the dark that something was happening, because I remember I didn't understand myself when I got to the classroom, completely frozen, and began tidying up and arranging the chairs and desks along the lines on the floor. And remember how I hoped that no one would come before I'd finished and after I'd finished hoping that no one would move them. Remember that every time I tried different spaces, just in the hope that it wouldn't change anything, that everything would remain the same and look perfect. Remember myself almost crying when the students came into the classroom and messed it all up.

I was a wreck. I felt like I didn't belong anywhere. In school, I searched for a figure I could rely on. I looked for a mother, like the one at home but who wasn't emotionally available to me. Trying to find a mother figure outside, but all these years beginning to understand that you can't change your mother, that I'd always be left with the same mother and father that were there.

I remember those years and all the things look the same to me. As though it was a kind of ritual, in the previous house in the shower as well and in the new house. And it went on like that virtually every week until Grade 3. Then I was supposed to get into the rhythmic-gymnastics team and that means getting out of the house every day. Almost never being at home. But Dad wouldn't let me. And I remember that . . . that already then, like, I so wanted my mother to understand that something was wrong. But because he didn't let me, so she didn't either. And then I continued to stay at home and . . . it carried on like that until they got divorced.

In Grade 4, we moved house. I had my own room upstairs, a long way away from my sister's room and my mother's room. I remember then it got more frequent. I already didn't know when he would come and when he wouldn't. In the previous house it would usually happen once or twice a week. In the new house, I sometimes already felt that it was every night. I'd get up in the morning and already not know whether it had happened or not, because even when it didn't happen I felt disconnected.

Every night it was the same thing, almost exactly the same time, very few words spoken. Like before, I would first have to undress and then he would caress and touch me, and that always felt painful. And then he would take his clothes off. And from there everything would happen very fast until the penetration. I remember that when he would take his clothes off that was the moment I couldn't breathe because I knew it was happening again. I remember being disconnected, but I still remember feeling. I remember wanting to cry but telling myself I couldn't because I was so afraid.

I think that all these years I still wasn't sure if it was alright or not, what was happening. I didn't talk to anyone about it, but I didn't see then how hellish and horrendous it was for me. Perhaps I couldn't see so I could go on living and surviving.

I never had friends to sleep over and I never spent the night with any of them. You weren't allowed. There were lots of limits at home. You had to come straight from school and if you didn't – the physical violence would begin. Nobody could get angry at you in school or something not be right. I had to eat everything on the plate, I had to shower every day after lunch. And then I had to my homework, without TV, without music. You couldn't go to friends most of the time, and if you did then you had to be home by seven.

Remember getting beatings over and again from my father. Remember being naked then. Remember observing it from the side. Remember my mother's helplessness in the face of my father's violence. Remember the moment when Mum went over to Dad's side and began to beat me as well. Today, if you ask her she'll tell you that that she never lifted a finger to me. Like whole parts of her life had also disappeared on her. Dad was violent to her as well.

He was jealous, a difficult man. Outside, with other people he knew, with his extended family, at work, he was a completely different person. Shy, smiling, generous, caring. At home, he became a monster, violent, shouting, hurting, watching everything that happened in the house. You couldn't speak loudly, you couldn't do anything he didn't agree to. A child in a prison. Being a bit late, getting less than 90 in an exam, saying the wrong thing, wearing the wrong clothes – everything ended in violence. Remember there were days when I hoped that someone would see the signs, but no one did – no one.

I remember that at some stage I would tell people that my parents were divorced, hoping for the moment that they would – and it came when I was eleven. I felt a miracle had happened. My father was unfaithful to my mother in such an unsurprising way and left home. It was something my sister and I knew. I mean, we knew that it was happening but we never said anything to Mum. We knew he'd been unfaithful to her with another woman. We were with him several times at her place. He would take us there and tell us not tell Mum. In the end, he told her and said that he was leaving her for this other woman.

For some reason, Mum was very scared of telling us that they were getting divorced. She was sure that we'd take it very hard. I remember the day she told us, and how happy we were. For a year he went back and forth, each time all over again. Came back to hurt us.

And then all of sudden it stopped. Both of us, my sister and I, each took it to the extreme in our way. I started with the eating disorder and she stopped studying at age . . . in Grade 8. Until today I don't know if he abused her as well. She's still in touch with him. They don't see each other often, but they see each other from time to time. We've never talked about it, my sister and I. So I don't know. I mean . . . I've asked myself lots of times, but it's not something that's ever come up with her because I don't have a good relationship with her either.

On the day he finally left for good, everything fell to pieces. Mum became depressed, lost twenty kilos, began to work long hours, and was almost never home. She began going out with female and male friends to clubs that sixteen year olds go to. My sister left school, even the truancy officer gave up on her. She went out with men over 20 and was violent towards me and Mum.

My father went to live in Palm Heights. It was sufficiently far for it not to happen anymore. He left anyone who was in touch with her and began to go out with a 22-year-old or something like that. He moved with her to Palm Heights and I virtually had no contact with him, until the hospitalization. I don't know if they're married, but he's still with the same woman, who today's around 30 or something, they've got two daughters. I see them at family events but nothing other than that. Like for example at my sister's wedding.

There was 'the secret of the eating disorder and repressing the secret of the incest': the eating disorder, hospitalization, and treatment

After he left, I was drawn completely into the eating disorder. And at school there was a place I could feel a bit normal. When I was eleven I threw up for the first time. I remember the first I vomited. It was late at night, I'd eaten six crackers, I got out of bed and went into the bathroom and threw up. I remember that I thought how easy it was and a moment later I promised myself that I wouldn't do it again. Since then I've not stopped.

From Grade 2, I did artistic gymnastics, which also contributed to the eating disorder. After my parents got divorced, my mother was hardly at home and I had the place more or less to myself. And I began to eat lots and to vomit. I remember myself living at age eleven with the secret of the eating disorder and repressing the secret of the incest. I ate in order to fill the hole inside and threw up in order not to feel anything and to get rid of everything that might hurt or be difficult. But five minutes afterwards it was already hard. That's how it began, and has never stopped.

I'd eat huge amounts: frozen food, milk, and meat, sweet and sour, ten thousand calories an hour. And then throw it all up in long minutes until I felt if I threw up again I would faint. Only then did I stop, when blood was coming already. Remember skipping classes in the middle of the day, going home, eating, and throwing up, and going back to school for the rest of the day.

My life revolved around the bulimia and at the same time I continued to play the part of the perfect child. Doing everything to be an excellent study, so that people would like me. And still feeling as though I was looking for a mother to replace the mother at home. The bulimia succeeded in disconnecting me from everything I went through, to numb the feeling, to blur the memories, and most of all to counter the awful loneliness. I really turned it into a 'friend'.

For three years I lived around the food. No one knew. It was all secret, a secret that was already too difficult to contain, but there was no one to share it with. I didn't know anything else. Everything revolved around the weight and food. Years before, in artistic gymnastics, they had told me to eat certain things and take off some weight. They would weigh me and I remember how embarrassed I felt. Today, I look at pictures and ask myself how stupid I could have been to believe that I needed to lose weight.

Up until I was fifteen, no one knew anything. In Grade 10, I had a friend who was dealing with anorexia and I told her. She went with me to the school nurse and told her. Without her I probably would be in a very different place in my life today. The nurse and the counsellor invited me for a conversation. I pleaded with them not to tell my parents and they agreed. I was sent for treatment through the health insurance company. I was treated in an adolescents' clinic and my parents didn't know, even though today I know that that's not allowed. I began treatment for a year without anyone knowing. There, too, no one thought to tell my mother. I just lived in fear that someone else would find out. It was a wasted treatment, full of lies. They made me eat lunch there and the moment I finished I'd throw up and leave. They didn't know anything about me, they just related to the food. And they didn't know about eating disorder either. When the summer holidays came, the treatment stopped. Afterwards I didn't get back in touch with them and they didn't come looking for me. It took the school nurse a while to understand that something was wrong and I was no longer being treated.

And then at sixteen they told me that I could not let my parents stay ignorant any longer, because they wanted to send me to hospital. I was sent for treatment again and this time for a diagnosis from a psychiatrist. The psychiatrist, who shouted at me that I was late while I'd waited outside while she gossiped on the phone with a friend and I didn't want to interrupt, didn't manage to get much out of me, but the final decision was to tell my parents. And that's when my mother found out. A month later I was hospitalized in Cedar Hills.

Hospitalization on the adolescent eating disorder ward

I was hospitalized for eight months on the adolescent eating-disorder ward. Dr. Palmer, the head of the ward, was my therapist. I treated the hospitalization like a summer camp. Really like that. I mean, at first, it was really hard. For the first month I thought for sure it would take a month and a half, because that's the minimum you have to be there, and then I would be released. And then when I understood that it was good for me to be there, I began throwing up and I didn't have a problem with it. And the truth is that there I also began cutting myself, because I saw other girls and so I learnt that as well. And somewhere I don't remember myself speaking about the . . . abuse there.

I was caught in some sort of fantasy about hospitalization, that it could save me from my home, and I couldn't see anything else. Without question, I matured there, I learnt to know myself. I got eight months break from the home that was destroying me, and someone actually saw me. But today I can remember and see things that I didn't attach must importance to before then, because in essence the only thing I really wanted was an embrace, nothing else interested me.

I think that during this period I was most occupied with finding a mother, because mine wasn't really there. So most of the treatment in effect centred around my wish for a relationship with a mother, knowing that it won't be my mother. All through the years, somehow I've always found some sort of figure that I could put in place of my Mum. And of course always in the end I've been the one hurt, I've always been the one left hurting, and always having to give her up.

The calming-down room on the ward where I was hospitalized was small and not very nice. On the new ward, there are two large ones with a window. I was in them, too, the second time I was hospitalized, which was for a month. And despite this, this experience of being put inside and the door shut before you, is a difficult one. I remember myself as a sixteen-year-old entering the ward for the first time and seeing the calming-down room, which one of the girls was in at the time, and saying to myself that there's no reason that I would ever go in there. And why in fact should I have a reason? A sixteen-year-old, sensitive and shy, only a kid. A calming-down room? Why?

I remember the first time they put me in it. By force. Don't remember the reason, but remember they pushed me in by force. Remember that they injected me with a tranquillizer in the room because I was resisting, crying. Remember the door being shut and locked behind me, and I'm lying on the floor, crying, scarcely breathing, and flashback coming up and overwhelming me. And it was very hard to calm down. Lack of control, the physical force the people supposed to be helping me were exerting on me, lots of tears and difficulty breathing, until the tranquilizer put me to sleep.

Remember this traumatic experience. And absurdly, afterwards, throughout the hospitalization I asked to put there. To go in there and not be outside. To be disconnected from the world, to be somewhere quiet, to disappear, to have everyone forget about me and not see (today I think it's very similar to other times when I was hurt but looked as though I was participating in the abuse and even initiating it). Lots of time I would go into the calming-down room in order to miss meals, in order not to have deal with food or with being together. Remember that when I was shut in there I hoped that someone would come and ask how I was, but they didn't always come. When I was hospitalized I remember being so hungry for attention, feeling so bad about that.

Remember the family therapy they forced me into and falling apart every week all over again. What happened was that in effect I didn't tell anything to anyone before the hospitalization. When I was hospitalized they did family therapy with the parents. To tell the truth, it seemed strange that they would ask the parents to come without suspecting that something might have happened with Dad. Today, now I'm a social worker myself, I know that lots of girls who are suffering from eating disorders were abused as children. But then, because I never told anyone that Dad abused me, they thought my parents should participate in the therapy.[1] At the beginning, I didn't say anything. It was awful. Only after about a month did I dare ask that they stop, like, bringing them. Then they understood that something was wrong. And yes, then first time in my life I said there'd been something. And they told my mother. I remember it was just . . . from that moment on I had no more family therapy on the ward. But we also didn't . . . didn't . . . didn't talk about it. I mean, I got released from the hospital. I told that to my therapist, Dr. Palmer. I said it once and then I . . . but there was no . . . It's possible that I really kept a lid on the whole thing. But it was very easy, because my mother didn't . . . didn't . . . didn't say anything after that day. And with my father, we really didn't talk after that. My mother and I never talked about it. I mean, what Prof. Palmer told her and that was it.

With my mother, the family therapy continued a bit longer and each time I fell apart all over again. I would go into the room, bury myself into my knees, not look at anyone, and cry. Remember that there absurd thoughts came up, the wish to die, the wish to disappear. The food was the centre and I simply sank into the awful secret that in fact had been exposed but I was left all alone with it. Because apart from stopping the family therapy with my father, they didn't do anything with it. One day after my release from the hospital, it's as though nothing happened, no eating disorder and no incest.

My therapist was amazing, I still stand by my words. Prof. Palmer is an expert in the treatment of bulimia. He's also an amazing guy, and he provided me with a healthy and supportive male/father figure. I think I simply wasn't in a place to give up on the vomiting as a way of coping with the severe abuse. Don't remember that the abuse came upon the therapy. It remained on the outside, not spoken about, don't know why. We dealt a lot with my need for a mother figure, my need for love, for hugging. The longing for something I didn't have, the self-harm, and above of the eating and vomiting. At another time and under different circumstances the hospitalization would have got me out of the eating disorder. But not in the case of sexual abuse that wasn't talked about and had no place. At least not as far as I was concerned.

In one place you quoted a sentence in which I said that I experienced the hospitalization at Cedar Hills as being like a 'summer camp' – and really, that's what it felt like for many years afterwards.[2] And now after I've read it, and haven't almost slept for two days, more and more things are coming up that I'd simply deleted, wiped out from my memory of the hospitalization. For me, Cedar Hills was an escape from reality and home. The further away and that no one should know. The ward protected me from the evil outside, from potential further abuse, from my family's anger, from attempting suicide (which happened in the end), and that's how I chose to remember it, as a 'summer camp', as a 'boarding school' that also happens to address the issue of food. I kept all the good memories and wiped out all the difficult and painful ones that I felt I'd dealt with there myself and no one else knew about them.

Everything comes up, the calming-down room, the pull towards it, the crying after the door was locked behind me, the difficulty in knowing that someone was controlling me and I had no means of escape, that I had no air and all the flashbacks and no one outside having any idea, and the more I cried the chances of getting out of the room soon went down. And eventually, after I fell asleep because of all the crying and pressure and pain, only then was there any possibility of getting out. And the getting out was even more frightening, going out into a place where you know you don't feel protected or safe, where no one understands you and no one knows.

The threats of infusions and the feeding tube because of the not eating. The 24-hour watch during the day and always having someone there when you go to the bathroom. The terrible anger because they knew and didn't do anything. Because I'd told them that my father had abused me and then nothing else was said about it. Cos I'd said that my father had hurt me and the next day, it was though I hadn't said a thing. And the revictimization wasn't delayed in coming after the hospitalization.

After the hospitalization: 'as though nothing had happened'

I was released from the hospital after eight months and I returned to a reality I didn't know how to deal with. After a week I'd already gone back to vomiting. The secret remained and I already couldn't contain it.[3] On top of all this, I was left completely alone. This whole experience of therapy, that there's someone with me, something there, someone for me, that all went when I was released.

When I was hospitalized, I told what had happened with Dad for the first time, but just as it came up so it was also closed. The family treatment stopped, and on the day I was released it was as though nothing had happened. Dad went out of my life and I continued to live my life as a secret. Actually, I didn't have to hide anything, Mum simply chose to shut her eyes. I continued to vomit and to eat through all the food in the house, and she made as though she didn't see. I continued to cry in my room and she made as though she didn't hear. Something in the hospitalization opened everything up from the beginning, all the memories came up, and the vomiting no longer helped me disconnect from the past.

Two weeks after my release I tried to commit suicide. I couldn't contain anything any longer. I swallowed 80 pills, but apparently I wasn't really ready to die because I told. And perhaps it was a cry for help, that someone would understand that I still wasn't alright. When I was hospitalized I lied and said that I wanted to live, but actually all I hoped for was to disappear. When I went home, I went back to living with the awful secret and the bulimia. In a second, I swallowed the pills and I regretted it. I knew that all I wanted was for someone to see me, for someone to hug me, for someone to take all the pain away and all the memories. I didn't want to die. I simply wanted to be normal. I told on the phone to the therapist from the hospital and he phoned Mum. She came back from Tel Aviv, took me to the hospital, and they pumped my stomach. A day and a half later, they released me, and as could be expected, the subject never came up again.

I went back to Grade 11 as sick as ever. Living in never-ending cycles of eating and vomiting. Even after I was released I continued to see Dr. Palmer for therapy every week for a year. I went to therapy but actually the eating disorder never stopped.

I think I was very disconnected from . . . from every feeling I had. I didn't feel anything and I was like that in school, too. I mean, I look at my report cards and . . . things the teachers wrote. I wasn't there. I was looking for a mother. Even . . . already at that age, I remember that I was really looking for that kind of figure in my teachers. But I wasn't . . . I mean, I wasn't connected to it at all.

Revictimization

It took me a long time to understand that I was addicted to the pain. I was addicted to it and I so I also couldn't stop what happened. At eighteen, I was very close to becoming a prostitute, I'd already met people who could get me into it. I could already see how easily I could be drawn into it. I wanted to be even more self-destructive. I wanted to have indiscriminate sex with anyone who wanted to. I wasn't interested in the money, I remember that that thought soothed me. And even today I still don't know why. It scares me to think how easily I could've gotten into it. Remember that I'd already fixed the first meeting, not far from the house. And it didn't happen. But the abuse I continued to experience was a substitute for that place. I was addicted to pain and to hurting myself and self-destruction. To self-violence, to disconnecting, to sleeping pills.

At the end of Grade 12, Mum met a guy. One of many she'd brought home. But this time was different. There was a feeling that this was serious between them. As a sign of the serious nature of the relationship mum gave him a key to the house. One day during the summer holidays before I went in the army, Mum asked me to go to lunch with him, to get to know him, and like a good, perfect child I complied. I put on a new dress I'd bought, which I'd soon regret. I remember this day as though it was yesterday. Remember the dress I wore, which I threw in the bin the next day. Remember I ate almost nothing while he ate a whole lot. Remember the song that was playing on the radio in the car on the way back home. Remember him asking me up for a cup of coffee, and me already knowing that something wasn't right. Something inside me froze, I didn't understand what he wanted. With all my power I forced a smile onto my face and said if he wanted he could go in remember him going up, making coffee, putting it on the table in the lounge, and remember him grabbing my arm and pulling me down on him and beginning to touch me. Taking my dress off. He raped me and I disconnected. Remember that in the first few second I fought him, and the next minute nothing. No crying, no shouting, no resisting, no saying no. Simply lying there like a doll, letting him do what he wanted. I didn't speak a word. I remember the tears rolling down, and not being there. I remember feeling he was stronger than Dad, more frightening than Dad.

He got up, looked at me with a serious expression, and went out. I cried for the first time so much and so hard that I nearly fainted. I was already in a different place. I was no longer the seven-year-old child who didn't understand what was happening, who wasn't sure what was allowed and what wasn't. I knew it wasn't right, but I still couldn't do anything. I knew it was forbidden, but I also knew I couldn't tell anyone. I hated myself so much, I disgusted myself. Everything comes up, it all comes up, feel that all the world's crashing down on top of me and that the end of the world has come. And then disconnect again, and again the eating and vomiting.

Then started seven of the worst years of my life. A week later, Mum and he broke up and Mum went to live abroad. She and her brother had a business, so there was talk of her going to live abroad as well and running the business. But it wasn't very realistic. I mean, it wasn't logical that she would leave the country because . . . with all this that she's not a Mum and isn't home, as though still . . . I wasn't yet eighteen, I hadn't gone into the army yet, I still hadn't. . .

And then she left, and he came to live nearby. He bought the whole upper floor and it was clear he wasn't thinking of moving. Mum never asked for the key back and he had an open door into the cage in which I continued to live for long, long years. I went into the army and he was still there, I finished the army and he was still there. I went to live in another city and went back after the eating disorder got worse, and he was still there. I started studying, and he didn't disappear. I finished my degree and nothing had changed.

He would be in the house before I got home, he was violent, he used to tear my clothes up, he'd often stand me in front of the mirror in my room and touch me, hurt me, push me down with force onto the bed and rape me. I remember that I couldn't disconnect like I did in the past. I'd take a whole load of sleeping pills afterwards to cope. After I started studying, I began to take pills every time before I went home, because I never knew what would happen.

And there's something else I've hidden. That I haven't told. Don't understand why but it's difficult to tell. When I was in the army, right at the beginning, I was raped. I went home with friends on leave after we'd finished the course for officer training. I went out with them and came home in a taxi. I got out on the other side of the bridge leading to the house and decided to go under, where the railway tracks are. I hadn't been there for years and I didn't go that way. Remember falling, so drunk that I could hardly walk straight. At the beginning, I thought I'd stumbled but when I tried to get up I understood I wasn't alone. He grabbed my head and shoved it to the ground. I didn't see anything, it was totally black. I couldn't breathe, I couldn't say a word. I was in shock. He stubbed his cigarette out on me and I couldn't breathe any more. I wasn't disconnected but from the fear, the shock, I couldn't move. I was frozen and couldn't utter a word. The tears rolled down my cheeks the whole time. I was convinced I was going to die, that I wasn't going to get out of this alive. I went home bruised all over. I sat down by the door of my room and fell asleep on the floor after crying and being in shock. He raped me, and that was the only time I told. In the morning, I phoned my commander and it felt ok to tell her. I didn't feel guilty except for the fact that I was drunk, and I was dressed revealingly. I told her and she took me to be checked at the hospital and afterwards I spent the holiday with her. Afterwards, I didn't talk about it, I didn't think about it. As though it had been completely wiped out. I went through all the required tests at the hospital and gave them my version. More than that I didn't want to do. I didn't have the energy. I was finished. I never talked about it. It's something that's completely disconnected from me. Remember it happened, remember slivers of a second, remember the scars afterwards, the cuts and the burns. Remember coming back to an empty house and falling asleep on the floor. Remember my commander coming to take me after I'd phoned her. Remember the tests, and afterwards remember how I put it aside and didn't talk about it. And I don't know why. Even when I tell my story to myself I omit that day. Everything I've gone through, and everything I've had to deal with, but this I couldn't cope with. I have no feelings with regard to that day, simply nothing. I don't even have to convince myself it didn't happen to go on living. It's simply not part of me.

When I got out of the hospital they threw me out of the officers' course. Where I was concerned, it was always going to happen. As far as the army was concerned, it was because of the eating disorder that I wasn't in control of. Prof. Palmer succeeded in convincing them to let me stay in the army despite them wanting to get me out completely.

So I continued in the army for another eighteen months, close to home. Every day I would go out, suffer abuse several times a week, and sometimes a fortnight get some peace. In the main it was when he wasn't in the country. I lived a double life, a double life that still goes on today.

I was released from the army and went to live far away from home and got a well-paying job reserved for released soldiers. There I was a completely different person. Everything was wiped out there. I even let myself get involved in a serious relationship for the first time. But sex was difficult. The nightmares didn't leave me alone, and touching was difficult.

And then my sister got married and I went to the wedding and when I got back I realized that I couldn't go on pretending anymore and I went back home. And he was still there. I started my BA and treatment at Sinai Clinic [a mobile eating disorders clinic near where she lived] at the same time. When I eventually told my therapist about it, she called it a 'relationship'.

I don't know why I didn't do anything. Why I shut up and am still shutting up. Why I have changed the lock, why I haven't gone to the police, why I haven't gone for help, why I don't say 'No', why I didn't flee from the house. I don't know! It's difficult to take the step and leave home. And in financial terms, I couldn't afford to.

Only six months ago, after my therapist stopped the therapy on the grounds that there was no progress and left me with everything that happened, I realized that I couldn't take it anymore and left home.

Dissociation

From an early age, it was like that, I disconnect. I know it happens to me and it happens a lot. It can also happen in other situations, when I'm sitting in group supervision or doing something . . . simply . . . after quarter of an hour I realize that I don't know what I was thinking about or where I was, but I wasn't there. Mostly in therapy, it would happen lots of time and when it happened . . . its whole parts that are wiped out. When he was abusing me for the most part it was when I was disconnected, but I was still there I just wasn't me. I do remember, I remember virtually everything. But I don't remember me there. I mean, I remember . . . I see the . . . me looking at myself, but I wasn't . . . I wasn't in my body, I saw myself from above.

I felt the pain. Yes, but all the time I tried not to feel it. I think when I was small I didn't feel it. I don't remember. Today, I can say that I went through afterwards, at a later age, yes, it was too great a pain. And then I began cutting myself often and I took lots of sleeping pills. Because obviously I couldn't be disconnected all the time. I . . . I would cut myself all the time and I took loads of pills for that whole time.

While I was in the army, there was a psychiatrist who would seem for me the eating disorder once a month, who gave me sleeping pills, and antidepressants I wouldn't take, but I stored them all up. Afterwards, when I got worse and I was in Sinai Clinic, I had lots of prescriptions from the psychiatrists there as well. I got pills from her and . . . I'd use the sleeping pills all the time. While I was studying as well, and before. That's what helped. I got addicted to them.[4]

Sometimes, I wasn't sure what was better – to remember everything or not to remember anything. I think that uncertainty about what happened is too difficult, but living with the memory of so many painful things is too painful.

I can't understand why while I'm writing this now I can scarcely move, the tears are streaming non-stop, and I want to scream. And yet at the same time nothing comes out. I think I was there but I didn't have any feelings, nothing! I was completely disconnected from myself. Gradually, I was simply not there, or I was but I couldn't see what was happening, I wasn't inside my body, I didn't feel anything – nothing. Up until today I can't understand that place.

In professional terms, I understand the mechanism of dissociation, and yet I can't understand how I managed to get through that.

The association between childhood sexual abuse and eating disorders: 'nothing helps like this does'

I remember the time when the eating disorder started. I don't remember much of it, but I remember those years. I remember it was hard at school. I remember feeling different. But then the eating disorder started. Sometimes people ask me if I don't want to erase the eating disorder – but I don't. Because I couldn't have coped without it.

As far as I'm concerned, the sexual abuse label is worse. It only came up in my last therapy, when I was in Sinai Clinic. It's much easier to talk about the eating disorder, much easier to throw up, much easier to focus on food and weight. And to talk about that, it's . . . too hard.

It's only in the last month or so that I've starting to understand that all the past ten years it's been much easier to stay with the eating disorder and hide behind that, to put that at the centre. And everyone let it be there because everyone has an eating disorder of some sort. And it's much easier not to talk about the sexual abuse.

When I started vomiting, I didn't see any connection. An eleven-year-old . . . I decided that I needed to lose weight and I started throwing up. And over the course of time, every time I felt bad I would throw up. And only after the hospitalization, when the things started coming up did I really realize that that's my way of not letting them come up. I mean, every time I throw up I . . . repress it a bit more and I . . . put it aside a bit more, and ignore it. It's also to put it out of mind and a sort of way of talking about it. I mean, that . . . that . . . that someone will see there's some sort of distress because . . . you can't show it any other way, at least that's how I felt. I mean . . . how can anyone see something's wrong? Only through the eating disorder. I couldn't see another way.

Even today I don't see that I could've coped with what I went through without the eating disorder. I mean, I don't see another way of dealing I could have chosen. There wasn't any other option. There was no supporting environment or anyone who understood, and no one to talk about it. I mean . . . I didn't hear anything about it. And the eating disorder was legitimate. Most of the girls in my grade had eating disorders. So in some place I also had to get to the place where my eating disorder was serious enough that someone would pay attention. Only that way could I get to someone, to talk with them at all, to create some sort of relationship. Because I couldn't come and say, 'This and this happened, I need help'. And it's also much easier to find treatment for eating disorders than for sexual abuse, if it's not private treatment then . . . at that age, I simply didn't know that rape centres existed. So there was no one to talk to.

With regard to choosing another form of addiction – drugs or alcohol – I was too good a child to do that. I mean, with all my self-destruction over the years, I was very aware of what could ruin my future. And the eating disorder felt to me as though it was something that I could live past. The pills, too, and the . . . cutting and everything. I mostly cut on my arms. But you can't see it. Most of the scars are on my feet; on my arms I tried not to leave scars. Because, again, from a place that was very . . . I was very aware of . . . if I decided at some stage that I wanted to live, then I wanted to keep all my options open. And the eating disorder let me do that. With regard to knowledge, I know it does damage, but I put that to the side.

In some place, I like the throwing up, it doesn't disgust me. Even from the most aspect of eating however much I want and then throwing up, or eating however much I want and not putting on weight. And also the feeling of afterwards, it's just not to feel anything. It's to throw up everything that happens at that moment and not let anything stay inside. No feeling, nothing. Even today I only do it for that reason. I mean, I go home and it's too hard and I already can't contain anything. It's my way of coping. It enables me to cope, I throw up and that's it, everything's gone, there's nothing left. True, it's only for a moment, and sometimes it passes, and then I start feeling bad again. And then either to throw up again or to cut or to find other ways that again, everything . . . self-destruction. Talking doesn't help – and there's no one to talk to anyway, because no one knows. So it's the only thing where I'm with myself, without the help of anyone else on the outside, can help myself. Yes, it's not that over the many years of therapy I've been through it didn't come up, to find other ways. It's just that nothing helps like this does. Nothing.

Mum – '"funny" that all my anger over what I've gone through in my life is directed towards her'

I think Mum knew. She can't not have seen, not noticed. Or perhaps she was so preoccupied with herself. Lots of times Dad would shower me, Mum knew, she let him, didn't see anything wrong with it. Today, this knowledge only makes me even angrier at her, hate her even more. 'Funny' that all my anger over what I've gone through in my life is directed towards her and not anyone else. Because I wanted her to be there for me. For seventeen years, I waited for her to notice what was happening with me. Seventeen years of suffering and nothing.

My mother introduced two men into my life who destroyed me. Destroyed every part, even the smallest, in my soul. Today, I can say that they completely destroyed my life. I'll never be able to be what I could have been without them.

Can't understand Mum. I want a mother, I want a mother who can hug, I want a mother who can contain and protect, and just be there. I want a mother whom I can tell that I've finished my studies and be there at the graduation ceremony for my BA, because no one was there. I want to tell her that I've become a social worker, I want to tell her about the crisis centre and the course. I want her to be able to contain what I went through. I want her to tell me she's sorry. I want her to tell me she didn't know. Because then it'll be easier to forgive her. I want her not to marry him. Six months after she left the country and left me alone with him, she came back and they moved back in together. My mother continued going abroad and coming back and he continued to come whenever it suited him. Now they're going to get married next month.

I want her to destroy his life for me as he destroyed mine. I want her to know! It hurts that she's not there. And at the same time, I'm angry at her, angrier than at anyone else in the world. I'm angrier at her than at Dad or her soon-to-be new husband. I'm angry at her because she didn't see, that she didn't protect me, that she isn't there today after so many years. Hate her. Want to scream at her and be angry at her. How could you leave your daughter like that? How could you not see me? Not feel me? I threw up, I cut myself, I tried to commit suicide, I cried, I tried to get you to see me every way I could – and you chose to shut your eyes in my direction. You're not a mother! You're not my mother! You'll never be!

Treatment in the eating disorder clinic

After I was released from the hospital the second time I was in therapy for three months at Sinai Clinic because I left Dr. Palmer. Then I went into the army and was treated by a mental health officer. There, too, the eating disorder continued. And after I finished the army and went back to Sinai Clinic, in fact 'on and off' [English original] at Sinai Clinic until last August.

So it's lot of years of treatment for the eating disorder and I'm still throwing up. Today, I'm doing it less, it's not like it was. It can be a week with four or five times. The average is about twice a week.

Until today the treatment I had focused on the eating disorder. I never went for treatment at a place that specializes in sexual abuse. And only this year did they tell me at Sinai Clinic that I can't go on having treatment there. After five years, they've finally understood that the problem isn't the eating disorder. That I don't need treatment for that, that that's been the easy thing all these years. They've referred me to sexual-abuse treatment centres and told me if after

I finish treatment there I still feel I need them, then I can go back. So I turned to the sexual-abuse treatment centre in August and they really weren't sure whether to take me or not, because of the eating disorder.[5]

When they told me that they were stopping my treatment at the eating-disorder clinic, I was really angry. Both because I'd had the same therapist there for two years, whom I'd really gotten into and really helped me. And because I didn't want to go to the sexual-abuse treatment centre. I mean, I also didn't understand why I had to be put under a sexual abuse rather than an eating disorder label. What's the problem with that? Like, it felt to me that it was all a matter of labels.

The eating-disorder treatment – for me, it didn't help. Not the hospitalization and not Sinai Clinic. But again, probably because I was in such a different place. I mean, the eating disorder was the symptom of something completely different that just didn't . . . didn't have a place. True, I didn't say anything about it either, but the feeling was also that that wasn't the place to talk about it. I went to be treated for the eating disorder, not for that. Everything centred around the eating disorder. That was the main thing, and I didn't have a problem with that.

In my last treatment, there was a change and things started to come up there already. But I . . . like, only . . . I think I found it very difficult to define it because I really liked and was really close to my therapist. But she didn't know how to talk to me about it. I mean, she used the wrong words. They really closed me down. She related to one of the abuses, which happened while I was with her, as a relationship. Up until today, I mean, I never corrected her. I never told her how it made me feel when she said it, nor did I tell anyone else, because I didn't talk about it with anyone. That was the two years of treatment at Sinai Clinic, where the central subject was the abuse, we didn't know how to touch it in therapy.

On the day therapist called the abuse from my mother's soon-to-be husband a 'relationship' I was broken. At that moment, I realized that there was no room for the abuse in the therapeutic alliance. She didn't understand me. Didn't understand what I was going through. Didn't understand that it was abuse, not a 'relationship'. Didn't understand that I didn't want it, even if I was the one who didn't leave home. As far as she was concerned, if I went and knocked on his door and thereby continued the abuse, it meant that I wanted it. After two years, they stopped the treatment on the grounds that I had to treat the sexual abuse before I could deal with the eating disorder. I'd just finished my studies. Just felt that I could perhaps make a change, and then they stopped the treatment.[6]

I looked for a way out from within the awful pain and I got addicted to the pain of the abuse, the dissociation, the numbness, the self-harm. I didn't know any other way. It was either that or dying. From the moment I tried to commit suicide at seventeen and a half, that was my way of living. In the knowledge that death was always around the corner, if I chose to go that way.

25 years and the only ones who knew were my therapists. My mother never asked, never took an interest, and never wondered. And my therapist? She did

nothing! I didn't ask her to, but I told her – I wanted her to do something to stop it all, but she didn't. She was like Mum, all the things Mum wasn't, but she also shut her eyes to the horror and the pain.[7]

Treatment at the sexual abuse centre

I turned to the sexual-abuse centre and there they wondered whether they should take me because of my active eating disorder. Ultimately, they did, and I left after two months because I couldn't take being there. I felt they weren't willing to accept all of me, who I was. That the eating disorder disturbed them, that there was no place for it there. The focus was completely on the sexual abuse. And I felt that I need to escape for a conversation about the eating disorder, that was very difficult to bring up there. I lost weight and there was no one to talk to, so I just left.[8]

At the same time, I started a course for volunteers at the rape-crisis centre. There was room to share about myself, something that really helped me talk about things. There I found people willing to listen to both things – both the bulimia and the abuse. I found a place to be there for others and to volunteer and give of myself. To give meaning, even if only a little bit, to my life, and a safe place.

Epilogue: the abuse destroyed me, the eating disorder saved me, and the two together are gradually finishing me off

I'm writing you this now from the place in which I am today, and I'm not sure what was there five years ago. How I coped. I don't remember what I told myself, how I explained it to myself so that I could go on living. I only remember one big disconnection. Without feelings, without anything. The child who never smiled. That's how they always saw me. And 'funny' today that now people tell me that I smile too much. Really, there's such a thing as 'too much'?

Today, when I look at my life I can't look back and see anything good. My life destroyed me and what I could have been if it wasn't for . . . continue to eat and throw up with intolerable frequency. Continue to be hurt once a . . . when I go home. Can't find a stable and good life. Am immersed in pain, immerse in difficult memories. Work 67 hours a week just to escape it, and find myself finding it hard to escape. Starting and ending relationships because of the intimacy issue. Fell more comfortable than in the past but still light years away from the ability to be in a relationship. The bulimia has got me into crazy debts because of the amounts of food I buy, which puts me even further behind. Thinking of going home, back to the abuse, the closest to death. Every day, I try to be dissociated from all these things and manage to survive one more day, and another, but when I put a mirror in front of my face I understand how much I'm under its control. The sexual abuse destroyed me, the eating disorder saved me, and both together are slowly ending my life.

Notes

1 Dawn's story confirms my reservations regarding family therapy as a routine approach to treating girls hospitalized on eating disorder wards. When treating populations that include many (up to 70 percent) who were sexually abused as children, frequently by a close family member, family therapy must take into account the likelihood that one of the parents was responsible for the abuse. It thus cannot constitute a routine therapeutic method. When employed as such, it signals to the victims that the therapist is collaborating with the denial and silencing, turning his or her gaze away from the abuse and leaving the client with the feeling that there is no escape or way to convey the awful secret except through symptoms such as eating disorders. These disguise the source of the problem.

2 Dawn wrote these paragraphs after she had read my doctoral dissertation.

3 When a patient gathers the courage to reveal the secret of the abuse, she has a desperate longing for her disclosure to be validated. When the therapeutic environment does not relate to the abuse, the patient is left in even greater despair than before. The silence with which the revelation of the secret is greeted left Dawn feeling helpless and hopeless, unable to deal with the abuse. This may explain the extent to which her situation deteriorated and the revictimization of which she speaks below.

4 Substance abuse frequently serves as a form of 'chemical dissociation', helping survivors dissociate from the pain of the abuse by using it to self-medicate (Gur, 2004).

5 Dawn's story illustrates the extent to which the absence of a CPTSD diagnosis and the lack of training for the staff of eating disorder clinics have in dealing with childhood sexual abuse characterize patients with eating disorders. Receiving inadequate and fragmented treatment, they are transferred from eating disorder specialists to sexual abuse experts. Hereby, their feelings of disconnection and alienation are magnified, reenacting the original trauma that included neglect and denial by those around them.

6 The treatment given in eating disorder clinics does not correspond with the principles guiding the treatment of CPTSD. This is exemplified by Dawn's description of the ending of her treatment, which was completely arbitrary and unilateral. The rules guiding the treatment of CPTSD leave room to decide about ending the therapy by mutual agreement. When the patient is given a decision, this reinforces her sense of helplessness, preventing her from feeling that she is regaining a measure of control over her life.

7 Dawn's harsh statement illustrates the way in which abuse survivors, who experienced neglect, indifference, and denial on the part of those around them, need active and involved therapists.

8 Dawn's account of her treatment at the rape crisis centre once again demonstrated the problem of services constructed according to separate principles and focusing on different symptoms.

Reference

Gur, A. (2004). *The experience of prostitution among women who involved in street prostitutions in Israel* (MA thesis). Tel Aviv University Publishing House (Hebrew), Tel Aviv, Israel.

Bibliography

Ajzenstadt, M., Soffer, M., & Steinberg, O. (2010). *In prison I rest: Women prisoners beyond the walls*. Bnei Brak: Hakibbutz Hameuchad (Hebrew).

Anderson, K. P., LaPorte, D. J., Brandt, H., & Crawford, S. (1997). Sexual abuse and bulimia: Response to treatment and preliminary outcome. *Journal of Psychiatric Research, 31*, 621–633.

Andrews, B. (1997). Bodily shame in relation to abuse in childhood and bulimia: A preliminary investigation. *British Journal of Clinical Psychology, 36*(1), 41–49.

APA (American Psychiatric Association). (1980). *Diagnostic and statistical manual of mental disorders* (3rd ed.). Washington, DC: American Psychological Association.

APA (American Psychiatric Association). (1994). *Diagnostic and statistical manual of mental disorders* (4th ed.). Washington, DC: American Psychological Association.

APA (American Psychiatric Association). (2013). *Diagnostic and statistical manual of mental disorders* (5th ed.). Washington, DC: American Psychological Association.

Appignanesi, L. (2008). *Mad, bad and sad: A history of women and the mind doctors from 1800 to the present*. Londen: Virago.

Arnold, R. P., Rogers, D., & Cook, D. A. (1990). Medical problems of adults who were sexually abused in childhood. *British Medical Journal, 300*, 705–708.

Ashur, D. (2006). Haqdama [Preface]. In H. Cixous & C. Clément (Eds.), *The newly-born woman* (pp. 7–23). Tel Aviv: Resling (Hebrew).

Beauvoir, S. de. (2010). *The second sex*. Trans. C. Borde & S. Malovany-Chevalier. New York, NY: Vintage.

Bell, L. (2003). What we can learn from consumer studies and qualitative research in the treatment of eating disorders? *Eating and Weight Disorders, 8*(3), 181–187.

Belluck, P., & Carey, B. (2013). Psychiatry's guide is out of touch with science, experts say. *New York Times*, May 6, 2013. Retrieved October 22, 2017, from www.nytimes.com/2013/05/07/health/psychiatrys-new-guide-falls-short-experts-say.html?pagewanted=all&_r=0

Berger, D., Ono, Y., Saito, S., Tezuka, I., Takahashi, Y., Uno, M., ... Suemastu, H. (1995). Relationship of parental bonding to child abuse and dissociation in eating disorders in Japan. *Acta Psychiatrica Scandinavica, 91*, 278–282.

Bordo, S. (1993). *Unbearable weight: Feminism, western culture and the body*. Berkeley: University of California Press.

Brewerton, T. D. (2004). Eating disorders, victimization and comorbidity: Principles of treatment. In T. D. Brewerton (Ed.), *Clinical handbook of eating disorders: An integrated approach* (pp. 509–545). New York, NY: Marcel Dekker, Inc.

Brewerton, T. D. (2007). Eating disorders, trauma, and comorbidity: Focus on PTSD. *Eating Disorders, 15*(4), 285–304.

Brewerton, T. D. (2011). Posttraumatic stress disorder and disordered eating: Food addiction as self-medication. *Journal of Women's Health, 20*(8), 1133–1134.

Brewerton, T. D. (2015). Stress, trauma, and adversity as risk factors in the development of eating disorders. In L. Smolak & M. Levine (Eds.), *Wiley handbook of eating disorders* (pp. 445–460). New York, NY: Guilford Press.

Briere, J. (1989). *Therapy for adults molested as children*. New York, NY: Springer.

Briere, J. (1992). *Child abuse trauma: Theory and treatment of the lasting effects*. Newbury Park, CA: Sage Publications.

Briere, J. (2013). Foreword. In C. A. Courtois & J. D. Ford (Eds.), *Treatment of complex trauma: A sequenced, relationship-based approach* (pp. vi–x). New York, NY: Guilford Press.

Bromberg, P. (1998). *Standing in the spaces: Essays on clinical process, trauma, and dissociation*. London and New York, NY: Routledge.

Brownmiller, S. (1975). *Against our will: Men, women and rape*. New York, NY: Simon and Schuster.

Bruch, H. (1974). The perils of behavior modification in treatment of anorexia nervosa. *Journal of the American Medical Association, 230*, 1419–1422.

Bruch, H. (1982). Anorexia nervosa: Therapy and theory. *American Journal of Psychiatry, 139*, 1531–1538.

Brumberg, J. J. (1988). *Fasting girls: The emergence of anorexia nervosa as a disease*. Cambridge, MA: Harvard University Press.

Carter, C. J., Beewell, C., Blackmore, E., & Woodside, D. B. (2006). The impact of childhood sexual abuse in anorexia nervosa. *Child Abuse & Neglect, 30*(3), 257–269.

Caslini, M., Bartoli, F., Crocamo, C., Dakanalis, A., Clerici, M., & Carrà, G. (2016). Disentangling the association between child abuse and eating disorders: A systematic review and meta-analysis. *Psychosomatic Medicine, 78*, 79–90.

Chefetz, R. A. (2006). Preface: Why should you read these articles on dissociation processes? *Psychiatric Clinics of North America, 29*, xv–xxiii.

Chesler, P. (1972). *Women and madness*. New York, NY: Avon.

Chesney-Lind, M. (1989). Girls' crime and women's place: Toward a feminist model of delinquency. *Crime & Delinquency, 35*(1), 5–29.

Chu, J. A. (1992). The therapeutic roller coaster: Dilemmas in the treatment of childhood sexual abuse survivors. *Journal of Psychotherapy Practice and Research, 4*, 383–390.

Chu, J. A., & Dill, D. L. (1990). Dissociative symptoms in relation to childhood physical and sexual abuse. *American Journal of Psychiatry, 147*, 887–892.

Cixous, H., & Clément, C. (1986). *The newly-born woman*. Trans. B. Wing. Minneapolis, MN: University of Minnesota Press.

Cloitre, M., Stovall-McClough, K. C., Nooner, K., Zorbas, P., Cherry, S., Jackson, C. L., . . . Petkova, E. (2010). Treatment for PTSD related to childhood abuse: A randomized controlled trial. *American Journal of Psychiatry, 167*(8), 915–924.

Cole, P., & Putnam, E. (1992). Effect of incest on self and social functioning: A developmental psychopathology perspective. *Journal of Consulting and Clinical Psychology, 60*, 174–184.

Courtois, C. A. (1988). *Healing the incest wound: Adult survivors in therapy*. New York, NY: W. W. Norton.

Courtois, C. A. (1997). Healing the incest wound: A treatment update with attention to recovered-memory issues. *American Journal of Psychotherapy, 51*(4), 464–496.

Courtois, C. A. (2008). Complex trauma, complex reactions: Assessment and treatment. *Psychological Trauma: Theory, Research, Practice, and Policy, S1*, 86–100.

Courtois, C. A., & Ford, J. D. (2009). *Treating complex stress disorders*. New York, NY: Guilford Press.

Courtois, C. A., & Ford, J. D. (2013). *Treatment of complex trauma: A sequenced, relationship-based approach*. New York, NY: Guilford Press.

Courtois, C. A., Ford, J. D., & Cloitre, M. (2009). Best practices in psychotherapy for adults. In C. A. Courtois & J. D. Ford (Eds.), *Treating complex traumatic stress disorders: An evidence-based guide* (pp. 82–103). New York, NY: Guilford Press.

Dalle Garve, R., Rigamonti, R., & Todisco, P. (1995). *Trauma and dissociative experiences in eating disorders*. Paper presented at the Fifth Annual Spring Conference of the International Society for the Study of Dissociation, Amsterdam.

Dana, M., & Lawrence, M. (1999). *Nashim okhlot et atzman: Al anorexiya, bulimiya ve-akhila kefiyatit [Women eating themselves: On anorexia, bulimia, and forced eating]*. Tel Aviv: Modan (Hebrew).

D'Andrea, W., Ford, J., Stolbach, B., Spinazzola, J., & van der Kolk, B. (2012). Understanding interpersonal trauma in children: Why we need a developmentally appropriate trauma diagnosis. *American Journal of Orthopsychiatry, 82*(2), 187–200.

Davies, J., & Frawley, M. (1994). *Treating the adult survivor of childhood sexual abuse: A psychoanalytic perspective*. New York, NY: Basic Books.

de la Rie, S., Noordenbos, G., Donker, M., & van Furth, E. (2006). Evaluating the treatment of eating disorders from the patient's perspective. *International Journal of Eating Disorders, 39*(8), 667–676.

Demitrack, M. A., Putnam, F. W., Brewerton, T. D., Brandt, H., & Gold, P. W. (1990). Relation of clinical variables to dissociative phenomena in eating disorders. *American Journal of Psychiatry, 147*, 1184–1188.

Elliot, D. E., Bjelajac, P., Fallot, R. D., Markoff, L. S., & Reed, G. B. (2005). Trauma-informed or trauma denied: Principles and implementation of trauma-informed services for women. *Journal of Community Psychology, 33*(4), 461–477.

Fairburn, C. G., & Bohn, K. (2005). Eating disorder NOS (EDNOS): An example of the troublesome 'not otherwise specified' (NOS) category in DSM-IV. *Behavior Research and Therapy, 43*(6), 691–701.

Fairburn, C. G., & Cooper, Z. (2010). Eating disorders, DSM-5 and clinical reality. *British Journal of Psychiatry, 198*, 8–10.

Fairburn, C. G., & Harrison, P. J. (2003). Eating disorders. *The Lancet, 361*, 407–416.

Fallon, P., Katzman, M. A., & Wooley, S. C. (1994). *Feminist perspectives of eating disorders*. New York, NY: Guilford Press.

Favaro, A., & Santonastaso, P. (2000). Self-injurious behavior in anorexia nervosa. *Journal of Nervous and Mental Disease, 188*, 537–543.

Fellitti, V. J., Anda, R. F., Nordenberg, D., Williamson, D. F., Spitz, A. M., Edwards, V. et al. (1998). Relationship of childhood abuse and household dysfunction to many of the leading causes of death in adults: The Adverse Childhood Experiences (ACE) study. *American Journal of Preventive Medicine, 14*(4), 245–258.

Felman, S., & Laub, D. (1992). Foreword. In S. Felman & D. Lab (Eds.), *Testimony: Crises of witnessing in Literature, Psychoanalysis, and History* (pp. xiii–xix). New York, NY: Routledge.

Finkelhor, D. (1979). *Sexually victimized children*. New York, NY: Free Press.

Finkelhor, D. (1994). Childhood sexual abuse: An evidence-based perspective. *Developmental Clinical Psychology and Psychiatry, 40*, 409–417.

Finn, S., Hartman, M., Leon, G., & Lawson, L. (1986). Eating disorders and sexual abuse: Lack of confirmation for a clinical hypothesis. *International Journal of Eating Disorders, 5*, 1051–1060.

Fonagy, P., Gergely, G., Jurist, E. L., & Target, M. (2002). *Affect regulation, mentalization, and the development of the self*. New York, NY: Other.

Ford, J. D., & Courtois, C. A. (2009). Defining and understanding complex trauma and complex traumatic stress disorder. In C. A. Courtois & J. D. Ford (Eds.), *Treating complex traumatic stress disorders* (pp. 13–30). New York, NY: Guilford Press.

Frances, A. (2013). *Saving normal*. New York, NY: William Morrow.

Frances, A. (2013). *Saving normal: An insider's revolt against out-of-control psychiatric diagnosis, DSM-5, Big Pharma, and the medicalization of ordinary life*. New York, NY: HarperCollins.

Fraser, S. (1987). *My father's house: A memoir of incest and of healing*. New York, NY: Harper and Row.

Fredrickson, B. L., & Roberts, R. A. (1997). Objectification theory: Toward understanding women's lived experiences and mental health risks. *Psychology of Women Quarterly, 21*, 173–206.

Freud, S. (1896/1962). Heredity and the aetiology of the neuroses. In J. Strachey (Ed.), *The standard edition of the complete psychological works of Sigmund Freud* (vol. 3, pp. 141–156). London: Hogarth.

Freud, S. (1932). Femininity. In *New introductory lectures on psycho-analysis*. Harmondsworth: Penguin, 1991.

Freud, S. (1986). *The complete letters of Sigmund Freud to Wilhelm Fliess, 1887–1904*. Cambridge, MA: Belknap.

Freud, S. (1995). The aetiology of hysteria. In P. Gay (Ed.), *The Freud reader* (pp. 96–111). New York, NY: W.W. Norton.

Freud, S., & Breuer, J. (1895). *Studies on hysteria*. Trans. J. Strachey. New York, NY: Basic Books. Retrieved October 10, 2017, from https://archive.org/stream/studiesonhysteri037649mbp/studiesonhysteri037649mbp_djvu.txt

Gadalla, T., & Piran, N. (2007). Eating disorders and substance abuse in Canadian men and women: A national study. *Eating Disorders: The Journal of Treatment and Prevention, 15*(3), 189–203.

Gagnon, J. (1965). Female child victims of sex offenders. *Social Problems, 13*, 176–192.

Gelinas, D. (1983). The persisting negative effects of incest. *American Journal of Psychiatry, 46*, 313–332.

Goldberg, A. (2006). Preface. In *Dominic LaCapra: Writing history, writing trauma* (pp. 7–27). Tel Aviv: Khidekel (Hebrew).

Goldfarb, L. A. (1987). Sexual abuse antecedent to anorexia nervosa, bulimia, and compulsive overeating: Three case reports. *International Journal of Eating Disorders, 6*, 675–680.

Goldstein, A., & Katz-Charny, J. (2004). Therapy with families that have who have experienced sexual abuse. In Z. Seligman & Z. Solomon (Eds.), *Critical and clinical perspectives on incest* (pp. 278–301). Tel Aviv: Hakibbutz Hameuchad and Tel Aviv University Publishing House (Hebrew).

Goodman, G., Bottoms, B. L., Rudy, L., Davis, S. L., & Schwartz-Kenney, B. M. (2001). Effects of past abuse experiences on children's eyewitness memory. *Law and Human Behavior, 25*, 269–298.

Gordon, R. A. (2000). *Eating disorders: Anatomy of a social epidemic* (2d ed.). Malden, MA: Wiley-Blackwell.

Gore, S. A., Vander Wal, J. S., & Thelen, M. H. (2001). Treatment of eating disorders in children and adolescents. In J. K. Thompson & L. Smolak (Eds.), *Body image, eating disorders, and obesity in youth* (pp. 293–311). Washington, DC: American Psychological Association.

Greenspan, M. (1983). *A new approach to women and therapy*. New York: McGraw-Hill.

Grubrich-Simitis, I. (1997). *Early Freud and late Freud: Reading a new studies on Hysteria and Moses and Monotheism*. Trans. P. Slotkin. London and New York, NY: Routledge.

Guillaume, S., Jaussent, I., Maimoun, L., Ryst, A., Seneque, M., Villain, L., . . . Courtet, P. (2016). Associations between adverse childhood experiences and clinical characteristics of eating disorders. *Scientific Reports, 6*. Retrieved October 10, 2017, from www.ncbi.nlm.nih.gov/pmc/articles/PMC5090200/

Gur, A. (2004). *The experience of prostitution among women who involved in street prostitutions in Israel* (MA thesis). Tel Aviv University Publishing House (Hebrew), Tel Aviv, Israel.

Gur, A. (2008). Mufkarot: Nashim Beznut. Women Abandoned. Tel Aviv: Hakibbutz Hameuchad (Hebrew), Tel Aviv Israel.

Gur, A. (2008). Nashim mechuarot le-samim: Ma'afiyenim ve-darkei tipul [Women addicted to drugs: Symptoms and treatment]. In H. Mell, M. Hovav, & M. Golan (Eds.), *Addiction, violence and sexual offense: Mandatory treatment* (pp. 93–117). Jerusalem: Carmel.

Gur, A. (2011). *The relationship between childhood sexual abuse and eating disorders from the perspective of women who experienced childhood sexual abuse and suffer from eating disorders* (PhD diss.). Bar-Ilan University (Hebrew), Ramat Gan Israel.

Hall, R. C., Tice, L., Beresford, T. P, Wooley, B., & Hall, A. K. (1989). Sexual abuse in patients in patients with anorexia nervosa and bulimia. *Psychosomatics, 30*, 73–79.

Halpern, R. (2012). *The body and its discontents: Israeli women's fiction 1985–2005*. Tel Aviv: Hakibbutz Hameuchad (Hebrew).

Hart, O. van der, Nijenhuis, E., Steele, K., & Brown, D. (2004). Trauma-related dissociation: Conceptual clarity lost and found. *Australian and New Zealand Journal of Psychiatry, 38*(11–12), 906–914.

Hieman, M. (2008). *Attacks on linking*. Tel Aviv: Museum of Art.

Hembree, E. A., Street, G. P., Riggs, D. S., & Foa, E. B. (2004). Do assault-related variables predict response to cognitive behavioral treatment for PTSD? *Journal of Consulting and Clinical Psychology, 72*(3), 531–534.

Herman, J. L. (1981/2000). *Father-daughter incest*. Cambridge, MA: Harvard University Press.

Herman, J. L. (1992). Complex PTSD: A syndrome in survivors of prolonged and repeated trauma. *Journal of Traumatic Stress, 5*, 377–391.

Herman, J. L. (1997). *Trauma and recovery*. New York, NY: Basic Books.

Herman, J. L. (2000). *Father-daughter incest*. Cambridge, MA: Harvard University Press.

Herman, J. L. (2009). Foreword. In C. A. Courtois & J. D. Ford (Eds.), *Treating complex traumatic stress disorders* (pp. xiii–xvii). New York, NY: Guildford Press.

Herman, J. L. (2012). CPTSD is a distinct entity: Comment on Resick et al. *Journal of Traumatic Stress, 25*, 256–257.

Herman, J. L., Perry, J. C., & van der Kolk, B. (1989). Childhood trauma in borderline personality disorder. *American Journal of Psychiatry, 146*, 490–495.

Herman, J. L., & Schatzow, E. (1987). Recovery and verification of memories of childhood sexual trauma. *Psychoanalytic Psychology, 4*, 1–14.

Herzog, D. B., Stoley, J. E., Carmody, S., Robbins, W. M., & van der Kolk, B. (1993). Childhood sexual abuse in anorexia nervosa and bulimia nervosa: A pilot study. *Journal of the American Academy of Child & Adolescent Psychiatry, 32*, 962–966.

Irigaray, L. (1985). *This sex which is not one.* Trans. C. Porter. Ithaca, NY: Cornell University Press.

ISSD (International Society for the Study of Dissociation). (2013). Retrieved July 16, 2017, from www.isst-d.org/default.asp?contentID=76#diss

ISSTD. (International Society for the Study of Trauma and Dissociation) (2013). *Adult treatment guidelines.* Retrieved from www.isst-d.org/default.asp?contentID=49

ISTSS (International Society for Traumatic Stress Studies). (2012). *ISTSS expert consensus guidelines for complex PTSD.* Retrieved February 15, 2017, from www.istss.org/ISTSS_Main/media/Documents/ISTSS-Expert-Concesnsus-Guidelines-for-Complex-PTSD-Updated-060315.pdf

Jacobi, C., Hayward, C. de Zwaan, M., Kraemer, H. C., & Agras, W. S. (2004). Coming to terms with risk factors for eating disorders: Application of risk terminology and suggestions for a general taxonomy. *Psychological Bulletin, 130,* 19–65.

Kaffman, A. (2009). The silent epidemic of neurodevelopmental injuries. *Biological Psychiatry, 66,* 624–626.

Kaplan, V. A., & Sadock, B. J. (1975). *Comprehensive textbook of psychiatry.* Baltimore: Lippincott Williams & Wilkins.

Kearney-Cooke, A. (1988). Group treatment of sexual abuse among women with eating disorders. *Women and Therapy,* 7, 5–22.

Kearney-Cooke, A., & Striegel-Moore, R. H. (1996). Treatment of childhood sexual abuse in anorexia nervosa and bulimia nervosa: A feminist psychodynamic approach. In M. F. Schwartz & L. Cohn (Eds.), *Sexual abuse and eating disorders* (pp. 155–175). Bristol, PA: Brunner/Mazel.

Kinsley, A. C., Pomeroy, W. B., Martin, C. E., & Gehard, P. H. (1953). *Sexual behavior in the human female.* Philadelphia: Saunders.

Kinsler, P. J., Courtois, C. A., & Frankel, A. S. (2009). Therapeutic alliance and risk management. In C. A. Courtois & J. D. Ford (Eds.), *Treating complex stress disorders* (pp. 183–201). New York, NY: Guilford Press.

Kluft, R. P. (1990). *Incest-related syndromes of adult psychopathology.* Washington, DC: American Psychiatric Press.

Kluft, R. P. (2001). The difficult-to-treat patient with dissociative disorder. In M. J. Dewan & R. W. Pies (Eds.), *The difficult-to-treat patient* (pp. 209–242). Washington, DC: American Psychiatric Press.

LaCapra, D. (2001). *Writing history, writing trauma.* Baltimore: Johns Hopkins University Press.

Lacey, J. H. (1990). Incest, incestuous fantasy and indecency: A clinical catchment area study of normal weight bulimic women. *British Journal of Psychiatry, 157,* 399–403.

Landis, J. T. (1956). Experiences of 500 children with adult sexual deviation. *Psychiatric Quarterly Supplement, 30,* 91–109.

Latzer, Y. (2002). Eating disorders as addiction. In H. Doitch, (Ed.), *Adolescents and addiction* (pp. 29–41). Jerusalem: Association for Psychosocial Rehabilitation for Adolescent and Young Adults (Hebrew).

Latzer, Y., Hochdorf, Z., Bachar, E., & Conetti, L. (2003). Treatment as a 'secure base': Family therapy as a secure-based attachment in eating disorders. *Sihot, 3,* 1–9 (Hebrew).

Levy, I. (2009). Afterward. In C. Bollas (Ed.), *Hysteria* (p. 262). Tel Aviv: Tola'at (Hebrew).

Light, A. (2008). Dialogues with madwomen: Allie Light. In G. Morris (Ed.), *In action! Interviews with directors from classical Hollywood to contemporary Iran* (pp. 227–234). London: Anthem.

Loewenstein, R. (1990). Somatoform disorders in victims of incest and child abuse. In R. Kluft (Ed.), *Incest-related syndromes of adult psychopathology* (pp. 75–111). Washington, DC: American Psychiatric Press.

MacKinnon, C. (1989). *Toward a feminist theory of the state*. Cambridge, MA: Harvard University Press.

MacKinnon, C. (2005). Difference and dominance: On sex discrimination. In A. E. Cudd & R. O. Andreasen (Eds.), *Feminist theory: A philosophical anthology* (pp. 392–402). Oxford: Wiley-Blackwell.

MacMillan, H. L., Fleming, J. E., Streiner, D. L., Lin, E., Boyle, M. H., Jamieson, E., . . . Beardslee, W. R. (2001). Childhood abuse and lifetime psychopathology in a community sample. *American Journal of Psychiatry, 158*(11), 1878–1883.

McCallum, K. E., Lock, J., Kulla, M., Rorty, M., & Wetzel, R. D. (1992). Dissociation symptoms and disorders in patients with eating disorders. *Dissociation, 5*, 705–708.

McFarlane, A. C., McFarlane, C., & Gilchrist, P. N. (1988). Post-traumatic bulimia and anorexia nervosa. *International Journal of Eating Disorders, 7*, 705–708.

McKann, I. L., & Pearlman, L. A. (1990). Vicarious traumatization: A framework for understanding the psychological effects of working with victims. *Journal of Traumatic Stress, 3*(1), 131–149.

McLean, L. M., & Gallop, R. (2003). Implications of childhood sexual abuse for adult borderline personality disorder and complex posttraumatic stress disorder. *American Journal of Psychiatry, 160*(2), 369–372.

Mendelsohn, M., Herman, J. L. Schatzow, E., Coco, M., Kallivayalil, D., & Levitan, J. (2011). *The trauma recovery group*. New York, NY: Guilford Press.

Micale, M. S. (1993). On the 'disappearance' of hysteria: A study in the clinical deconstruction of a diagnosis. *Isis, 84*, 496–526.

Miller, K. J. (1996). Prevalence and process of disclosure of childhood sexual abuse among eating disordered women. In M. F. Schwartz & L. Cohn (Eds.), *Sexual abuse and eating disorders* (pp. 36–51). Bristol, PA: Brunner/Mazel.

Molendijk, M. L., Hoek, H. W., Brewerton, T. D., & Elzinga, B. M. (2016). Childhood maltreatment and eating disorder pathology: A systematic review and dose-response meta-analysis. *Psychological Medicine, 49*(8), 1402–1416.

Molnar, B., Buka, S. L, & Kessler, R. C. (2001). Child sexual abuse and subsequent psychopathology: Results from the National Comorbidity Survey. *American Journal of Public Health, 90*(5), 753–760.

Murnen, S. K., & Smolak, H. W. (2009). Are feminist women protected from body image problems? A meta-analytic review of relevant research. *Sex Roles, 60*, 186–197.

Nagata, T., Kiriike, T., Iketani, Y., Kawarada, Y., & Tanaka, H. (1999). History of childhood sexual or physical abuse in Japanese patients with eating disorders: Relationship with dissociation and impulsive behaviors. *Psychological Medicine, 29*, 935–942.

Newton, T., Robinson, P., & Hartley, P. (1993). Treatment for eating disorders in the United Kingdom, Part 2: Experience of treatment: A survey of numbers of the eating disorders association. *Eating Disorders Review, 1*, 11–21.

NIMH (National Institute of Mental Health). (2008). *What are eating disorders?* Retrieved October 10, 2017, from www.nimh.nih/health/topics/eating disorders?/index.shtml

NIMH (National Institute of Mental Health). (2015). *Eating disorders*. Retrieved October 10, 2017, from www/nimh.nih.gov/health/topics/eating disorders/index.shtml

Oppenheimer, R., Howells, K., Palmer, L., & Chaloner, D. (1985). Adverse sexual experiences in childhood and clinical eating disorders: A preliminary description. *Journal of Psychiatric Research, 19*, 157–161.

Orbach, S. (1986). *Hunger strike: The anorectic's struggle as a metaphor for our age*. Harmondsworth: Penguin.

Orbach, S. (2006). *Fat is a feminist issue: The anti-diet guide*. London: Arrow.

Orbach, S. (2009). *Bodies*. New York, NY: Picador.

Orbach, S. (2015). Give us back our bodies. *Huffington Post*. May 22, 2015. Retrieved October 10, 2017, from www.huffingtonpost.co.uk/2011/03/08/give-us-back-our-bodies_n_7411178.html

Padua, A. (2004). The body can tell: Issues in the medical treatment of survivors of childhood sexual abuse. In Z. Seligman & Z. Solomon (Eds.), *Critical and clinical perspectives on incest* (pp. 483–497). Tel Aviv: Hakibbutz Hameuchad and Tel Aviv University Publishing House (Hebrew).

Pearlman, L. A., & Caringi, J. (2009). Living and working self-reflecting to address vicarious trauma. In C. A. Courtois & J. D. Ford (Eds.), *Treating complex traumatic stress disorders* (pp. 202–224). New York, NY: Guilford Press.

Pearlman, L. A., & Courtois, C. A. (2005). Clinical applications of the attachment framework: Relational treatment of complex trauma. *Journal of Traumatic Stress, 18*(5), 449–459.

Polivy, J., & Herman, C. P. (2002). Causes of eating disorders. *Annual Review of Psychology, 53*, 187–213.

Putnam, F. W. (1989). *Diagnosis and treatment of multiple personality disorder*. New York, NY: Guilford Press.

Putnam, F. W. (1997). *Dissociation in children and adolescents: A developmental perspective*. New York, NY: Guilford Press.

Reed, M. (2002). *Shvuya: Kroniqa shel gilui arayot miqtzo'i – Sipur autobiografi* [*Captivity: A chronicle of professional incest – An autobiographical account*]. Tel Aviv: Tammuz (Hebrew).

Reed, M. (2012). *Zehut disotziativit ve-yitzuga ha-akshavi be-media [Dissociative identity and its representation in the contemporary media]*. Retrieved October 10, 2017, from www.hebpsy.net/articles.asp?t=0&id=2869

Root, M. P. (1991). Persistent disordered eating as a gender-specific, post-traumatic stress response to sexual assault. *Psychotherapy, 28*, 96–102.

Root, M. P., & Fallon, P. (1988). The incidence of victimization experience in a bulimic sample. *Journal of Interpersonal Violence, 3*, 161–173.

Rorty, M., & Yager, J. (1996). Speculations on the role of childhood abuse in the development of eating disorders among women. In M. F. Schwartz & L. Cohn (Eds.), *Sexual abuse and eating disorders* (pp. 21–35). Bristol, PA: Brunner/Mazel.

Rosen, E. F., & Petty, L. C. (1994). Dissociative states and disordered eating. *American Journal of Clinical Hypnosis, 36*, 266–275.

Rosenvinge, J. H., & Klusmeier, A. K. (2000). Treatment for eating disorders from a patient-satisfaction perspective: A Norwegian replication of a British study. *European Eating Disorders Review, 8*, 293–300.

Ross, C. A. (1994). *The Osiris complex: Case studies in multiple personality disorder*. Toronto: University of Toronto Press.

Ross, C. A., Miller, S. D., Bjornson, L., Reavor, P., Fraser, G. A., & Anderson, G. (1991). Abuse histories in 102 cases of multiple personality disorder. *Canadian Journal of Psychiatry, 36*, 97–101.

Rozmarin, M. (2003). Acharit devar: Me-hiot gever ke-hithavut ke-isha – Teoriyat ha-hevdel ha-bein mini shal Luce Irigaray [Epilogue: From being a man to becoming a woman – Luce Irigaray's theory of the inter-sex difference]. In L. Irigaray (Ed.), *This sex which is not one* (pp. 81–93). Tel Aviv: Resling (Hebrew).

Russell, D. E. (1983). The incidence and precedence of interfamilial and extra-familial sexual abuse of female children. *Child Abuse & Neglect*, 7, 133–146.

Russell, D. E. (1986). *The secrete trauma: Incest in the lives of girls and women*. New York, NY: Basic Books.

Russell, G. F. M. (1986). The changing nature of anorexia nervosa. In G. I. Szmukler, P. E. Slade, P. Harris, D. Benton, & G. F. M. Russell (Eds.), *Anorexia nervosa and bulimic disorders* (pp. 101–112). Oxford: Pergamon.

Russell, G. F. M. (1995). Anorexia nervosa through time. In G. Szmulkler, C. Dare, & J. Treasure (Eds.), *Handbook of eating disorders: Theory, treatment and research* (pp. 5–17). Chichester: Wiley-Blackwell.

Salter, A. C. (1992). *Epidemiology of child sexual abuse*. New York, NY: Lawrence Erlbaum.

Sands, S. (1991). Bulimia, dissociation, and empathy: A self-psychological view. In C. L. Johnson (Ed.), *Psychodynamic treatment of anorexia nervosa and bulimia* (pp. 34–50) New York, NY: Guilford Press.

Schechter, I. D., Schwartz, H. P., & Greenfield, D. G. (1987). Sexual abuse and anorexia nervosa. *International Journal of Eating Disorders, 6*, 313–316.

Schwartz, H. (2000). *Dialogues with forgotten voices: Relational perspectives on child abuse trauma and treatment of dissociative disorders*. New York, NY: Basic Books.

Sesan, R. (1994). Feminist inpatient treatment for eating disorders: An oxymoron? In P. Fallon, M. A. Katzman, & S. C. Wooley (Eds.), *Feminist perspectives of eating disorders* (pp. 251–271). New York, NY: Guilford Press.

Sillon, B. (1992). Dissociation: A symptom of incest. *Individual Psychology, 48*, 155–164.

Silverman, S. W. (1996). *Because I remember terror, father, I remember you*. Athens, GA: University of Georgia Press.

Sloan, G., & Leichner, P. (1986). Is there a relationship between sexual abuse or incest and eating disorders? *Canadian Journal of Psychiatry, 31*, 656–660.

Smolak, L., & Murnen, S. K. (2002). A meta-analytic examination of the relationship between child sexual abuse and eating disorders. *International Journal of Eating Disorders, 31*, 136–150.

Somer, E. (1999~~1994~~). *Dual relationships: Seduction and sexual exploitation in counseling and psychotherapy*. Tel Aviv: Papyrusa and Tel Aviv University Publishing House (Hebrew).

Somer, E. (2004). To be or not to be: Childhood trauma and dissociative disorders. In Z. Seligman & Z. Solomon (Eds.), *Critical and clinical perspectives on incest* (pp. 164–192). Tel Aviv: Hakibbutz Hameuchad and Tel Aviv University Publishing House (Hebrew).

Somer, E., & Saadon, M. (1999). Therapist-client sex: Clients' retrospective reports. *Professional Psychology: Research and Practice, 30*(5), 504–509.

Spiegel, D., Loewenstein, R. J., Lewis-Fernandez, J., Sar, V., Simeon, D., Vermetten, E., Carden, E., & Dell, P. F. (2011). Dissociative disorders in DSM-5. *Depression and Anxiety, 28*, 824–852.

Striegel-Moore, R. H., & Bulik, C. B. (2007). Risk factors for eating disorders. *American Psychologist, 62*, 181–198.

Swain-Campbell, N. R., Surgenor, L. J., & Snell, D. L. (2001). An analysis of consumer perspectives following contact with an eating disorder service. *Australian and New Zealand Journal of Psychiatry, 35*, 99–103.

Thomas, J., Vartanian, L. R., & Brownell, K. D. (2009). The relationship between Eating Disorders Not Otherwise Specified (EDNOS) and officially recognized eating disorders: Meta-analysis and implication for DSM. *Psychological Bulletin, 135*(3), 407–433.

Tice, L., Hall, R. C. W., Beresford, T. P., Quinones, J., & Hall, A. K. (1989). Sexual abuse in eating disorders. *Psychiatric Medicine*, 7, 257–267.

Tierney, S. (2008). The individual within a condition: A qualitative study of young people's reflecting on being treated for anorexia nervosa. *Journal of the American Psychiatric Nurses' Association, 13*, 368–375.

Tjaden, P., & Thoennes, N. (2000). *Full report of the prevalence, incidences, and consequences of violence against women: Findings from the national violence against women survey (NCJ 183781).* Washington, DC: US Department of Justice.

Torem, M. S. (1986). Dissociative states presenting as an eating disorder. *American Journal of Clinical Hypnosis, 29*, 137–142.

Tripp, M. M., & Petrie, T. A. (2001). Sexual abuse and eating disorders: A test of a conceptual model. *Sex Roles, 44*, 17–32.

United Nations. (2006). *UN Secretary-General's study on violence against children.* Retrieved from www.unviolencestudy.org/

Vandereycken, W. (1985). Inpatient treatment of anorexia nervosa: Some research-guided changes. *Journal of Psychiatric Research, 19*, 413–422.

Vandereycken, W., & Vansteenkiste, M. (2009). Let eating disorder patients decide: Providing choice may reduce early drop-out from inpatient treatment. *European Eating Disorder Review, 17*, 177–183.

van der Kolk, B. A. (1989). The compulsion to repeat the trauma. *Psychiatric Clinics of North America, 12*, 389–411.

van der Kolk, B. A. (2001). The assessment and treatment of CPTSD. In R. Yehuda (Ed.), *Traumatic stress* (pp. 1–29). Washington, DC: American Psychiatric Press.

van der Kolk, B. A. (2009). Afterword. In C. A. Courtois & J. D. Ford (Eds.), *Treating complex stress disorders* (pp. 455–466). New York, NY: Guilford Press.

van der Kolk, B. A. (2014). *The body keeps the score: brain, mind, and body in the healing of trauma.* New York: Penguin Books.

van der Kolk, B. A., Roth, S., Pelcovitz, D., Sunday, S., & Spinazzola, J. (2005). Disorders of extreme stress: The empirical foundation of a complex adaptation to trauma. *Journal of Trauma Stress, 18*(5), 389–399.

van der Kolk, B. A., Weisaeth, L., & van der Hart, O. (1996). History of trauma in psychiatry. In B. van der Kolk, A. C. McFarlane, & L. Weisaeth (Eds.), *Traumatic stress: The overwhelming experience on mind, body, and society* (pp. 47–76). New York, NY: Guilford Press.

Vanderlinden, J., & Vandereycken, W. (1993). Dissociative experience and trauma in eating disorders. *International Journal of Eating Disorder, 13*, 187–194.

Vanderlinden, J., & Vandereycken, W. (1997). *Trauma, dissociation, and impulse dyscontrol in eating disorders.* Bristol, PA: Brunner/Mazel.

Vanderlinden, J., & Vandereycken, W. (1996). Is sexual abuse a risk factor for developing an eating disorder? In M. F. Schwartz & L. Cohn (Eds.), *Sexual abuse and eating disorders* (pp. 17–35). Bristol, PA: Brunner/Mazel.

Waller, G. (1991). Sexual abuse as a factor in eating disorders. *British Journal of Psychiatry, 159*, 664–671.

Walsh, B. T., & Garner, D. M. (1994). Diagnostic issues. In D. M. Garner & P. E. Garfinkel (Eds.), *Handbook of treatment for eating disorders* (pp. 24–33). New York, NY: Guilford Press.

Wolf, N. (1991). *The beauty myth: How images of beauty are used against women.* London: Vintage.

Wonderlich, S. A., Brewerton, T. D., Joice, Z., Dansky B. S., & Abbott, D. W. (1997). Relationship of childhood sexual abuse and eating disorders. *Journal of the American Academy of Child & Adolescent Psychiatry, 36*(8), 1107-1115.

Woodside, B. D. (2005). Treatment of anorexia nervosa: More questions than answers. *International Journal of Eating Disorders, 37*, 541–542.

Wooley, S. C. (1990). *Contribution of psychology of women and the treatment of eating disorders.* Plenary Session II presented at the Fourth International Conference on Eating Disorders, New York, NY.

Wooley, S. C. (1994). Sexual abuse and eating disorders: The concealed debate. In P. Fallon, M. A. Katzman, & S. C. Wooley (Eds.), *Feminist perspectives on eating disorders* (pp. 171–211). New York, NY: Guilford Press.

Wooley, S. C., & Kearney-Cooke, A. (1986). Intensive treatment of bulimia and body-image disturbance. In K. D. Brownell & J. P. Foreyt (Eds.), *Handbook of eating disorders: Physiology, psychology, and treatment of obesity, anorexia and bulimia* (pp. 476–502). New York, NY: Basic Books.

World Health Organization. (2017). *Violence against women.* Retrieved February 15, 2017, from www.who.int/mediacentre/factsheets/fs239/en/

Yen, S., Shea, M. T., Battle, C. L., Johnson, D. M., Zlotnick, C., Dolan-Sewell, R. et al. (2002). Traumatic exposure and PTSD in borderline, schizotypal, avoidant, and obsessive-compulsive personality disorders. *Journal of Nervous and Mental Disease, 190*, 510–518.

Zerbe, K. J. (1995). *The body betrayed: A deeper understanding of women, eating disorders, and treatment.* New York, NY: Gürze.

Index

abandonment 147, 150, 175, 195–196
ABC Model 203
abuse 17, 25–26, 191, 195–196; suspected *vs.* certain 167; *see also* child abuse; childhood abuse; childhood sexual abuse; physical abuse; sexual abuse; substance abuse
acting out 142, 192–193, 197–198
acute-stress disorders 68
addiction(s) 21, 40, 67, 71, 85–86, 89n5, 153, 175, 177, 181–182, 192, 204, 207–208, 213; alcohol 21, 85, 87, 233; as chronic disease 89n5; drug 21, 85, 87–88, 233; eating disorders as 85–88; gambling 86, 160; to pain 228, 235; 'patient identity' 86; to sense of control 57; sexual 41; -treatment centres 115
adolescence 21, 69, 88, 94, 108, 110, 132, 184
adolescent eating disorder wards 125, 130–131, 139, 144, 151, 205n3, 225
adolescent psychiatric wards 136, 138, 143, 145, 152, 205n3
adulthood 19, 21, 70, 94, 178, 185, 216
affect dysregulation 184
affective detachment 82
aggression 184, 202
agoraphobia 21
alcohol 61, 78, 85, 87–88, 179, 233; *see also* addiction; alcoholic
alcoholic 41
alienation 95, 237n5; relational 183; spiritual 183
amnesia 23, 25, 66, 68–70, 72, 79, 83, 122, 130, 192; episodic 186n5; full 2, 41, 72, 74, 79, 208; partial 2, 41, 72, 77, 208; psychotic 23; *see also* dissociative amnesia
anger 55, 104, 112, 131, 140, 148, 181, 200, 219, 227, 233
anger attacks 140, 167
anorexia *see* anorexia nervosa
anorexia nervosa (AN) 3, 5–10, 12, 23, 32–33, 35, 41, 46–47, 53–54, 57–60, 73, 75, 87, 102, 109–110, 112–113, 117, 120–121, 135, 137, 155, 177–179, 186n1, 224; binge-purge 35
anorexics 9, 33, 117, 121, 135, 137, 155, 176
antisocial personality disorder 215
anxiety 34–35, 58, 71, 146, 181, 191; body 9, 93
anxiety disorders 21, 185
Arendt, Hannah 205n4; 'banality of evil' 205n4
army 6, 13, 15–16, 75, 96, 100, 110, 140, 156, 219, 229–231, 234
asceticism 9
asexuality 109
attachment/relational disorders 175
attention and cognitive disorders 178
authority 7, 21, 118, 161, 167, 193–196, 199, 207, 209, 217; abuse of 196, 207; figures 167, 183, 196
autonomy 194; of client 207, 209
avoidant/restrictive food intake disorder 5

battering 20, 192–193, 215; wife 193
behaviour: addictive 40; aggressive 167, 197; promiscuous 21
bell jar 141–142, 164n4
betrayal 21, 150, 196, 199, 202, 217
betrayed/betraying body 40, 91–113, 113n3
Big Pharma 216
binge eaters 6, 99, 176
binge eating 5, 72, 120

binge-eating disorder (BED) 5–6, 32
bingeing 4, 6, 10, 15, 47, 60, 72, 74–75, 85, 99
body anxiety 9, 93
body hatred 9, 93
body image 93, 111; distorted 94; female 9, 93; low 35; negative 8; poor 98; women's 180
body language 9
borderline personality disorder(s) (BPD) 67, 140, 177, 183, 196, 200, 208, 215
boundaries 26, 35, 59, 61, 87, 92, 106, 117–118, 132, 146, 161, 167–169, 173, 186n4, 189, 194, 197–199, 203, 209; personal 197
brain development 190–191
breasts 94, 108–109, 111
Breuer, J. 180, 186n4
Britain 119
Brown, Natalie 142, 187n7
bulimia *see* bulimia nervosa
bulimia nervosa (BN) 3, 5–8, 14–15, 32–35, 41, 47, 49, 53, 56–57, 72, 75, 85, 100, 102, 137, 146, 177, 224, 226, 228, 236
bulimics 8, 33–34, 137, 176
bystanders 162, 210
bystanding 210

calming-down room 138, 161, 225–227
cancer 15, 49, 74, 175
chemotherapy 59–60, 179
Chesler, Phyllis 141, 177–178
child abuse 32, 176; emotional 32; physical 32–33; sexual 32–33; *see also* childhood sexual abuse; childhood sexual exploitation
childhood abuse 21, 24, 32–34, 36, 42–43, 69–70, 80, 115, 159, 162, 178, 180, 184, 200, 216; *see also* child abuse; childhood sexual abuse; childhood sexual exploitation
childhood maltreatment exposure 32
childhood sexual abuse (CSA): and addiction 85; and dissociation 1, 69; and eating disorders 1–2, 10, 26, 32, 34–35, 39–44, 46, 58, 65, 78, 115, 163, 178–181, 207; effects of 21, 176, 207–208; history of 1, 32, 34, 147, 207, 211; rates of 1, 208, 211; study of 70; survivors of 21, 24, 39–40, 42, 52, 54, 62, 70, 94, 112, 118, 121, 140, 150, 159, 162, 164n5, 166–167, 174n1, 175–176, 180, 201, 208, 211, 215–216; symptoms of 40, 75, 166, 176, 212; trauma of 22, 35, 39, 147, 181; treatment of 25, 65, 115–116, 162, 166, 175, 199; victims of 19, 25–26, 81, 119, 164n4, 183, 197, 211, 213n1; *see also* sexual abuse treatment; survivors; trauma
childhood sexual abuse centres 166
childhood sexual abuse treatment 115–116, 166, 170
childhood sexual abuse treatment programmes 166
childhood sexual exploitation 26, 93, 177
childhood trauma, Interpersonal childhood trauma (as a separate concept?) 32, 41, 65–66, 166, 178, 191
children: day 21, 83; night 21, 83
Christianity 92
clean addict 88, 89n5; *see also* addiction
Clément, C. 93
'coerced collaboration' 136
comorbidity 85, 163, 181, 185–186, 189, 204, 211; multiple 185–186
complex post-traumatic stress disorder (CPTSD) *see* CPTSD
conduct disorders 178
consciousness 19, 39, 67–68, 70, 183, 186n5; altered states of 70; other states of 21, 70–71; split 23
control (regaining control) 3, 5, 9–10, 12–13, 20, 30, 35, 39–41, 56–59, 67–68, 70, 72, 80, 83–85, 91, 94, 118, 121, 126–128, 136, 139, 151, 154, 156, 167, 176, 178, 180, 191–193, 209, 225, 230, 236, 237n6
coping 39, 50, 71, 104–105, 137, 153–154, 159, 169, 196, 198, 204, 212, 216, 226, 233
coping mechanisms/skills/strategies/tools 25, 41, 47, 67, 71, 94, 153, 159, 160, 175, 184, 189, 192, 203, 209–210, 216; *see also* coping
countertransference 189, 200–204; traumatic 200
counting calories 85
Courtois, C.A. 19–22, 24–25, 69–70, 148, 163, 166–167, 182–183, 189–191, 194, 202, 211
CPTSD 40, 66, 140, 148, 150, 159, 162–163, 176, 178–179, 182–186, 189–196, 202–205, 207–208, 211–212, 216, 237n5; clients 195, 202–204, 207;

symptoms 150, 183, 207–208, 212–213; treatment 163, 176, 189–190, 194, 211–212, 237n6; *see also* meta-model
cruelty 195, 199–202, 204, 217
cutting 65, 100, 112, 139, 152, 154, 155, 169, 225, 231, 233–234

death 3, 22, 29, 53–54, 60, 75, 100, 112, 117, 127, 155, 235–236; risk of 3
de Beauvoir, Simone 92, 113n2
defence mechanisms 70, 160, 192, 201, 212
delinquency *see* juvenile delinquency
delusions 177
demon possession 23, 91, 93, 177; hysterical 93
denial/looking away/indifference 19–20, 24, 69, 118, 136, 147, 162, 186n1, 192–193, 195–196, 199, 237n1, 237n5, 237n7
depersonalization 66–72, 81, 94, 184
depersonalization/derealization disorder 68–69; *see also* depersonalization; derealization
depression 21, 23, 34, 52–53, 60, 86, 102, 142, 181, 184; clinical 13; post-partum 177
derealization 67–69, 72
detox centre(s) 150–152
diagnosis 6, 8, 20, 23, 25, 63n2, 69n5, 140, 150, 175–179, 181–186, 189, 191–192, 196, 201, 211, 215–216, 224, 237n5
Diagnostic and Statistical Manual of Mental Disorders (DSM) 178; *see also* DSM-III; DSM-IIIR; DSM-IV; DSM-5
diagnostic labels 162, 195
Dialogues with Madwomen 84, 177
diets/dieting 4, 10, 12–14, 16, 72, 159
dirtiness, feeling of 101–102
discrimination 177
disgustingness 99, 101–105; *see also* self-disgust
dissociation 1, 22, 26, 41, 46–47, 49, 54, 65–73, 75–76, 79, 82–83, 85, 89n1, 122–123, 128, 126–127, 140, 153, 159, 163, 175, 177, 183–185, 192, 199, 201, 208, 212, 218, 232, 235; chemical 85, 237n4; *see also* dissociative disorders
dissociation disorders 140; *see also* dissociative disorders
dissociative amnesia 68, 73–81
dissociative disorders 2, 21, 39–42, 54, 65–72, 84, 94, 115, 175, 178, 180–181, 185, 190, 200–201, 208, 212, 216; *see also* depersonalization/derealization disorder; dissociative amnesia; dissociative identity disorder (DID); other specified dissociative disorder; unspecified dissociative disorder
dissociative episodes 98
dissociative experiences 67, 72
dissociative identity confusion 83
dissociative identity disorder (DID) 66, 68–72, 83–85, 177, 212; *see also* multiple personality disorder (MPD)
dissociative mechanisms 42, 70, 159
dissociative responses 70, 166
dissociative states 40
dissociative symptoms 67–70, 72, 212
domestic violence 184, 186n5, 192
dominance 118, 181, 193; dynamics of 167
double standards in clinical practice 177
drive-control disorders 178
drug addicts 152, 212, 215–216; *see also* addiction
drugs 11, 68, 71, 85, 87–88, 179, 208, 233
DSM-III 7, 25, 115, 184, 201
DSM-IIIR 186n2
DSM-IV 7, 183–185, 186n2, 216
DSM-5 2, 4, 6, 68, 83–84, 183, 185, 216

eating disorder centres/clinics/facilities 44, 115, 120–121, 126, 133–134, 149–150, 153, 156, 163, 166, 168, 170, 180, 207, 212, 234, 237n5, 237n6
eating disorder field 147, 160, 175, 180–181, 211–212
eating disorders (EDs): as addiction 85; atypical eating disorders 7; and childhood sexual abuse 1–2, 10, 26, 32, 34–35, 39–44, 46, 58, 65, 78, 115, 163, 178–181, 207; as control 56–59; as cultural disease 179; definition 4–7; and depersonalization 81; and dissociation 72; and dissociative amnesia 73; and dissociative identity disorder 83; as distraction 85; 'eating disorder not otherwise specified' (EDNOS) 7; and gender 2, 4, 8–10; history 7; and identity confusion 83; risk factors for 8; as secret language 65; *see also* anorexia nervosa; avoidant/restrictive food intake disorder; binge-eating disorder; bingeing; bulimia nervosa; pica; rumination disorder

eating disorder symptoms 7, 35, 120–123, 136, 153–154, 159–160, 182, 186
eating disorder treatment(s) 119–122, 124–126, 130–133, 135, 144, 147–149, 155, 158–159, 163, 169, 176, 211–212, 235
eating disorder wards 43, 47, 54, 59, 73, 77, 122–123, 125–127, 130–131, 136, 138–145, 148, 151–152, 155, 158–159, 160, 168, 197, 203, 213n1, 237n1; *see also* adolescent eating disorder wards
Einstein, Albert 207
emotional detachment 82
emotional dysregulation 140, 178, 183
emotional numbness 68, 72
emotional regulation 63n1, 190
empowerment model 209; *see also* personal empowerment
existential crisis 21
exorcism 23
exploitation 71, 95, 118, 132, 147, 160, 192–193, 196; *see also* childhood sexual exploitation

'false memory syndrome' 25
False Memory Syndrome Foundation 25
fasting 5
fatness *see* obesity
feeding tube 125, 127–129, 137, 227
female/feminine body 2–3, 91–95, 110, 112; betrayed/betraying 93–95, 113n3; degradation of 92; exploitation of 95; objectification of 92, 95, 122, 136, 160; oppression of 91; politicization of 91; *see also* body image
female 'madness' 8, 141, 176, 177–178, 181, 215
female oppression 9, 178, 181
female prisoners 197, 215–216
female sexuality 40, 94
feminine subjugation 20, 36
femininity 39–40, 91, 94, 106, 108–112, 113n2; fear of 110
feminism 19, 92
feminist analysis 20, 92, 193
feminist critique 121, 160
feminist eating disorder therapists 121
feminist movement 19, 25, 177, 184, 186n5
feminist perspective 35
feminist therapists 121, 136
feminist writers 36, 92, 136, 181
fight-or-flight reactions 191
flashbacks 25, 44, 68, 76, 127, 132, 138, 147, 181, 225, 227
food 4–6, 9, 11–12, 14, 16–17, 41–42, 48, 56–63, 78, 80, 82, 86–87, 93, 102–106, 109, 120, 122, 124–126, 128–130, 132, 135, 137, 144, 146, 155, 160, 178–180, 211, 224, 226–228, 232, 236
forced eating/feeding 117, 118, 126, 136, 161, 211
frameworks 150, 216; conceptual 92, 182, 215–216; coping 203; cultural 179; diagnostic 215; eating disorder 122, 125, 130, 160, 163, 168, 172, 212; therapeutic 121, 197, 202–203; treatment 122, 126, 147, 150, 162–163, 168, 197, 202, 207
framing story 58, 178
Freud, Sigmund 19, 23–24, 35, 36n1, 92, 178, 180, 186n3, 186n4

gambling 86, 122, 160
genitalia 107, 110
'genital wound' 92
guilt 6, 11, 17, 21–22, 28, 35, 52, 54–55, 67, 94, 98, 101, 103, 157, 192–193, 230

hallucinations: auditory 177; visual 177
hegemonic male establishment 23
hegemonic patriarchalism 92
hegemonic patriarchal society 175
helplessness 35, 56, 69, 167, 195, 200, 222, 237n6
Herman, Judith 22, 47, 56, 70, 121, 176, 181, 183–185, 186n5, 192, 194, 205n1
Holocaust denial 192
homeless girls 208
hospitalization 54, 63n3, 77, 119, 125, 131, 135–136, 138, 140–145, 148–149, 151–152, 155, 179, 218, 213n1, 223–228, 232, 235; general psychiatric 116
hypervigilance 181, 191
hysteria 8, 19, 23–24, 91, 177; *Studies on Hysteria* 35
hysterics 92, 144, 177, 179

identity: confusion 83; -formation 21, 83, 140, 167; fragmented 67; patient 86, 141; personal 67, 83
identity disorders 69, 72, 140, 175, 197; *see also* dissociative identity disorder (DID)
imaginary friends: communication with 177

incest 20, 24, 26–30, 34, 41, 66, 70, 148, 218, 223, 226; father-daughter 26–27, 29–30, 148
indifference 69, 118, 147, 162, 195–196, 199, 237n7
inner 'homelessness' 164n5, 174n1
International Classification of Diseases (ICD) 7, 183
interpersonal 178, 192–193, 195, 208, 217
interpersonal childhood 178
interpersonal childhood trauma 178
interpersonal difficulties 34
interpersonal-relationship disorders 178
interpersonal traumatic stressors 178
invasiveness 117–118, 161
Irigaray, L. 93
isolation 138, 144–147, 167, 193, 196, 203, 211
Israel 136, 219

Japan 72
Jung, Carl 180, 186n4
juvenile delinquency/crime 21, 207–208, 212–213

Kearney-Cooke, A. 1, 33–35, 95, 121, 136, 187n6
Kristeva, Julia 93

Lacan, Jacques 113n2
laxatives 4–5, 11, 13, 15, 44, 55
Levi, Primo 205n4
Light, Allie 84, 177
listening 10, 125, 169, 199, 201–202, 213n1

'madness' *see* female 'madness'
male body 92
male control 20
male dominance 181, 193
male-dominated society 91; patriarchal 141, 181
male hegemonic establishment 178; medical 8
male interest 108, 177
male sexual gaze 92
male subjectivity 113n2
male superiority 181, 193
mania 177
masturbation 104
medicalization 179–180
melancholy 177
memories 22, 25, 27, 44, 63, 65–66, 67–68, 73, 75–79, 79, 81, 85, 88, 121, 134, 150, 162, 194, 224, 227–228, 236; fake 25; partial 42; real 79; recovered *vs.* unbroken 167; repressed/recovered 25, 70; traumatic 25, 68, 81, 134–135, 190–191, 199
menstrual cycle 6, 94, 113
menstruation 12, 94, 97, 106, 108, 111–113; fear of 112–113; *see also* menstrual cycle
mental health 13, 19–20, 24–25, 65–67, 70, 121, 124, 140, 177, 181, 184, 193–194, 196, 199–200, 204, 212, 215–216, 234
mentalization 39–40, 63n1, 159, 200–201; non- 40; un- 72, 179
mentoring services 210
meta-model 190
'Metamorphosis' 142, 187n7
Middle Ages 23, 177
molestation 1, 19, 26, 93, 175, 186n3
monasticism 9
morbidity 3; *see also* comorbidity
mother-daughter relations 148–150; and anger 148
multiple personality disorder(s) (MPD) 22, 68, 72, 84
mutuality 122, 167, 169, 193–195, 207

Narcotics Anonymous 89n5
National Institute of Mental Health 70
neglect 67, 91, 97, 99–100, 118, 147, 160, 162–163, 176, 182–183, 191, 195–196, 201, 203–204, 210, 237n5, 237n7
neurobiological 190–191
neuropathology 24, 178
neuroscience 183, 190
neuroticism 177
nodding therapists 162
non-kosher food 60
Norway 120
numbing 3, 89n4

obesity 7, 16, 40–41, 83, 94, 102, 106–107; childhood 8; as defence 106–107
objectification 92–93, 95, 136, 160
objectivized body 39; *see also* objectification
obsessive/compulsive symptoms 34; *see also* OCD
obsessive washing rituals 101; *see also* OCD
OCD 88, 177
oedipal stage 92
oral sex 62–63, 126

Orbach, Susie 36, 93
other specified dissociative disorder 69
overeating 4, 7, 17, 106
Ovid 187n7

paedophiles 84, 199
panic 21–22, 69, 136; attacks 22
pathologization: of clients 211
pathology 159, 161–162, 210; of eating disorder 120, 156, 161
patriarchal families 147
patriarchal hegemonic establishment 180
patriarchal hegemony 181
patriarchal language 92
patriarchal society 91–92, 95, 141, 175, 179, 181
patriarchy 20, 22, 193
peer support 203–204
'penis envy' 92
perception 59, 67–69, 92–93, 122, 142, 160, 177, 180, 191, 198; *see also* self-perception
perpetrator 21–22, 25, 35, 52, 60, 93, 106, 117–118, 122–123, 147–148, 160, 162, 182, 184, 192, 195–197, 199, 210
personal empowerment 194; *see also* empowerment
personality disorders 26, 33, 40, 175, 181–182, 185, 186n2, 196–197, 200, 215; *see also* borderline personality disorders; multiple personality disorders
personality-structure disorders 166
phobias 21, 177
physical abuse 33, 67
pica 4
Plath, Sylvia 141
politics of diagnosis 178
polypharmacy 185
post-traumatic distress 7, 175
post-traumatic stress disorders
post-traumatic symptoms 35, 85, 166, 178
power 161, 210; abuse of 196, 207; arbitrary 167; disparities 209; exploitation of 160; exploitative 167; exploitative exercise of 196; male 20, 193; misuse of 167
pregnancy 16, 22, 94, 112, 218
privacy 161, 209; invasion of 129; lack of 137, 161; respect for 161, 209
professional supervision 202–204
projection 162
projective identification 125–126
promiscuity 23, 171
prostitution 7, 21, 40, 104, 122, 172, 192, 207–208, 212, 213, 216, 228
PSTD 25, 68, 115, 216, 181–185, 201; chronic 67
psychiatric disorders 3–4, 21, 34, 179, 185, 186n2
psychiatric institutions 208
psychiatric wards 115, 136, 139–140, 144–147, 150–151, 163, 177, 203; *see also* adolescent psychiatric wards
psychoanalysis 24, 35, 92, 162, 180; Freudian 92; as male product 92
psychoanalytic movement 19
psychodrama group 43
psychopathology 34; adult 21
psychosomatic symptoms 22
psychosomatic ward 49–50
psychotherapy 185, 189, 193; psychodynamic 119
psychotic episodes 140
punishment 35, 52, 61, 96, 99–100, 117, 128–129, 136, 144, 150, 160, 198; *see also* self-punishment
purging 6, 41, 43–44, 72, 94–95, 137

radical self-care 202, 205
rape 20, 29, 33, 35, 44, 51, 63n4, 70–71, 74–75, 81, 84, 93–94, 101, 106, 112, 115, 129–130, 145, 163, 172, 179–180, 187n7, 192–193, 215, 229–230, 233, 236, 237n8; gang 20, 193
rape crisis centres 51, 115, 163, 170, 172, 236, 237n8
reactivation 209; *see also* reenactment
recovery 120–121, 155, 162, 167, 175, 178, 182, 190–196, 203, 205n1, 207, 209–210
reenactment 21, 115, 118, 121–124, 146, 151, 160–163, 182, 189, 195–196, 198, 201, 209–210, 237n5
regression 120, 134–135, 139, 170, 189, 191
rehab centres 152, 197
rehab programme 144, 152
rejection 150, 163, 182
relational collaboration 209
relationships (relations): caregiving/client 209; healing 121, 192–193, 196, 199, 210; interpersonal 63n1, 195–196; reparative 199; therapist-client 194; traumatic 195–196; *see also* therapeutic relationship
religious ecstasy 23
resilience 195
restraint 117–118, 126–127, 145–146, 161, 169, 211; physical 126–127

revictimization 7, 40, 63n4, 75, 80, 89n2, 113n4, 118, 121, 131–132, 161, 172, 183, 197, 200, 210, 218, 227, 237n3
revulsion 94–96
at-risk women 212–213
rumination disorder 5
runaways/running away 21, 208, 213
Russell, D. E. 7–8, 19–21
Russia 27

safe boundaries 118, 132, 197–198
safety/feeling safe 102, 154, 190, 195, 209
secondary victims 201
Second World War 184
secrecy 1, 115, 122, 179, 193
secularization 180
self, sense of 22, 67–69
self, the 22, 68, 71, 184, 201; fragmentation of 22
self-anger 157
self-blame 52
self-care 202–203, 205
self-control 3, 35
self-cutting *see* cutting
self-definition 194
self-destruction 21, 40, 52, 54, 101, 103, 160, 228, 233
self-destructive behaviour/tendencies 40, 141, 161, 168–169, 172, 175, 228
self-disgust 98, 103, 105, 157
self-evaluation 5
self-guilt 101, 103
self-harm/ing 52, 54–55, 57, 100, 123–124, 136, 145, 152–154, 160, 171, 177, 181, 227, 235
self-hatred 35, 184
self-healing 39
self-help groups 119–120
self-hurting 54; *see also* self-harm/ing; self-injury
self-image 8, 34, 99, 118, 140–141, 147, 161, 210
self-injury 7, 21, 33, 40, 67, 75, 94; *see also* self-harm/ing
self-management skills 167
self-medication 60, 85
self-perception 191
self-punishment 52, 54–55, 101, 103
self-regulation 190–191
self-starvation 7, 47, 85, 94, 99, 112–113, 177
self-transparency 203, 210
self-violence 228
self-worth 21
sexual abuse 72, 78, 93; history of 33, 35, 72; internalization of 157; rates of 33; survivors of 54; treatment of 122; victims of 51; *see also* childhood sexual abuse; sexual assault
sexual abuse centres/clinics 115–116, 133, 150, 166, 168, 170, 172–173
sexual abuse programme 151
sexual abuse therapy 45, 155
sexual abuse treatment 166, 168; specialized/specialist 132, 151, 166–174; *see also* childhood sexual abuse treatment
sexual abuse treatment centres 133, 155, 163, 170, 235–236; *see also* childhood sexual abuse treatment centres
sexual assault 58, 70, 78, 87, 131, 181, 207; adolescent 75
sexual assault centres 207, 212
sexual assault victims 78, 87, 172
sexual attractiveness/attraction 106, 110
sexual crimes 20, 22
sexual exploitation 26, 93, 132, 147, 177; *see also* childhood sexual exploitation
sexual gratification 93, 160
sexual harassment 93, 186n3, 193
sexuality 7, 9, 12, 39, 40, 93–94, 106–108; concept of 39
sexual molestation 19, 26, 93
shame 1, 10, 20–21, 24, 27, 34, 67–69, 71, 92–95, 98, 111, 115, 121, 190, 192–193, 208, 221
silence 1, 9, 19–20, 22, 24, 26, 29, 42, 47–48, 78, 92–93, 135–136, 142, 187n7, 193, 215, 220, 237n3; conspiracy of 48; decree of 147
sleep: disorders 94, 177; problems 181
slimness 9, 106; culture of 7
social support 184, 204
sociocultural 7–8, 178, 192–193
somatic disorders 39, 183
somaticization 94, 184–185; problems 94
Spielrein, Sabina 186n4
spiritual renewal 202, 204
stigma 67, 140, 178, 190, 193
stigmatization 177, 204
strength 3, 14, 48, 55, 87, 147, 156–157, 160–162, 167, 182, 190, 194–195, 205n2, 210
substance abuse 71, 122, 212, 237n4
suicidal ideation 21, 40, 52; adolescent 23
suicidal signs 152

suicide 11, 54, 145, 147, 155, 228, 234–235; attempt 40, 52–53, 122, 147, 151, 153, 156, 161, 182, 212, 227; risk 54; slow 52–53; threats 73
support group 172
support system 184, 198–199, 204
survival mechanisms/strategies 3, 26, 40, 65–67, 70, 94, 109, 153, 160, 175, 179, 218
survivors 21, 24, 39–40, 42, 52, 54, 62, 66, 70, 71, 93–94, 106, 112, 118, 121, 122, 133, 140, 147, 150–151, 159, 160, 161–162, 164n5, 166–167, 174n1, 175–176, 180, 182, 179, 186n5, 190, 192, 194, 196, 200–202, 204, 208, 211, 215–216, 237n4, 237n7

therapeutic alliance 34, 120, 122, 162, 167, 190–191, 193–198, 200, 217, 235
therapeutic contract 153; *see also* treatment contract
therapeutic interactions 193
therapeutic process 162, 190
therapeutic relations 196–197
therapeutic relationship 118, 167, 189, 195–198, 201
therapeutic setting/space 118, 148, 167, 199–201
therapy 13, 42–47, 51, 59, 66, 77, 79–81, 83, 87, 122, 133, 167, 172, 200, 209, 237n6; behavioural 119–120; cognitive-behavioural (CBT) 119, 121; family 119–120, 126, 131, 136, 147–149, 161, 163n1, 218, 226, 237n1; group 120, 130, 136, 150; individual 120, 136; interpersonal 119; pharmaceutical 119; *see also* psychotherapy; therapeutic alliance
thinness 40–41, 50, 58, 87, 94, 105, 159, 178; culture of 87; social normativity of 50
throwing up *see* vomiting
transfer 136, 138–139, 143–145, 150–152, 162–163, 182, 208, 237n5
transference 162, 189, 200–204; sexual 200; traumatic 200; *see also* countertransference
trauma 26, 67, 68, 70, 71, 72, 75, 79, 80, 85–86, 89n1, 104, 123, 133, 140, 145, 153, 147, 150, 159, 167, 168, 178–179, 182, 190–193, 195–196, 199–201, 203–204, 210–211, 215; acute 162, 185; childhood sexual 24–25, 166; chronic 176, 182–183; chronic childhood 65; complex 40, 119, 153, 176, 182, 185, 189, 195, 202, 208, 211, 215–216; definition 39; interpersonal 178, 192–193, 195, 208, 217; interpersonal childhood 178; interrelational 20; mental 63n1, 186n5; ongoing 183–184; original 21, 47, 118, 160–161, 163, 189, 196, 198, 209–210, 237n5; prolonged/protracted 182–183, 185; psychic 186n2; psychological 56, 70, 182, 194; relational 20, 162, 192, 196, 200; repeated 182–183; secondary 201; secondary effects 201; sexual 33, 42, 47, 50, 58, 65, 89n2, 102, 122–123, 127, 133, 151, 158, 180–181, 192, 207; sexual abuse 163; single-event 216; socially non-recognized 192; unrecognized 42; vicarious 201–204; victim 89n1, 201, 211; war 25; *see also* reenactment
trauma-informed/oriented services/treatment 160, 176, 190, 208–210, 216
traumatic narrative 190, 197, 201–202
traumatization 184, 204
treatment: aggressive 126; authoritarian 118; 'CBT' 158; coercive 118, 126–127; dietetic 126; non-empowering 161; pharmacological psychiatric 145; punitive 127; reward and punishment 128–129; *see also* childhood sexual abuse treatment; eating disorder treatment(s); hospitalization; psychotherapy; sexual abuse treatment; therapy; trauma-informed/oriented services/treatment
treatment contract 117
trust 21–22, 71, 120, 127–129, 132, 138, 145, 151, 157, 167–171, 173, 187n8, 190, 192, 195–198, 200, 203, 210

United States 20, 24, 70, 136, 175, 178, 184
unspecified dissociative disorder 69
unwanted sexual reactions 94

Van der Kolk, B. 19, 33, 35, 176, 178, 183–185, 191, 204, 216
vicarious/secondary trauma (as a separate concept) 163n3, 201–204
victimization 195, 208–209; *see also* revictimization
Victorian England 7
Victorian era 23, 177
Vietnam War 25, 184

violence 19, 24, 118–119, 126, 144, 146–147, 161, 167, 193, 203, 208–209, 222; effects of 208–209; gender-based 181, 193; interpersonal 25, 193, 204, 209; intimate-partner 19; mental 80; physical 80, 146, 219, 222; sexual 19–20, 24–25, 184, 186n5; against women and children 192–193; against women and girls 192; *see also* domestic violence
vomiting 4–7, 14–15, 35, 41, 47, 50–51, 54–55, 76–77, 85–86, 94, 95–96, 100–105, 111, 118, 120, 122, 130, 136, 137–139, 144, 146, 151–152, 155–156, 158–160, 180, 224, 226–229, 232–234, 236; self-induced 5
vulnerability 94–95, 108
West, the 3, 4, 93
Western civilization/culture 3, 92–93
Western Europe 184
Western society/world 19, 93, 177; industrial-capitalist society 7
witchcraft 23, 91
witches 92, 177
women: demon-possessed 23, 177; oppression of 36, 176, 181; social oppression of 23
Women's Liberation Movement 24
Wooley, S. C. 9, 32–34, 121, 181, 187n6
Woolf, Virginia 92
World Health Organization 181, 183

Made in the USA
Monee, IL
13 September 2026

62978986R20155